W9-BYL-711

PRAISE FOR *CARY GRANT*

"Reminds us that everyone wanted to be Cary Grant. Even Cary Grant."
—ATLANTA JOURNAL-CONSTITUTION

"Well-researched and competently written. . . . Even strangers to his work might feel they know the star—and the man—after reading this fast-moving biography."
—ST. LOUIS POST-DISPATCH

"Eliot's fascinating, sympathetic portrait is of a consummate performer who hid inner demons and used filmmaking to distance himself from reality (and four of his five wives)."
—PUBLISHERS WEEKLY

"This new treatment by the author of the acclaimed WALT DISNEY undoubtedly will garner popular attention."
—BOOKLIST

"Showbiz biographies tend to be all play and no work, but Eliot is as good on the movies as he is on the man . . . I am tempted to say of CARY GRANT what CHARADE's Audrey Hepburn says of Cary Grant: 'You know what's wrong with you? Nothing.'"
—DAILY TELEGRAPH

"Marc Eliot tells Grant's life story briskly and knowledgeably. Unusually for a showbiz biographer, he also has a snappy turn of phrase."
—IRISH INDEPENDENT

Also by Marc Eliot

DEATH OF A REBEL:
Starring Phil Ochs and a Small Circle of Friends

ROCKONOMICS:
The Money Behind the Music

DOWN THUNDER ROAD:
The Making of Bruce Springsteen

WALT DISNEY: Hollywood's Dark Prince

THE WHOLE TRUTH

TO THE LIMIT:
The Untold Story of the Eagles

DOWN 42ND STREET: Sex, Money,
Culture, and Politics at the Crossroads of the World

Cary
Grant

A BIOGRAPHY BY

MARC ELIOT

 THREE RIVERS PRESS • NEW YORK

Previous page: Photograph courtesy Hulton-Deutsch Collection/CORBIS

Copyright © 2004 by Rebel Road, Inc.

All rights reserved.
Published in the United States by Three Rivers Press,
an imprint of the Crown Publishing Group,
a division of Random House, Inc., New York.
www.crownpublishing.com

THREE RIVERS PRESS and the Tugboat design
are registered trademarks of Random House, Inc.

Originally published in hardcover in the United States
by Harmony Books, an imprint of the Crown Publishing Group,
a division of Random House, Inc., New York, in 2004.

Library of Congress Cataloging-in-Publication Data

Eliot, Marc.
Cary Grant: a biography / Marc Eliot. — 1st ed.
1. Grant, Cary, 1904–86. 2. Motion picture actors and actresses — United
States — Biography. I. Title.
PN2287.G675E45 2004
791.4302'8'092 — dc22   2004004115

0-307-20983-0

Printed in the United States of America

Design by Lauren Dong

10 9 8 7 6 5 4 3

First Paperback Edition

David M, Sarah M, Ernest G, Karen H,
Phil O, David B, Shen Z.

CONTENTS

Everybody wants to be Cary Grant. Even I want to be Cary Grant. I have spent the greater part of my life fluctuating between Archie Leach and Cary Grant; unsure of either, suspecting each. I pretended to be somebody I wanted to be until finally I became that person. Or he became me.

—CARY GRANT

He was the best and most important actor in the history of the cinema . . . The essence of his quality can be put quite amply: he can be attractive and unattractive simultaneously; there is a light and dark side to him but, whichever is dominant, the other creeps into view . . . He was rather cheap, and too suspicious . . . he was, very likely, a hopeless fusspot as man, husband, and even father. How could anyone be "Cary Grant"? But how can anyone, ever after, not consider the attempt?

—DAVID THOMSON

Where among Screwball stars William Powell, say, was one-dimensionally debonair, Ray Milland bland, Don Ameche plebeian and suspiciously Latin, Henry Fonda the soul of uprightness, and Gary Cooper a prodigy of plain speaking (though in some of these cases they played against type), Grant is marvelously protean, the multifarious embodiment of all these qualities and more.

—BRUCE BABINGTON AND PETER WILLIAM EVANS

The "heterosexual" couple of classical cinema encompassed within them and between them all sorts of shifting alliances: dyads, triangles, quartets, the great stuff of Freudian narrative, concealed and revealed. You don't *have* to see the perverse shadings and alternative readings in the old films, but they are there: to deny all the homosexual, bisexual, and heterosexual possibilities inherent in the coming together of, say, Dietrich or Garbo and their lovers; Grant and his; or practically all of the screwball couples; or practically all star couples, is to read film literally and to insist on making unequivocal something whose very charm, whose layered inferences, were based on the equivocal.

—MOLLY HASKELL

Star-gazing can be said to constitute one of the mass religions of our time.

—ANDREW SARRIS

Out of chaos comes the birth of a star.

—CHARLIE CHAPLIN

INTRODUCTION

Although he would go on to star in six more Hollywood features, Cary Grant's thirty-four-year film career crested with his dual performance as George Kaplan/Roger O. Thornhill in Alfred Hitchcock's *North by Northwest.** Released in 1959, the film signaled the commercial and artistic peak not just of Grant's magnificent body of work but of Hitchcock's as well. One of the celebrated director's cleverest (and silliest) movies, *North by Northwest* afforded the increasingly maudlin filmmaker the chance to muse upon his most primal obsession, his own mortality, in this instance projected onscreen by the adventure of his favorite leading man, Cary Grant, in what would become for both their wildest flight of cinematic fancy.

Kaplan's faked murder two-thirds of the way through the film forces the question of whether he actually is who the others believe him to be, someone entirely separate — Roger O. Thornhill — or whether he really ever exists at all. Out of this question a larger one emerges: is Kaplan the creation of the Hitchcock-like CIA operative (Leo G. Carroll) who has, thus far, remained largely unseen while cleverly *directing* the either/or/neither Kaplan/Thornhill's every move? Or is he someone, or something, else, an externalized elaborate fantasy, perhaps, of Thornhill's most repressed desires for an idealized life of exciting adventure, of romance, of *meaning*?

Grant must have found *North by Northwest*'s multiple plot twists enor-

---

*The final six were Blake Edwards's *Operation Petticoat* (1959), Stanley Donen's *The Grass Is Greener* (1960), Delbert Mann's *That Touch of Mink* (1962), Donen's *Charade* (1963), Ralph Nelson's *Father Goose* (1964), and Charles Walters's *Walk, Don't Run* (1966).

mously appealing, as they so clearly reflected his own lifelong struggle to balance the great circus ball of fame with a desire to live an intensely private real life, a life whose very survival depended upon the enormous popularity of his synthetic movie star persona.

Indeed, onscreen Cary Grant was nothing less than perfect, "the man from dream city," as Pauline Kael once described him, the handsome devil every man dreamed of being and the devastatingly handsome lover every woman dreamed of being with. To the world that knew and loved him only through his films, he was worthy of worship and adoration, even if everything from his famous self-confident swagger and unflappable romantic charm to his magical name's ultra-British iambic flow was as calculated and artificial as — well, as George Kaplan.

In 1966, SEVEN YEARS AFTER the release of *North by Northwest,* Cary Grant officially retired from making movies for the third and final time; by then his place high in Hollywood's pantheon of cultural icons was well assured. In the twenty years of life he had left, his gait inevitably slowed, his skin thickened, his hair grayed, and his shoulders stooped, until, at eighty-two, he quietly joined Hollywood's league of legendary dead. Yet because of the glorious legacy of his films, to present and future fans he would remain forever young, eternally alluring, and preternaturally beautiful, the quintessential motion picture personification of the middle third of the American twentieth century's definition of "tall, dark, and handsome." Once he became a star, with few notable exceptions, Cary Grant never ventured too far from "Cary Grant" and was always readily identifiable by the crystalline dazzle of his smile, the rolling shuffle of his slightly bow-legged walk, the suede slip-slide of his voice, that irresistible cleft in his chin, and those unforgettably piercing topsoil-brown eyes that connected him to the world — the twin-beam projectors of his inner emotions.

Movie stars are the magnified external images of society's idealized dreams, hopes, and fantasies. Filmgoers associate with these stars to such a degree that their physical beauty becomes a social metaphor for moral and emotional perfection. It is the reason they are so worshiped at the peak of their popularity, and why the crest of their stardom rarely lasts longer than five years. In film time this translates into perhaps a half-dozen major roles for a leading man, and even fewer for a woman, before reality crashes their endless party and irrevocably separates them from their fans. A once-flawless face's first wrinkle often signals the beginning of the descending arc of one's cinematic shooting star.

How much more remarkable, then, that Cary Grant remained a top box office draw *for thirty-four years.* Not only did he defy the relentless downward curve of box office decline, he actually became *more* popular the older he became and the longer he made movies. His forty-eighth, Michael Curtiz's 1946 *Night and Day,* a bit of Hollywood fluff masquerading as Cole Porter's biography, was only his first color feature, and the first of his films that would ultimately make the list of his top twelve box office grossers. His number one top-grossing film was his sixty-second, Blake Edwards's *Operation Petticoat,* made in 1959 when Grant was fifty-five years old. And his seventy-second and final film, Charles Walters's *Walk, Don't Run,* released in 1966 when Grant was sixty-two, would place twelfth, more popular (i.e., profitable) than sixty of the other movies he made.

During this most astonishing of Hollywood long runs Grant was, with one or two exceptions, every major Hollywood director's favorite actor, the first choice to star again and again in the best movies they made, opposite and often enhancing the luminosity of many of the most beautiful women ever to grace the silver screen.

The list is as impressive as it is long. The highlights include Josef von Sternberg's *Blonde Venus,* with Marlene Dietrich (1932); Lowell Sherman's *She Done Him Wrong,* with Mae West (1933); Norman McLeod's *Topper,* with Constance Bennett (1937); Howard Hawks's *Bringing Up Baby,* with Katharine Hepburn (1938); George Cukor's *Holiday,* with Hepburn again (1938); George Stevens's *Gunga Din,* with Joan Fontaine (1939); Hawks's *Only Angels Have Wings,* with Jean Arthur (1939); John Cromwell's *In Name Only* (1939), with Carole Lombard, who first appeared with Grant in his second film, Alexander Hall's *Sinners in the Sun* (1932); Hawks's *His Girl Friday,* with Rosalind Russell (1940); Garson Kanin's *My Favorite Wife,* with Irene Dunne (1940); Cukor's *The Philadelphia Story,* with Hepburn (1940); Alfred Hitchcock's *Suspicion,* with Fontaine (1941); H. C. Potter's *Mr. Lucky,* with Laraine Day (1943); Delmer Daves's *Destination Tokyo,* with Faye

Emerson (1943); Frank Capra's *Arsenic and Old Lace*, with Priscilla Lane (1944); Clifford Odets's *None but the Lonely Heart*, with Jane Wyatt (1944); Michael Curtiz's *Night and Day*, with Alexis Smith (1946); Hitchcock's *Notorious*, with Ingrid Bergman (1946); Irving Reis's *The Bachelor and the Bobby-Soxer*, with Myrna Loy (1947); Henry Koster's *The Bishop's Wife*, with Loretta Young (1947); Potter's *Mr. Blandings Builds His Dream House*, with Loy (1948); Hawks's *Monkey Business*, with Ginger Rogers (1952); Hitchcock's *To Catch a Thief* (1955), with Grace Kelly; Leo McCarey's *An Affair to Remember*, with Deborah Kerr (1957); Stanley Donen's *Indiscreet*, with Bergman (1958); Melville Shavelson's *Houseboat*, with Sophia Loren (1958); Hitchcock's *North by Northwest* (1959), with Eva Marie Saint; Blake Edwards's *Operation Petticoat*, with Dina Merrill (1959); Donen's *The Grass Is Greener*, with Kerr (1960); Edwards's *That Touch of Mink*, with Doris Day (1962); Donen's *Charade*, with Audrey Hepburn (1963); Ralph Nelson's *Father Goose*, with Leslie Caron (1964); and Charles Walters's *Walk, Don't Run*, with Samantha Eggar (1966).

Just as amazing, if not even more impressive, the film career of the actor whom *Time* magazine once described as "the world's most perfect male animal" began relatively late, according to Hollywood's quick time clock. Grant was twenty-eight years old when he first went west to seek his fortune in films, having spent the better part of his twenties as a steadily rising leading man in a succession of Broadway musicals and comedies.

Over the next three and a half decades, his impact on movies was so enormous, he would virtually redefine the cinematic image of the romantic American male. In the hands of Hollywood's immigrant-bred, mostly Jewish studio moguls endlessly obsessed with female WASP beauty, British Archie Leach was reborn as the projection of their own idealized American selves and presented to the world as Cary Grant.

Yet, despite his physical beauty (and that was, with rare exception, all the moguls ever really required of him), Grant early on sensed something was lacking in his acting, that there was an internal disconnect between his manufactured cinematic image and his inner being. Indeed, without a masterful script to provide a compelling character, without a brilliant costume designer to dress him up, without an artful makeup man to apply the sheen to his skin, without a tasteful set designer to enshrine him, without a skillful editor to exact his comic timing, without a sharp-eyed cameraman to place him in the most favorable light, without a beautiful costar to externalize desire, and without a director to impose his own unifying personality, Grant feared that, at heart, he was less than the sum of his movie-star whole, a spiritless cinematic symbol.

Moreover, once a performance was constructed and frozen on film, he knew he would forever have to compete with that symbol in a battle against time in reality he could never win. That is why, into the fifties (both his own and the century's), he became increasingly more selective in his choice of screen roles and directors, choosing only those parts and the men who guided him in them, directors who best knew how to help him perform that special Grant sleight-of-hand on audiences over and over again without ever once giving the trick away.

In 1953, after having turned down three great roles—Norman Maine, eventually played by James Mason in George Cukor's *A Star Is Born* opposite Judy Garland; reporter Joe Bradley, which went instead to Gregory Peck in William Wyler's *Roman Holiday* with Audrey Hepburn; and Linus Larrabee, which Humphrey Bogart grabbed on the rebound in Billy Wilder's *Sabrina* opposite Audrey Hepburn (the latter two having directors and costars Grant had never worked with)—he chose instead to return to safer, if shallower, waters opposite one of his favorite leading ladies, Deborah Kerr, in *Dream Wife*, a strictly by-the-numbers romantic comedy for MGM, written and directed by his good friend Sidney Sheldon, who had penned the hugely successful 1947 Grant vehicle *The Bachelor and the Bobby-Soxer*.

When *Dream Wife* proved a major failure, Grant, just shy of his fiftieth birthday, was convinced that the magic had finally gone and announced his intention to retire. It took one of his favorite directors, Alfred Hitchcock, the so-called master of suspense and the supplier of many of Hollywood's most unforgettable corpses, to bring Cary Grant back to life. Grant accepted the lead in *To Catch a Thief*, a film whose plot centers on whether suave, urbane John Robie, the most notorious jewel thief in Europe, has in fact retired or is still on the job. Robie insists somebody must be imitating him—*that he is not really who everybody thinks he is*—a notion that perfectly captured both Grant's and Hitchcock's real-life ongoing professional and emotional issues of identity, image, and self.

The enormous success of *To Catch a Thief* returned Grant to widescreen glory. This intended one-time-only encore lasted for eleven years and twelve pictures, each of which allowed him to reprise some aspect of his by-now-familiar repertoire of onscreen characters — romantic leading man, verbal wit, athlete, bon vivant, urbane hero. As with the previous two pictures he had made for Hitchcock (*Suspicion*, 1941, and *Notorious*, 1946), Grant's comedic instincts had been darkened, and therefore deepened, by the great director, who knew better than anyone how to use the extraordinary talents of one of his most favored leading men. Indeed, *Suspicion*, in which Grant may or may not have been a wife-killer, arrived at a time when he was considered essentially a comic actor, after such films as *The Awful Truth* (1937), *Bringing Up Baby* (1938), *Holiday* (1938), and *The Philadelphia Story* (1940), among the best of his screwball and light comedy work. His departure into melodrama immediately preceding *Suspicion* was *Penny Serenade* (1941), for which Grant was nominated for an Oscar but which was not as popular at the box office. *Suspicion*, on the other hand, was a smashing success and restored Grant to the front line of Hollywood's most desired leading men.

It was not until Charles Walters's *Walk, Don't Run*, released in 1966, that Grant, no longer able to pass for the romantic leading man and with no desire at all to age gracefully into "uncle" or "grandfather" character roles, took himself off the cinematic treadmill this time for good, content to let "Cary Grant" live on through the endless recycling of his old movies. Having never been able to make the connection between his real life and the world his cinematic other had so successfully created, and with his movie persona as the great leading man firmly in the past, he could no longer find any romantic passion for making movies. Instead, he pursued the ongoing drama of his own real life. Away from the screen and with the help of therapy and psychotropic drugs, a brief fourth marriage that yielded the child he had so dearly wanted, and a fifth and final wife who became his devoted companion to the end, Grant managed in the last twenty years of his life to get closer than he ever had to reconciling his long struggle between person and persona, vision and visionary, dream and dreamer, movie star and man.

That is why, for those of us who seek to find ourselves in the movies, to discover in them the projected passion of our own hopes and dreams; who believe we know ourselves better when we sit in the dark (but not the darkness); for those of us who see in our heroes what we hope to discover in ourselves, the story of Grant's lifelong pursuit of happiness cannot help but enlighten and inspire us all.

PART ONE

PREVIOUS PAGE: *A long-overdue moment as Frank Sinatra hands an emotional Cary Grant his only Academy Award, a noncompetitive Honorary Oscar at the 42nd annual awards presentation in Hollywood, April 7, 1970.* (BETTMANN/CORBIS)

1

On the night of April 7, 1970, four years after starring in his last feature film, sixty-six-year-old Cary Grant, who had never won an Oscar, was awarded a special noncompetitive Academy Award for his lifetime of achievement in motion pictures. Although to his great legion of fans it was an honor scandalously overdue, for a number of reasons, some less obvious than others, it very nearly did not happen.

The original concept of the Academy of Motion Picture Arts and Sciences had been the brainstorm of Louis B. Mayer, who in 1926 came up with the idea of an interstudio house union open to all studio employees, including actors, run by moguls, to offset the growing problem of independent trade organization in Hollywood. The notion of annual awards was meant to placate those employees who sought the more practical benefits of better salaries, job security, health insurance, and retirement plans. At the time virtually everyone connected to the motion picture industry, from set painters, costume makers, and prop men to screenwriters, actors, and directors, was subject to the whims and fancies of the sweatshop mentality of the pioneering generation of Hollywood moguls.

The first actor to successfully break the hitherto ironclad contract system for performers was Cary Grant, who became a freelance actor-for-hire on a per film basis in 1937, after his original five-year exclusive deal with Paramount expired (as had the studio itself, in its first incarnation as Paramount Publix). During his half-decade studio tenure he had appeared in twenty-four features (including three made on loan-out to other studios) at a salaried basis that had begun at $450 a week in 1932 and ended at $3,500 in

1936, far below the $6,500 per week that Gary Cooper, his main competition at Paramount, earned that same year.

Money, however, was not the only reason Grant chose not to remain a contract studio player. In 1934 MGM, the studio "with more stars than there are in heaven!" and the one he felt was more suited to his style and image, wanted to borrow him from Paramount to costar as Captain Bligh's first mate in Frank Lloyd's *Mutiny on the Bounty*. It was a film Grant desperately wanted to be in, believing it would be the one to finally make him a major star. When Adolph Zukor, the head of Paramount, refused to allow the loan-out, MGM gave the role instead to its own relatively unknown contract player, Franchot Tone. *Bounty* went on to win the Best Picture Oscar for 1935, and its three stars—Clark Gable, Charles Laughton, and Tone—were all nominated for Best Actor. (None won; the award that year went to Victor McLaglen for his performance in John Ford's *The Informer*.)

Grant never forgave Zukor, and a year later, when his contract was up, he refused to re-sign with a reorganized Paramount, then surprised everyone when, after fielding offers from all the majors, he announced he was not going to sign an exclusive studio contract with any and instead would sell his services on a nonexclusive per film basis. To underscore the finality of his decision to go independent, he canceled his membership in the Academy, an action everyone in Hollywood considered professional suicide. At the time no one except Charlie Chaplin had been able to survive without the security of a weekly paycheck in Academy-dominated Hollywood, and to do it he had to start his own studio, United Artists (with Douglas Fairbanks, D. W. Griffith, and Mary Pickford).

No one, that is, until Cary Grant. The same year his deal at the studio expired, Grant appeared in George Cukor's *Sylvia Scarlett* for RKO, a role that showcased his unique talents as his screen acting at Paramount had not. And, although Grant's performance in the film was arguably just as good as, in some cases notably better than, William Powell's in *My Man Godfrey*, Paul Muni's in *The Story of Louis Pasteur*, Gary Cooper's in *Mr. Deeds Goes to Town*, and Walter Huston's in *Dodsworth*, he was pointedly ignored at Oscar time by a still-resentful Academy. To the conservative moguls, he was now officially an outsider, an enemy of their system, as reviled as any independent trade union activist. Their anger was exacerbated, no doubt, by his early, frequent, and indiscreet flaunting of his eleven-year "marriage" to actor Randolph Scott.

IT WAS A RESENTMENT THAT was to last for a very long time. Of the seventy-two movies he would make, only two of his performances—in *Penny Serenade* (1941) and *None But the Lonely Heart* (1944), both made during Hollywood's wartime male talent drain—earned him nominations for Best Actor, and both times he lost (first to rival Gary Cooper, who won for *Sergeant York*, and then to Bing Crosby, who won for *Going My Way*).

Nevertheless, his pioneering individualism had helped to redefine the notion of what creative freedom meant in Hollywood, and played a key role in the complex, multifaceted movement toward industrywide independence. Aided by a 1948 landmark antitrust lawsuit brought against the studios by the government to end the moguls' absolute control of the production, distribution, and exhibition of movies, Grant was among the handful of individuals whose actions eventually helped transform Hollywood from a factory that manufactured movies by mass production, much the way Ford made cars, to a place where outside, independently financed films could be produced by the actors themselves and sold for distribution to the highest bidder.

As much as the studios resented Grant, he resented them in turn for what he believed was their stubborn refusal to properly acknowledge via Oscar not only his individual success but all that the success of his movies meant to the industry. To him, their intentional slight was not only an offense to his ego but cost him (and them) potential millions in profits at the box office for the many pictures he not only starred in but owned a piece of; one of the truisms of Hollywood is that no matter how successful a film, the awarding of an Oscar significantly increases its profits.

In fact, many in the industry steadfastly believed that it was the money far more than the rejection—after all, how much more popular with the public could Grant be?—that kept the notoriously penny-pinching actor's finger on the legal hair-trigger of the pistol he continually pointed at the heads of the studios. From the early 1930s until he left the business entirely, Grant brought numerous if mostly frivolous lawsuits against the heads of the industry, and almost always with the same accusation: that they had somehow conspired to cheat him out of what was rightly his. As late as the summer of 1968 he was still going at it. That August he and his partner, director Stanley Donen, filed a multimillion-dollar suit against MCA (Universal Studios) for its "poor judgment" in failing to obtain television distribution of the four films they had coproduced. The lawsuit, eventually settled out of court and like all the others, did nothing to ameliorate the industry leaders' long-term hostility toward Grant. That same year the members of the Academy angrily vetoed newly elected Academy president Gregory Peck's decision to award Grant a rare Honorary Oscar for his lifetime of achievement as an actor. Only after Grant "voluntarily" rejoined the Academy in 1970 did Peck finally get the votes he needed and Grant his award.

MORE THAN TWO HOURS into the Awards ceremony, held that year at the Dorothy Chandler Pavilion in downtown Los Angeles, a nervous, tuxedoed Cary Grant was escorted by a hostess from the green room to the immediate backstage area, where he stood behind a fly curtain and listened through a small technician's cue speaker as Frank Sinatra finished his brief but spirited introduction.

A onetime rival of Grant's for the affection of Sophia Loren (in 1956, during the filming of Stanley Kramer's *The Pride and the Passion*), Sinatra had been Peck's last-minute choice to replace Princess Grace (Kelly) Rainier. At Grant's insistence, Kelly had bowed out of what would have been her first live appearance at the Oscars in fifteen years (she had appeared in 1967, but on film shot in Monaco), after Grant announced that he could not, for "personal reasons," show up to accept his Oscar.

Those "personal reasons" had to do with an about-to-erupt sex scandal involving just the kind of gossipy scrutiny into Grant's personal life he had more or less succeeded in avoiding for most of his career. In March, less than a month after the Academy announced its intention to award Grant his Honorary Oscar and just two days after Grant assured Peck he would end his personal twelve-year boycott of the ceremonies to accept it,* Cynthia Bouron, a former Hollywood call girl and self-proclaimed actress, filed a paternity suit against Grant, claiming he was the father of her seven-week-old baby girl. Within hours word of the publicly filed lawsuit swept across the Hollywood trades and on to the front pages of newspapers across the country and around the world. Grant, who had been tipped off the day of the filing by a friend at the Los Angeles courthouse, immediately flew to Bristol, England, to visit his suddenly sick mother.

Many felt the timing of the lawsuit could not have been mere coincidence. After it became a matter of public record, more than one columnist claimed to have known it was coming for weeks and that he had been asked by unnamed parties to sit on the story until the Academy's decision to give Grant his Oscar had been publicly announced.

The day the story broke it became the subject of choice over morning coffee in Beverly Hills. How, everyone in the business wondered, could Grant possibly have allowed himself to become ensnared in one of the studios' oldest tactics, the moral smear? The widespread belief among Grant's supporters was that if the hardliners at the Academy had not been able to prevent Grant from getting his award by ballot, they would do it another way, by publicly humiliating him and forcing him to bow out of the ceremonies.

Once the lawsuit was filed, except for his conversations with Peck via long-distance telephone, Grant carefully avoided direct contact with anyone but his closest friends and his lawyer, spokesperson and personal manager Stanley Fox. Despite their well-known diligence, the British paparazzi had very little success tracking Grant down, the reason being that after making a brief, highly publicized appearance in Bristol, Grant secretly flew to the Bahamas in one of good friend Howard Hughes's private planes, where he remained in seclusion at the billionaire's private villa.

During his absence, Bouron held a press conference to announce that *she* intended to show up at the Academy Awards, hold a press conference in front of the red carpet, reveal her new baby's full name, and if Grant dared to show, hand him the subpoena that he had thus far been able to avoid.

---

*Grant had made only two appearances since the Oscars became a television show; once in 1957, to accept the Best Actress Oscar won by Ingrid Bergman, another Hollywood outsider, and again in 1958, acting as stand-in for Bergman, to present the Best Actor Oscar to Alec Guinness.

Grant had reason to worry. The truth was that he had had a brief sexual affair with Bouron the year before. The nature of the mutual attraction between the sixty-six-year-old Grant and the thirty-three-year-old Bouron was most likely a clever sting of sorts, made possible by Grant's enduring attraction to much younger women and his desire to have a second child. When the scandal broke, it was Fox who had advised Grant to get out of town and make no public comment about anything and, to prevent Bouron from making further potentially damaging comments, filed a countersuit, knowing her lawyers would then prevent her from saying anything more.

The potential for trouble, however, still loomed. Questions concerning Grant's long and bitter divorce from his fourth wife, actress Dyan Cannon, had recently flared up over the question of Grant's visitation rights to his four-year-old daughter, Jennifer. Bouron's paternity suit, he feared, might adversely upset the already delicate balance of the rights he had fought so long and hard to win.

And finally there was Princess Grace. The last thing Grant wanted was to have his dear friend associated in any way with scandal. That was the real reason why, the day after the Bouron story broke, Princess Grace sent, at Grant's insistence, her reluctant but irrevocable regrets to the Academy.

The last week in March, Grant authorized Fox to accept service of Bouron's subpoena and then quietly slipped back in to Los Angeles. The next day, under an agreement reached by his and Bouron's attorneys, he gave blood samples to the authorities. Bouron was also required to do so, but did not show at the appointed time, or at two subsequent occasions. Fox seized upon this to petition Judge Laurence J. Rittenband to dismiss Bouron's lawsuit. At a hastily convened hearing, Fox's request was granted, and just like that, her paternity case against Grant was over.

The scandal, however, refused to die. A new gust of rumors quickly blew through Hollywood that Grant had secretly met with Bouron and paid her off not to show up and give blood. While this made for good gossip, the reality of that having taken place was highly unlikely. Had the baby proved to be his, Grant, who had suffered a lifetime dealing with his own boyhood abandonment issues, and who desperately wanted a second child, would not likely have turned his back on it.

Nevertheless, the front-page persistence of the story convinced Grant that, despite Peck's continuing pleas, he should not show up at the Oscars. Then on the first of April, at the behest of Howard Hughes, Grant flew to Hughes's Desert Inn hotel in Las Vegas to talk over the situation. The reclusive billionaire told him that the only way he could put an end to the whole sorry situation was to act as if he had done nothing wrong and had nothing to hide, and the only way to do that was to show up at the ceremonies and accept his Oscar. (It was ironic advice from the increasingly reclusive Hughes, who, having summoned Grant to Las Vegas, had conducted the meeting via telephone, suite to suite.)

On April 2, Grant called Peck and said he would show up after all but wanted his decision to be kept secret. Peck agreed. Nonetheless the story appeared the next day in an item by local columnist John Austin, who said he had been tipped to Grant's appearance by a "close friend." (The only other person besides Peck who knew of Grant's decision was Hughes. Austin's column hinted it was indeed Hughes who had convinced Grant to show. It remains a matter of conjecture as to why Hughes would have told Austin, but the most likely reason is that he felt that once the story appeared in print, Grant would not be able to change his mind again.)

Peck then called Sinatra and asked him to be the presenter, and he said yes. As the night of the Awards approached, Grant spent several days and at least one evening at Cannon's home, both to give support to and seek comfort from his ex-wife. Cannon, as it happened, had been nominated that year as Best Supporting Actress for her performance in the wife-swapping comedy *Bob & Carol & Ted & Alice.**

As THE AUDITORIUM LIGHTS slowly dimmed, a six-minute montage of clips from Grant's best-loved movies played on a large screen behind the podium, punctuated by outbursts of spontaneous laughter from the audience and ripples of applause. When the film ended and the lights came back up, Sinatra finished his introduction by praising Cary Grant for the "sheer brilliance of his acting that makes it all look easy."

And then at last the moment was upon him. With tears rolling down his cheeks, Grant emerged from the wings and walked slowly to the microphone

---

*She lost to Goldie Hawn, who won for her performance in *Cactus Flower.*

while the audience rose as one to stand and cheer for him. He nodded appreciatively several times, quickly wiped one eye with a finger, and waved gracefully to the crowd. As the crescendo of their applause began to wane, he slipped on his thick-rimmed black glasses, and in the familiar voice so beloved by his fans all around the world, humbly delivered his carefully prepared words of acceptance and appreciation.

"I'm very grateful to the Academy's Board of Directors for this happy tribute," he began, "and to Frank, for coming here especially to give it to me, and to all the fellows who worked so hard in finding and assembling those film clips."

He squinted into the audience, looking for those he was about to thank. He spotted Hitchcock, nodded slightly toward him, then once again spoke, departing from his notes and holding up his Oscar. "You know, I may never look at this without remembering the quiet patience of the directors who were so kind to me, who were kind enough to put up with me more than once — some of them even three or four times. There were Howard Hawks, Hitchcock, the late Leo McCarey, George Stevens, George Cukor, and Stanley Donen.

"And all the writers. There were Philip Barry, Dore Schary, Bob Sherwood, Ben Hecht, Clifford Odets, Sidney Sheldon, and more recently Stanley Shapiro and Peter Stone. Well, I trust they and all the other directors, writers, and producers, and leading women, have all forgiven me what I didn't know."

At this point he paused, glanced at his notes, and then looked up again. "I realize it's conventional and usual to praise one's fellow workers on these occasions. But why not? Ours is a collaborative medium; we all need each other. And what better opportunity is there to publicly express one's appreciation and admiration and affection for all those who contribute so much to each of our welfare?"

A longer pause followed, during which he appeared to be trying to hold back his tears. He softly cleared his throat, then continued, coming closer than he ever would to explaining if not apologizing for his long and rancorous boycott of the Academy: "You know, I've never been a joiner or a member of any—oh, particular—social set, but I've been privileged to be a part of Hollywood's most glorious era. And yet tonight, thinking of all the empty screens that are waiting to be filled with marvelous images, ideologies, points of view, and considering all the students who are studying film techniques in the universities throughout the world, and the astonishing young talents that are coming up in our midst, I think there's an even more glorious era right around the corner.

"So before I leave you, I want to thank you very much for signifying your approval of this. I shall cherish it until I die, because probably no greater honor can come to any man than the respect of his colleagues. Thank you."

As the audience rose once more, he turned slowly and left, out of sight even before the ovation ended. For Cary Grant, these last few steps signaled the end of the long and wondrous journey that had started so long ago, when as little Archie Leach of Bristol, England, the first, sweet dreams of destiny had come to him in the night.

And the horrid nightmares as well.

PART TWO

FROM BRISTOL
TO BROADWAY

PREVIOUS PAGE: *Archibald Alec (Alexander) Leach, age 4, Bristol, England, 1908.*
(Courtesy of the private collection of the Virginia Cherrill Estate)

2

"I'm reminded of a piece of advice my father gave me regarding shoes; it has stood me in good stead whenever my own finances were low. He said, it's better to buy one good pair of shoes than four cheap ones. One pair made of fine leather could outlast four inferior pairs and, if well cared for, would continue to proclaim your good judgment and taste no matter how old they become. It is rather like the stock market. It makes more sense to buy just one share of blue chip than 150 shares of a one-dollar stock."

—CARY GRANT

Bristol is the seventh-largest city and third-largest seaport in Great Britain. It is situated to the south of Cardiff, Wales, to the west of Bath, and to the southwest of Gloucestershire. In 1497, John Cabot, the discoverer of Newfoundland, first sailed to the New World from Bristol. Noted natives of Bristol include England's seventeenth-century poet laureate Robert Southey; William Penn, for whom Pennsylvania is named; and the celebrated Shakespearean actor Sir Henry Irving. During the first years of the twentieth century, Bristol was the designated port of departure for those who wished to sail via luxury liner from England to the United States. It is adored by the rest of the world for its celebrated cream sherry.

Bristol is also one of England's many great theatrical districts, home to the famous Theatre Royal on King Street, which first opened in 1766 and remains in operation to this day. The other major stops on the British vaudeville circuit at the turn of the twentieth century were Bristol's Empire and Hippodrome. All three venues were the first signposts on the journey to dreamland for the boy whose destiny it was to become Bristol's most beloved progeny, young Archibald (Arch-*eee*-bald) Alec (Alexander) Leach.

Archie, as everyone called him, was the second child born to Elsie Maria Kingdon, the daughter of an Episcopalian shipwright, and Elias Leach, the son of an Episcopalian potter. Although Elias had big dreams of one day becoming a famous entertainer, he earned his living wage as a tailor's presser at Todd's clothing factory. The Kingdons generally presumed, in the waning days of the staunch Victorian epoch, that their prudent daughter had, unfortunately, married beneath her class. They did not consider Elias — at thirty-three, twelve years their daughter's senior — socially acceptable or sufficiently established in business for a man his age.

Nevertheless the slight, attractive, cleft-chinned, and prohibitively shy Elsie did not turn him down when he proposed. How could she? He was tall, slim, dashing, and a charmer, the mustachioed man of her dreams. She resolutely believed in Elias, even if her parents didn't, and was certain that he meant it when he promised her that the type of fancy coats and suits of the wealthy he pressed at the factory would one day belong to him as well, that the manual labor in the steamy, windowless shop in which he toiled six days out of seven was but a brief stepping-stone to a better life for the both of them.

Elias could dream with the best of them, and he also knew well how to make at least some of those dreams come true. By the time he walked his twenty-one-year-old wife down the aisle, he had already played through the field of Bristol's most (and least) eligible women, using his good looks to insinuate himself into their beds if not their lives. When he met Elsie, he sensed that her father might provide a rich dowry and, later on, a comfortable inheritance. It was enough to lure him to renounce his wild ways and seek Elsie's hand in marriage.

They settled in to one of the newly built working-class semidetached homes along Hughenden Road, just off Gloucester, a dwelling too chilly and damp in the winter, the air roughened by the smelly choke of poorly ventilated coal heating, and too sweaty in the clumping humidity of summer. In dire need of fresh stimulation, Elias soon returned to his carousing ways. At least part of his problem was sexual frustration. Less than a year into the marriage, he discovered he was no longer able to raise Elsie's temperature, no matter what the time of year. Her Victorian disposition toward romance dictated that procreation was the only justification for engaging in the act of sex. Doing it for pleasure was unproductive, a sacrilegious waste of time, at least as far as she was concerned.

Filled with many splendorous churches and lively music halls, Bristol provided ample opportunity for Elsie to worship God, at least as much as the numberless pubs and music halls accommodated her husband's more secular devotions. Indeed, Elias's relapse into roguishness found easy pickings in the traveling vaudeville companies that continually played the local theaters, where that sort of entertainment itself was seen by Elsie and the church folk as nothing more (or less) than the work of the devil himself.

Victorian society believed that no crime went unpunished. If the authorities of the state did not arrest and prosecute those who broke the legal code, a higher authority surely would avenge those who broke the moral one. Such was the only explanation Elsie could fathom to explain the unexpected death of her firstborn, John William Elias Leach.

She had given birth at home on February 9, 1899, and from the moment baby John took his first breath, Elsie devoted herself to his every need. She showered him with all the love and affection she withheld from her husband, who, she believed, had not remained true. He was surely the cause of God's retribution on their home when, in his eighth month of life, the child developed a cough, followed by violent convulsions and the onset of a fever that would not break. John died of tubercular meningitis on February 6, 1900, two days before his first birthday and one day before Elsie's twenty-third.

She would not allow herself to cry at baby John's funeral. Throughout the solemn service she sat tearless, cloaked in black, and stared straight ahead into the private world of her overwhelming grief. God had indeed punished

Elias for his sins and in so doing had brought His wrath down upon her as well, taking back the fruit of their corrupted marriage. After his burial, baby John's name was never spoken again by either Elsie or Elias.

In the spring of 1903 Elsie became pregnant once more, a sign, she believed, of a merciful God. She had Elias redecorate the room that had been her firstborn's and add more insulation to the walls and ceiling to prevent any deathly drafts from blowing onto her new baby.

Archibald Leach was born on January 18, 1904. Early on, to ensure his good health and moral righteousness, Elsie imposed her obsessive orderliness upon the lad, a prudent upbringing that would stay with him the rest of his days. "As a little boy," he would remember nearly eighty years later, "I was fined for spilling things on the tablecloth. Thruppence a blib. But that wasn't so bad. I had a shilling a week for allowance, so I had four blibs — and we only put the tablecloth on the table on Sundays."

Elsie enjoyed keeping little Archie's hair long and curly and dressed him in frilly clothes that resembled nothing so much as a little girl's dresses. Much has been made elsewhere of this early treatment as the speculative root of Cary Grant's later bisexuality, and while it may indeed have been a factor, this was the common style of Victorian childrearing in pre-Freudian England. A toddler's sexuality was presumed to be nonexistent, and the so-called cross-dressing of boys was nothing more provocative than a mother's innocent "dolling up" of her baby, without regard to gender. Nevertheless links are links, and Freud did establish that sexual feelings are present in children, and that preadolescent emotional connections are often retained, in one form or another, for a lifetime. In his thirties Cary Grant and his housemate and lover Randolph Scott often showed up at costume parties dressed as women, and in his mid-fifties Grant surprised reporter Joe Hyams by admitting that he still often preferred wearing women's nylon panties under his regular clothes when he traveled because they were easier to pack than men's underwear and he could wash them out himself, which saved on hotel laundry bills.

As likely to have influenced the young Grant's psyche as his too-close physical attachment to his mother was Elias's frequent absences, which deprived him of a father's normalizing presence. In truth, her husband's nights away from home no longer worried Elsie. Instead, she saw them as an opportunity for additional uninterrupted playtime with her perfect little Archie.

And yet even as the boy grew more attached to his mother and her possessive ways, he still strongly identified on some level with his father. If Archie had become the surrogate husband to his mother, receiver of her smothering affection and perhaps a bit of her misplaced rage, on some primitive or instinctive level he probably knew why Daddy wasn't always around. The few nights Elias did stay home, he and Elsie had loud arguments over money (or the lack of it), which only deepened the emotional split in the boy's loyalties between the two and secured the groundwork for his well-known lifelong thriftiness and later conflicted views of adult love — his uneasy acceptance of the public's at-times-wild adulation, the chaste pursuit of women he believed he unconditionally loved, his failure at marriage, his preference for the company of men over women, or the choice of no company at all. "My parents tried so hard and did their best," Grant said later on. "The trouble was that they weren't happy themselves. The lack of money for my mother's dreams became an excuse for regular sessions of reproach, against which my father learned the futility of trying to defend himself. But that isn't really to say that either one of them was 'wrong' or 'right.' They were probably both right."

Elias (Jim to his friends) was, if anything, relieved by his exclusion from his fatherly responsibilities to his son. He preferred the aroma of cigar smoke and ale spilled on wood at a local pub to the hot cabbage and cold wife waiting for him at home. Whenever Elias did get to spend time alone with his son, it was that much more fun for the both of them. When Archie was just five, his father began taking him to the pressing factory on Saturdays, where the boy loved to stand amid the loud machinery until closing time, then walk through town holding his hand above his head to reach his father's big one as Elias made the rounds of the local pubs and the traveling cribbage games. Archie always received two rewards for "assisting" his father at work. The first was a wrapped candy he was encouraged to fish for with his fingers in the well-pressed pants Elias wore for after-work activities. The second was the advice of a man who admired fine clothing, who believed that visual presentation, despite one's social standing, was the best way to self-promote. One afternoon Elias, after noticing the inferior quality of Archie's shoes, gave him a stern but loving lecture about the importance of proper footwear. Elsie, ever thrifty and practical, had bought Archie four pairs of inexpensive shoes. It was the kind of thrift Elias did not approve of. To him, the dress-up shoes his son wore looked "cheap" and "wouldn't last." Better to have just one good pair, he advised the young boy, than several that were worthless. "Buy less at higher quality" was a lesson Archie would remember the rest of his life.*

One of Elias and Archie's favorite Saturday-night pastimes was to go to a Bristol music hall or vaudeville theater to see pantomime — a particularly raucous and quite popular entertainment where men played both male and female parts, and the male lead was always played by a young and usually attractive woman — and the song-and-dance routines of the newest performers.

In 1909, at just five years of age, young Archie caught his first glimpse of the performer he would be obsessed with for much of of his life. Charlie Chaplin was a member of the Karno Players, a traveling vaudeville group that regularly toured the music hall circuit that included Bristol. A year later, Karno took Chaplin and others to America, a journey from which Chaplin would not return. He became a solo sensation first in the New York City vaudeville houses along Forty-second Street, then in short film comedies, and triumphed in Hollywood when he gave the world, and Archie, the gift of "the Little Tramp."

ELIAS WAS A BIT OF a piano-roller himself, and soon enough young Archie could plunk out some pretty fancy rhythms on the pub's beer-stained clanky uprights. When Elsie learned of her son's musical talent, in a gesture of kindness perhaps tinged with parental competitiveness, she had her father buy a fancy brand-new upright for the family living room. The arrival of the piano angered Elias, not because he didn't enjoy the boy's playing but because he

---

*This sartorial philosophy was reflected in the relatively sparse wardrobe of the highest-quality clothing that Grant maintained, even at the height of his great wealth and enormous popularity. Once he became an independent player, to the end of his career, he contracted to keep, at his discretion, all the clothing he wore in his films, more than once green-lighting a script out of consideration of the wardrobe. Grant was quoted (Davis, "Cary Grant") as saying that his favorite film in terms of fashion was *That Touch of Mink* (1962) because of the luxurious and exclusive custom-made Cardinal suits his character wore. At the end of shooting he kept the entire wardrobe of blues and grays that so perfectly offset his then blue-gray hair.

hadn't paid for it himself, and his loud but hollow complaints about not wanting to live off her father's charity set off yet another squabble over money that was anything but music to young Archie's ears.

At Elsie's insistence, Archie began studying classical piano, while at his father's urging he continued to develop his music hall style. The conflicted direction of his percussive abilities confused the boy, even as it became yet one more focal point of his parents' polarization, to the point where, while he loved to play, he rarely did for either of them.

Soon enough Elsie, ever the practical puritan, decided that her young boy's God-given talents (aided by the strong left hand, which he naturally favored) qualified him for early admission to one of the best schools in the area, the Bishop Road Junior School in Bishopston. She was rightly proud when Archie's musical abilities convinced the board he was fit to take one of the few available vacancies. The only thing that concerned her was Archie's left-handedness, something she feared might keep the school from allowing him to enroll.

Once enrolled, five-year-old Archie played the piano far less often than he kicked a football, and his unusually deft playground skills won him the friendship and admiration of the other boys his age and older. With all the good food and exercise he got, he spurted upward like a bean weed, stretching to a full six foot one before his thirteenth birthday. What then became apparent to everyone at school, students and teachers alike, was how unusually handsome young Archie was, tall, strong, and blessed with a face that was embossed with his mother's dimpled chin and rich brown eyes and his father's thick black wavy hair and ready smile.

If life seemed better for him at Bishop Road, his absence from home only made things worse between Elsie and Elias. Without Archie as the restraining buffer, their bickering became more frequent, and always centered on either Elias's philandering or his lack of sufficient income. More than once their fights turned physical. For Elias, as he saw it, at times the only way to deal with his stubborn wife was to beat her into proper submission.

Whenever things became too intense between them, Elsie simply left until thing cooled down. It eventually became clear to Elias that the situation between them was hopeless and that he had to leave for good. Unable to pay for a divorce, he figured out a route to freedom by taking a factory job in Southampton, eighty miles southeast of Bristol near the southern shore, to make uniforms for both militaries in the ongoing Italian-Turkish conflict.

Years later Grant would recall in this revealing description the traumatizing incident of what he took as his father's abandonment and his own culpability in helping to drive him away: "Odd, but I don't remember my father's departure from Bristol. *Perhaps I felt guilty at secretly being pleased, but now I had my mother to myself . . . anyway, I don't remember my father's going, but I missed him very much despite all his, and therefore my, faults*" (emphasis mine).

In Southampton, Elias quickly took a young mistress by the name of Mabel Alice Johnson and set up a second household. They soon had a baby, born out of wedlock, while back home, Elsie and Archie were forced to move to even smaller quarters.

Whenever Archie made the occasional visit to Southampton to visit his father, Elias made no secret of his new live-in relationship, and rewarded the boy's arrival with a trip to the local cinema to see the latest Chaplin–Mack Sennett two-reeler. Archie always laughed out loud at Charlie's put-upon character and exasperated glances through the camera—straight at him!—that brought a special brightness and joy to his otherwise lonely life.

IT WAS A JOY THAT would not last. One day in 1914 when he was ten years old, Archie came home from school and could not find his mother. With the war imminent, relatives had begun to live together to share ration books. Despite their smaller house, Elsie had taken in two of her brother's children, both of them older than Archie; now they silently watched as he ran from room to room looking for his mum. When he finally asked where she was, they said she had gone to a seaside resort for a little while. Why, Archie wondered, would she do that without taking him along? Without even telling him? And who was going to take care of him while she was away?

Elsie's sudden disappearance deepened Archie's increasingly tortured feelings of abandonment, guilt, and despair that would, in one form or another, stay with him for the rest of his life. Years later, Grant had this to say about his many failed marriages: "I [made] the mistake of thinking that each of my wives was my mother, that there would never be a replacement once she left. I found myself being attracted to [women] who looked like my mother — she had olive skin, for instance. Of course, at the same time I [often chose] a person with her emotional makeup, too, and I didn't need that."

What did happen to Elsie? Where had she gone? Not to a seaside resort, and not for a little while, as his relatives first told him. That story was quickly replaced by another; his mother had died of a heart attack.

The news devastated the young boy, who soon began to act out both his rage at being abandoned again, this time by his mother, and his guilt for somehow having caused both his parents to leave him. He soon turned to petty thievery and kept at it, even when, mostly out of pity, the community awarded him a scholarship to the prestigious Fairfield Secondary School. It was there he met his first girlfriend, someone he would still remember decades later as "plump, pretty, and frankly flirtatious" but utterly beyond his reach. The daughter of a local butcher, the girl so turned Archie's head that one day while staring at her, he walked straight into a lamppost and very nearly knocked his own teeth out.

That summer, Archie relocated himself to Southampton. He longed to move in with his father, but Elias said no, claiming that the woman he lived with and their baby, Archie's half-brother, took up all the room in the house. Archie then volunteered for summer work as a messenger and gofer on the military docks, often sleeping in alleys at night if he didn't make enough money to rent a cot in the local flophouse. This was wartime, and one of his daily chores was to hand each soldier a life belt before he set out from the English Channel in a transport ship, many of which were sunk by German submarines only a few miles offshore. Out of his sense of patriotism, Archie refused to accept any tip money from the soldiers for whom he ran these errands. Instead, he would take a military button or a regimental badge. He coveted these as if they were the true reflection of his self-worth and proudly wore as many of them as he could fit on his own belt.

Archie reluctantly returned to Bristol that fall for school, still consumed with grief over the death of his mother. He often spent his nights alone in his room, staring at a photo of Elsie, weeping softly as he prayed for God to watch over her soul. On weekends he would take himself to the local docks to watch the schooners and steamships that, he would later recall, "came right up the Avon River into the center of town." During these periods his notion of leaving Bristol forever intensified: "While most of my school friends were playing cricket, I'd sit alone for hours watching the ships come and go, sailing with them to far places on the tide of my imagination, trying to release myself from the emotional tensions which disarranged my thoughts."

In many ways, his longing to "release" himself was not all that different from, in many ways an emulation of, Elias's having found a way out of Bristol. Archie wished to escape as well, but no longer just to Southampton — his dreams now stretched much farther than that. Like his (and every Brit's) hero, Charlie Chaplin, he wanted to travel to the land of magic and dreams. America — *that* was where he longed to go.

THE NEXT SERIES OF EVENTS have often been described as "a lucky happenstance," the "fateful meeting of a boy and his mentor," or as Grant himself would later recall, "a coincidence of destiny zeroing in on my future." Thirteen-year-old Archie, although at best an average student with a bit of an aptitude for chemistry, was nonetheless befriended by his science professor's part-time assistant, brought in one day to help conduct a class experiment.

The assistant was actually a close friend of the teacher and an electrician who worked at the newly rebuilt Bristol Hippodrome (which then replaced the old Empire). Archie eagerly asked to be taken backstage to see the theater's modern switchboard and lighting system. It was a request his friend happily granted, and Archie quickly learned the technical aspects of putting on a show; he got to watch the performers from the privileged perspective of the wings, from where he could see the awestruck faces of the young boys in the first few rows lit by the spill of stage lighting as they bounced up and down with delight. According to Grant, "That's when I *knew*." Like Charlie Chaplin, he too would join the theater and see the world!

Archie's electrician friend then introduced him to the house manager of the Hippodrome, who also took a liking to the boy. He often invited young Archie to sit with the backstage crews and occasionally help them pull curtain and lighting cables and change scenery between acts. Archie did so well he was eventually promoted to help the lighting men handle the special twin arc lamps, or limelights, as they were known (for their tendency to throw a pale green halo around performers). They hung from the ceiling at either side of the stage and had to be manually focused to keep the star performers in their special sharp, double-spot illumination.

Eventually Archie was allowed to operate one of the limelights on his own and was good enough with it to operate the all-important center "moving white" at the back of the house. All went well until one time during a performance he misfocused the center spot on a couple of back mirrors that gave away the secret to a headlining magician's best trick. At the magician's insistence, Archie was permanently barred from ever again working at the Bristol Hippodrome.

He was devastated and vowed to never set foot inside another theater, but soon found himself once again hanging around the fringes of Bristol's many playhouses, spending time with the actors he had gotten to know during his brief career as a lighting man. On the odd occasion he was even able to get some pickup work at the Hippodrome as a call boy after school for ten shillings a week, which is how he first heard about Bob Pender's troupe of young knockabout comedians.* Pender's was a specialty act whose performers padded their skits with intricate slapstick numbers, stilt-walking choruses, and intricate mime routines complete with matching costumes and oversize masks. Pender, whose real name was Bob Lomas, had first made a name for himself as a performer in the tradition of the great Drury Lane clowns before forming his own company, intending to follow the path of the legendary Fred Karno traveling shows.

Lomas's entourage was a decidedly family affair. His wife, Margaret, a former Parisian Folies-Bergère ballet mistress, gave the Pender troupe the benefit of her specialized training in movement and balance. Among the lead performers were Lomas's daughter Doris, his brothers Tom and Bill, his widowed sister-in-law, and her son.

Like all companies made up of mostly young performers, Pender's was forever in need of trainable talent to replace those who grew too quickly, got bored and left, fell in love, married, or went into the military. After getting to know young Archie, Lomas invited him to try out as a member of the traveling company. Archie was beside himself! After hanging on the backstage fringes of the business for what seemed like forever, he was, at last, going to have a chance at performing.

---

*Variously known as "Bob Pender's Little Dandies," "The Pender Troupe of Giants," "Bob Pender's Nippy Nine Burlesque Rehearsal," and by Grant in later recollections as "The Bob Pender Acrobats."

He worked up a series of athletic moves he had learned from the older footballers in school, with a couple of flips he had always been able to do, and also showed that he could walk on his hands, a trick his father had taught him. Lomas liked what he saw and offered him a position with the company, provided that Elias give his written approval. Archie immediately accepted, went home, forged a letter of permission from his father, and brought it back to Lomas, who then sent him off to observe the troupe in Norwich.

Unfortunately, Archie's first tour ended abruptly ten days later, while the troupe was still in Norwich, by the sudden and unexpected arrival of Elias. He had been told by Archie's Bristol relatives that the boy had run away. He quickly tracked his son down, confronted Lomas, and informed him that Archie was not yet fourteen, the legal work age in England at the time. Elias demanded that he be returned to school at once and threatened to press criminal charges of abduction of a minor against Lomas. Reluctantly, Archie packed his few things, said good-bye to everyone, and returned to Bristol without ever having appeared on stage.

Back home, Archie longed to return to the theatrical life and came up with a clever plan to make it happen. Years later, according to Grant, he "investigated" the girls' lavatory at school, meaning that he drilled a small peephole through one of the walls to watch the girls go to the bathroom. Other sources claim he reverted to his old ways and was caught stealing. Whatever the reason, his official expulsion, for "inattentiveness, irresponsibility, and incorrigibility," occurred in March 1918, just two months after his fourteenth birthday. The school's decision conveniently freed him to rejoin the Pender troupe.

That August Archie eagerly signed a three-year contract, this time actually cosigned by Elias, that officially granted him permission to join Pender's troupe, at a weekly salary of ten shillings with board and lodging included and technical training to be provided by Lomas. By now Elias was more than happy to give his son over to Lomas, for reasons that had less to do with Archie's budding talents than his own present needs. When the boy got in trouble at school, the local authorities had investigated why he was living with relatives in Bristol rather than with his father in Southampton. The last thing Elias wanted was the Bristol authorities sniffing into his personal life. Finally, when Elias discovered that Lomas was a fellow Mason and a family man, he gave his full consent, believing his boy would be well cared for.

ARCHIE PROVED an apt pupil when he wanted to be, especially in the more physical aspects of British music hall entertainment. His specialties became stilt-walking, tumbling, and pratfalls, to which he brought his natural athleticism and the same kind of natural rhythm and timing he had shown at the piano. At Lomas's urging, he also began to work on his speech to lose his pronounced West Country Bristol brogue. Unable to master "cultured English talk," he developed a unique vocal mix of rhythms, raspy voice, and hesitant diction, the sound of which would one day be instantly identifiable to movie audiences all over the world.

For the next two years Archie and the troupe traveled the British music hall circuit, occasionally jumping over to the European mainland and the larger theatrical outposts of the Middle East.

By the age of sixteen, six-foot-one Archie Leach, with his handsome face, great smile, easy laugh, and natural athletic ability, had developed a charismatic stage presence that brought him to the front ranks of the Pender touring company. And then it happened. In 1920 Lomas's organization was invited by famed New York impresario Charles Dillingham, Oscar Hammerstein's chief competitor, to come to the United States, to perform at 42nd Street's Globe Theater as the opening act for Fred Stone, one of vaudeville's biggest stars. With room for only eight of the twelve resident young men in his company, Lomas was forced to eliminate one-third of his male leads. Archie could hardly contain himself when he saw his name posted on the bulletin board along with the other youngsters who had survived the cut.

He arose at dawn the morning of July 21, the day of the troupe's departure, and was the first to arrive at the Southampton docks, accompanied by Elias, who wanted to be there to say farewell. After kissing his father goodbye, he boarded the luxury liner RMS *Olympic* (the *Titanic*'s sister ship), bound for America.

Also aboard were two of the most famous Hollywood film stars in the world. Douglas Fairbanks and his bride, Mary Pickford, whose marriage had caused an international newspaper and newsreel frenzy, were completing their six-week European honeymoon with a first-class cruise back to the States. It was just before leaving for the Continent that Fairbanks and Pickford had signed their historic deal, along with Chaplin and D. W. Griffith, to create their own studio, United Artists, with the intention of gaining their artistic freedom and financial independence from the other studios.

When word got out that Fairbanks and Pickford were on the *Olympic*, it thrilled the other passengers, but none more than Archie. Every day he watched the people stream in and out of the dining room until he got his nerve up to approach the glamorous couple for their autographs. Fairbanks and Pickford proved remarkably gracious, and when Archie asked permission to have his picture taken with them, they happily complied. Archie told them how much he admired their movies, and how he hoped one day to be as great a physical actor as Fairbanks, famous for his astonishing acrobatic stunts often filmed in single, uncut sequences. Fairbanks thanked the boy, and then, to Archie's surprise, asked if he would like to join him in his daily on-deck morning calisthenics. Would he! Doing jumping jacks next to the well-tanned, immaculately dressed, and perfectly coiffed actor thrilled Archie and inspired him to "doggedly strive" to keep himself as fit and well groomed as his first famous Hollywood friend.

And so it was, late every afternoon, while the *Olympic* steamed westward and the other passengers took their daily naps, played cards, or stole away for a romantic interlude, Archie Leach stood by himself on deck, leaning over the rail trying to see the face of his future. Freed at last from the prison of British provincialism, he vowed that once in America, he would never again look back at the loneliness and sadness of all his yesterdays, left buried somewhere with Elsie in her Bristol grave.

3

"I never associated him with being a working-class kid. I must say, I don't want to sound snobbish about it, but he never had any sort of Bristol accent. From the first time I met him, he always impressed me as the model gentleman. I thought he was Cary Grant offscreen, in real life. But that's what made him such a good actor."

—PETER CADBURY

Archie's dreams of the future stretched across the ocean like expanding tubes of a telescope until, on July 28, the tip of lower Manhattan finally came into view. As the *Olympic* slowly pulled into New York's harbor and the Hudson River, Archie stood on deck with the hundreds of other passengers, the salt spray cooling his face in the hot sun as they sailed past the silent, welcoming gaze of the Statue of Liberty. When he turned his head in the other direction, while the great ship was carefully tugged into West Forty-sixth Street's White Star pier, he could see for the first time the magnificent tall buildings of Manhattan.

Mr. and Mrs. Fairbanks and the other first-class passengers disembarked to fireworks and a live brass band, while hundreds of photographers and newsreel cameramen and hordes of well-wishers celebrated the return of the larger-than-life screen legends. By the time Pender's troupe deboarded, much of the pomp, press, and people had gone. Archie and the others had missed all the excitement because of getting bogged down in the extra-long tedium of customs reserved for steerage passengers. His first steps onto American soil were taken over dead streamers and punctured balloons strewn along the wooden pier, as he and the others made their way to the waiting taxis that Lomas had arranged to take them to their hotel. The entire troupe had been booked into a Fifty-eighth Street "We Cater to the Theatrical Trade" residential hotel, just west of Eighth Avenue, about three-quarters of a mile from where they had docked.

After lugging his own bags up four flights to his small room, Archie barely had time to unpack when a slip of paper under his door informed him that the company was to attend a reception that evening personally arranged and supervised by Charles Dillingham, to be held on the stage of his famed Broadway Globe Theater. Archie was ready to go an hour before departure time.

Dillingham intended the welcome party as a way to formally introduce the Penders to Fred Stone, the star for whom they had been booked to open. The evening went well enough, with relations between Stone and the troupe cordial, if not warm. They cooled even more the next day when Stone caught a glimpse of the troupe rehearsals. He didn't like what he saw—not because they were so bad, but because they were too good. Stone feared that the Penders' spectacular physical feats, far better than he had heard, particularly the stilt-walking routine, would be impossible for him to follow, and he insisted they be taken off the bill.

It was a blow for the Penders and for Dillingham, as well. He had invested a lot of money in this booking, personally financing the trip over from England, and needed to find a way to recoup. The next day Dillingham released a statement to the press saying that because of the physical limitations of the Globe, Pender's stilt-walking "Giants," as his players were advertised in the American trades, would not be appearing after all, and he had arranged to book them instead into another of his contracted venues, the cavernous New York Hippodrome, billed by the showman as "The World's Largest Theater" (its front curtain was a full city block long). The Hippodrome was the permanent home of his *Good Times* revue, meant to compete with the *Ziegfeld Follies*, the talk of the town at the New Amsterdam Theater.

Good Times was a world-class extravaganza, complete with elephants, zebras, monkeys, horses, acrobats, fireworks, dazzling light shows, solo singers, cyclists, dancers, chorales, musicians, magicians, and a self-contained water show that featured dozens of female swimmers and male divers in a stage tank containing 960,000 gallons of water. Dillingham hoped the Penders' stilt act would now give the show a dash of old-world music hall. In a sequence squeezed in between the elephants and the zebras the producer billed as "The Toy Store," the stilt-walkers were all made up to look like toys that came alive at night after all the people went home.

On August 9, barely a week and a half from the day he arrived in America, Archie made his Stateside debut as one of the stilt-walkers in Dillingham's *Good Times* revue. The act received great notices in the press, and the group settled in for a long run. Between performances Archie and the others quickly developed a regular routine of performing, laundering their own clothes, and cooking their own meals on hot plates in their rooms. To avoid homesickness, several of the boys paired off and roomed together.

At one point Archie developed a strong crush on a gorgeous, leggy blonde in the *Good Times* chorus by the name of Gladys Kincaid, his first case of show-business-related unrequited love. As Grant would later recall, "Here I was, seventeen, and incapable of sufficient progression toward testing that birds-and-bees theory." The self-confessed still virginal Archie never even got to hold Gladys's hand. He spent one afternoon shopping for a present for her at Macy's, but rather than buy her a lover's lure—some fancy lingerie or imported perfume—he chose a multicolored woolen coat-sweater-scarf combination, which got him nothing more from Gladys than a puzzled look followed by a motherly pat on his handsome cheek. (The only physical comfort Archie managed in these days was back at the hotel, engaging in the kind of adolescent games of sexual exploration and experimentation typical of British all-boys boarding school residents.)

The revue ran on Broadway for another nine months, then embarked on a year-long tour on the famous B. F. Keith vaudeville circuit, which took them to the major cities east of the Mississippi. As it happened, the Keith circuit traveled the same route as the New York Giants baseball team, and because all the games were played in daylight, Archie was able to see a good number of them. Having never heard of baseball before coming to America, he became endlessly fascinated by the intricacies of the game and developed a love for it that would last a lifetime.

He also met quite a few successful actors on the circuit (and a few unknowns, mostly understudies and last-minute fill-ins, among them a young New York hoofer by the name of James Cagney), but none amused him or impressed him more than the Marx Brothers, whose vaudeville routines later became the basis for many of their zany movies. While the rest of the country preferred Groucho, Zeppo, the good-looking straight man and romantic lead, was Archie's favorite, the one whose foil timing he believed was the real key to the act's success. Not long after, Archie began to augment his already well-practiced "suave" Fairbanks look and dress with a Zeppo-like fancy bowtie (called a jazz-bow, or jazzbo, during the Roaring Twenties) and copied his brilliantine hairstyle, adding Dixie Peach, the favorite pomade of American black performers and show business leads, by the palmful to his thick dark mop, to give it a molded, comb-streaked blue-black Zeppo sheen.

THE KEITH CIRCUIT TOUR ended in January 1922, just days shy of Archie's eighteenth birthday, which roughly coincided with the expiration of his original contract. After four years in America, Lomas was exhausted by all the traveling, especially by the long distances between stops that made touring much more difficult in the States than back in England. He was ready to bring the boys home and assumed that Archie and the others would be eager to depart as well. To his surprise, not only Archie but most of the others chose to stay in America. Lomas agreed, gave them all the equivalent of their passage money and some additional funds to help settle in, and bade them all a warm farewell. He then sailed with his family back to England and obscurity, never again to achieve the level of popularity there he had enjoyed prior to his voyage west. In his absence the world of British music hall had all but vanished, its theaters converted to accommodate the working public's newest favorite form of entertainment, feature-length motion pictures.

BACK IN AMERICA, Archie, who quickly split from the others, was, for the first time, now on his own in New York City and loving it. Freed from the never-ending regimentation and grind of traveling and performing, he now intended to relax and enjoy the city. He loved traveling around in open-air buses down Fifth Avenue to Greenwich Village, then back uptown in the enclosed ones that went up Broadway all the way to Harlem. He marveled at the tall residential apartment buildings all along the West Side that were so unlike the one- and two-family dwellings that dotted Bristol. He also enjoyed riding the IRT subway all the way to the Bronx and then back to the Battery. On sunny days he liked walking through Central Park, or visiting Grant's Tomb, or taking the ferry to see the Statue of Liberty up close.

All too soon, however, the little money he had left ran out, and in the fall of 1922 he found himself broke and out of a job. He reluctantly moved out of his single room at the hotel and into the apartment of another struggling artist, George (Jack) Orry-Kelly, who had a small loft on Barrow Street in the Village, situated behind a legitimate theater.

Orry-Kelly, originally from South Wales and named by his mother after her favorite garden flower, was one of the few new friends Archie had made in America, although exactly when and how remains unknown (Grant makes no mention of Orry-Kelly in his "autobiography"). When Archie told him of his current situation, the set designer offered to let him share his living space, and the out-of-work actor quickly and gratefully accepted. It is not difficult to understand why Archie liked him. At twenty-four, Orry-Kelly was seven years Archie's senior, smart, sophisticated, city-seasoned, tall, and good-looking. He dressed impeccably, presented himself with confidence, and benefited from a quick and verbal wit. Like Archie, Orry-Kelly was the son of a tailor (Archie's father, primarily a presser, had done some tailoring for the military while he lived in Southampton). Like Archie, he had migrated at an early age to America to find work in the theater. But unlike Archie, he was extremely effeminate and openly and unashamedly gay. During all the time they lived together, Archie would try to cherry-pick those qualities he most admired in Orry-Kelly, even as he struggled to deal with an undeniable physical attraction to his new and charismatic roommate.

With time on his hands, Archie began to frequent the National Vaudeville Artists (NVA) Club on West Forty-sixth Street, a gathering place for performers like himself in search of a lead on a new job, or word of a traveling company that was passing through and needed a pickup performer. Most often all he found was a soft chair and a courtesy cup of tea.

Archie auditioned for several Broadway shows, but the advantages of his handsome face and tall, athletic body were offset by the still noticeable traces of his working-class British accent, which made casting directors reluctant to hire him. He became increasingly intimidated by the act of auditioning—a fear (he later recalled) that manifested itself in the form of a recurring dream. Standing in the center of a lighted stage, Archie is surrounded by a large cast of actors and unable to remember his lines. The result is always the same: public humiliation for not being able to perform and deliver. The dream, with all its socio-sexual implications, appears by all accounts (including Grant's) to have begun approximately the same time period Archie moved in with Orry-Kelly.

Also around this time, Archie managed to earn some money by serving as a male escort to several of the most socially acceptable women in the city. He fell into this type of work after he befriended a fellow he would later identify only as "Marks," an easy-time hustler of the type that operated on the fringes of the New York theater community. One night Marks set him up to accompany Lucrezia Bori, the world-famous Metropolitan Opera lyric soprano, to a swank Park Avenue affair.

The idea of "acting" the role of a black-tie escort appealed to Archie, and Marks easily convinced him that his good looks made him well equipped to play the part. The evening with Bori proved to be the successful debut of a character who would one day be recognizable to all the world—a handsome, charming rake, dressed in the finest tux, with an appealing manner, cleft chin, and devastating smile.

That night, mingling with the upscale crowd, Archie met a fellow by the name of George Tilyou Jr. Over cognac and small talk, a relaxed Archie revealed his "secret" to Tilyou, that he was, in fact, less than he appeared to be. Beneath all his gloss, tails, and sheen, he told his new friend, he was just one more out-of-work actor picking up a few dollars playing Bori's "date." Tilyou got a great kick out of it, and when Archie told him his best talent was walking on stilts rather than carrying on airs, Tilyou burst out laughing and told him he might be able to help him out with a real job. His late father, he said, had created—and his family still owned and operated—Coney Island's famous Steeplechase Park amusement attraction.

They exchanged phone numbers, and when Archie called the next day, Tilyou proved as good as his word. He had managed to secure a park job for Archie as, of all things, a stilt-walker. A few hours later Archie found himself dressed in a bright green coat, jockey's cap, and long black pants. Tilyou directed him to walk around the boardwalk on stilts, wearing a wooden sandwich board advertising that the steeplechase was open. It was undeniably a step down, and Archie knew it, but escort work was far from steady, and he desperately needed the money to extend his stay in America. The forty dollars a week he received from Tilyou, in a job that earned him the nickname "Rubber Legs," was almost enough to make ends meet.

To get the rest, besides occasional escorting gigs, he sold hand-painted ties that Orry-Kelly made in their Greenwich Village apartment, which had lately become a bit more cramped when Orry-Kelly took in another roommate, an Australian fellow by the name of Charlie Phelps, whose financial contribution was badly needed. How and when Phelps first appeared in Orry-Kelly's life remains unknown, although it may actually have been Archie who met him first, aboard the *Olympic* on his voyage across the Atlantic, for which Phelps, a bit of a vagabond, had hired on as a steward in order to gain his passage to America.

Archie sold Orry-Kelly's ties on street corners during the day and at night served as the household cook, specializing in the fried and breaded Dover sole and crisp chips all three were so fond of from their youth. Fresh sole was available daily at the nearby docks, and after spending several hours selling his wares, Archie always enjoyed walking over and picking out a couple of freshly caught fish, then buying his other ingredients from the many small ethnic shops that flourished on the streets of the West Village, in preparation of that evening's "family dinner."

A FEW MONTHS LATER, Dillingham announced auditions for *Better Times*, his sequel to *Good Times* scheduled to play that summer at the Hippodrome. Archie quickly contacted the other members of the Penders still in America and suggested they reunite, train, and try out as a unified act for the show. When they felt ready, they auditioned for Dillingham, who immediately hired their stilt act as a featured spot for his new extravaganza.

Better Times opened on Labor Day weekend (August 31) of 1922, and after seven months that had felt like a lifetime of unemployment, Archie was back working on Broadway. The show ran for six months, and when it closed, Archie was able to convince the others to stay together and form their own company, the Lomas Troupe, named after the man who had first brought them together. Archie proved a diligent manager and soon had the group booked onto the Pantages circuit, a national vaudeville trail that traveled across the country, including a few stops in Canada, before arriving in Los Angeles to play the circuit's namesake theater on Hollywood Boulevard, the West Coast equivalent of New York's famed Palace.

On his first day off in L.A., Archie explored Hollywood just as he had New York City—alone, unplanned, and unhurried. He traveled once more by bus and by the many trolleys that crisscrossed the city and mostly, as everyone else seemed to in those days, on foot. He strolled up and down the sparkling pavement of Hollywood Boulevard, marveling at the palm trees along the sidewalks, the first real ones he had ever seen, and tried to keep his head tilted toward the sky to catch some of the glorious sunshine that quickly and beautifully bronzed his face.

During one of his evening performances at the Pantages Theater on Hollywood Boulevard, Archie was visited backstage by Douglas Fairbanks, who'd read about the show in the trades and remembered the youngster's name from their voyage to America aboard the *Olympic*. Archie was delighted both by the visit and by Fairbanks's invitation for him to visit the set of his latest production, *The Thief of Bagdad*. The next afternoon Archie did just that. As if he were in the eye of a hurricane, he stood motionless off to the side of the massive film stage while dozens of behind-the-scenes workers scurried all around him. Then suddenly he heard his name being called, and he spotted Fairbanks, a wide smile on his face, waving him over for a quick but friendly chat before he shot his next scene. It was a day young Archie Leach would never forget.

When the troupe's engagement at the Pantages ended, Archie reluctantly returned to New York, dreaming of the day he would be able to return to Hollywood and make movies of his own.

Back in Manhattan, Archie fell into his familiar routines of escorting, selling ties on the street, keeping house with Orry-Kelly and Charlie, and spending many an afternoon at the NVA Club. Acting work was, as always, hard to find, and Archie took whatever morsels came his way. Because he could move well, he'd get an occasional booking as half of a song and dance "duo," his partner being whatever young out-of-work actress was available. For the union scale of $62.50 a night, he and his assigned partner would trot out into one of the many new and cavernous movie houses that had sprung up in the suburbs across the river in New Jersey and dance to scratchy recordings played between features while indifferent audiences filed in and took their seats.

Among the younger theatrical casting directors he regularly stopped by to see was Jean Dalrymple, who eventually put him in a vaudeville skit called *The Woman Pays*, which played several months on the junior Orpheum circuit. The gig is notable because it marks his first speaking role. The skit, written by Dalrymple, centered on Archie, "the handsomest man in town," being the unwitting object of two overzealous women vying for his affections.

By the time the tour ended, Archie and Dalrymple had become good friends, and slowly, with her guidance, he developed a strong reputation as a willing and reliable "straight man" for whatever vaudeville stars came to town for one-offs (one night of performances). Straight-man work was unpopular among the more established actors, who disliked playing the fool, the foil, or the mark, setting up jokes for comedians who made them, and only them, look good. Archie, however, was more than willing to do that kind of work, but soon ran into new problems no one, including Dalrymple, had anticipated. Comics like Milton Berle were reluctant to use him because his good looks made it too difficult for audiences to accept him as "the dummy." Berle was a particularly physical pie-in-the-face type who, like so many jokesters, considered himself also something of a ladies' man and did not appreciate being upstaged by someone as attractive to women as Archie.

At the opening night party of one of these gigs Archie found himself among many of the glitterati of New York vaudeville, including comedians

George Burns and Gracie Allen. Burns had heard about Archie and wanted to meet him.

Archie invited Orry-Kelly to accompany him to the party. Things had not been going well between the three roommates, and Archie saw this as a chance for just the two of them to get out of the apartment and have a good time. While Archie was away on tour, Orry-Kelly had begun to get steady work on Broadway as a costume designer for such theatrical luminaries as the great Ethel Barrymore. Archie had wanted him to stay home and leave the wage-earning to him. But for Orry-Kelly, career was not just the first but the only priority.

Unfortunately, things came to a head at the party, when Archie and Orry-Kelly got into a loud shouting match that horrified the other guests. Burns, in particular, was disgusted by the public display and asked friends why everyone had to be a witness to all this "homosexuality."

Believing he and Orry-Kelly had come to an impasse in their relationship, Archie began seeing more of Lester Sweyd, a vaudevillian star ten years his senior whom he had first met when both were appearing at the Hippodrome. Sweyd had made a name for himself playing Fonzo, the Boy Wonder in Skirts, before retiring from the stage to become a full-time agent. Shortly after the argument with Orry-Kelly at the party, Archie began spending nights at Sweyd's apartment.

He also began to accept more of the constant offers from Marks to do escort work. His good looks had made him quite popular among the wealthy women around town, and it was an open secret among them that the "social services" of this handsome young actor could be acquired for an entire evening at a quite reasonable cost.

Socializing with the tuxedo allowed Archie to observe, up close, the physical mannerisms of the wealthy and helped him iron out many of the lingering cultural wrinkles from his own limited upbringing. He listened carefully to the way these people spoke and worked incessantly on modulating his lingering British singsong lilt into a more descending American rhythm. He practiced his walk to eliminate his street roll, the result of his slightly bowed, naturally acrobatic "Rubber Legs."

All this physical fine-tuning resulted in his becoming even more attractive to the women who hired him. And while his increasing presence among the upper strata of the New York social scene may have been mostly decorous, it bothered Orry-Kelly that Archie was rapidly gaining a name as the number one gigolo in town, and that such a reputation could hurt both of their careers. One night over dinner Orry-Kelly made it official. Their relationship was over, and Archie would leave the apartment for good.

With his love life in shambles, a tainted reputation, and not a penny to his name, Archie moved out. For the next year and a half he rented a room in an SRO at the NVA Club in Times Square. Fearful that escorting was ruining any chance he might have at making a living on Broadway, he took a series of dead-end jobs waiting on tables or wearing a billboard for a Chinese restaurant across the street from Macy's department store.

Years later, to cover up the failure and humiliation of these times, Grant insisted that in 1925, at the age of twenty-one, he returned to England to appear in repertory with the Nightingale Players. In fact, he never left America at all. Instead, he remained in New York City, lost, lonely, and knocking around, until 1927, the same year he later claimed to have returned from British rep to the United States and New York City.

One thing is certain: the year 1927 would signal the creative rebirth of Archie Leach.

4

"I had quite a run of stage successes, both in New York
and on tour. After . . . I thought a visit to Hollywood would
be quite an idea, and I made the trip by car all the way
from New York."

—CARY GRANT

That spring, desperate for money, Archie swallowed his pride and called
upon Orry-Kelly, to whom he had not spoken for two years, and who had
during that time become a highly sought-after Broadway set and costume
designer. Orry-Kelly was happy to hear from him, but was still not willing to
take him back. Instead, he agreed to pay for a small studio apartment for Archie
on East 80th Street, in the Yorkville section of Manhattan. This new neighborhood felt strange to Archie. It seemed light-years from Times Square, with
a huge influx of German immigrants and many crowded restaurants that specialized in that country's heavy cuisine. He much preferred the more familiar
show business surroundings of Rudley's, the theatrical bar and grill on 41st and
Broadway where he now was a familiar face, nicknamed "Kangaroo" by fellow
drinking buddies because of his accent and funny walk. Among them were
some of the biggest up-and-coming names in show business, including screenwriter Preston Sturges, playwrights Moss Hart and Edward Chodorov,
Broadway song-and-dance man George Murphy, and a stage actor with the

unusual name of Humphrey Bogart. Although Archie became extremely pop-ular among this heady crowd and was granted the privilege of sitting at their large, Algonquinesque table, he felt a bit intimidated and tended to say little. According to Chodorov, "He was never a very open fellow, but he was earnest and we liked him."

Orry-Kelly was also part of the elite gay Broadway social scene, and at a party one night producer Reginald Hammerstein, the younger brother of Oscar Hammerstein II (grandson of the legendary Broadway impresario), told him he was casting his big new fall musical, *Golden Dawn*. Orry-Kelly replied that he ought to check out Archie Leach, an actor he thought would be perfect for it.

The next day Reggie set up an appointment for Archie and during the audition developed an immediate and intense crush on him. Archie, who would later on recall Reggie only as a "happy acquaintance," nevertheless began a romantic relationship with the young producer. They were seen together at many of the best nightclubs in town, and before long Reggie told Archie the role in *Golden Dawn* was his. He also convinced his uncle, Arthur Hammerstein, now in charge of the theatrical dynasty's business end, to sign Archie to a one-year personal management contract to run through the 1927–28 theatrical season. The agreement gave the Hammerstein organiza-tion exclusive rights to Archie's services at a starting salary of $75 a week, renewable through 1933 at pre-set increases to $800 a week. Archie eagerly signed on the dotted line, and that fall the show opened on Broadway.

Golden Dawn is the story of a white goddess who rules an African tribe, a flimsy premise that allowed for extravagant sets and numerous musical numbers with touches of minstrelsy, lots of jazzy pop, and a finale notable for featuring mainstream Broadway's first topless chorus line. Its main attraction (besides the naked bodices of its beautiful chorines) was the appearance of Metropolitan Opera star Louise Hunter.

The show opened on November 30, 1927, to largely negative reviews (the most memorable coming from the *New York Daily Mirror*'s Walter Winchell, who dubbed it *The Golden Yawn*) and quickly closed.

Archie, who was cast in a secondary role of a youthful Australian POW with one song and a single line of dialogue, was, ironically, the only person who benefited from *Golden Dawn*. His appearance, brief as it was, proved good enough to get him signed by Billy "Square Deal" Grady, a young hustling William Morris agent. Grady was convinced that Archie could be a star, and he worked closely with the Hammersteins, who still held exclusive rights to Archie's services on Broadway, to get him into *Polly*, slated for Broadway later that year.

Polly, a musical adaptation of a 1917 stage comedy, *Polly with a Past*, starred British music hall sensation June Howard-Tripp, vaudevillian Fred Allen, and comedienne Inez Courtney. Archie was cast as a society playboy opposite Howard-Tripp, a poor girl masquerading as a rich one.

Unfortunately, June took an instant dislike to Archie, and despite (or perhaps because of) his strong out-of-town reviews, she complained to the producers that he was unsuited to play opposite her. His British working-class accent, she said, made a mockery of his rich playboy character, and besides not being able to act, in her opinion, he also could neither dance nor sing.

To appease their star, the producers reluctantly fired Archie, although he was still in the show when it had its out-of-town tryout in Philadelphia, where the great Florenz Ziegfeld happened to see him in it and decided he wanted him to star in the national tour of his Broadway hit *Rosalie*.*

Ziegfeld's world-famous Follies had by now taken up permanent residence in the New Amsterdam Theater on 42nd Street, built shortly after the turn of the century, the Klaw and Erlanger Booking Agency. By 1910, Marc Klaw and Abraham Erlanger's professional differences with the Hammersteins had escalated into a personal feud (which would eventually help bring down the Hammerstein empire). The Hammersteins hated Ziegfeld, who was firmly in the Klaw and Erlanger camp, believing he had stolen much of the original Hammerstein concept of style, flash, and glitter for his Follies.

When Ziegfeld offered Archie the romantic lead in the prestigious touring company of one of his biggest hits, Ziegfeld thought he would have no problem signing him. Although Archie's contract with the Hammersteins still had a few months left on it, he was sure his appearance in two consecutive flops would, if anything, give them the excuse they needed to get out of their

---

Polly received devastating reviews and closed after only sixteen performances. Its worst review was also the funniest. Robert Garland, writing in the *Telegram*, paraphrased Robert Browning's 1845 poem "Home Thoughts, from Abroad" by writing, "Oh, to be in England now that June is here!"

deal with him before it officially ended. What neither Ziegfeld nor Archie counted on was the emergence into the mix of the Shubert Organization, headed by J.J. and his brother Lee. Having heard of Ziegfeld's interest in Archie, they quietly bought out the remainder of his contract from the cash-hungry Hammersteins, who were willing to sell it to the Shuberts to prevent the hated Ziegfeld from getting him.

All this back-door dealing infuriated Archie, who resented being the pawn in a power game in which he held no financial advantage and that, to his way of thinking, cost him his chance to break into the big time as the star of the already hugely successful *Rosalie*.

The Shuberts immediately cast Archie opposite Jeanette MacDonald in their new musical farce, *Boom Boom*, scheduled to open at their wondrous new Broadway Casino Theater on January 28, 1929. Archie's role was a small but important one that included a little singing and a lot of what he did best—looking good.

Boom Boom opened to so-so reviews, with most of the praise going to Jeanette MacDonald, whose costumes happened to have been designed by Orry-Kelly. During the run of the show, Archie and Orry-Kelly briefly rekindled their romantic friendship, but if Archie had any hope of making a permanent go of it, it ended when Orry-Kelly took a permanent job in St. Louis to design costumes for that city's Municipal Opera Company.

Boom Boom closed after seventy-two performances, another instantly forgettable star vehicle. It did, however, bring both MacDonald and Archie overtures from the Paramount Publix film studios. Oscar Serlin, Paramount's leading New York–based talent scout, had caught a performance of *Boom Boom* and thought MacDonald might do well in films opposite Paramount's newly signed French cabaret star, Maurice Chevalier. He also liked Archie's stage presence and decided to invite them both to take a screen test in the studio's Astoria headquarters. Paramount was among the last of the majors to keep a working base on the East Coast, at the insistence of Adolph Zukor, who believed that Broadway was a fertile pool for new talent and an important cultural base from which to maintain his film studio's level of sophistication.

Archie and Jeanette each spent an afternoon before the cameras in Queens, but neither was offered a Hollywood contract, although MacDonald did receive the more favorable grading. The unanimous verdict on Archie was that his seventeen-and-a-half-inch neck was too thick, his long legs too bowed, and his handsome face too pudgy.* Nowhere in Archie's evaluation is there any mention of his acting ability.

THE STOCK MARKET CRASH OF '29 hit the New York theater industry particularly hard, sending almost every working actor to the unemployment lines. Suddenly Archie's contract with the Shuberts, which he had at first so resented, became his lifeline. For the next three years he dutifully appeared in a number of their cookie-cutter shows, grateful for the steady employment. He spent as little as possible and saved whatever and wherever he could. Apparently, nowhere during this period is there evidence of his involvement in any personal relationship with either a man or a woman. He was young, single, well-to-do, extremely popular, and, apparently, utterly alone. Years later, reflecting on these times, Grant noted, "Without the ability to fully love or be fully loved, so many of us [used] the acquisition of money [to] provide self-esteem and happiness." In other words, money had become the only tangible measurement Archie had to assess his self-worth; and performing was the way to attain both. Whenever he received less than a rave notice or a show closed early, his fears of a return to poverty quickly resurfaced, along with an acknowledged dip in his self-esteem.

One time during a particularly difficult period he happened to run into Fred Allen, who had befriended him when they'd appeared together in *Polly*. Archie poured his heart out to Allen, who by way of response invited Archie to accompany him to the observation tower atop the Woolworth building in Lower Manhattan. It was a rainy day, and the city was blanketed with a thick gray fog. Allen told Archie to look out as far as he could see, which was not very far. Nevertheless, Allen said, there surely was a whole wide world out there. Just because they couldn't see it at the moment didn't mean it didn't exist. Faith, he told Archie, was the belief in the existence of the world and of one's place in that world. The individual may be small and relatively

---

*This comment about his neck, thickened from years of acrobatics, caused Grant, for the rest of his life, to wear custom-made shirts with unusually high collars.

unimportant by comparison, but nevertheless he existed, and his importance was not always measurable by immediate circumstances or surroundings. Archie, who was not much of a spiritual or intellectual contemplator, put a great deal of value on Allen's words and thanked him profusely for taking the time to try to explain his way of looking at life. Allen's philosophy was the most sensible thing he had ever heard; he was living in a fog, and fogs sooner or later lifted.

If that wasn't exactly what Allen had meant, for Archie it was close enough. He would remember Allen's words for years, and whenever he got depressed he would think of himself as being engulfed by a metaphorical fog; he would work his way out of it by having the faith that it would pass. Just because he wasn't happy at that moment didn't mean he never would be. That afternoon with Fred Allen became an important first step in Archie's journey of self-discovery, one that would take a lifetime to complete.

ARCHIE'S NEXT SHUBERT SHOW was A *Wonderful Night*, a reworking of Johann Strauss's *Die Fledermaus*. The show received mixed reviews and managed only 125 performances before it closed in February 1930. This latest failure forced the Shuberts to pare down their stable of contract players. They wanted to keep Archie, but only if he would agree to work that summer in their open-air Municipal Opera in, of all places, St. Louis. Archie was delighted. This was the excuse he needed to rejoin his former lover, Orry-Kelly. He was so happy he bought himself a brand-new bright yellow Packard to make the drive to the Midwest. Once there he and Orry-Kelly once again became physically involved, and while the Shuberts had arranged for Archie to have his own hotel room, he spent most evenings that summer with Orry-Kelly in his apartment.

When the season ended, Archie convinced Orry-Kelly to come back to New York City with him, where they moved into a new apartment and bought a nearby speakeasy. On nights when neither of them was working, they tended bar together.

That fall, Billy Grady, Archie's agent, got the Shuberts to agree to loan him to producer William Friedlander, who was looking for a male lead to star opposite Fay Wray in *Nikki*, a new play headed for Broadway written by

Wray's husband, Hollywood screenwriter John Monk Saunders. Friedlander had commissioned Saunders to write the show after he won an Academy Award for his work on the 1928 blockbuster film *Wings*. Saunders agreed on the condition that Friedlander cast Wray in the lead. He then took one of his own magazine serials, *The Last Flight*, and adapted it for the stage. *Nikki*, as it was retitled, told of the romantic adventures of three American soldiers in Paris during World War I. To custom-fit the vehicle for Wray, Saunders changed one of the three leading male characters to a woman and turned it into a love triangle. Friedlander then enlisted the services of Phil Charig, an up-and-coming Broadway composer (another client of Grady's), to turn it into a musical, complete with lavish production numbers and a chorus line of leggy dancing girls.

Archie was cast as Cary Lockwood, one of the two soldiers competing for the love of Nikki. The role paid him $375 a week, a seventy-five-dollar cut from his Shubert-guaranteed salary, the difference held back by the Shuberts as their fee for allowing the loan-out. If the show ran longer than five weeks, Archie's salary was to increase to $500 a week, with the Shuberts' cut to be made up by Friedlander.

Unfortunately, *Nikki* did not get that far, closing in November 1931 after only thirty-nine performances. At the final-night party, held at the Waldorf, Archie confided in Irene Mayer Selznick, daughter of legendary Hollywood mogul Louis B. Mayer and a friend of Fay Wray and her husband, that he "loved" Wray and was seriously thinking of following her to Hollywood just to be near her. It was an odd comment to a friendly but total stranger that foreshadowed the chaste infatuations and bizarre confessionals the actor was to form with and make to women for the rest of his stage and film career.

As brief a run as it had, *Nikki* did provide the key review that changed the course of Archie Leach's life. In his influential *New York Daily News* show business column, Ed Sullivan singled out the actor's performance, predicting a big future in movies for the "young lad from England." The mention was enough to get him a recall from one of Paramount's Astoria studio's casting directors for a brief appearance as a sailor in *Singapore Sue*, a ten-minute short the studio was making to introduce Anna Chang, their newest acquisition. Meanwhile, Orry-Kelly had received an invitation from Jack Warner to come to Hollywood and work as a contract costume designer for the studio.

It was the big break he had been waiting for. When he told Archie about it, Archie promised that as soon as he finished *Singapore Sue*, he would join him in L.A.

The timing couldn't have been better. *Nikki* completed Archie's contractual obligation to the Shuberts, whose bad run of flops had forced them into receivership and because of it were in no position to enforce their option to re-sign him or anybody else. Upon completing his one-day shoot on *Singapore Sue*, and just short of his twenty-eighth birthday, Archie packed up his belongings, arranged for the sale of the bar, and said good-bye to his few friends. One of them was composer Phil Charig, who also wanted to head west and volunteered to make the drive with him. Another was early mentor Jean Dalrymple, with whom he took one last lunch at the Algonquin. When she could not get him to change his mind and stay in New York to pursue what she believed was a promising stage career, she cautioned him not to get caught up in the false glamour of Hollywood and asked him to promise to sooner or later return to the "pure" world of the theater.

That made him laugh.

The next day Archie and Phil slipped into the front seats of the yellow Packard. Archie kicked over the engine, pressed down on the accelerator, and pointed the front wheels in the direction of his future.

ARCHIE AND PHIL ARRIVED in Hollywood the first week of January 1932 and took up nominal residence together in a small courtyard apartment on Sweetzer, just north of Melrose Avenue, that Orry-Kelly had helped them secure, one of the so-called DeMille flats Paramount had built in the early 1920s to house its employees. Archie's next order of business was to make an appointment with the casting people at Paramount who, at Adolph Zukor's directive, were eagerly awaiting his arrival.

With good reason. The studio was in need of a new leading man to rejuvenate its continuing box-office slump that had begun even before the Depression, with the unexpected departure followed by the sudden early death in 1926 of its biggest male silent movie star, Rudolph Valentino. Valentino's silent "Sheik" movies made him a sensation, and his loss left a gaping hole in Paramount's already slim roster of bankable leading men.

Zukor, nicknamed "Creepy" and "Creepy Jesus" by his employees for his self-described visionary abilities in picking future stars, had, besides discovering Valentino, taken all the credit for German sensation Marlene Dietrich — Paramount's answer to MGM's Greta Garbo — who had become an overnight star following her appearance in Josef von Sternberg's *The Blue Angel* (and he gave the director, who had actually discovered Dietrich, none). His only other big box-office male lead, Gary Cooper, had skyrocketed in popularity following his appearance opposite Dietrich in Sternberg's follow-up to *The Blue Angel, Morocco* (1930), but was considered by Zukor to be too quirky and rebellious for the long run. Cooper, born of British immigrant parents, had been discovered by Clara Bow, who helped launch the tall, lanky, handsome actor to the top ranks of Hollywood's leading men. *Morocco* had indeed catapulted him into the superstar stratosphere, but the experience of working with Sternberg, who was hopelessly in love with Dietrich and all but ignored him during shooting, left him angry and frustrated. He retaliated first by having an affair with his costar and then taking a year-long vacation in Africa, from where he sent word to the studio that he was considering permanently retiring from the movie business. Zukor needed to find another actor to challenge Cooper's position as the studio top male, and he thought handsome Broadway actor Archibald Leach just might be the one to do it.

Although Paramount was making what many regarded at the time the best Hollywood movies, MGM was generally considered more glamorous because of its lustrous roster of players who so perfectly idealized and reflected the popular cultural icons of the time: the Teddy Roosevelt toughness of Clark Gable; the suaveness and Lost Generation sensitivity of John Gilbert; the Roaring Twenties sheen of Norma Shearer, the "First Lady of the Screen" (who also happened to be married to studio head Irving Thalberg); and the exotic old-world majesty and mystery of Greta Garbo, the woman the studio cannily referred to as "the European." And, while MGM and Warner Bros. had survived the industry's shift from silent films to talkies with only minimal disruption, sound had plunged Paramount into financial disarray and eventual bankruptcy, primarily due to the reluctance of its founders Zukor and Jesse Lasky, general manager Benjamin Percival (B. P.) Schulberg, and head of production Walter Wanger to switch quickly enough to talkies. Worse, for the studio, the onset of sound movies happened at approximately the same time as the 1929 stock market crash. Bank money quickly dried up, which made it more difficult for the lagging studio to bolster its inventory of expensive actors with those who not only looked right but sounded good as well.

Lasky eagerly anticipated the arrival of Archie Leach after word had come to him out of New York, via *Singapore Sue* director Casey Robinson, that the studio ought to lock up the actor immediately, before MGM got a look at him. Zukor ordered Schulberg to do whatever was necessary to sign him. Schulberg invited director Marion Gering, his wife, and Archie to dinner at his home, an honor usually reserved for the studio's biggest stars. Over coffee, Gering told Archie that Schulberg happened to be screen-testing his wife the very next day. At that point Schulberg butted in, put an arm around Archie, and as if he had had a sudden revelation, said, "Why don't you make it with her?"

Archie knew he had tested well when the next day Schulberg called him into his office and asked him to think about changing his name to something that sounded more all-American, something like, say, Gary Cooper. That night Archie had dinner with Fay Wray and her husband, John Saunders, during which Wray told Archie that she was about to sign with RKO to star as the unrequited love object of a giant ape in Merian C. Cooper's forthcoming *King Kong*. The subject of Archie's impending name change then came up.

He asked her if she had any suggestions, and without hesitating she smiled and said he should use Cary Lockwood, the character he'd played in *Nikki*. The next day, Archie brought it to Schulberg, who loved the first part because it rhymed with Gary, but was less satisfied with Lockwood. For one thing, the studio already had a contract player with that last name. For another, short last names were better because they showed up larger on a marquee and were easier for the public to remember. He handed Archie a list of names that he had had the studio publicity department compile and told him to pick one. Archie scanned the list and matter-of-factly chose Grant.

"I like it," Schulberg said. "Let's go with that one."

Archie smiled and said nothing.

The next day Schulberg sent Bill Grady, Archie's agent, a contract for the services of Paramount's newest acquisition, Cary Grant.

GO MAE WEST, YOUNG MAN

PART THREE

PREVIOUS PAGE: *Movie poster for the original theatrical release of* She Done Him Wrong (1933), *with Mae West receiving star billing over Cary Grant.* (CinemaPhoto/CORBIS)

5

"Some men squeeze a line to death. Cary tickles it into life."

—MICHAEL CURTIZ

In February 1932, only six weeks after his arrival in Hollywood, Archie Leach had become Cary Grant by way of a name change that was industry real if not legally official and had signed a five-year exclusive-services contract with Paramount Publix at a starting salary of $450 a week, with incremental raises to be made at the studio's discretion.

Grant was convinced the movies would not only magnify every inch of his face, body, and movement, they would, in turn, enlarge his personality as well. The better he looked, he believed, the more of his personality his acting would project onto audiences. As a result, he became obsessed with his physical appearance even more so than he had while living in New York City. Every morning after his first shower (he took at least three daily) and shave, he would closely examine his face in the round extension wall mirror, pulling it close in to search for the tiniest of skin nicks or flaws. He declined to have his teeth "painted" white by the studio, a technique they used to increase the dazzle of a smile during shoots. He was especially proud of his great teeth and practiced fixing his smile in such a way as to show them off to their fullest advantage. He brushed them compulsively, several times a day, often until his gums bled. He started as soon as he woke up, and sometimes did it in the morning while still in bed with a dry toothbrush, always after every meal, and at night just before he went to sleep. He carried a brush with him at all times and in company would often excuse himself after smoking a cigarette to get to a men's room, where he would scrub any dulling residue, real or imagined, from his one-pack-a-day habit.

He also refused to allow the studio to send him to Max Factor's face specialists, who were adept at perfecting the slightest facial flaw. (Although throughout his life Grant denied he had ever had a nose job, it does look noticeably slimmer in photographs taken after 1932, with the slightly thick Roman curve somewhat reduced, the bridge a bit narrower, and the tip more smoothly planed.) He put weights in his bedroom and worked out every morning and every evening. He carefully monitored his diet and greatly reduced his intake of alcohol.

As a personal reward for the physical progress he was making, he bought himself a beautiful Sealyham terrier he jokingly referred to as his alter ego. Owning a dog in New York had been impossible for him. Now that he could afford one, he wanted the best he could get. He named the hound Archie Leach.

GRANT'S FIRST FEATURE FILM was Frank Tuttle's *This Is the Night*, an adaptation by George Marion Jr. of Avery Hopwood's Broadway sex comedy *Naughty Cinderella*, in which he played the role of a cuckold opposite Lily Damita and her costar, the comedic Roland Young. It was a thankless role in which Grant cheerily loses his wife to another man, and it annoyed him, not for the character he played, but because he was cast as a second-string support player behind such A-listers as Charles Ruggles, Young, and Damita. He was further dismayed when he saw the film's final pre-release cut. He thought that even though he came off sleazy and weak-willed, no one would ever believe that someone so good-looking would lose his wife to the funny but unattractive Young. If the public bought him in this type of role, he feared they would never accept him as a legitimate leading man.

After the screening, he left the studio, stopped off, had a few drinks, then a few more, and sometime around midnight returned to the house on Sweetzer and solemnly informed Charig he was heading back to New York City. Charig managed to calm down the obviously inebriated Grant and, while forcing coffee down his throat, placed a call to Orry-Kelly, who had lately not been all that available to Grant. Orry-Kelly had claimed it was simply due to his heavy workloads, but the truth was, he had moved on, and while neither had admitted it to the other, both knew it was so. On the phone Orry-Kelly talked to Grant for a long time and tried to explain to him the reality of Hollywood. He was a working film actor now, and regardless of his roles, he should be grateful he had a studio contract.

The next morning a hungover Grant returned to the studio, where he was to begin shooting scenes for his second feature, Alexander Hall's *Sinners in the Sun*, starring Carole Lombard. Schulberg had personally selected Grant for this role and, because the actor was still doing retakes on *This Is the Night*, had him delivered by golf cart between the sets of the two films, often without so much as time for a regular costume change, forcing Grant to slip into a tux while in transit. In *Sinners*, Grant was cast as a sophisticated man-about-town, a role he felt was a bit more suited to his abilities but still not the type he felt he could play.

Because of it, he believed his acting days in Hollywood were likely numbered, and he used some of his earnings to become a silent partner in Neale's Smart Men's Apparel, a retail clothing operation on Wilshire Boulevard. Neale was L. Wright Neale, whom Grant had met socially and liked, even though the man often referred to Grant as "Sister Cary" (a cutesy reference to the Theodore Dreiser novel *Sister Carrie* that Grant didn't particularly appreciate). The shop was located on Wilshire and Vermont, near all the new and fashionable retailers and large department stores that catered to the town's big movie money. Grant wanted to invest in a non–show business venture and chose tailoring because as a child he had learned something about the trade from his father. His participation in the business was, on some level, a tangible link to happier memories of childhood.

To Grant's surprise, the *Daily Variety* called his performance in *This Is the Night* "striking," and noted that "he looks like a potential femme rave," *Variety*-speak to describe his good looks. The only thing about the review that bothered Grant was the critic's having mistakenly referred to him as "Gary."

Still in 1932 he was put into yet another film, Dorothy Arzner's *Merrily We Go to Hell*, starring Fredric March and Sylvia Sidney, who also happened to be Schulberg's mistress. Grant, meanwhile, quietly invested in a second retail branch of his clothing business, this one in New York City.

In *Merrily*, March was badly miscast (comedy was never his forte), which allowed Grant to walk off with the film as a character-within-a-character in playwright March's play-within-a-play. His small but well-received performance was strong enough to convince the still self-exiled Gary Cooper to hasten his return to the studio after his good friend March had sent word to the safari-ing actor that this new fellow Grant was apparently being groomed as his possible replacement. He also sent along the *Variety* review with Grant's misspelled first name.

At a huge reception thrown by Zukor to hail its returning star, Cooper, whose feathers were still ruffled by the Cary/Gary name incident, delivered a personal gift he'd brought back from Africa for the studio head—a monkey on a chain. He also intentionally snubbed Grant by bypassing him in the reception line and ignoring him when Grant introduced himself and tried to make polite conversation over cocktails. It was the start of a personal animosity between the two that was to last for many years.*

To further placate their reluctant superstar, Zukor cast Cooper in a role he had, in fact, been considering for Grant, the lead in Marion Gering's *Devil and the Deep*, costarring Charles Laughton and Tallulah Bankhead, relegating Grant to a small and completely forgettable part. Nevertheless, Grant's performance was good enough to convince the studio to make him one of the leads opposite Dietrich in *Blonde Venus*, the fifth Josef von Sternberg/Marlene Dietrich film. The cast also featured British West End sensation Herbert Marshall as Dietrich's cuckolded husband, while Grant played Dietrich's guilty-conscienced lover.

In the movie, American scientist Ned Faraday (played by Marshall in full-tilt British accent and manner) marries sultry German nightclub singer Helen Jones (Dietrich), a familiar echo of the *Blue Angel* scenario. Marshall, Sternberg's obvious onscreen surrogate, in this instance an intellectual not all that different from *The Blue Angel's* Professor (Emil Jannings), falls for his (Sternberg's) real-life obsession, the easy showgirl Marlene Dietrich, and

---

*Decades later in an interview Cooper gave to actress/journalist Suzy Parker, he confessed his long-standing "hate" for Grant, adding a swipe at his looks and acting style by mentioning that his "mannerisms always got on my nerves."

then proceeds to punish her brutally for the very thing that attracts her to him: her beauty and sexuality. When Faraday develops radiation poisoning that can be cured only by expensive treatments, Helen returns to work as the nightclub sensation "Blonde Venus," making her first entrance dressed as a gorilla (Sternberg's inside joke on Cooper's gift to Zukor upon his return to the studio. Ever since *Morocco*, during the making of which Cooper and Dietrich had had a torrid affair, there was no love lost between and the actor and the director).

While performing in the club, Dietrich's character meets and falls for millionaire Nick Townsend, played by a slicked-up Grant, who promptly puts her out on the street as his slave-lover and high-priced prostitute. Nick is, in reality (if that is the right word), a pimp. Through him, Helen raises enough money to send her husband to Germany for medical treatment, but upon his return when he discovers she has been unfaithful, he leaves her and tries to take their child with him. Desperate, Dietrich flees to Paris, resumes her nightclub career, and once again takes up with Grant. This time he realizes he is in love with her, proposes marriage, and she agrees. Upon their return to America, her husband forgives her, and reluctantly she leaves Grant for Marshall.

What is remarkable about this otherwise soapy film, besides the luminous cinematography that captured Dietrich's always extraordinary beauty and overt sexuality, is the undeniable flash of dark brilliance Grant brought to his first substantial role. Von Sternberg usually allowed Dietrich to intimidate her male costars (Emil Jannings, Victor McLaglen, Warner Oland, Adolphe Menjou, and Clive Brook; only Gary Cooper managed to come off as heartless, clever, sexual, and charming, a first-class womanizer too good-looking for his — or Dietrich's — own good). But Grant was able to deflect Dietrich's brute force — and play to the audience's sympathies — by showing compassion for Marshall's plight. He came off more noble and forgiving than weak and heartless. Audiences, women especially, loved it when Marshall took his wife back in the final scene (a plot turn hotly contested by Sternberg, who thought the studio-imposed ending was neither happy nor realistic, and that Dietrich should have wound up alone in the gutter where she belonged).

The trickiest aspect of Grant's character, and what also made his playing of it so convincing, was his ability to sustain an evil yet appealing irresistibility. For the first time Grant showed the blueprint from which he would construct his style of acting—the suggestion of an emotional darkness beneath the brightness of his surface attractiveness. In the end, Grant managed to make Townsend's broken heart not merely comprehensible to audiences, but broodingly compassionate, all conveyed through a single last look on his wounded beautiful face that became even more beautiful *because* it was wounded.

Throughout the filming of *Blonde Venus* (and throughout his career), Sternberg maintained his brilliant if eccentric sense of visual perfectionism. During the filming of Grant's first scene, Sternberg took a comb and parted his star's hair on the right side rather than the left, the way Grant had always combed it before. The change gave Grant's already remarkable face an added symmetrical beauty. For the rest of his life Grant would comb his hair in the manner first prescribed by Sternberg. The director also lit Grant in his trademark shadow-and-light stylistics, which kinetically enhanced his emotionally textured performance.

Blonde Venus came very close to being rejected by the censorial Hays Office for its depiction of Dietrich's character having an adulterous affair with Cary Grant, *enjoying* it, and then returning to her husband and child to live happily ever after. With enough alterations to satisfy the censors, *Blonde Venus* was released, and while it didn't make Grant a star, it did well enough to solidify his reputation as one of Hollywood's new crop of fast-rising actors, one of the band of British "colonists," as they were known in Hollywood, that included C. Aubrey Smith, Ronald Colman, Basil Rathbone, Victor McLaglen, Boris Karloff, John Loder, David Niven, Charles Laughton, and of course Grant's longstanding idol and role model, Charlie Chaplin.

Grant finished out 1932 making his sixth and seventh films, William Seiter's *Hot Saturday* and Marion Gering's *Madame Butterfly*. That same year, for economic reasons Paramount eliminated many of its highest-paid performers, among them Tallulah Bankhead, George Bancroft, Buddy Rogers (who was unable to make the vocal transition to sound), the Marx Brothers (who would be picked up by Irving Thalberg at MGM and become the most successful comedy team of their era), Richard Arlen, Jeanette MacDonald, and Maurice Chevalier. This bloodletting created a casting vacuum that helped suck surviving newcomer Cary Grant into the vacancies left by the studio's decimated top-of-the-line stars.

When trouble erupted over the casting of *Hot Saturday*, the story of a love triangle, Grant was perfectly positioned to step in. At Schulberg's directive, he took over the starring role of Romer Sheffield when Gary Cooper refused to play it on the advice of his friend Fredric March, who had also flatly turned down the part, believing the supporting role of Bill Fadden was the more sympathetic one. Schulberg then cast another studio newcomer, Randolph Scott, in the supporting role of Fadden, which had originally belonged to Grant. *Hot Saturday* wasn't much of a movie but did have a profound effect on Grant's personal life, as it marked his first meeting with Scott and the beginning of one of the longest, deepest, and most unusual love relationships in the history of Hollywood.

Grant's satisfaction at being cast in the lead of *Hot Saturday* was tempered by the studio's having to shelve its planned big-budget sound remake of its 1922 silent blockbuster *Blood and Sand*, in which he was to have played the role that the late Rudolph Valentino had created. Schulberg had been the driving force behind the remake and wanted Grant to star because of his dark-haired, tall, sleek, and sexually appealing screen presence. Schulberg, whose huge $6,500 weekly salary had afforded him far too much time to gamble, drink, and bed every starlet on the lot, had also caused him to lose sight of the financial realities that were closing in on Paramount. When, in 1932, Paramount could no longer make its mortgage payments on the studio's expansive real-estate holdings, and even after firing so many of its star players could not make payroll, Zukor, whose studio now hovered on the brink of bankruptcy, blamed Schulberg's philandering for much of Paramount's problems, fired him, and canceled *Blood and Sand*. Grant was extremely disappointed at both the firing, as he had come to like Schulberg a great deal, and a lost opportunity to become the logical successor to the still manically worshiped and so far irreplaceable Valentino. Grant feared such a star-making role might never come his way again.

His next film seemed to bear this fear out: a musical version of *Madame Butterfly*, whose script he found all but incomprehensible. The thankless role of Lieutenant Pinkerton, who drives Cho-Cho San (Sylvia Sidney) to suicide, was yet another that Cooper had flatly refused to play.

Madame Butterfly was one of many Hollywood films of the 1930s that catered to the country's growing interest in Eastern culture. Unfortunately, to make the film "comprehensible" to the general public, Paramount chose to Westernize the Japanese characters, giving all the leads to well-known Anglo Hollywood actors and actresses. The film captured Grant's already dated singing style in his solo "My Flower of Japan," a music-hall hiccough that infringed on his thin, reedy tenor. It remained to the very end (along with *Singapore Sue*) one of the films that Grant most detested. In later years he actually tried to buy the negative in order to destroy it.

WHILE THE FORWARD THRUST of Grant's early film career seemed to have been stalled by *Madame Butterfly*, Zukor decided to bet the studio's future on one final extravaganza, a film version of Mae West's 1928 scandal-splattered Broadway stage hit, *Diamond Lil*, the sequel to her 1926 self-written stage smash, unsubtly titled *Sex*, very loosely based on Somerset Maugham's short story *Rain*. The project had originally been signed by Schulberg, who believed its sensational star and vehicle couldn't help but make a fortune for the studio. In New York the stage version had caused many highly publicized police "raids" for "lewdness, nudity and profanity."*

What worked on Broadway was one thing; turning it into a hit movie would prove to be quite another. With the Hays Office gaining power in Hollywood, the major studios had become increasingly hesitant to make movies that Will Hays deemed too controversial, too antisocial, or too sexually explicit. Carl Laemmle, the head of Universal, was the first to consider a screen version of *Diamond Lil* but was ultimately pressured by Hays into giving up the idea, even after signing West to a generous contract.

Indeed, West's persona as a fleshy, smirky sex goddess without modesty or morals had made her as pervasive a pop culture phenomenon as Chaplin's celebrated "Little Tramp." One of West's favorite publicity stunts was to allow herself to be photographed in her famous "swan" bed, whose headboard looked like nothing so much as the bare upper thighs of a Victorian woman with skirts hiked high up the front. Her enduring popularity—her audiences wanted to know everything about her, including what she wore in the

---

*Schulberg likely was aware that the so-called raids were actually staged by the producers to sell tickets, a clever scheme that turned an ordinary show into a box office sensation. It made West the biggest star on Broadway, and that was enough for Schulberg to want to bring her to Paramount.

boudoir ("a black lace nightgown, sometimes with black stockings") — translated into money, a lot of it, and her talent for making it finally convinced Zukor to greenlight Schulberg's offer to West of a $5,000-a-week salary (above the negotiated rights for *Diamond Lil*) to star in the movie version of her play for Paramount.

Less than six weeks after her arrival in L.A. in the fall of 1932, Zukor, eager to see some return on his investment, put West into a quickie film role as Maudie Triplett, opposite another Paramount Valentino-hopeful, song-and-dance man George Raft, who bore a slight physical resemblance to the dead actor but lacked his charm, mystery, and heat.

The seventy-minute film, *Night After Night*, proved a huge winner at the box office, and West received rave reviews, while Raft was all but ignored. *Photoplay*, one of the most influential film magazines of the time, said, "Wait till you see Mae West. An out-and-out riot!" Zukor then hired Schulberg back on a freelance basis to produce *Diamond Lil*, having promised the Hays Office a complete rewrite of the original stage version and a cleaned-up, sanitized film version, not just of the play but of the West persona, as well. After changing the project's name to *She Done Him Wrong*, the film was added to the fall production schedule. George Raft, originally cast by Zukor as the love interest, was at Schulberg's directive replaced by Cary Grant, who had always been the producer's first choice to play opposite West.

ONE OF THE MOST ERRONEOUS yet persistent myths about Cary Grant is that he was discovered by Mae West while both were strolling the Paramount backlot, that she took one look at him and said, "If that guy can talk, I'll take him — he's the only one who could do justice to the role of 'The Hawk.'" Several versions of this "moment of discovery" exist; the most popular comes from West's own memoirs.* Here she recalls visiting the Paramount lot one day in 1932 prior to signing on to film *Diamond Lil* and seeing "a sensational-looking man walking along the studio street . . . the best thing I'd seen out

---

*A highly fanciful bit of self-promotion ghostwritten by Martin Sommers in 1933 for the News Syndicate Co., which ran it in several installments. It later appeared in book form under the title *Goodness Had Nothing to Do with It*.

there." According to West, she then insisted that Grant be her costar or there wouldn't be a film.*

Grant himself flatly denied the story many times, always claiming, "It wasn't true. Mae West didn't discover me. I'd already made four pictures before I met her."[†] In an interview he gave to *Screen Book* in December 1933, he gave this version of the story: "I had met Miss West one night at the [American] Legion [Friday night] fights at the Hollywood American stadium. I understand that she had already seen me and asked for me to play 'The Hawk' in her picture. It seems that during her search for a suitable leading man, she had seen me getting out of my studio car and decided I was the type to play opposite her. I suppose it was because she is blond and I am dark and we make a suitable contrast. Another factor in my getting the role in *She Done Him Wrong* was that Lowell Sherman, the director, had liked my work with Miss Dietrich in *Blonde Venus*."

In fact, both West's and Grant's version were likely made up, and for good reason. Grant and West had appeared on Broadway at the same time for several seasons and became quite well acquainted during this period. As it happens, while West was developing her sex goddess stage image, she was also running a highly successful male escort service. One stresses that there is no smoking gun, but because of how perfectly the timings mesh (West was running her service before, during, and after the two-year period when Grant "disappeared"), it is tantalizing to wonder if Grant worked for her, and if she was, in fact, the otherwise unknown, unidentified "Marks."

Because of the studio's financial difficulties, the film was given an eighteen-day shooting schedule (instead of the fifteen to twenty weeks normally allotted a "big" picture). Filming began on November 21, after the full seven-day rehearsal period that West had insisted upon. Set in a Bowery bar at the turn of the twentieth century, the sanitized but still raunchy story centers on Lady Lou, the proprietor of the Dance Hall (a standard euphemism

---

*Another version of the Grant discovery story, from West herself, went like this: "In 1932 I was standing with William LeBaron, the producer of the film I was going to make, *She Done Him Wrong*. I saw Cary across the studio street. I says, 'What's this?' I says, 'If this one can talk, I'll take him.' He says, 'What part will you use him for?' I says, 'The lead, of course.'" West recounted this version of her "discovering" Cary Grant to Richard Gehman in *American Weekly*, October 21, 1962.

[†]*She Done Him Wrong* was actually Grant's eighth full-length feature film.

for a house of prostitution), corun by West's husband (Noah Beery Sr.), which sells beer to the boys while also dealing in a little white sexual slavery on the side. Captain Cummings, aka "The Hawk" (Grant), is an undercover cop running a nearby missionary and is bent on "saving" her. One of the most famous (and often misquoted) lines in all of film history is uttered in *She Done Him Wrong* with a moistness hard to misinterpret, when Lil meets Cummings for the first time and says, "Why don't you come up sometime, see me. I'll tell your fortune." By the end of the film, after a series of bizarre plot twists, love changes and redeems them both. In the final scene, Cummings leads her away, with the strong suggestion he is going to reform her first, then marry her. They get into a cab and Grant removes all the rings on her fingers so he can slip a single small diamond on one. Lou looks into his eyes and murmurs, "Tall, dark, and handsome," to which he replies, "You bad girl." "You'll find out," she says, sucking in her cheeks and smiling wickedly as the film ends.*

She Done Him Wrong, West's second film, was, in retrospect, the best performance of her career. It was loosely based on her own early experiences in New York, the saloon being a substitute for the stage, white slavery a reference to her (and possibly Grant's) escort days, and her arrest at the end reminiscent of the legal troubles her shows had run into with the city's moral squads.

It was also the eighth and final film Grant made in 1932 and, after this highly productive year, the one that brought him closer than ever to the first rank of Paramount's leading men.† Ironically, it was Grant's approach to play-

---

*Other memorable Mae West lines that came from *She Done Him Wrong*: When asked if she had ever met a man who made her happy, West replies, "Sure. Lots of times." A woman admires her diamonds and says, "Goodness!" West replies, "Goodness had nothing to do with it!" When Grant resists her advances, she says, "That's right, loosen up, unbend. You'll feel better." When Grant apologizes for taking her time, she replies, "What do you think my time is for?" An updated, suggestive version of the song "Frankie and Johnny" is sung by West, along with several others, including "A Guy What Takes His Time."

†In his first year in Hollywood, Cary Grant made eight movies, a little more than 11 percent of the seventy-two features he would appear in between 1932 and 1966. In the next thirty-three years (beginning in 1933), Grant made sixty-four additional movies, an average of two a year, although once he became a free agent, he deliberately slowed down the pace. In 1940 he made his thirty-sixth film, the halfway mark of the total output of films he would make in his lifetime, when he starred in Garson Kanin's *My Favorite Wife*. In the next twenty-six years he would make the same number of films he had in the first eight of his Hollywood career.

ing the romantic lead in *She Done Him Wrong* that did it. His onscreen aloofness, a reflection of nothing so much as his own uncertainty as to how to play a love scene opposite the voracious West, was taken by the public to be just the opposite — manly, moral resistance to Lil's many charms — and created a new type of romantic sophisticate, not only for Grant but for the legions of actors who would thereafter try to imitate him. Grant's "Hawk" was underplayed and always gentlemanly, resistance translated into self-assurance and moral righteousness, all highly glossed with what would become his trademark shimmering elegance.

No one was more surprised than Grant at how successful he was opposite the voracious West. As in the past, he had tried to mask what he thought of as his own lack of any true acting style by emulating his performing idols, Chaplin, Noël Coward, Jack Buchanan, Rex Harrison, and Fred Astaire. Years later Grant perceptively and graciously summed up his acting in *She Done Him Wrong* as a combination of pose and impersonation. "I copied other styles I knew until I became a conglomerate of people and ultimately myself," he told an interviewer. "When I was a young actor, I'd put my hand in my pocket trying to look relaxed. Instead, I looked stiff and my hand stuck in my pocket wet with perspiration. I was trying to imitate what I thought a relaxed man looked like."

Nevertheless, the physical image of Cary Grant seemed even more perfect on the big screen than it had on stage. In his early movies especially, the camera quickly discovered and magnified the perfection of his features, the beautiful dark and sharp eyes that sat carved beneath his thick black brows, the handsome nose, the flawlessly smooth skin, the thick, slick hair always perfectly cut and parted, and that remarkable cleft in his chin, whose two smooth and curved bulges resembled nothing so much as a beautiful woman's naked behind while she was on her knees in sexual supplication before the godlike monument of his face.

Opposite West, Grant's arched body language seemed to react with bemused distaste, an apparent product of calculated wit. He smartly held his own by not allowing himself to get engaged in a competition he could not win. In the silvery sheen of sharp black and white, all Grant had to do was show up and let his irresistible face be photographed in shadowed cuts, as if caught in the flash of lightning. Holding his own, however, was not enough.

Working with West had taught him a valuable lesson. As long as he was the pursuer, the focus was always going to be on the object of his affection. The thing to be in any movie was the one pursued. It was what all front-rank stars in Hollywood benefited from, and why he was not yet in their league. Should he ever have the opportunity to call the shots, as West had, he promised himself, he would make himself the object of his co-stars', and by extension the audience's, heated pursuit. Eventually this decision would come to define the essence of, and the reason for, Cary Grant's superstar persona.

The enormous profits generated by *She Done Him Wrong* were enough, for the time being at least, to save Paramount from impending bankruptcy. Costing what was then a risky $200,000, the film earned more than $2 million in its initial three-month domestic run, making it one of the highest-grossing and most profitable films Hollywood had ever produced. It would go on to gross an additional million dollars worldwide in first release (despite being banned in Australia after its premiere and in several other smaller markets), and it remains to this day one of West's few films still shown on the theatrical revival circuit and on cable TV's classic movie channels.

For her next movie, Paramount agreed to pay West $300,000 plus writing royalties to star in *I'm No Angel*.* Grant was once again assigned to costar, and in appreciation for his contribution to the success of *She Done Him Wrong*, Paramount raised his salary from $450 to $750 a week. By contrast, he knew, West was being paid a mint. Not because she was a better actor than he was (although that might have been the case), but because she was a better businessperson. Like his idol, Chaplin, she had managed to remain a per-picture independent, able to demand and get her price, one that, unlike Broadway money, could be parlayed into a real fortune. In the theater, an actor (with rare exceptions, such as run-of-the-play contracts) was paid for a single performance, or number of performances, and if asked to go on the road, paid again. An actor in film was also paid once, but the film could earn residual money as long as it could be run and rerun. The only way, Grant realized, to get some of that money was to do what Chaplin and West had done, to find a way to own a piece of the pie.

---

*The screenplay was adapted by West from a script by studio screenwriter Lowell Brentano, originally called *The Lady and the Lions*. West kept the general story and rewrote all the dialogue.

Even before production began on *I'm No Angel* (during which time Grant made three more nondescript studio "quickies"),* he had already begun to formulate a plan for his own financial emancipation.

SHORTLY AFTER THE SUCCESS OF *She Done Him Wrong*, as if on the studio's cue, Cary Grant's steady ride to stardom was threatened by rumors that were being spread by the studio-controlled gossip columnists. Everyone in the business knew these journalists-cum-rumormongers were organs of the industry, used to keep their players in line. Hedda Hopper, Sheilah Graham, and Louella Parsons owed their success to easy access behind the studios' iron gates, where all the "good" stories were. The hard truth was, no matter how talented a director, screenwriter, or producer, no matter how crucial they may have been to the success of their movies, no one cared about them or went to see a film because of them, at least not knowingly. The only real attraction factor in the studio era was star power. For this reason the studios carefully stroked the egos of their stars and at the same time sought to control them by resisting union movements, never grooming noncontract players for stardom, and most effectively, imposing the so-called morals clause. The public, the studios knew, would tolerate a lot, was in fact titillated by the endlessly reported bouts of drinking, fighting, illicit but consentual sex, and even, for a while, subversive politics (like liberal Hollywood's romance with the Lincoln Brigade). Everyone, however, drew the same line in the moral sand when it came to the three absolute no-nos: heterosexual rape, child molestation, and male homosexuality.

No star, however big, ever completely escaped the gossip rumor mill — those who had affairs, those who didn't, those who weren't gay, those who were, those who were suspected, and those targeted by a rival studio. Gary Cooper, known in the industry for the size of his penis (huge) and his love of gorgeous women (insatiable), because of his extremely pretty face and enormous box office clout was a favorite target of rival studios, who used to continually hint that he really preferred men to women (ridiculous).†

---

*Paul Sloane's *Woman Accused*, Stuart Walker's *The Eagle and the Hawk*, and Louis Gasnier and Max Marcin's *Gambling Ship*.

†Paramount countered those stories by letting it be known through the same gossips that women knowingly referred to Cooper as someone who "talked softly and carried a big dick."

But the same stories about Grant—who, unlike Cooper, had never been romantically attached to any woman during his New York years and now not in Hollywood—made the heads of Paramount a bit nervous. Their anxiety grew after their biggest female star, Marlene Dietrich, who made a habit of literally taking the measure of her male costars—during the filming of *Morocco* she raved about the size of Cooper's sex organ and his ability to use it—let it be known among her inner circle, who then informed the gossips, that in the love department, Grant got an "F for fag." He was, she claimed, "a homosexual." Grant's angry and unconvincing response was to hint at Dietrich's well-known penchant for women, saying, "If women want to wear men's clothes, let them do men's work." He didn't mean construction.

The niggling rumors about Grant's sexual preferences, generated by competing houses and spread by the gossips, took a giant step into the public's consciousness when Tallulah Bankhead, his costar in *Devil and the Deep*, who had tried and failed to bed Grant, publicly echoed Dietrich's evaluation of his lack of sexual interest in women. Next to give him the failing grade was his *Sinners in the Sun* costar Carole Lombard. This landslide of negative evaluations that began to show up in the gossip columns became increasingly difficult for either the studio or the public to ignore.

To counter the running rumors, Paramount arranged for a torrent of sanctioned newspaper "interviews" and "inside stories" to be published about Cary Grant—"The Lover," "The Ultimate Ladies' Man," "The All Around Athlete"—and flooded magazines with photos of him taken with every leading woman it had under contract. Grant, for his part, seemed willing to play the publicity game, hoping that in the end it would result in his greater value to the studio, and therefore to himself. Another reason he was reluctant to rock any boats was that Neale's Smart Men's Apparel—in which he had invested, hoping it would turn into a nationwide franchise and make him a millionaire—had turned into a bottomless money pit and sucked him dry of nearly every penny he had before it finally went under.

On the other hand, much to Paramount's dismay, the rumors about Grant's standoffishness with women failed to induce him to behave with caution. A few months earlier, in the fall of 1932, Grant and Phil Charig had moved out of their small Sweetzer apartment into a larger, although still cozy house by Hollywood-movie-star standards, on West Live Oak Drive in

Griffith Park, nestled just below the giant-lettered HOLLYWOODLAND sign, a place that afforded them a fabulous view of the night-lighted sky of Tinseltown.* Then, just before Grant began shooting *She Done Him Wrong*, Charig sat his roommate down and broke the news that he was giving up trying to break into the motion-picture-scoring business, had packed his things, and was returning to New York City to work on Broadway.

If Charig thought Grant might try to convince him to change his mind and stay, he was mistaken. Instead, Grant told him he understood, thought he was doing the right thing, wished him well, and asked him how soon he could leave.

One week after Charig's departure, Grant put out a permanent welcome mat for his new roommate: the young, single, handsome, and athletic contract player he had met during the filming of *Hot Saturday*, Randolph Scott.

---

*The fifty-foot-tall HOLLYWOODLAND sign was originally erected in 1923 at the top of Beechwood Drive as an advertisement for real estate. In 1945 it was abandoned by the original owners and claimed by the city, which shortened it to HOLLYWOOD.

6

Question to Randolph Scott: Was there pressure on you or Cary Grant to wed, in the '30s . . . after you and Cary were together for some time?

Randolph Scott: When said properties get on a bit in years, there is pressure, more pressure for a star who's foreign-born.

—INTERVIEWED BY BOZE HADLEIGH, 1996

At first, the decision to live together seemed perfectly normal. For economic reasons more than any other, unmarried actors (and actresses) shared housing all over Hollywood. It made sense since all they needed was a place to crash for a few hours between the days they spent working at the studios and nights they spent on the Strip, unwinding along the two-mile slither of no-man's-land where they could hang till dawn having all the sex, drugs, booze, or any other illicit be-bop they could think of.

Except that Cary Grant and Randolph Scott hadn't crashed. They'd fallen into something that resembled conventional love and didn't give a damn who knew it. Randy (as he was called by everyone who knew him) first met Grant on the set of *Hot Saturday*. Six years older, he was born in 1898 into a Virginia family that had made its fortune in textiles. When he was still a very young boy, the family moved to Durham, North Carolina, where he was raised in an atmosphere of traditional southern gentility. By the time he was a teenager, Scott was six foot four, lean, muscular, and tough, with enough athletic ability and social connections to get him into Georgia Tech. He became the star of the football team with a bright future in sports when an injury forced him to give up his dream of a professional playing career. He then transferred to the University of North Carolina, where he graduated with a degree in textile engineering and manufacturing, planning to follow in his father's footsteps. But he appeared in a school play, was bitten by the acting bug, and decided, against his parents' strong objections, that upon graduation he would go west and pursue a career in movies.

He arrived in Hollywood in 1927, at the relatively late age of thirty, and promptly looked up the son of one of his father's old friends, who was in a position to help him. Howard Hughes hailed from a southern family of wealth far greater even than the Scotts'. Born and raised in Houston, he moved to California while still a teenager to study engineering at the California Institute of Technology, until the sudden death of his father in 1923 left him the sole heir to the family's billion-dollar empire. While continuing to oversee the family-owned industrial tool company, Hughes, with the help of his uncle Rupert, a successful Hollywood screenwriter, set up shop as an independent film producer.

At their first meeting, Scott handed the young billionaire a formal letter of introduction from his father. Hughes took an immediate liking to the actor and decided to take him under his wing, arranged for him to study acting at the state-funded Pasadena Playhouse, and used his influence to get him some extra work at Fox. A short time later Hughes made a personal phone call to Adolph Zukor that resulted in Scott's getting an audition at Paramount for Cecil B. DeMille's upcoming 1929 production of *Dynamite*. Although he lost out on the lead role to Joel McCrea, the studio hired him as Gary Cooper's dialect coach, because his speech still held traces of the British accent he had inherited from his parents. They wanted Cooper to sound more southern, the way Scott naturally did, for his role in Victor Fleming's scheduled western epic *The Virginian*. Scott managed to land a small role in the film and did well enough that he was awarded a five-year player contract, similar to the one Grant would sign two years later.

When Grant and Scott met on the set of *Hot Saturday*, the physical attraction between them was immediate and strong. Despite the six-year age difference between them, they physically resembled each other to a startling degree. A short time later, when Charig told Grant he was moving out, Grant immediately asked Scott to move in, an offer the actor accepted without hesitation.

Cary enjoyed having Randy around the house, even more so when he discovered how much they liked the same things: drinking, smoking, and expensive clothes. They also shared a wicked sense of humor that allowed Scott to pick up on and guffaw at every understated joke Grant tossed his way.

They were also a good match sexually. Like Scott, Grant's physical needs and desires were not particularly overheated. Sex was almost an afterthought, a natural extension of the buddy-buddy British-schoolboy-type friendship they shared.

It wasn't merely the fact that Grant and Scott lived together that fueled the rumors that had begun to shadow Grant; it was the style in which they did it. While Grant was a material minimalist when it came to furniture and decor, never willing to waste money on such things, Scott was much more the homey type and enjoyed curtains and throw rugs and carved furniture reminiscent of the ornate environment of his childhood. He was in charge of decorating the place, and Grant made the decisions about what they wore and kept the wine and spirits closet well stocked.

Cary and Randy soon became well known in Hollywood as the Damon and Pythias of Tinseltown for their lack of caution in how they chose to display their affection in public. They often attended parties dressed in similar harlequin costumes, and at one Halloween soirée, for a howl, they both arrived dressed as women. When word of their incautious public displays first reached the studios, and the innuendos in the columns grew louder, Schulberg commenced to impose the publicity-defined lifestyle on them that included the endless stream of Hollywood starlets photographed with either one or both men in or near their "Bachelor Hall."

Nonetheless, it was often impossible for the studio to disguise the presence of the "coupling" that neither felt compelled to hide. When magazine reporter Ben Maddox was dispatched to do a piece on two of Hollywood's "most eligible bachelors," he wrote what he observed this way: "Cary is the gay, impetuous one. Randy is serious, cautious. Cary is temperamental in the sense of being very intense. Randy is calm and quiet. Need I add that all the eligible (and a number of the *in*eligible) ladies-about-Hollywood are dying to be dated by these handsome lads?"

Another quote the studio attributed to, of all people, Carole Lombard that was widely circulated also didn't help. It was actually written by a PR writer for the studio and showed up in all the columns. It claimed that Lombard was a frequent visitor to "Bachelor Hall" (she wasn't), and "marveled" at the way the two men divided their chores: "Cary opened the bills, Randy wrote the checks, and if Cary could talk someone out of a stamp, he mailed them." The quote did not amuse Grant. Moss Hart, a frequent houseguest, was another oft-quoted source. He remembered Grant's parsimonious brand of hospitality, noting that if he stayed more than a few days, he would receive an itemized bill for his laundry, phone calls, and incidentals. Grant didn't find any humor in this, either.

Nor did it help matters any that photos of the two men at home wearing aprons somehow found their way into the newspapers, causing Hollywood gossip hack Jimmie Fiddler to go against the personal request of Schulberg to ignore the gay angle and openly wonder in print and on his syndicated radio show if the two actors weren't "carrying this buddy business a bit too far."

Grant and Scott reluctantly accepted the studio's insistence on what it called "protective publicity" as long as it didn't interfere with their private life. Whenever asked, Grant would say he did nothing special to keep himself in shape, that his body was just naturally the way it was, but in truth he and Scott were obsessed with physical fitness. To keep themselves in peak condition, they made a competition out of it: if either one ever exceeded his designated body weight, he had to pay the other $100 (later on it became $1,000 and would be given to charity). As it happened, neither ever had to pay off the bet. Grant remained a constant 180 pounds, while Scott always kept to 190. Whenever they were home together, they worked out for two hours every morning before breakfast. Their favored routine was barbell reps, after which they would take a quick swim in the ocean. They spent their free afternoons together riding horses, Scott's favorite physical pastime.

Grant's attraction to Scott's manly attributes and southern-bred ways was nicely burnished with the one quality Grant envied most in his partner and that he considered requisite for anyone he would ever be involved with — financial security. Grant was particularly interested in Scott's family connections to Howard Hughes and often expressed his desire to meet the famous billionaire. Scott, for his own reasons, kept the two far apart. It was one thing to cavort in outlandish costumes in Hollywood and be linked to female starlets for the sake of public consumption. It was quite another to have a family friend get too close to the real deal. Polite caution, the spine of southern upbringing, was Scott's mantra, a way of life that he vigorously applied to his relationship with Grant.

Then, on the night of September 16, 1932, when Grant and Scott attended the gala Hollywood premiere of *Blonde Venus* together, everything between them became infinitely more complicated.

Grant had been asked by the studio to accompany one of its contract starlets to the opening, and he agreed. He then slipped up and let it be known to one reporter that his "date" for the opening was actually Scott, a fact that found its way into print. Schulberg blew a gasket, but there was nothing he could really do about it. Grant refused to take the starlet if Scott could not also come along.

The premiere was a typical black-tie-and-klieg-light affair, with all the resident glitterati and paparazzi present for the occasion. Schulberg held his breath as Grant, his female date, and Randy all emerged from their limo and strolled up the red carpet awash in the *pop pop* of endless gunpowder flashbulbs. After the screening, Grant quickly and quietly ditched the girl and went with Scott to the Brown Derby on Wilshire Boulevard for a light after-supper of hors d'oeuvres and iced champagne. At midnight they made a final round of handshakes and cheek-kissings, then stepped out into the warm September night to await the arrival of their limo. Grant lit a cigarette, filled his lungs with smoke, turned his head to exhale, and noticed for the first time the attractive woman standing nearby.

He recognized her immediately. It was Virginia Cherrill, the female star of *City Lights* who had been discovered, made into a star, and — it was rumored — romanced and rejected by Charlie Chaplin.

7

"Her shapely form in a blue bathing suit did not inspire the thought of her playing such a spiritual part as the blind girl."

—CHARLIE CHAPLIN

Most accounts of the relationship between Cary Grant and Virginia Cherrill depict him as the victim of a young and cold beauty emboldened by fierce ambition, a calculating Hollywood wannabe who, via a steamy, if opportunistic, romance with Chaplin followed by a brief and stormy marriage to Grant, managed to sleep her way to the forgettable middle. But the personal recollections of friends who knew her for most of her life and the private diaries she left behind reveal a far different and hitherto unknown side to the woman who was to become the first Mrs. Cary Grant.

Born and raised in Carthage, Illinois, at the age of eighteen the five-foot-five, blue-eyed, already-ravishing blonde caught the eye of prominent Hollywood agent Irving Adler. Always on the lookout for a pretty face he could represent, he first noticed Cherrill at a local beauty contest she had entered as a lark and won while in her sophomore year at Northwestern University. Adler managed to arrange to meet her and, after a year's proper courtship, proposed marriage. Cherrill, bored with school and looking for a way up and out, accepted. They were married in Chicago, after which he moved with her to his home in Beverly Hills.

The relationship was not a very good one; the gap in their age and the difference in their lifestyles posed insurmountable problems; in less than a year they were divorced. Although she still had no interest in anything like an acting career (fearing he would lose her, Adler had forbidden Cherrill to look for film work, which had been perfectly fine with her), she thought it might be fun now to see more of Hollywood while still young and, happily, free.

She rented a little beach house for herself in Venice and summoned her mother, who had since divorced, to come and live with her. Then, one night in the spring of 1930, the twenty-one-year-old Cherrill had a chance personal encounter with the world's most famous film star, forty-three-year-old Charlie Chaplin, that was to profoundly change her life.

It took place in downtown Los Angeles at the American Legion fights (the same arena where Grant later claimed he first met Mae West). Chaplin noticed Cherrill, who was sitting nearby with her first husband's uncle (with whom she was still friendly and who was now wheelchair-bound—the reason she often accompanied him to the bouts, in which she otherwise had no interest). What caught Chaplin's attention was the way Cherrill squinted as she watched the action (being extremely nearsighted and too vain to wear her glasses in public). At the time, Chaplin was having trouble casting the lead for his new movie, *City Lights*, because he felt none of the actresses he had interviewed knew how to play "blind," which the main female character, the flower girl, was, and he thought this beautiful girl might actually *be* blind.

Without hesitation, he went over and politely asked her if she could see. When she laughed and said of course, he invited her to audition for the film.

Exactly one month later Cherrill found herself in front of Chaplin's camera, starring as the heartbreakingly beautiful blind flower girl. After Louella Parsons visited the set that day, in her next column she breathlessly described Cherrill as "Hollywood's greatest beauty."

Although virtually every account has them involved in a passionate romance by the time the cameras started to roll, Cherrill always insisted she never had any romantic interest in Chaplin. In fact, when they met, she was already engaged to the well-known New York–based millionaire Rhinelander William "Willie" Stewart, and all during the filming of *City Lights*, she was regularly traveling east to join him on weekends. However, Stewart, like Adler, did not approve of acting as a suitable career for a married woman, and when she refused to quit the movie, he broke the engagement. The timing of their split fueled speculation in the gossip columns that she and Stewart had parted because she had become involved with Chaplin.

Not that Chaplin would have minded, and not that he didn't try. But when she turned down his advances, he began to complain about her limited acting abilities. According to Chaplin, she didn't even know how to hold a flower properly, or to mouth her one crucial line, "Flower, sir," that Chaplin wanted to shoot in close-up. According to Cherrill, once he lost sexual interest in her, he no longer wanted her in his film. "Most of the actresses that worked for him became involved with him," Cherrill said later. "He suddenly thought I was too old. After all, I was twenty and had been divorced."

Things got so bad between them that Chaplin actually fired Cherrill midway through *City Lights* and intended to replace her with Georgia Hale, the star of his 1925 *The Gold Rush*, until he realized how costly the casting change would be. As the principal financier of his own movies, he found himself caught in a financial squeeze when Cherrill insisted that before she would return, her salary would have to be doubled, from $75 a week to $150. Chaplin reluctantly agreed.

Despite all the off-screen folly, advance word on *City Lights* was extremely positive, so much so that even before its 1931 release, Cherrill was signed to a contract by Fox studios and immediately cast opposite a young and still-unknown contract player by the name of John Wayne, in Seymour Felix's instantly forgettable 1931 campus comedy, *Girls Demand Excitement.**

The night Cary Grant met her, because of *City Lights*, she was a bigger star than he was. He had recognized her outside the Brown Derby and—uncharacteristically for him—walked right up and introduced himself. As they both waited for their partners and their cars, he asked if they might have lunch together some time. Cherrill happily gave the handsome actor her phone number. By now she and her mother had moved to a small apartment in Hollywood, and it was there she received a phone call the next morning from Grant, inviting her that same afternoon for a bite to eat at the Paramount

*In the film, Wayne plays the head of a group of boys whose goal it is to oust all girls from their college. The issue is finally decided by a basketball game. Virginia Cherrill, the female lead, seduces Wayne in an attempt to change his mind about the necessity of women in a man's life. *Variety* summed up the B movie this way: "Theaters playing to a clientele of class will find nothing in it." To the end of his life Wayne laughingly referred to *Girls Demand Excitement* as the silliest film he had ever made.

commissary. Over coffee he asked Cherrill to dinner and she accepted. That night when he showed up at her apartment, she told him she hoped he didn't mind, but she had invited her mother along. Not at all, Grant said. In truth, he found the idea altogether delightful.

They began dating regularly and continued to see each other all during the making of *She Done Him Wrong*, a development that delighted Zukor, who arranged for photographers and reporters to follow the two whenever they were out in public. If all this media attention bothered Grant, he didn't show it. Again, uncharacteristically, he dutifully and happily posed for as many pictures as the paparazzi wanted. Scott, meanwhile, sat home and stewed with jealousy. While he usually found the women with whom the studio provided for him and Grant to be a hoot, he found nothing amusing about Cherrill. He told Grant he didn't approve of her, that she was an opportunist, and refused to socialize with the two of them. Grant calmly told him he was wrong about Cherrill, and then let it go at that.

Upon completion of *She Done Him Wrong*, after only a few days off that he spent with Cherrill, Grant returned to the studio at Zukor's insistence to begin shooting *Woman Accused*, his first film of 1933. *Woman Accused* was based on a highly popular magazine article that had been commissioned by *Liberty*, wherein ten famous authors of the day* combined their talents to write a murder mystery, each tackling a separate chapter.

He followed that one without a break by appearing in Stuart Walker's *The Eagle and the Hawk*, costarring opposite Fredric March in a World War I melodrama in which a heroic lieutenant (March) is destroyed by the ravages of war. Although March and a fellow officer (Grant) dislike each other at the start of the film, by the end, through March's moral humanitarianism, Grant's character comes to understand the true meaning of heroism. Strongly antiwar in its sentiment, Paramount hoped to cash in on the populist sentiments of the so-called Lost Generation.

Schulberg, hired once again by Zukor to produce the film, had originally wanted Gary Cooper and George Raft to play the leads, but they considered the film's ending too downbeat—Raft's character commits suicide—and

*Rupert Hughes, Vicki Baum, Zane Grey, Viña Delmar, Irvin S. Cobb, Gertrude Atherton, J. P. McEvoy, Ursula Parrott, Polan Banks, and Sophie Kerr.

both refused to be in it. The film was then recast with March in Cooper's role and Grant in Raft's, and Carole Lombard and a romantic story line were added to make March's character more appealing to women. Shooting was completed in four weeks.

Grant, despite suffering a back injury during an especially elaborate special-effect stunt-bomb explosion, was immediately put into yet another production the day after he finished his last scene. This time it was Louis Gasnier and Max Marcin's *Gambling Ship*, a sorry mishmash involving gamblers, gangsters, and lovers, in which Grant played a character who was all three, opposite Glenda Farrell and Benita Hume. In the film, Grant had little more to do than look good in a tuxedo—something at which he was by now quite adept.

His schedule left little time for Cherrill and even less for Scott. Nonetheless, because of all the studio-encouraged publicity, Grant and Cherrill had become Hollywood's newest hot couple and were invited everywhere. Although, by necessity, they had to turn down most offers, one place Grant especially wanted to go to with her was Hearst's castle at San Simeon, where, despite Cherrill's history with him, he hoped to finally meet Charlie Chaplin. The first time Grant and Cherrill made the three-hour drive from L.A. up the coast highway to the castle, the silent-screen legend, who had been invited by Hearst specifically to meet Grant, failed to show.

THE GRANT/CHERRILL RELATIONSHIP as presented to the public was a picture-perfect romance and, for a time, it actually was. Cherrill felt a strong sexual attraction to Grant from the first time she laid eyes on him, and eagerly looked forward to spending every weekend she could with him, soon charmed by his quick wit and polite manner as well as his astonishing good looks.

Early on, during a black tie dinner one night at the Mocambo, one of Grant's acrobatic partners from his early years with the Pender troupe happened to walk in. Grant recognized him, called him over, and threw his arms around the fellow. He asked him how he was, what he was doing, where he was staying. At one point he asked Grant if he still remembered how to do a backflip. "Of course," Grant said.

"I'll bet you fifty dollars you can't do it right here and now."

Without hesitation Grant went up to the bandleader and asked if he could have a drum roll. The room quickly hushed, and everyone's focus shifted to the center of the dance floor, where Grant did a fast half-dozen backflips straight across it, after which the room broke out in whistles and applause. Smiling, Grant returned to his table and stuck his hand out to collect his fifty dollars. Cherrill, by now in hysterics, would often recall that night as one of the funniest and most enjoyable she had spent with Grant. For his part, for the rest of his life, Grant would tell friends that Virginia Cherrill had the best sense of humor of any of his wives.

However, according to Cherrill's longtime friend Teresa McWilliams, it was not all backflips and giggles between the two. Far from it. "From the beginning, they were inseparable, even with Scott around nearly all the time. Inseparable and, almost from the beginning, fighting with each other. The essential problem was Cary's incredible jealousy. Virginia had this lovely laugh, and a naturally flirty way, and he was absolutely nuts about her, but it was those very qualities that also drove him nuts whenever any other man paid the least bit of attention to her. And some of those who did were pretty formidable. She was always either at his studio or working on a picture somewhere in those days, or just hanging out at one of the studio commissary soda fountains where men like Humphrey Bogart and Spencer Tracy were always after her. When Grant heard about these goings-on, he made time in his day no matter what else he was doing, even shooting a picture, to drop in to visit Cherrill without letting her know he was coming, and if she was working, he would stand off to the side and watch, for hours if necessary, to make sure no one got too close to her.

"Often, at night, when Cary was either away, busy rehearsing or, as it was most of the time he just didn't want to go out, she'd take herself to the Brown Derby, where every man would flock around her, and she'd have a drink or two, laugh, tell jokes, and be the lighthearted girl she really was."

Every man, that is, except Randolph Scott, who, Cherrill couldn't help but notice, despite his obvious dislike for her, seemed now to always be present. Having realized that Cherrill was not going to go away that quickly, Scott had changed his tactics and decided he had better make himself a visible factor in her relationship with Grant. He often came along whenever the two of them went to dinner and would then hang around, waiting in the car until after Grant took her home. Studio executives noticed it as well, especially in the publicity photos that usually included the three of them, and often offered to supply Scott with a female starlet to serve as his companion on these "double dates," a suggestion the actor flatly refused.

Scott's jealousy was tempered by the fact that the studio had continued pressing him to counter the growing rumors about his "odd" relationship with Grant, who at least had a girlfriend. The last thing Scott wanted was a woman. Several years older than his partner, he was committed to their private way of life, less certain of a successful career in film, and wished to live out his years only with Grant.

To remind him of just that, midway through the filming of *Gambling Ship* the wealthy Scott gave Grant an expensive present—a house on the Santa Monica beach, one block south of Wilshire Boulevard, to use as their private getaway from the relentless Hollywood publicity scene (and Virginia Cherrill).

The house, adjacent to the fabled Malibu Beach, stood along an exclusive spit of waterfront known as Millionaire's Row. Scott had bought it from Norma Talmadge, a silent-screen star whose career had ended with her inability to make the transition to sound. He customized it with every luxury imaginable, including a private gymnasium, an indoor heated swimming pool, and a sumptuously appointed kitchen, and presented the keys to Grant as if to show him that he could provide him with the kind of good things in life that his actress girlfriend couldn't. Even though Scott gave the house to Grant, he put the lease in both their names, his only proviso being that if either of them got married, the other would have the right to buy out the rest of the property.

Grant immediately took to the place and brought in his favorite piece of furniture, in fact his *only* piece of furniture—his bed, which he installed in his own, separate bedroom. Eight feet long and six feet wide, it came with a headboard complete with bookshelves, lights, radio, clock, mirror, telephone stand, even a fold-down writing desk. At one point, he told a reporter lucky enough to get a personal tour of the beach house that his goal was to retire at sixty and spend the rest of his life in bed, as long as it was *that* bed.

Although he tried not to show it to either Scott or Cherrill, the growing tension caused by their uneasy three-way relationship, on top of his nonstop work schedule, was starting to take its emotional toll on Grant. His one-pack-a-day smoking habit increased to two. He began drinking more than ever. He developed serious insomnia and took pills to help him drop off into an always fitful sleep.

After several months of their odd public threesome, stories began to appear in the press of Grant's impending marriage to Cherrill. When Grant confronted Zukor, he denied having anything to do with it. He then asked Cherrill if she was the source, but she vehemently denied that the rumor had come from her. She pointed the finger at Scott, figuring he was doing it to cause problems between them. (She was wrong. The source, in fact, was Schulberg.)

Scott blew up over the press releases and insisted Grant promise him he was not interested in anything long-term with Cherrill. To keep Scott happy, Grant told any and all reporters or columnists who asked that his schedule was simply much too busy at the moment to permit him to concentrate on something as important and life-changing as marriage.

These comments in turn infuriated Cherrill, who retaliated by openly revisiting one of her former Hollywood lovers. In 1930, shortly after divorcing her husband and arriving in L.A., and prior to her second engagement and working for Chaplin, she had had a passionate, if brief, affair with pianist and actor Oscar Levant. Throughout the making of *City Lights*, Cherrill, although engaged to Stewart, resumed seeing Levant. From the time she met Grant, she had carefully avoided a still-smitten Levant until Grant's comment about his being too busy to consider marriage was published. One night after Cherrill had left for the evening, Grant, who suspected she was seeing somebody else, followed her in his Packard to her house in Hancock Park, where she was now living, still with her mother, and became incensed when he saw Levant pull up a few minutes later in his green Ford. Grant waited until Levant went inside, then repeatedly rammed the back of the car with his much heavier yellow Packard. Years later Levant recalled this peculiar incident by noting with bemusement, "The only thing I got out of [my] love [affair with Cherrill] was a bill for damages to my car. I thought it was a peculiar way of anyone's showing his strength, even though I sympathized with Grant's mood."

On a drive to Santa Barbara the following weekend, Cherrill tried to discuss with Grant what had happened, but his unwillingness to admit he had acted like a lunatic only angered her more. She then asked him to pull into a bus depot so she could go to the bathroom. He did, she got out, went to the ladies' room, and then slipped out a side door and boarded the next bus back to L.A. Grant waited nearly an hour before he finally realized what she had done. He irately turned the Packard around and gunned his way home.

Other times when she was angry or frustrated with Grant, Cherrill simply left Los Angeles without telling him where she was going, or with whom. On more than one occasion she would go to the airport, get on a plane, and fly to New York to rendezvous with Stewart. She always made sure their liaisons made it into the columns, so that Grant could not help but find out. These actions sent him into romantic somersaults.

GRANT BEGAN FILMING Wesley Ruggles's *I'm No Angel* in the summer of 1933. He had mixed feelings about returning to the screen in what was essentially another star vehicle for Mae West in which he had little more to do than feed her straight lines.

In *I'm No Angel* West plays Tira, a circus performer who specializes in lion-taming while hustling rich men on the side. Grant is Jack Clayton, a wealthy, sexually shy socialite who easily falls for Tira's calculated charms. He asks her to marry him but then breaks up with her, she sues him for breach of promise, he lets her win, and in the final reel true love provides the real settlement. They reconcile, at least for the time being, with neither one having changed in the least.

In real life, the relationship between Grant and West was anything but loving. He resented what he considered her on-set star trips, in which she dictated everything from camera angles to light focus, and this time around she made Grant's character, as she insisted he portray him, as exciting as a wet mop. Lacking the inner fire and passion needed to play against each other, the film's conflict fell flat.

West was so dissatisfied with Grant that she refused to film her love scenes with him. Instead, she had them shot in single isolated takes, so that her face and dialogue would be shot one day, and his the next, edited later on to make it seem as if they had played the scene together. Grant was humiliated and told the studio in no uncertain terms that he would never work with West again.

For the public, however, Grant appeared gracious. When a reporter from the *Los Angeles Times* asked him if the legendary West sexual "magic" had worked on him, he said, carefully choosing his words, "I can't say that I'm in love with Miss West, or that she is in love with me, but I don't hesitate to admit that her screen loving really gets to you. Mae is a great actress because she is so thoroughly genuine."

Despite all the on-set problems, their pairing once again struck box office gold, and Schulberg, who had produced the film, despite knowing how much they disliked each other, hoped to make them a permanent screen team, on the order of Sternberg and Dietrich, or Chevalier and MacDonald. Completed in September (at a cost of $225,000), *I'm No Angel* reached theaters in November, in time to catch the Christmas holiday rush, and proved an even bigger hit than *She Done Him Wrong,*

Audiences packed houses to see the spectacular scenes in which West wickedly played with the lions, cracking leather whips like a professional dominatrix to keep them in their places, and to hear her familiar double entendres:

She: "I like sophisticated men to take me out."
He: "I'm not really sophisticated."
She: "You're not really out yet, either."

He: "You haven't a streak of decency in you."
She: "I don't show my good points to strangers."

He: "Do you mind if I get personal?"
She: "I don't mind if you get familiar."

He: "If I could only trust you."
She: "Hundreds have."

The script was written by West, who of course gave herself the best lines.

In its first eight weeks of release *I'm No Angel* grossed more than $4 million. In New York City it opened at the Paramount, where it set a new record for attendance, with 180,000 people buying tickets the first week alone.

WHILE GRANT WAS FILMING *I'm No Angel*, Cherrill took a role in a small independent film, Lois Weber's *White Heat*, shot on location in Hawaii.* According to Cherrill, during this period of enforced separation Grant hired private detectives to spy on her. To make matters worse, while Grant spent more and more time at the Hollywood apartment to be closer to the studio during filming, Scott preferred to remain at the beach house with a new girl-friend all his own—studio contract starlet Vivian Gaye. Grant tried to take Scott's new involvement in stride. He knew he couldn't complain, with Cherrill having become a permanent part of their relationship, and he knew Scott wasn't seriously involved with Gaye. In those uncertain financial times at Paramount, Zukor had stepped up the pressure on Scott to once and for all put an end to his relationship with Grant. If they didn't, Zukor warned Scott, the studio was willing to lose him before his more popular cohabiting partner. Soon after the studio's ultimatum, Scott became involved with Gaye.

A beauty of Swiss and Russian ancestry, Gaye had fallen hard for the tall, handsome, square-jawed Scott after being personally assigned by the studio to be his date one evening in 1933 (she replaced Sari Maritza, who had become his regularly assigned companion for public double dates with Grant and Cherrill when Maritza became involved with another actor).

Although he never actually proposed to Gaye, Scott thought it wise to let her believe, for his own sake, that there was a possibility of marriage in the future, and he did not object when she told friends they were going to get married, not even when it reached the gossips. As Scott knew it would, it pleased Zukor and—for the moment at least—the heat was off.

Meanwhile, Grant was hard at work on yet another movie role, this time playing the Mock Turtle in Adolph Zukor's last-ditch effort to save the studio from going under: an all-star musical production of *Alice in Wonderland*. By now bankruptcy appeared all but inevitable, and Zukor, who had managed

*Not to be confused with Raoul Walsh's 1949 *White Heat*, which starred James Cagney and Virginia Mayo. Because of the same first names of the female leads, these two films are often mistaken for each other.

to wrest total control of the studio from cofounder Jesse Lasky, put everything and everyone he had into *Alice*, hoping its success would save them for at least one more year.

Serving once again as producer, Schulberg assigned Norman McLeod to direct the Joseph L. Mankiewicz and William Cameron Menzies script, based on the Lewis Carroll classic, and he had McLeod cast every available Paramount star in it, including Gary Cooper as the White Knight, W. C. Fields as Humpty Dumpty, Sterling Holloway as the Frog, Edward Everett Horton as the Mad Hatter, Roscoe Karns as Tweedledee, Jack Oakie as Tweedledum, and Baby LeRoy as the Joker. Grant, not included in the original cast, was inserted at the last minute to play the Mock Turtle, after Bing Crosby angrily turned down what he considered an insult of a part. The film opened to mixed reviews and was taken by the public for what it was, a top-heavy novelty.

Shortly afterward, an exhausted Grant, having made five pictures in 1933, thirteen in two years, suffering from a variety of physical ailments made worse by his shattered nerves, decided it was the perfect time for himself and Cherrill—who had completed her film and returned to L.A.—to take a vacation. Now was as good a time as any, he figured, to show her England. Scott believed this choice of locale was no accident, and correctly figured Grant was taking Cherrill home to meet his family and get married.

To Grant's surprise, Cherrill was less than thrilled at the notion of a long cruise to London; not because she didn't want to make the trip—especially since Cary had begun to hint the end result would indeed be marriage—but because he insisted on waiting for Scott to finish acting in a film he was making called *Broken Dreams* so he could come along. When she asked him why Scott had to be there, Grant replied with a smile that every fellow needed a best man. Cherrill did not find it at all amusing.

The next day she accompanied Grant to Monogram Studios, where Scott was filming, all the while continuing to try to persuade him to leave his "pal" home. Their disagreement exploded into a furious argument on the set that interrupted shooting; it was a dust-up that made the local gossip columns.

The next day Scott announced his engagement to Vivian Gaye.

The day after that Grant booked passage for three on the French liner *Paris*, set to depart from New York, destination Southampton, England.

And the day after that, an enraged Cherrill flew by herself to New York City, from where she wired Grant that she was not going if Vivian Gaye wasn't. Grant wired back saying that under no circumstances was Gaye going to join them. Cherrill's response was to book passage for herself on the next liner bound for England.

And so it was that on November 23, a distressed and heavily sedated Cary Grant, accompanied by Randolph Scott, flew to New York City, headed straight for the pier to board the *Paris*, and set sail for England, where he hoped to find Cherrill and salvage their relationship.

Romantic salvation, however, would serve only as the point of departure, for upon his triumphant return to England after thirteen years in America, awaiting Grant was nothing less than a miraculous resurrection, one far more unexpected and shattering than anything he could ever have imagined or dreamed of.

WIVES AND MOTHERS

PART FOUR

PREVIOUS PAGE: *Virginia Cherrill and Cary Grant arrive in Hollywood after their tumultuous wedding in London, February 1934. (Courtesy of the private collection of the Virginia Cherrill Estate)*

8

"The first day that Cary, the perfectionist, walked into my house, he went immediately into high gear. He pursed his lips, made clucking noises, and set about straightening the pictures. Through the years to come he made generous efforts to straighten out my private life by warning me of the quirks and peculiarities of various ladies . . . enthusiasm was a most important ingredient in Cary's makeup, and it shone out of that side of his character which he presented to his friends; the other side was as mysterious as the dark side of the moon."

—DAVID NIVEN

Cary Grant was miserable because Virginia Cherrill had not come on the trip to England with him, and Scott was miserable because Grant was. So they locked themselves inside their first-class cabin and stayed drunk for the entire voyage. They never even bothered to get dressed, preferring to stay in their silk pajamas, flannel robes, and ascots while they ate, drank, and chain-smoked. All day every day Grant loudly and mournfully played the grand piano the captain had installed as a courtesy.

Grant crucified Bach while he rambled through his besotted mind and put together a rescue plan. Should he be able to find Cherrill, he would immediately ask her to marry him, believing now that that was what it would take to get her back.

As for Scott, he had already gone public with the announcement of his engagement to Gaye and had promised to marry her in time for them to spend Christmas together as husband and wife, but when he told her she wasn't allowed to come on the trip to England, she became angrier than he'd ever seen her before, or ever imagined she could get. Although neither made it public at the time, she had abruptly broken off their engagement. Before Scott returned from England, she began dating director Ernst Lubitsch, whom she would eventually marry.

Upon disembarking in Southampton, the two were driven directly to the Savoy in London and taken by private elevator to the top-floor suite that Paramount Publix had reserved for Grant, all expenses paid (for the hotel and everything else for the entire length of his stay, in return for his agreeing to make a single public appearance at the gala London opening of *She Done Him Wrong*).

Even before his bags were unpacked, Grant began to search for Cherrill. He spent much of his first day in London in his suite, calling every hotel in the city until he found her. They talked on the phone, he went to her hotel and waited for her in the lobby, she came down, they kissed and made up, and she checked out of her suite and moved into his. At this point a fed-up Scott decided to return to the States. He had no desire to get between the two of them again.

Alone with Cherrill, Grant spent that night and the next day with her in the suite and because of it missed the London premiere of *She Done Him Wrong*. As the time approached and with Grant nowhere in sight, a desperate studio representative called the hotel, managed to get Grant on the phone, and reminded him of his obligation. Grant angrily replied that he was under no such obligation because he hadn't as yet been paid what he insisted was an appearance fee, separate and apart from his travel expenses. When the distraught Paramount executive explained to him that his "fee" was the pickup of all his expenses, Grant insisted he was mistaken and hung up. What Grant really wanted was to be left alone with Cherrill, to mend his romantic fences, and he wasn't about to leave her alone again while he went to the opening of Mae West's movie.

They didn't emerge from the hotel until days later, with a much calmer Grant eager to give Cherrill a tour of his homeland. They traveled by limousine from London to Bristol to revisit all the familiar sites of his youth — the Fairfield School, and the local music halls and playhouses where he had begun his career. To his utter amazement and delight, he was greeted by throngs of cheering fans who had waited for days to welcome home their most famous son.

In charge of all the planned festivities were several of the Kingdons, his mother's side of the family, including Aunt May and cousin Ernest, who had looked after him once his father had relocated to Southampton. They hosted a private reception at Picton Street, where Ernest Kingdon had hung pictures of the young Archie Leach all over the walls. Also in attendance was his stepbrother, Eric, the child of Elias and Mabel, his Southampton mistress. During the festivities Eric informed Grant that his father wanted to meet with him, in private and at his convenience, to discuss a matter of great importance.

HE KNEW IT WAS NOT going to be easy. They hadn't been face to face in fifteen years, since the day Elias had seen him off to America, after which time Elias had committed himself to his new life in Southampton. Since then there had been no contact between the two. Now Grant hoped he and his father could somehow revive their relationship.

On the night of the meeting, Grant dressed in his best dark blue suit, pressed as sharp as a razor's edge to impress his father, and took Cherrill along. Grant made the appropriate introductions, and they all had dinner together, after which Grant left Cherrill with Mabel and Eric while he and Elias went to a local pub to talk. They found one Elias liked, went to a table in the rear, and got down to serious business — the nature of which Grant was totally unprepared for. Even after being warned by relatives that his father had become a bad drunk, Grant had been shocked at how Elias's once-handsome face had been raked by sun and scotch, with sagging jowls, piloted by a pair of dead eyes. He waited to see if this was going to be a genuine rap-prochement or, more likely, a touch-up for money. Grant was prepared for and ready to go along with either or both.

He couldn't have been farther from the mark.

After two pints, Elias stared into his third and said, softly, "Now, son, would you like to see your mother?"

"*What?*"

Elias took a deep breath, slurped some foam, and then began to calmly explain the truth about Elsie's "death." He took his boy back to that day when young Archie came home from school to find his mother gone. He told him that Elsie had not died after all, that for all this time she had been only a few miles away, involuntarily committed to Fishponds, the Country Home for Mental Defectives on the outskirts of Bristol, after she had suffered what he called a severe "nervous breakdown."* Elias expected Elsie to remain at Fishponds for the rest of her life, which was why, he said, he had thought it better that Archie, for his own sake, be told she was dead.

Grant was devastated. By the time he left the pub to return to his hotel, he had lapsed into a fog of depression, unreachable even by Virginia Cherrill, who became frightened by his bizarre demeanor.

A million miles away in his mind, Grant wondered how his father could have done it to his mother. *To him.* All those years thinking she was dead, she had been alone, locked up, shunned. For Grant, learning the truth meant that he had not been abandoned after all, at least not by his mother, but he *had* been abandoned by Elias, lied to and tricked by the father he had so adored.

That night, Grant fitfully tossed and turned through nightmarish visions of his mother made to suffer for his father's sins. Cherrill was unable to soothe him with her voice or her arms around him, as he wrestled until dawn with the recast demons of his reawakened youth.

---

*No one can be sure of Elsie's mental condition, as all of her medical records will remain sealed until the year 2073. But such were the times that it was not unusual for Victorian and Edwardian women to be committed by the British State for suffering what were then perceived as "abnormal" mental conditions that would today be easily recognized as nothing more serious than a hormonal imbalance. Elsie's incarceration also served as a convenient escape route for Elias from his unhappy marriage. Unable to afford a divorce, with his wife officially indisposed he was then able to openly maintain his relationship with Mabel in Southampton. And because Elsie was still alive, Elias could not be pressured into another marriage.

After dropping off at the first sign of morning light, Grant awoke late the next day and seemed relatively composed. After an afternoon breakfast in the suite with Cherrill, he telephoned Elias and requested his help in arranging a visit to his mother at Fishponds. Elias said he would take care of everything.

The next day, alone, Cary Grant hailed a cab and took the fifteen-minute ride to the insane asylum. Upon his arrival, he stepped through the stone-and-gate front entrance and was escorted by the administrator and the head nurse to a reception room where Elsie was sitting, waiting for him. The shock of actually seeing his mother stunned Grant. There she was, alive and . . . *smiling.*

The thirty-year-old actor and his fifty-six-year-old mother sat side by side on a stiff lounge, she doting on him as if he were still a little boy, *her* little boy, while he smiled and brushed away a tear as he gazed at a woman he only vaguely recognized, whose strong voice had turned high and thin, whose thick lovely hair had turned mousy gray, and whose bones seemed to stick out of their joints.

It quickly became apparent to Grant that Elsie was a bit more than out of it. Apparently, she had no idea how much time had passed, that he had gone to America and become a movie star. To her he was still precious little Archie. They talked for a long time, and before he left Grant promised his mother he would get her released by her next birthday, coming up in February, and that they would celebrate it together on the "outside." Then he put his arms around her and held her tight. He could feel a slight giggle pass through her as he held back his tears.

To the end of his life, Grant never spoke to anybody except Virginia Cherrill of that first, shocking reunion with his mother, nor about much of anything having to do with his early life in Bristol, nor the purposeful deception perpetuated by his father, other than the few romanticized memories he included in his memoirs.*

As the days passed in the hotel, Cherrill noticed that Grant's mood continued to darken. It slowly dawned on the woman he had so desperately pursued throughout Hollywood, then across America and on to the other side of

---

*Grant's reactions to his initial visit to his mother, and his subsequent discussions about it with Cherrill, are from her private tapes and diaries.

the Atlantic, that she was no longer the only living female worthy of his deepest affections. Nevertheless, Cherrill determined not to let anything interfere with their plans to be married. She continued to refer to herself, to the gossips of London's daily press, as Cary Grant's "fiancée."

The only problem was that he hadn't as yet formally proposed. Amid all the confusion and emotional upheaval, the conflicting forces of his emotions snapped through him like static electricity. He retreated once more into the confines of his hotel room—and sought the shielding comfort of expensive scotch.

His drinking dramatically increased and soon he began to complain to Cherrill, who tried as best she could to stay out of the line of fire, of his continuing physical aches and pains, including a return of his old back problem from the explosion on the set of *The Eagle and the Hawk*.

After Cherrill met with the press and blithely talked of a possible Christmas wedding in London, Grant's physical condition worsened. He imagined himself the victim of every illness imaginable, as if he were a magnet and the metal shavings flying through the air were germs of disease seeking to attach themselves to him. Psychosomatic or not, real physical symptoms began to exhibit themselves. When he began bleeding heavily from his rectum, Cherrill insisted he see a doctor.

The initial diagnosis was a bad case of hemorrhoids, aggravated by Grant's fragile emotional condition, a conclusion the hypochondriac actor rejected in favor of his own more dramatic one: that he was suffering from terminal rectal cancer. His fears grew worse the next day, when the physical symptoms intensified. While he was brushing his teeth, pulses of blood shot out of the upper left side of his mouth. It was enough to convince him to check into a clinic on Fulham Road in preparation for cancer surgery.

Although later on Grant (and others) would insist that he had suffered from either "cancer" or a "pre-cancerous" condition, there is absolutely no medical record of any such condition having actually existed. Equally in question are the "radiation treatments" Grant claimed to have taken in the weeks that followed. Radiation for cancer was still heavily experimental at the time, and it is unlikely that the private clinic where he stayed would have been equipped to administer such sophisticated treatment. In addition, there is no recorded evidence, no medical charts, no photos, nothing to document any of the side effects of radiation—temporary baldness (almost always), vomiting, weight loss, weakness, and constant bed care. Nor are there any medical records to show that he had any type of chemotherapy.

On the other hand, it is quite possible, judging from photos taken of Grant before and after this visit, that he was hospitalized for, among other things, a touch-up of the nose work he had first had in the States. Or equally plausible, drinking as heavily as he was, he might have used the time at the hospital to dry out, or was never in the hospital at all but went instead to a rehab clinic. No matter what the actual series of events, one thing is certain: Grant and Cherrill's so-called wedding plans were indefinitely postponed.

Almost as bad for her was the thought of having to play nurse to Grant for the prescribed four weeks or more of hospital bed rest. Cherrill, already on edge, developed a severe bout of laryngitis that Grant was certain was throat cancer. She continued to make plans for their wedding, setting a January date, until she discovered that her final divorce papers (from Irving Adler) were still in Hollywood and she could not obtain a marriage certificate without them. It would take at least a week or two for them to arrive in London. She then picked February 9, 1934, as their proposed wedding date (one day after Grant's mother's fifty-seventh birthday). Grant, too weak to argue, gave his consent.

When the news hit the papers, Grant tried to call Scott several times and finally reached him at the beach house, but despite his pleas, Scott refused to return to England to stand up as best man. Grant asked no one else, including his father, to do the honors.

On February 9, the day of his wedding, the mobs outside his hotel were so big, he somehow got separated from Cherrill, with whom he was supposed to drive to the Caxton Hall marriage registry office in London.

They arrived separately, in time for an altogether joyless civil ceremony. Afterward they were taken directly by limousine to the train station, where they traveled by rail to Southampton. Upon their arrival they directly boarded the luxury liner *Berengaria*, bound for the United States, with first-class accommodations once again provided by the studio. With new film deadlines pressing, Grant had no choice but to forgo any honeymoon, return home with Cherrill, and resume making movies, knowing all the while a disgruntled Scott was waiting for him.

Worse for Grant, Elsie had rejected his impassioned pleas to come to America with him, and he was not even able to stay in England long enough to keep his promise about celebrating her fifty-eighth birthday together on the outside. It wasn't until Grant and his new wife were still at sea that Elsie Leach was, thanks to Grant's efforts, officially declared "sane" and released from Fishponds after nineteen years of incarceration. She quietly returned to the same house in Bristol from which she had forcibly been taken; her sister May and other members of the Kingdon family waited there to receive and care for her.

Grant had been miserable without Cherrill on the journey over to London. On the return trip to America, he was miserable for having married her. Cherrill, meanwhile, who had at the very least hoped for a romantic honeymoon at sea, was bitterly disappointed by her bridegroom's ignoring her the entire voyage.

9

"Movie stars operate in an ether as intimate to us as dreams. That's why movie stars often seem as close, or closer to us, than loved ones."

—PETER RAINER

Even before the *Berengaria* docked in New York City, Cary Grant knew his marriage to Virginia Cherrill was over. During the voyage she had talked about the type of home she wanted to make for them. The more elaborate and elegant she imagined it, the more Grant cringed. Even while living with Scott, who loved to decorate with the kind of ornate flourish that only inherited southern wealth could provide, Grant was content to have nothing more in the house in the hills than a chair or two, a version of his favorite bed, running water, a radio, and a refrigerator. Scott had filled the place for the both of them, and Grant had gone along with it primarily to please him. He did not have the desire to similarly accommodate his bride.

There were other problems as well. Cherrill had become extremely chatty during the long journey home—talking about everything from poetry to cooking. Unfortunately, nothing she went on about held the least bit of interest for Grant. He had had little formal education and did not consider himself an intellectual in any sense, or a gourmand. Whenever he and Scott talked, they mostly theorized about ways to increase their creative control and financial stake in the films they worked on, via approval of script, casting, directors, profit participation, salary guarantees against gross, and so on. Cherrill, on the other hand, was completely uninterested in discussing the art *or* the business of acting. She told Grant she was more than willing to give up her movie career, such as it was. She may not have been the domestic type, but she knew she could offer Grant her beauty and the promise of good sex that went with it—two things in which Grant, at least as far as Cherrill could tell, now seemed utterly uninterested. It was almost as if all the action for Grant had been in the pursuit; as in the movies, when the couple married, the story ended. In the morning after of what should have been the biggest day of his life, he almost seemed surprised she was still there.

Upon arriving in New York City, Grant's mood seemed to brighten, and in lieu of an official honeymoon, he stole forty-eight hours from the studio and booked a suite in the Raleigh Hotel in midtown Manhattan. For the next two days he took delight in giving Cherrill an informed walking tour of the city as he had known it in the 1920s, and he showed her all his personal landmarks: the hotel he'd stayed in while with the Pender troupe, the small apartment he'd shared with Orry-Kelly, the beautiful turn-of-the-century theaters he'd performed in, and the spirited dives he'd frequented when he had little or no money. It was a repeat of his Bristol tour without the accompanying emotional trauma.

Cherrill noted with some surprise Grant's affinity for what she took to be the seamier side of the city. When she made a joke about all the adolescent boys from England he'd had to live with, Grant never broke stride as he matter-of-factly related to her stories about the games they used to play with one another, the measuring of their penises to see who had the biggest, the "circle jerks," the rubbing up against one another at night for comfort—all the things, he said with a half-smile, that go on in boys' dormitories all over England, from Eton to Oxford. As she would tell friends and acquaintances later on and note in her diaries, it was the closest Grant ever came to admitting to her that he was bisexual. Not surprisingly, Grant's "confession," his way of trying to explain himself to her now that they were man and wife, further dismayed Cherrill. Unable to see much without her glasses and always unwilling to wear them in public, she walked speechless with Grant mile after mile in a blind haze along the city's cement streets.

By the end of the two days (during which time their marriage was, according to Cherrill, still not officially consummated), she was more than ready to board the Santa Fe Chief at Grand Central Terminal for the three-day journey back to Los Angeles.

At Union Station in downtown L.A., they were met by dozens of paparazzi, tipped by the studio on their arrival and eager to photograph the newlyweds. To avoid the gauntlet that Cherrill actually looked forward to, Grant insisted they duck out a side exit and into a limousine he had ordered in anticipation of the crush of the press.

They went directly to the house on West Live Oak Drive. To Cherrill's dismay, Randolph Scott was there, waiting for them at the front door. That was when she realized he had not moved out, that he was still living in the small house with, apparently, no intention of leaving. As Grant carried Cherrill over the crowded threshold, his other full-time live-in, Archie Leach, barked loudly at Cherrill, then ran out the back door and disappeared. The dog's running away threw Grant into a new funk that lasted the entire week until, seven days later, the tired-looking hound came loping back home.

Grant barely had time to celebrate, as the studio, which had given him a few extra days to search for his dog, now demanded his immediate return to work. Zukor needed him to put as much filmed product in the can as possible, anticipating the studio's imminent bankruptcy and the selling off of its assets, the most valuable of which were finished movies.

THE FIRST FEATURE GRANT APPEARED IN after returning to Hollywood was Marion Gering's *Thirty Day Princess*, costarring Sylvia Sidney and produced by B. P. Schulberg's new independent production company (distributed by Paramount), formed while Grant was in London. Schulberg's official departure from Paramount upset Grant, as he had always believed Schulberg was his strongest supporter at the studio.

Thirty Day Princess is a variation on the old prince-and-pauper plot of switched identities and roles. A princess (Sidney, sporting an odd Asian-sounding accent despite her character's supposedly European origins — the "mythical kingdom of Taronia") comes down with the flu at a particularly inopportune time. An actress (also Sidney) is hired to impersonate her to fool a New York newspaper publisher (Grant), who has been critical of the princess. Upon "meeting" her, he falls in love with her stand-in. This slapstick rondo goes around in circles for seventy-three tedious minutes. Grant hated everything about the film, including the haste with which it was made and the fact that once again he was cast in a role that Gary Cooper had rejected. The film was ready for release that May, barely four months to the day Grant and Cherrill had returned from England.

Cherrill, meanwhile, continued to feel uneasy living under the same roof with Grant *and* Scott, and as soon as *Thirty Day Princess* was finished, insisted that she and Grant move to a place of their own. Grant obligingly, if reluctantly, leased an apartment at the La Ronda complex, on Havenhurst just east of Hollywood. The next day Scott rented the one next door, and Cherrill threw a fit. While Scott moved in his things, a loud argument ensued between her and Grant that lasted deep into the night. By now Grant was convinced that divorce was going to be the only remedy for the misery he had inflicted upon himself by marrying Cherrill. He would have already filed if not for two considerations. The first was practical: his inherent thriftiness made him fear divorce and alimony in a state where mandatory "irreconcilable differences" settlements were based on residency, not the location of the wedding, and was almost always a fifty-fifty split of assets. He didn't feel like handing over half of everything he had because of a stupid mistake he'd made. The second consideration was more complex. More than anything else, he hated the notion of appearing to abandon anyone, even his wife — *especially* his wife — which would have been a clarion echo of his father's abandonment of Elsie. As a result, Grant was emotionally paralyzed and withdrew even further from Cherrill. When they did communicate, he passively avoided the big issue by arguing with her over the smallest and most insignificant ones.

Their constant bickering continued through the release of four more unremarkable Cary Grant "tuxedo" movies that he was happy to lose himself in, if for no other reason than to get away from the situation at home. They were all made in the space of seven months, and none earned back its cost. Lowell Sherman's *Born to Be Bad* costarred Loretta Young and was released May 18, 1934, with Grant on cash loan to Darryl F. Zanuck's 20th Century. In Harlan Thompson's *Kiss and Make Up*, opposite Helen Mack, Grant sang

"Love Divided by Two," written for him by Leo Robin and Ralph Rainger. In Frank Tuttle's *Ladies Should Listen*, Grant played opposite Frances Drake, and in one of Paramount Publix's final films, Elliott Nugent's *Enter Madame*, Grant starred opposite Elissa Landi.

In these movies, Grant can be seen with his hands in his pockets, trying to act suave, even interested. His reversion to pocket-posing was a manifestation of his boredom with playing the same uninteresting character over and over again, and his resident insecurity as an actor that always surfaced whenever he felt unprotected by the lack of a strong script, a solid director, a talented lighting designer, or a perfectionist cinematographer. Indeed, what is most notable about these movies is how similarly unremarkable they are, how glossy without shine their black-and-white photography appears, and how mechanically their mise-en-scène is presented. These were, pure and simple, product, the final churn-out of the Paramount Publix factory that in its endgame specialized in these hurried, repetitious, and banal feature films.

Of the actresses Grant played opposite in this cluster of features, Landi was the one he most favored, but not for the reasons one might suspect. At the time Landi was struggling to make it as an actress without having signed to any studio (although she had been offered a contract by several, including Paramount). She would not go on to become a star, despite her good looks and appealing onscreen personality, at least in part because of her unwillingness to become a contract player for any of the majors — an act of courage and tenacity Grant admired. Landi's failed attempt at autonomy became an early reference point as well as an object lesson for Grant, whose growing desire to gain control of his own cinematic destiny made him feel, more than ever after these last pictures, like a mouse in a wheel toy, running faster and faster and still getting nowhere.

Not long after, Grant petitioned Zukor and his collapsing studio to loan him out to MGM, where a film version of the popular book *Mutiny on the Bounty* by Charles Nordhoff and James Norman Hall was being planned. By now loaning had become so common among studios that Irving Thalberg, the legendary head of production at MGM, thought nothing of mentioning to Grant at a party that they both happened to attend just how much he would like to have him play the part of Midshipman Roger Byam in *Mutiny*. It was a special role, the always charming and articulate Thalberg explained, one that called for a personality of enormous intelligence and positive appeal with a rational eloquence, a balance between the extremes of the evil Captain Bligh and the idealistic Fletcher Christian. The film was to be one of MGM's spectacular star-studded showcases. Charles Laughton was set to play the role of Captain Bligh, and Clark Gable was the only actor the studio would even consider for the role of Fletcher Christian.

Grant envied Gable's swaggering success (and his $4,000-a-week salary) and wanted more than anything to appear in a movie with him, knowing that it was bound to be a box office smash and elevate the careers of all who appeared in it. He quickly read the book and then the script and believed he was perfect for the part of Byam. Thalberg then contacted Paramount to arrange Grant's loan-out, which the MGM head of production believed at this point was nothing more than a mere formality. As far as Thalberg was concerned, there was no way the financially strapped Paramount could refuse the deal, especially the hefty fee it would collect for Grant's services while continuing to pay him his $750-a-week salary.

Thalberg consulted with Zukor, who feared the very thing Thalberg predicted—that *Mutiny* would make Cary Grant one of Hollywood's biggest stars. With a year left on Grant's contract, Zukor believed it was not in the studio's best interest to escalate Grant's value. Better, he thought, to keep him at a level where his contract could be renewed at a bargain rate. It would prove a costly mistake on Zukor's part, and one that would permanently alter the direction of Grant's career.

Grant was, predictably, infuriated at Zukor's decision not to let him appear in *Mutiny on the Bounty* and vowed that when his contract was up, he would not re-sign with Paramount, no matter what they offered. It didn't help matters any that Franchot Tone, cast in the role that Thalberg had wanted to give to Grant, earned an Oscar nomination for Best Actor of 1935.*

As all this was taking place, Grant's marriage to Virginia Cherrill continued its precipitous decline. His gathered anger and confusion curdled into

---

*No one was less happy to see Tone get the role over Grant than Gable. He and Tone had been bitter rivals for the affections of Joan Crawford and did not like each other at all.

an overall insecurity and paranoia. He became irrationally jealous of any man he suspected of having a sexual interest in his wife—an ironic twist for a man who had no sexual interest of his own in her. (In truth, had he been thinking clearly, he would have realized that her running off with someone would have given him the perfect excuse to sue for divorce *and* come out of it for the most part financially intact.)

That September, while they were out having dinner, Grant mistook Cherrill's familiar squinting at the menu for flirting with someone at another table. They bickered about it, an argument that continued until they got home, where it escalated until, according to Cherrill, Grant slapped her hard across the face.

The next morning she packed her things and returned to her mother's apartment in Hancock Park, vowing never to live under the same roof with a madman.

"She liked to flirt, there was no question about it, whether or not the incident that sparked the violence actually happened," recalled Teresa McWilliams. "And he was incredibly jealous. She had this lovely laugh, and enjoyed men playing up to her, while Cary was just unbelievably possessive. I suppose it was his way of being nuts about her. What made her finally leave, though, was the night he hit her. She still loved him, but she became afraid of him, and because of that slap it was a fear that could never go away."

Grant knew he had gone too far. The next day all traces of his anger were gone, replaced by a profound remorse. In the days and weeks that followed, he began to drink more heavily and was often seen at the studio during rehearsals or going over lines holding a paper cup of scotch that he tried to pass as tea.

At night he turned to Scott for sympathy, but got none. Scott was glad Cherrill had finally left. Besides the fact that she had managed to crash his private party of two, he simply couldn't stand anything about her. He considered her pretentious, self-centered, boring, and ill-mannered, and her incessant laugh drove him crazy. He told Grant he ought to count his lucky stars he was rid of the woman.

Instead, Grant desperately tried to reestablish contact with Cherrill. The last week in September, he finally managed to get her on the phone and begged her to return to their apartment at La Ronda. She agreed to meet with him at a party, believing she would be safe in a crowd. But once they were together, Grant could not control his rage. He angrily accused her of being unfaithful to him during their separation, demanding to know with whom she had been staying. He dismissed her moving back in with her mother as nothing more than a flimsy cover story.

They never made it back to his apartment. Cherrill stormed out of the party alone, and the next morning contacted gossiper Louella Parsons, with whom she had become good friends, to give her the "exclusive!" on "The Cary Grant–Virginia Cherrill Separation!" In Parsons's next column, she reported that Cherrill had told her the following: "Whether it is permanent or not is up to Cary. I will not discuss the reason for our trouble, but things have been going from bad to worse. I left Cary two weeks ago and consulted a lawyer, but we later patched things up, and I hoped we might make a go out of our marriage because I am in love with my husband."

For Grant, who had no use for gossip columnists, especially after they had begun to write with annoying regularity about his relationship with Randolph Scott, this latest attempt on Cherrill's part, to use one to send him a personal message, was intolerable. Despite the hint their marriage might still be salvageable, Grant knew enough about how Hollywood operated to understand that Cherrill's interview had as much to do with her lawyer's building a case for a lucrative settlement than anything else.

To make matters worse, Scott was horrified at the appearance of Grant's marital problems in the columns (although it was something of a relief to have him linked with a woman rather than the usual innuendo about the two of them).

By the end of the following week Grant's drinking increased, his telephoned pleas to Cherrill became more desperate (and only made her more resolute), and he sank even further into twisted despair. On the evening of October 4, just after dining out alone, he returned to the apartment he had shared with Cherrill and called his closest friends, including Scott, who was right next door, offered rambling apologies for all his bad behavior, and made what sounded like nothing so much as vague farewells. He then placed one final call to Cherrill, begged her to come back, and when she refused, told her he was going to kill himself.

Following a few moments of silence, Cherrill, a seasoned player in the ongoing emotional push-pull of their relationship, hung up, waited, and when the phone didn't ring, called Grant back. The phone was answered by Grant's part-time Filipino houseboy, Pedro, who conveniently just happened to be on duty that night. Cherrill told him she was worried that Cary himself had not picked up. Pedro said he would check on Grant, who was in his bedroom. He put the phone back in its cradle, entered the room, and found his boss stretched out on the bed, clad only in boxer shorts, with a pitcher of water and a large, nearly empty bottle of sleeping pills on the night table. In a panic, Pedro called the police emergency services, and at 2:28 in the morning an ambulance came screaming up to the front of the house, several medical personnel rushed in, hooked Grant up to a respirator, put him on a stretcher, and took him to Hollywood Hospital. There his stomach was pumped, his blood was tested, and despite Cherrill's initial fears that he had fatally overdosed, he quickly revived. Later on the doctors told her they had found no more than a single tablet's worth of sleeping medication in Grant's blood, but that his alcohol level had been dangerously high.

Somehow, the story of Grant's "attempted suicide" made headlines in the next afternoon papers, and working with the publicity department at Paramount, he scrambled to come up with a story. He was instructed by the studio to tell the reporters that "I had been at a party with friends, and when I got home they tried to play a joke on me. They called the police after I lay down. It was all a colossal gag."

And a colossal lie.

There is absolutely no evidence that anybody was with Grant that night, but telephone records confirm the series of calls he made on the evening of October 4. Later on, in fact, Grant himself would change his story and describe the incident this way: "You know what whiskey does when you drink it all by yourself. It makes you very, very sad." So much for being "at a party with friends." He went on to say, "I began calling people up. I know I called Virginia. I don't know what I said to her, but things got hazier and hazier. The next thing I knew, they were carting me off to the hospital."

The incident might have been more easily written off (as it has by most of Grant's biographers), if not for his mysterious and never fully explained hospital stay in England the previous December, immediately following Grant's discovery that his mother was, in fact, still alive. What had really made Grant so ill back then that required several weeks of hospitalization? It is safe to say that the one thing it wasn't was rectal cancer. A truism says a single event is an incident, a series a pattern. It is difficult to see these two relatively close and emotionally traumatic episodes as unrelated. Curiously, all relevant hospital records in both instances have disappeared.

THE DIVORCE PROCEEDINGS WERE NOT particularly lurid, but because they involved a handsome movie star and his beautiful ingenue wife, they were front-page news. Preliminary hearings began on December 11, 1934, in Los Angeles Superior Court, before the ironically named divorce court judge William Valentine. At the hearing Cherrill testified that in the three months since their separation Grant had almost completely cut her off financially, and because of it she had had to pawn her engagement ring and diamond watch and take a second loan against her car just to have enough money for food. In all that time, she claimed, Grant had given her a total of only $125. Now she demanded a thousand dollars a month, pending the finalization of their divorce, so she could properly prepare for her return to a career in films.

Grant, through his lawyer, made a counteroffer of $150 a month. When called to the bench by the judge to explain how he had arrived at his figure, Grant said, "She managed to [get along on that much] before we were married, so she could do it again."

That was enough for Valentine. He ordered Grant to immediately start paying Cherrill $725 a month until the final settlement and subsequent dissolution of their marriage. In addition, Grant was required to post a $20,000 bond, to ensure his payment of both his and Cherrill's legal fees. Last, he was prohibited from selling any of his property.

A week later Cherrill amended her complaint to include accusations that, during their marriage, Grant "drank excessively, choked and beat her, and threatened to kill her."

If Cary hit the roof, Zukor went through it. The last thing he needed was to lose his best and least expensive contract player to this kind of scandal. On Christmas Eve he brought the lawyers from both parties together in a secret meeting at the backlot, during which he warned Cherrill's attorneys that before any settlement could be reached, she would have to drop the charges against Grant regarding his drinking and threats of violence. They agreed, knowing that at this point it didn't make much difference, as the columns had already headlined the accusations for the public's eager consumption.

By the time the divorce proceedings began, a still depressed Grant failed to show up in court, claiming he had to do last-minute reshoots of his two latest movies, Elliott Nugent's *Enter Madame* and James Flood's *Wings in the Dark*. It was a reasonable excuse, and Grant was allowed to have his lawyers stand in for him.

A single one-hour divorce session was held on March 26, 1935, and produced enough "revelations" from a well-rehearsed Cherrill for the next morning's papers. Her lawyer, Milton Cross, who specialized in Hollywood divorces, got her to claim, through her tears and in such a reluctantly soft voice that Valentine had to continually ask her to speak up, that her husband was "sulky, morose, took to drinking . . . and would argue with me on every point. He said I was lazy and ought to go to work, but when I tried to, he discouraged me and refused to let me work . . . he was tired of me and said he didn't want to live with me anymore." To reinforce her claims, Cherrill's lawyers brought her mother to the stand, who testified she had seen Grant "mistreat" her daughter several times.

At Zukor's insistence, Grant had instructed his lawyers in advance not to cross-examine Cherrill or anyone else, including her mother, and to make no further comments of any kind on his behalf, either outside the courtroom to the press or inside before the judge. Grant agreed that the best thing to do was to get it all over with, even if he had to pay a premium price. In the end, the judge formally declared the eleven-month marriage over and awarded Cherrill half of Grant's property, estimated to be worth $50,000.

Less than a month later Cherrill left alone for an extended vacation in England.

Grant, meanwhile, reluctantly gave up the apartment at La Ronda and Scott quickly gave up his place next door. They returned together to the house under the HOLLYWOODLAND sign on West Live Oak Drive. Scott was delirious to have Grant back and chose to pretend that nothing involving Cherrill had ever happened.

An inconsolable Grant didn't have to pretend. Nothing had, and he hated himself for it.

PART FIVE

INDEPENDENCE AND SUPERSTARDOM

PREVIOUS PAGE: *On the Columbia Pictures set of* The Awful Truth *(1937), Cary Grant mirrors the physical style of his director and first comic mentor, Leo McCarey. (Courtesy of the Academy of Motion Picture Arts and Sciences)*

10

"My first great chance came in 1936, when I was borrowed by RKO for *Sylvia Scarlett* playing opposite Katharine Hepburn. This picture did nothing to endear its female lead to the public, but it helped me to success. . . . After this picture I made one after another, probably too many."

—CARY GRANT

Once he and Randolph settled back into West Live Oak Drive, Grant became something of a social recluse, refusing to leave the house for any reason except to go to the studio, fearing he would be laughed at by his friends because Cherrill had left him and because of the sordid details of her testimony. On weekends he took to sitting alone in the sun for hours at a time, with a glass of straight scotch in one hand, a lit cigarette in the other.

He did some last-minute reshoots for James Flood's *Wings in the Dark*, a weeper with Grant as a blind man who learns to "see" through the love of a good woman, played by Myrna Loy, in many ways a reversal of Chaplin's *City Lights* scenario, but without any of *Lights*'s humor, depth, or emotion. Grant showed up for the reshoots with his face deeply tanned and insisted the studio come up with light pancake to match the skin tone of his earlier scenes. Thus began what was to become a pattern for the rest of his moviemaking days, using the sun's rays for makeup.

AFTER *WINGS IN THE DARK,* because of Paramount's financial problems, Grant's next film was a long time coming. While waiting for a new script, he became involved in an odd relationship with a significantly older woman who called herself Countess di Frasso, a fifty-year-old heiress whose real name was Dorothy Taylor and whose New York–based family had become wealthy in the decidedly nonroyal leather goods trade. She had acquired her title by marrying an Italian count, her second unsuccessful foray into legal bliss. He turned out to be a deadbeat with no appreciable earning skills. Their fortune, such as it was, all came from her, and it was barely enough to pay the mortgage on their beautiful Italian villa.

Nevertheless, the count and countess loved to lavishly entertain at their villa, especially visiting Hollywood celebrities, one of whom, Gary Cooper, arrived in 1931 and returned to Beverly Hills with Countess di Frasso dutifully in tow. Cooper and the countess carried on an open affair in Hollywood until he surprised everyone, including her, by suddenly marrying socialite Veronica Balfe.

The jilted countess decided that rather than return to her villa she would stay in Hollywood and soon enough, after following the details of Grant's divorce in the newspapers, marked him as her next Hollywood paramour. While it is highly unlikely that he sexually serviced her with anything like the passionate fervor that Cooper did (if he serviced her at all), they met and somehow managed to become, if not lovers, good friends. Hovering over this new relationship was the ever-present professional rivalry and personal animosity between Cooper and Grant. This time Grant got to "replace" Cooper in a way he knew would annoy his heavily narcissistic competitor.

For the next several years, the countess occasionally blew through Grant's life like an unpredictable breeze, depending upon her availability and his. Their noticeable age difference (she was twenty-two years older), his great looks (she loved being seen with him in public), her financial generosity (she paid for everything), and his appetite for social status (she was, after all, a countess) made him the ideal companion. On Grant's side, his serial melancholia about Elsie made the countess an ideal mother-surrogate: a doting older woman willing to spoil her precious and beautiful "little boy." In the parlance of the *real* golden days of Hollywood, as one who was there at the time rather crudely recalled, "Cary was the perfect central-casting fag to Taylor, a rich, old, self-delusional hag."

MEANWHILE THE STUDIO, deep into reorganization and temporarily unable to get major bank funding for any new films, tried to raise cash by loaning Grant to Warner Bros. as a last-minute replacement for an ailing Robert Donat in that studio's big-budget production of Michael Curtiz's *Captain Blood.** Grant, with his natural athletic abilities, would fit perfectly into the part of the swashbuckling British pirate. But when Zukor offered him to Curtiz, Warners unconditionally turned him down. According to one version, Grant was rejected by the studio for being "too effete." Although the quote has been often repeated, it is rarely attributed. It was actually made by Warner Bros. contract director Michael Curtiz himself, his angry reply to Jack Warner for even making the suggestion. Curtiz—the "wild Hungarian," as he was known—had little use for Grant and his "type." Instead, he cast *über*-heterosexual Errol Flynn to play the role that would go on to make the handsome, rugged Australian a star.

WITH TIME ON HIS HANDS and his skin cooked to a golden tan roughly the tone and consistency of a holiday turkey, Grant continued to ignore Scott's advice to get out of the sun, out of the house, and back into the social scene. To make that happen, Scott finally agreed to introduce Grant to Howard Hughes, one of the few Hollywood celebrities besides Chaplin he still wanted to meet. Scott figured if anyone could get Grant's head out of his own rear end, it was Hughes; after all, MGM may have had more stars than there

---

*Donat had suddenly taken ill, and the studio decided that it was still early enough into the production to reshoot the entire film.

were in heaven, but Hughes had all the starlets. If Grant still wanted to play with girls, a couple of nights together out on the town, Scott believed, would make him forget all about Virginia Cherrill.

Scott's reasons for wanting to put Grant and Hughes together were not completely selfless. Already thirty-seven years old, Scott had a far less successful movie career than Grant, and even fewer prospects. He figured that if he supplied Hughes with something he wanted, Hughes might give him something more in return. Hughes loved beautiful women, and Scott knew that Cary Grant was the ultimate lure.

Meanwhile, to replenish his nearly depleted post-divorce bank account, Grant accepted radio work in New York. Appearing on radio was something he had previously been opposed to, believing that giving away a performance for free would make audiences less inclined to pay to see or hear an actor perform onscreen. Nevertheless, with no films in his immediate future, on May 5, 1935, he made his debut on the airwaves starring in a live broadcast of the Lux Radio Theater, opposite Constance Cummings, a thirty-minute onetime performance for which he was paid $1,750, plus airfare and hotel.

To his surprise, he quite enjoyed the whole experience. For one thing, no physical preparation was required, and for another, it exposed him to a new group of performers, mostly East Coast types who, for a while, dominated the prime time airwaves. Throughout the next twenty years, whenever he had the opportunity, Grant worked on the radio, either as a character in a drama or as a guest on a celebrity variety show, most often with Groucho Marx on his *Kellogg Show*, *The Eddie Cantor Show*, and George Faulkner's talk show, *The Circle*. Whenever Grant did Faulkner's show, he would find himself alongside other Hollywood luminaries, such as his good friend British actor Ronald Colman. One time he even recorded a full-length radio version of his blind-man opus, *Wings in the Dark*, that, as it turned out, worked far better on the sightless medium than it had in the movies.

He returned to making movies after the dust settled around Paramount's 1935 reorganization. Paramount Publix became Paramount Pictures and emerged from bankruptcy. In some ways, at least as far as Grant was concerned, day-to-day operations at the studio had changed little; mostly it was business as usual.* Gary Cooper had recently scored a tremendous success starring in Henry Hathaway's *The Lives of a Bengal Lancer,* but when Zukor wanted to make a sequel, *The Last Outpost,* both Cooper and Hathaway rejected the idea, and the project fell to studio hacks Charles Barton and Louis Gasnier, who cast Grant in the Cooper role and told him to prepare for the role by trying to look more manly. Grant's response was to grow a mustache that made him a ringer for Douglas Fairbanks.

His costar in the film was Claude Rains, who upstaged everyone else in it, including Grant. *The Last Outpost* was released in October 1935 and quickly disappeared, after which Zukor lent Grant to RKO Radio Pictures to costar opposite a new up-and-coming actress by the name of Katharine Hepburn. The move would prove crucial to Grant's career and forge two professional relationships that would profoundly affect both his career and his personal life.

KATHARINE HEPBURN, "the Magnificent Yankee," had been born into a line of bluebloods of Scottish descent from West Hartford, Connecticut. Her father was a noted urologist and surgeon and an early pioneer in the fight against syphilis. He was tall, good-looking, and athletic, a highly skilled investor who had become wealthy from stocks and real estate. Her mother, known to everyone as Kit, was a Boston Houghton (accounting for all six of the Hepburn children having the same Houghton middle name) and a cousin of the ambassador to Britain.

Under her father's strict guidance, Hepburn became a superb athlete, with considerable skills in wrestling, tumbling, trapeze, water sports, and golf. She was intrigued by acting at an early age, a drive that became supercharged in a twisted way after her older brother Tom tried to duplicate a trick they had seen in a stage production of *A Connecticut Yankee in King Arthur's Court* and

---

*The studio went into receivership in 1934 and, after its reorganization a year later, still had outstanding debts of $95 million. In 1936, the newly formed Paramount Pictures made a $6 million profit. By 1941, the end of the Depression and the emergence of a movie-hungry, star-worshiping war generation pushed that profit to nearly $11 million. By 1944 that figure had swelled to $16 million, and peaked at $44 million the following year. By 1946, the studio had paid off all its remaining debt.

accidentally—or as some claim, deliberately—hanged himself. She attended Bryn Mawr and, while exhibiting superior learning skills, nearly flunked out because she spent most of her time in the drama department.

Upon graduation she joined a Baltimore theatrical company and soon made the jump to Broadway, where she appeared in several shows, most of them flops. Then in 1928 she surprised everyone by marrying Ludlow Ogden Smith, a Philadelphia socialite. Upon her return from their honeymoon she agreed to understudy the Broadway star Hope Williams in the lead role of Philip Barry's *Holiday* (a role she would perform only once during its entire year-long run). That led to a starring role in 1932 in *The Warrior's Husband*, a contemporary version of *Lysistrata*. The part gave Hepburn the chance to showcase her considerable athletic skills and also to display a lot of her body, including her previously undisplayed gorgeous long legs.

Word of her audience-pleasing performance eventually reached Merian C. Cooper, the executive producer of RKO Radio Pictures, who sent his then production head, David O. Selznick, to New York, to offer the young actress an exclusive acting contract with the studio for $150 a week. When Selznick met with Hepburn, he asked what it would take to get her to come to Hollywood, and she pulled a figure out of her head that she was certain would send Selznick running. Through her agent, Leland Howard, she had demanded a starting salary of $1,500 a week. Selznick agreed without hesitation, and when *The Warrior's Husband* ended that summer, she flew to Hollywood to begin her film career.

Her first fearure was *A Bill of Divorcement*, in the leading role that every young actress in Hollywood had fought for. It was based on the New York stage play by Clemence Dane that had made a star out of Katharine Cornell in 1921. Once the studio had acquired the rights to the play, it was given to one of its hot new directors with a Broadway pedigree, George Cukor, who, because of his success with Cornell and his superior stage work with Ethel Barrymore, Laurette Taylor, and Helen Hayes, had developed a reputation as a "woman's director." When film legend Dorothy Gish committed to making her long-awaited Broadway debut in *Young Love*, she'd insisted George Cukor direct her.

Even before Cukor officially took up residence at RKO, Selznick had purchased *What Price Hollywood?* for him, a film that in many ways anticipates

Cukor's later *A Star Is Born* (1954). *What Price Hollywood?* made a star out of its lead, the previously unknown Constance Bennett, and Selznick hoped Cukor would repeat his success by turning Hepburn into the studio's next female box office sensation. Selznick's instinct proved correct; on the strength of her performance in Cukor's *A Bill of Divorcement* (1932), Katharine Hepburn did indeed become the newest star of the silver screen.

In addition to reaffirming George Cukor's reputation as a "woman's director," the film erased any lingering doubts about his talent and commercial viability. It also began what amounted to a half-century of continually successful film collaborations between Hepburn and Cukor.

After two more hits — *Morning Glory* (for which she won her first Oscar) and Cukor's *Little Women* — Hepburn completed her obligations to the studio in 1935 and was then hesitant to re-sign with RKO after Selznick left to join his new father-in-law, Louis B. Mayer, at MGM. She finally accepted an offer of $300,000 from RKO for six films still to be chosen, with script approval and choice of role. Nevertheless, Selznick's absence proved as damaging as Hepburn had feared, and her next three films — John Cromwell's *Spitfire*, Richard Wallace's *The Little Minister*, and Philip Moeller's *Break of Hearts* — were major disappointments at the box office. The producer of all three was Pandro S. Berman, who had been given the nearly impossible assignment of replacing the legendary Selznick. His shepherding of the trio of Hepburn films was so disastrous, it nearly ended her film career as well as his own.

Her next film, George Stevens's *Alice Adams* (1935), another Berman production, was a standard Depression-era fantasy of a poor girl successfully climbing the social ladder. Fortunately for Hepburn (and Berman), the film hit a nerve with audiences and helped restore some of the luster to her Hollywood career. It not only proved a winner at the box office but earned Hepburn a second nomination as Best Actress.* Once again she was the hottest female star in Hollywood.

For her next project, she turned once more to her favorite director, Cukor, who this time had what he believed was the perfect Hepburn vehicle. It was based on a 1918 Compton MacKenzie novel, *The Early Life and*

---

*The film was also nominated for Best Picture. It lost in both categories, Hepburn to Bette Davis in Alfred E. Green's *Dangerous*, and the film to Frank Lloyd's *Mutiny on the Bounty*.

Adventures of Sylvia Scarlett, loosely based on the sensational British Crippen case, which Cukor wanted to somehow turn into a comedy.

Once he had his star in place, Cukor hired the distinguished novelist Evelyn Waugh to write the script.* The story of the film begins in France and concerns the adventures of young Sylvia Scarlett, whose father is an embezzler and must flee the country to escape imminent capture and imprisonment. Arriving in London, Sylvia, disguised as a boy to throw off the authorities tracking the duo down, and her father meet up with Jimmy Monkley, a swaggering con-artist cockney lad with whom they team to roam and loot the countryside. Eventually, Sylvia's father marries a wacky servant girl named Maudie Tilt, while Sylvia meets a successful artist, Michael Fane, and must revert to being a "girl" in order to win his affections.

For the part of Henry, Sylvia's father, Cukor cast curmudgeonly Edmund Gwenn, and to play Michael Fane, he chose Brian Aherne, a well-known British actor who was nevertheless regarded as a standard-issue trunk-jawed Hollywood leading man. The one part he had the most difficulty casting was Jimmy Monkley. No one at RKO could master to Cukor's satisfaction the essential cockney accent of Monkley's self-proclaimed "gentleman adventurer." It was Hepburn who suggested that Cukor try to borrow Cary Grant from Paramount for the part, something the director was at first, to Hepburn's surprise, reluctant to do.

Cukor's hesitancy was fostered by a longstanding skepticism about Grant's acting ability, based on the movies he had seen him in. "I could never get weak-kneed at the idea of Cary Grant," he had told one studio head early on, when considering suggestions as to who should play opposite Hepburn in *A Bill of Divorcement.* The role eventually went to John Barrymore.

More than likely the real reason for Cukor's hesitancy had to do with the director's private life and the increasingly repressive atmosphere that surrounded and affected both Cukor's and Grant's social and sexual proclivities. Cukor was unabashedly homosexual, his reputation as a "woman's director" industry code for his own sexual sensitivities. Actresses, knowing they were never going to have to submit to a Cukor casting couch, adored him for

---

*Little of Waugh's work made it into the final production.

his manner as much as for his manners. He came from the theatrical world of Broadway, where the gay life was not merely tolerated but prevalent. Once he made the change to Hollywood, he found the atmosphere more restrictive, even more so after the onset of the Hays Code. The lavishly appointed living room of Cukor's Hollywood home became a kind of private if informal West Coast Algonquin room, which many of the industry's most interesting (and often, but not exclusively, gay) luminaries regularly attended, including Sinclair Lewis, Theodore Dreiser, Fanny Brice, Ferenc Molnár, Tallulah Bankhead, Greta Garbo, Somerset Maugham, Noël Coward, Tennessee Williams, and Katharine Hepburn. These gatherings caused Joseph L. Mankiewicz to publicly characterize Cukor as "the queen of the roost."

Cukor and Grant had both spent approximately the same decade working in the New York theater. It is therefore difficult to believe that they did not know, or at least know of, each other in some capacity, if only in passing, having crossed paths at one opening or another, or party, or social seasonal gathering. Yet both maintained that prior to Cukor's casting Grant in *Sylvia Scarlett*, they had never met. Moreover, Grant's longtime personal secretary, Frank Horn, whom he had hired in the early 1930s, was a Hollywood hillside neighbor of Cukor's, with a legendary collection of male pornography and, it was believed, extensive contacts in that field. Horn and Cukor were intimates, making it even more unlikely that Grant and the director were total strangers.

All of this suggests not so much that Cukor and Grant were ever romantically involved or that they had anything to hide, but how pervasive the gay fear factor was for so many of Hollywood's biggest actors and directors. Cukor especially was extremely afraid of risking his livelihood by going "above the line" in his unquenchable thirst for male lovers, and on more than one occasion his homosexuality did negatively affect his career (his notorious firing a few years later as director of *Gone With the Wind* at the insistence of Clark Gable, who refused to take direction from a homosexual).

Nevertheless, Hepburn insisted on having Grant as her costar, and in the end Cukor would not refuse her and went to Zukor to see if he could borrow

Grant for the film.* As far as Zukor was concerned, Grant was, these days, available for rental to whatever studio was willing to meet his premium fee. Paramount agreed to pay Grant a $15,000 bonus for the scheduled six-week shoot, about twice his normal salary, which had by now reached $2,500 a week, applied against what it received from RKO—about half—while Hepburn received $50,000 *and* her regular contract salary.

Grant was understandably unhappy with this financial arrangement, as well as with the relatively small size of his role and what he considered the relatively uninteresting parameters of his character. The film, as he saw it, was nothing more than a star vehicle for Katharine Hepburn, and the only other real role was the part of her father.

When producer Pandro Berman became aware that Grant was upset, he in turn was miffed. He considered the casting of the actor in a Hepburn movie a gift, an automatic and much-needed boost for a career that, as far as Berman was concerned, had already fizzled and was not likely to reignite. Like so many Hollywood producers, he thought Grant largely uncastable— too old for young romantic leading roles (for which James Stewart and Joel McCrea were perfect), too "precious" for action parts (Fairbanks, Gable, Flynn), too pretty to play stubbled hard-edgers (McLaglen, Colman), too prissy for genre and period pieces (Laughton, Tone), and too weak for traditional heroes (Cooper, Gable, William Powell). Furthermore, Berman knew that Zukor had much the same opinion of Grant and because of it had given up on trying to turn him into a top-of-the-line star at Paramount. Grant, meanwhile, sensing his position at the studio was becoming increasingly shaky, accepted the role and the money despite his misgivings.

ONE OF THE PEOPLE most pleased with Grant's being cast in the film was Randolph Scott, who used the opportunity to finally put Howard Hughes and Grant together. Scott convinced Grant that, with his contract nearing an end,

---

*There is at least one other possible explanation for Cukor's casting of Grant. The Countess di Frasso always insisted that it was her "influence," such as it was, that got Cukor to hire Grant for *Sylvia Scarlett*. As it happened, she and Cukor were good friends, and although the story is most likely apocryphal, neither Cukor nor Grant ever publicly disputed the countess's often-made claim.

the time was finally exactly right for him to become friendly with the billionaire independent filmmaker. What's more, Hughes had lately become interested in Katharine Hepburn, and a friendship with Grant, Scott knew, would give him a reason to be on set while they filmed.

Grant and Hughes hit it off immediately and were soon fast buddies. Hughes appreciated Grant's understated sense of humor and lack of pretense. He particularly liked Grant's aloofness when it came to the press. And because Grant had little apparent interest in women, Hughes felt no competition for any of the ones he wanted, especially Hepburn. As far as Grant was concerned, Hughes was just the type of male whose social company he enjoyed. He found him unpretentious, rough-edged, nonjudgmental, and with a genuine taste for adventure tinged with danger that Grant found exciting. During the filming of *Sylvia Scarlett*, Hughes invited Grant to take a ride with him in his new H-1 plane over Los Angeles. Grant agreed, and soon they were soaring together above the coast, above the country, above the world.

For the first time since Randolph Scott, Grant felt he had found a kindred soul, someone who was interested in and liked him. Hughes felt the same way, his own reserve perfectly meshing with Grant's coolness, two sides of the same antisocial coin. Moreover, through his friendship with Grant, Hughes got to know Katharine Hepburn better, and they soon began a blazing affair.

Finally, the Grant-Hughes friendship solved one more problem for Scott, who had recently decided to get married. Unable or unwilling to break the news to Grant until almost the day of his wedding, Scott was relieved to have successfully passed Grant off to Hughes—if not in exactly the same fashion of friendship that he enjoyed, nevertheless in a way that benefited all three of them.

Scott had quietly been seeing his childhood acquaintance Marion duPont Somerville, daughter of William duPont, the man who had invented nylon and rayon and gone on to amass one of the greatest American fortunes. The day after his ex, Vivian Gaye, married film director Ernst Lubitsch in 1934, Scott had flown home to visit his family in Orange, Virginia, to lick his emotional wounds, and it was during this trip that he rekindled his friendship with Marion.

Scott and Marion shared two interests: horses and money. His fiancée had a personal fortune estimated to be in excess of $100 million. Scott believed that marriage was a contract of shared wealth and mutual convenience as much as love, and on those terms he considered Marion the potentially perfect wife. She was certainly not the kind of gold digger he believed Virginia Cherrill was, and she was happy to continue on with her own non–show business life, separate and apart from his. The rumor that persisted throughout her life, that she was a whip-wielding lesbian (her horses was the reason she always gave for carrying a riding crop tucked under her arm), didn't bother Scott at all. Nor did it bother him that she had just been divorced from jockey Tom Somerville. If anything, Scott was amused by all of this and saw no problem with her "individualism." Or with the fact that shortly before they married, Marion was rumored to have invested heavily in Paramount Pictures, the studio where Scott was a contract player.

Still, just as Grant had had with Cherrill, Scott began experiencing problems with Somerville from the moment he announced they were officially engaged. To begin with, she had an intense dislike of Hollywood. She considered it vulgar, an unseemly place for people of wealth to live. She made it clear to Scott that there was no way she would ever consider relocating to Los Angeles. Scott, on the other hand, was equally adamant about never permanently moving back to the South. To him, it was a place that represented repression, guilt, and loneliness. By contrast, Hollywood had allowed him to live out his greatest desires, with a man he loved and respected, in a way that would likely have gotten him lynched in Virginia. Of course, neither of these obstacles proved a deal-breaker, once both realized that Scott could simply stay in L.A. The impending marriage also solved Scott's ongoing "confirmed bachelor" problem with the studio. The one remaining obstacle that had stood in his way was the lonely and morose post-Cherrill Grant, a problem he solved finally by hooking him up with Hughes.

AT A PRE-RELEASE SCREENING OF *Sylvia Scarlett* open to the public, Cukor, Hepburn, and Grant slipped in through a side door, anticipating nothing but laughter and applause. Instead, they witnessed the film playing to a silent, bewildered audience. The biggest laugh the film got was a shot of the northern coast of Malibu, whose nearby mountain ranges were meant to pass for the fabled white cliffs of Dover. Less than half the audience stayed for the entire picture. Those who departed early included B. B. Kahane, the new head of RKO.

Hepburn in particular was aghast at what she saw, and right up to the official opening implored Berman not to release the film, promising him a "free" performance in exchange. The picture's world premiere, which took place on January 3, 1936, at Radio City Music Hall, proved her instinct correct: it was soundly rejected by critics and public alike. Everyone seemed to intensely dislike the film for one reason or another; it did not fit easily into any specific genre, as its story was too difficult. Was it an adventure, a romance, a comedy, or a crime flick? And finally, the miscasting of Katharine Hepburn as an androgyne more boyish than Peter Pan did nothing to help either the movie or her career.

After its disastrous opening, Hepburn's movie career was considered to have reached a financial dead end. Her defiant (and confusing) cross-dressing in the film was taken by some as a flaunting of her presumed lesbianism in those carefully morally coded Depression times. Other aspects proved equally suggestive, such as Brian Aherne's "crush" on the disguised Hepburn that causes him to say, "There's something queer going on here." A bit later on in the film Hepburn, still dressed as a boy, is kissed by a maid and told she is "very attractive." In yet another, Grant reaches for Hepburn (still in drag) and says, "It's nippy out tonight. You'll make a proper hot water bottle . . . but there's something that gives me a queer feeling every time I look at you." And, at one point, a maid paints a mustache on "Sylvester" and kisses her.

Apparently, audiences weren't the only ones to read things into the film. Shortly after it opened, it was officially condemned by the Legion of Decency and would go on to earn the dubious honor of being RKO's biggest financial disaster of 1936. Pandro Berman was so humiliated by the magnitude of the failure that he tried to distance himself from it, Hepburn, and Cukor, insisting he would never work with them again (pointedly leaving Grant out of this declaration). In fact, the only one to come out of the film with any positive reaction was Cary Grant. His Cockneyed performance was the breakthrough that freed him from the endless run of stilted lovers and cardboard "tux" heroes he had suffered through, by his winning portrayal of a wholly realized and thoroughly likable character. His quick wit and effortless physicality were a revelation for audiences. Cukor summed it up best later on, when he said of Grant's amazing performance, "Until then he was a successful young leading man who was nice-looking but had no particular identity . . . Suddenly, in *Sylvia Scarlett,* he blossomed. It was a well-written part, well directed, he knew what this character was, and he gave a marvelous performance." For years, in fact, Cukor (as West did with *She Done Him Wrong*) claimed that he had discovered Grant and that *Sylvia Scarlett* had made him a star. Statements of such immodesty and exaggeration did nothing to endear him to Grant.

The critics' praise for Grant, and only Grant, was unqualified. *Variety* proclaimed, "Cary Grant . . . virtually steals the picture." *Time* magazine did the same: "Cary Grant's superb depiction of the Cockney almost steals the show." *The New York Times* said that "Cary Grant, whose previous work has too often been that of a charm merchant, turns actor in the role of the unpleasant Cockney and is surprisingly good at it."

Grant felt professionally liberated. For the first time, he did not have to be told he was good in a movie. This was, after all, his meat, the kind of physical performing with rhythmic comic timing that he had sharpened to a fine edge in his years of stage performing. "*Sylvia Scarlett* was my breakthrough," he would recall years later. "It permitted me to play a character I knew." Although he was, in private, less than thrilled with Cukor, Grant, in a publicity interview, made a point of thanking him in public for allowing him to play the role "as I saw it."

It wasn't until after the film's opening that Scott finally broke the news to him that he intended to marry Marion duPont. The next day a devastated Grant quietly packed his bags and caught a plane back to New York City. Once there he booked passage on a luxury liner bound for Mother England.

11

"I am most keenly reminded of what director-writer Garson
Kanin had told me once about Leo McCarey's extraordinary
influence on Cary Grant, the American screen's longest-
lived leading man, equally adept at comedy and drama: that
in *The Awful Truth*, Grant was in fact imitating McCarey's
own urbane manner as well as his infectious zaniness."

—PETER BOGDANOVICH

During the filming of *Sylvia Scarlett*, Cary Grant had quietly and directly—that is to say, not through Paramount—received an offer to star in a small independent British film, Alfred Zeisler's *The Amazing Quest of Ernest Bliss*, a remake of a 1920 Henry Edwards silent comedy, that was to be shot entirely in Great Britain. The timing couldn't have been more perfect. After Scott's marriage bombshell, Grant couldn't wait to get out of town, and England now seemed to him the perfect place to go to. Grant had told Zukor about the offer, and the studio head had unhesitatingly given him a green light. The studio had nothing for Grant coming up, and Zukor was relieved that his talented but increasingly fussy actor—he was now making Hepburn-like noises about script approval—had found a project that would keep him not only occupied but out of everyone's hair for a while.

Grant was excited about playing another British character in a role that allowed him to show off some of his ability to do physical comedy. Although he could as yet not fully articulate it, his growing dissatisfaction with Paramount lay in how the studio had continued to misuse his talent. This bothered him as much as any complaints he had about salary, billing, or the studio's seemingly neverending rules of morality. He no longer wanted to serve the house; he wanted it to serve him. And, if he ever had, he no longer sought the title of the next Valentino, or the second-string Gary Cooper, but the one and only Cary Grant. It was that goal as much as his feeling of having been abandoned by Scott that led him to fly to England to star in the independent production of *Bliss*.

In it, Grant plays the title character, Ernie Bliss, a working man who unexpectedly inherits $5 million, then sets out to discover "the real meaning of life" by spending a year earning his living without any help from anyone or anything, including his own newly enriched bank account. Along the way he falls for a woman (played by Mary Brian, dubbed "the sweetest girl in pictures!" for her portrayal of Wendy in Herbert Brenon's 1924 silent version of James M. Barrie's *Peter Pan*), who comes to love him for who he is rather than what he has. The film is yet another variation on the theme of Chaplin's *City Lights* — the power of inner beauty — but unlike *Wings in the Dark* contains a great deal of wit, humor, grace, and insight.

Grant was enormously pleased with his work in *Bliss*. Save for occasional flashes of brilliance (in *Blonde Venus, She Done Him Wrong,* and *Sylvia Scarlett*) in the five years and twenty-one movies he made before it, he had not appeared in a feature that fully showed off his unique physical and verbal comedic abilities as much as his particular romantic appeal. Without a tuxedo, murder weapon, period costume, physical affliction, or femme fatale in sight, *Bliss* finally allowed Grant to give the kind of performance he was capable of, the first true glimpse of what was to become the classic Cary Grant persona of charm, looks, wit, and decency.

Mary Brian, seduced by Grant's charismatic performance, took an immediate liking to him away from the camera as well and responded with genuine affection when Grant developed what resembled a schoolboy's crush on her. Before long they were being photographed together in London nightclubs and restaurants, their "affair" played up in the gossips on both sides of the Atlantic. Despite all outward appearances, however, Grant had no sexual interest in the strikingly beautiful actress. Still, there were many in the industry and out who believed that something must have been going on between the two of them, a belief bolstered by two significant factors: Brian's strong resemblance to Virginia Cherrill, and Randolph Scott's impending marriage. The studio, sensing a good opportunity, went so far as to intimate through its reliable posse of gossip-mongers that Grant and Brian were engaged.

The story was, of course, completely fabricated, but it gained a measure of believability when Grant, for whatever reason, was slow to deny it. Directly confronted by the press, he offered only a vague response that could be interpreted any way the entertainment reporters wanted. In truth, Grant was enjoying his friendship with Brian and may also have wanted to send a message to Scott that he wasn't suffering, although he knew all too well that Scott wouldn't interpret his relationship with Brian the way the public did. If there was any real message Grant was sending to Scott, it had to do more with loneliness than one-upsmanship.

There may have been yet another reason why Grant publicly welcomed Brian's companionship, and that was to please his mother. During the filming of *Bliss*, Grant intended to spend as much time as possible with Elsie, unencumbered by any drama surrounding the presence of a fiancée. He looked forward to enjoying the incredible gift of his mother's "coming back to life" — and coming back to *his* life. He was, therefore, quite unprepared for the reality that awaited him.

The first shock came after spending a day with Elsie, when he suddenly realized that she didn't exactly remember who he was. She seemed to treat him more like an old acquaintance than her son. The second came when he realized that she preferred to stay indoors as much as possible, in the same grimy house in Bristol from which she had been forcibly taken all those years before. It was as if she still believed she was being held in confinement. Grant once again offered to move her permanently to America so that she could live near him in comfort and style such as she had never known, but she laughed off the notion as completely absurd. At fifty-eight years old, she told him, the thought of moving to a foreign country was as comical as it was frightening.

Perhaps worst of all, she began to nudge him about the prospect of marriage, seemingly unaware that he already had done it once. He was old enough, she insisted, to finally take on that sort of responsibility. If he didn't watch out, she warned him, he could wind up a lonely old man. This last part completely unnerved him.

Grant did manage to convince Elsie to accompany him to London so she could watch some of the filming of *Bliss*. The visit, unfortunately, was interrupted by the news that his father, Elias, had fallen gravely ill. Decades of carousing, hard drinking, and chain smoking had finally taken their toll. At the age of sixty-three, his body had given in to all the self-inflicted abuse. On December 1, 1935, Elias Leach died of acute septicemia and gangrene of the bowel.

Distraught at missing the chance to say good-bye to his father in person, Grant remained grimly terse toward the press, especially in the face of hard questions regarding Elias's decades-long double life and the heretofore unknown existence to the public of "only child Archie's" half-brother, Eric, with whom Grant would now attempt to forge a closer friendship.

It all added up to a difficult replay of all the old traumas. Once again he was forced to deal with abandonment, this time by his father's death—which was real—and by his mother's resurrection, which in many ways had proven illusory.

The only official comment he made regarding his father's passing was at the funeral, held in Bristol, before friends and family, in which he said, simply, "He was a wise and kindly man and I loved him very much."

The day after filming was completed, Cary Grant boarded a luxury liner and set sail with Mary Brian back to the States.

BECAUSE IT HAD TROUBLE SECURING an overseas distributor, *The Amazing Quest of Ernest Bliss* did not arrive in American theaters until the spring of 1937, more than a year after it was made.* By then, everything in Grant's Hollywood career and personal life had completely changed.

---

*The film had a bit of trouble finding a release date in England as well, not arriving in British theaters until New Year's Eve 1936. It was released in the United States three months later, under several different titles (because of varied licensing arrangements), including *The Amazing Adventure*, *The Amazing Quest*, *Romance and Riches*, and *Riches and Romance*. Several biographies mistakenly report these as separate Cary Grant films. The film was never released in U.S. theaters under its original title but has been released as *Bliss* on VHS and DVD.

Grant returned to Los Angeles early in 1936 to the bad news that *Sylvia Scarlett* had bombed at the box office, so much so that Katharine Hepburn was now considered all but unemployable by the major studios. In the wake of the film's failure, her personal relationship with Howard Hughes had also floundered. She was tough and singular and disinclined to let Hughes gloss over the deep wound of her career nosedive with a palliative high-fly among the clouds. She was, Grant knew, far more grounded than that.

Despite the film's commercial failure, his outstanding reviews had put him at the top of everyone's popularity list. Adolph Zukor, who had by now been kicked upstairs to the supervisory position of chairman of the board as part of Paramount's reorganization, no longer had the studio under his absolute control. Two next-generation low-profile but high-powered executives, Barney Balaban and Y. Frank Freeman, had taken control over the actual making of movies. Unlike Zukor, they wanted to take advantage of Grant's popularity by casting him in Otho Lovering's *Border Flight*, opposite the studio's newest female discovery, Frances Farmer. It would prove the breaking point for Grant.

He so disliked the script he decided to test his newfound popularity by taking a page out of Gary Cooper's playbook: he unequivocally refused to appear in *Border Flight*. He sent word directly to Zukor that the studio should not expect him to show up on the set for the scheduled first day of shooting. Moreover, Grant informed Zukor, from now on he must have complete approval over all the projects he was to be involved in, as well as a long overdue raise. At his present salary of $2,500 a week, Grant was by no means starving, but he was still earning less than half the $6,000 a week that Cooper was bringing in, and that truly galled him.

Zukor went ballistic. As far as he was concerned, Cary Grant didn't deserve Gary Cooper's salary, because Cary Grant wasn't Gary Cooper. In his five years at Paramount, Grant had appeared in twenty-six films that—with a few notable exceptions, including *Blonde Venus* and *She Done Him Wrong*—were unremarkable product churned out factory-style by forgettable directors whose work more closely resembled that of assembly-line supervisors than of visionaries exploring the landscape of imagination.

By comparison, Cooper, who had been with the studio for eleven years, had made fifty-nine films. His first major screen appearance was in William Wellman's 1927 *Wings*, the first film to win the Academy Award for Best Picture, a level of success, achievement, and prestige that neither Grant nor any of his films had yet to match. Among the highlights of Cooper's career (through 1937) were Josef von Sternberg's *Morocco* (1930), a far more successful Dietrich vehicle than *Blonde Venus*; a segment in the eight-part *If I Had a Million* (1932), a panoramic multistar vehicle from which Grant was omitted because of his relatively low star-wattage;* Frank Borzage's *A Farewell to Arms* (1932), nominated for Best Picture of the Year; Ernst Lubitsch's terrific *Design for Living* (1933); Frank Capra's *Mr. Deeds Goes to Town* (1936, on loan to Columbia), for which Cooper received a Best Actor nomination; Lewis Milestone's hugely successful *The General Died at Dawn* (1936); and Cecil B. DeMille's neoclassic star vehicle western, *The Plainsman* (1937). At this point in time, there was simply no comparison between the two actors' achievements.

Which, Grant might have insisted, proved his point. It wasn't that Gary Cooper was a "better" actor—meaning a more popular and bigger money-maker for the studio—it was that he was always given the superior scripts. More often than not, his discards and rejects went to Grant, who like most actors was almost always only as good as the films he appeared in and the directors he worked with.

Nevertheless, Zukor took Grant's demands as the ungrateful tantrum of a second-tier actor whom the studio had carried while he walked through most of his contract years delivering a series of undistinguished performances, and who was still gainfully employed only through the good graces of Zukor's generosity, who had personally insisted on keeping him employed through the studio's roughest times and at the height of a national depression.

Because Grant did not have an agent—he didn't know anyone whom he felt he could trust to negotiate financial terms for him—it was all the harder for Zukor, who abhorred negotiating directly with actors about anything, to deal with him. (Zukor didn't think actors were intelligent enough to know a good deal when they were offered one.) Still, to keep Grant happy, and over

---

*The film was made up of eight segments, each helmed by a different director. Cooper's episode, "The Three Marines," was directed by Norman McLeod.

Balaban and Freeman's strong objections, he released him from *Border Flight* (John Howard was given the role) and offered him a thousand-dollar raise, to $3,500 a week, the highest among the second-tier performers at the still financially shaky studio. Zukor considered his offer more than generous and felt that if Grant didn't like it, he could leave at the expiration of his soon-to-expire contract. The way he saw it, Grant had failed to make the big break-through to the level of superstar. Besides, the studio's real A-list — of which Cooper, Dietrich, and West occupied the top slots — were all demanding huge salary increases to re-sign with the "new" studio. If he had to let someone go, Zukor figured, it would be Grant before any of them.

Still, Zukor hadn't completely given up on him, especially after the surprising critical reception for his work in *Sylvia Scarlett*. In one final attempt to mollify Grant, Zukor asked producer Walter Wanger to cast him as the lead in Raoul Walsh's upcoming *Big Brown Eyes*, opposite Joan Bennett, a film that Zukor considered important and prestigious for the studio, a role that could finally elevate Cary Grant to the A-list.

In truth, *Big Brown Eyes* was not as great a project as Zukor had thought, as it was little more than an imitation *Thin Man*. Grant read the script and decided to accept the role, although he correctly believed that he wasn't really right for the character of Danny Barr, a fast-talking, tough gumshoe type more suited to James Cagney. Grant used a clumsy stepped-up pace to his speech to convey "street smarts" and otherwise reverted to his familiar comfort zone of pocket-posing throughout the performance. Predictably, *Big Brown Eyes* did nothing at the box office.

In the wake of the film's failure, Zukor finally gave up on Grant, and when MGM asked to borrow him for George Fitzmaurice's *Suzy*, to star opposite the red-hot Jean Harlow, he quickly gave his approval.

Despite Dorothy Parker's clever dialogue contributions, the script for *Suzy* was a mishmash of three genres: romance, war, and espionage. Harlow, set adrift in the blanched cinematic ether of the sanitizing Hays Office, despite her character's romantic involvement with a man while still married to a presumed-dead but very much alive husband, was being rendered wholesome by the studio, with the result that she appeared unappealingly wholesome. Meanwhile, the sight of Grant in a military uniform playing a macho romantic two-timing aviator brought a round of back-of-the-wrist snickering from

Hollywood's knowing insiders. Grant's rival in the film for the affections of Harlow was none other than Franchot Tone. (Ironically, the reason Grant was offered the part was that MGM's regular roster of male A-list stars—Clark Gable, Robert Taylor, Robert Young, William Powell, Robert Montgomery, and Spencer Tracy—were all considered too important to appear in the smaller role opposite Tone.)

Despite Grant's decent-enough rendition of the song "Did I Remember," which went on to become a modest sheet-music hit, the film was quite ordinary, jacked up by flying sequences that were far superior to and did not match the rest of the film's scenes (with good reason: they were outtakes from Hughes's self-produced 1930 *Hell's Angels*, which he leased to MGM for a hefty fee).

Suzy was not an out-and-out flop, but it was by no means the major hit MGM had anticipated, and it did nothing for Grant's career. Shortly after its release, Grant made an extraordinary decision. He was not only not going to re-sign with Paramount, no matter what offer Zukor might come up with (if indeed he came up with one at all), but he would not sign an exclusive contract with *any* Hollywood studio. After his experience on Broadway with Hammerstein and the Shuberts, and now in Hollywood with Paramount, he had had enough of what he considered to be the actor's fate—indentured servitude.

After *Suzy*, A-line stardom seemed less reachable now for Grant than ever. Just behind Cooper, Crosby, and Henry Fonda, a new crop of younger leading men were already nipping at his heels, among them Jimmy Stewart, Fred MacMurray, Ray Milland, and Robert Cummings, all with smiles almost as dazzling and hair nearly as dark and luminous as Grant's.

And some could even act.

If Zukor was still at all interested in trying to keep Grant at Paramount, it wasn't apparent from the next assignment he gave him, the last under his existing contract. In the summer of 1936 Grant starred in Richard Wallace's *Wedding Present*, once again opposite Joan Bennett, with only costar credit, his name significantly placed after the title.

Wedding Present was a dull newsroom romance that once again gave Grant little opportunity to display his comic talents. After its release and quick fade (like *Suzy* and *Big Brown Eyes*, it was released prior to the

American premiere of *Bliss*), Grant officially notified Zukor that he was not going to re-sign with Paramount.

Zukor was surprised, not at the decision itself, but at Grant's audacity. At the time, in the Academy-controlled closed shop of major studios, contract players who became free agents rarely succeeded, and everyone in the business, including Grant, knew it.

Nonetheless, it was a risk he was willing to take. According to Grant, "If I had stayed at Paramount, I would have continued to take pictures that Gary Cooper, William Powell, or Clive Brook turned down. Refusing a renewal of my contract wasn't the first time I took what seemed [to everyone else] like a step backward."

AT THE END OF 1936, Cary Grant became Hollywood's first star-without-a-studio. It was a bold move, to be sure, but a move everyone predicted would do to him what it had done to everyone else who had tried to go up against the insular Hollywood system: help him commit career suicide. Those who had previously tried to go freelance and failed included Rudolph Valentino and Ronald Colman. Valentino had died before he could act upon his decision. Colman, who in his studio contract years, from 1917 through 1936, had appeared in forty-two films, once he went solo made only fifteen in the next two decades, despite a 1947 Best Actor Oscar for his performance in George Cukor's *A Double Life*. Gradually eased out of the movie business, Colman, unlike Grant, who continued to make important films for the next two decades, spent his last productive years mostly in radio and TV. Charlie Chaplin, who had made dozens of short and feature films while under contract to Keystone, Essanay, Mutual, and First National, had to start his own studio, United Artists, to be independent, after which his output fell to an average of two features a decade.

Both Randolph Scott and Howard Hughes warned Grant not to go through with his plan. Scott reminded Grant that he owed his very survival in movies to the contract system, and Hughes continued to have his share of trouble getting distribution for his independently produced movies — his enormous personal wealth the only way he had been able to keep himself going.

Grant, however, remained resolute. He was going to do things his own way, with no studio, no morals clauses, no forced parts, and nobody looking over his shoulder. To celebrate his decision, and to underscore what he saw as his victory over the morally oppressive system from which he was proudly liberating himself, early in 1937 he and the newly married Scott (whose wife remained safely tucked away in Virginia, allowing Grant and Scott to resume their exclusive live-in arrangement) showed up in identical skin-tight circus acrobat outfits, complete with tutus, at a well-publicized costume ball thrown by Marion Davies for her paramour, the flamboyant William Randolph Hearst.

Predictably, the event provided juicy fodder for the gossip columnists, which was fine with Grant. In fact, he welcomed it. He had put his career on the high wire, with all the safety nets taken down. Now he would either soar higher than ever before or fall into the abyss. Either way, he knew, it would be the most fanciful flight of his life.

12

"As the tall, dark, and handsome male star, 'Cary Grant'
always stands for male beauty and desirability, whether
in a Thirties screwball, a Forties film noir, or a Fifties
romantic comedy. He consequently turns around the
orthodox gendered difference between the one who looks
(and so desires) and the one who is looked at (and so is
being desired) . . . As a result Grant's trademark performance
style is inseparable from his screen persona as the
quintessential leading man of American romantic comedy."

—STEVEN COHAN

During his exit negotiations with Paramount, Grant, aware that he was about to challenge the freelance jinx, put together a team of experts to help him do so. For the first time in his acting career, he officially signed with an agent. To find one he liked, he reached all the way back to his early days with the Pender troupe, where he had first met Frank W. Vincent, at the time a young manager for theatrical talent. Vincent had taken a liking to Archie Leach and, at Lomas's request, had kept an eye on him the entire time he toured on the Orpheum circuit. Vincent had since become a successful Hollywood agent, forming a business partnership with Harry Edington. By the time Grant signed on, the agency's formidable roster included Greta Garbo, Marlene Dietrich, Douglas Fairbanks, Leopold Stokowski, Rita Hayworth, Mary Martin, Rosalind Russell, Claire Trevor, Louis Jourdan, Nigel Bruce, Joel McCrea, and Edward G. Robinson.

The first thing Vincent did for Grant was to negotiate the terms of his exit from Paramount. He did it cleverly, offering to have Grant renew for $75,000 a picture, plus story approvals. Grant wanted to break out of his tuxedo roles and venture into comedy. As Vincent knew he would, Zukor rejected that proposal and countered that Grant must make a onetime payment to the studio of $11,800 to buy out the remaining months on his contract (based on his present weekly salary and the days he still owed Zukor) and agree to one final loan-out, for which Paramount would collect the fee. Vincent quickly agreed, and just for that Grant was a free agent.

The loan-out was to Harry "King" Cohn, the iniquitous, self-styled-tough-guy head of Columbia Pictures, the so-called Poverty Row of the majors. Zukor may have done it at least in part as an act of vengeance against Grant, for Cohn's reputation as a vulgarian, womanizer, and tantrum-throwing tyrant often overshadowed and undervalued the quality of the films his studio produced, at times to the detriment of the actors, producers, and directors who made them.

Cohn wanted Grant for one movie, Robert Riskin's *When You're in Love*. Vincent, however, saw an opportunity to make a unique deal for Grant and offered Cohn and Columbia a nonexclusive four-picture deal that came reasonably close to the magic figure that had sent Zukor running for the medicine cabinet—a guaranteed $50,000 for the first two pictures (above Paramount's fee) and $75,000 for the final two. The only proviso Cohn wanted, and it was a smart one, was that Grant had to make at least one movie a year for Columbia. To Grant, who had been averaging five films a year at Paramount (for approximately one-tenth of the money), that seemed the easiest part of the bargain. Then Vincent showed what he was capable of, why he was regarded as one of the best agents in the business. Before the ink was dry on the Columbia deal, he went to RKO Radio and struck the same nonexclusive four-picture deal, guaranteeing them as well a Grant movie a year for the next four years.

Vincent knew what he was doing when he chose these two studios with which to negotiate Grant's future. Both Columbia and RKO desperately needed a new leading man to compete with the big guns locked in at Paramount, MGM, and Warners, and in Cary Grant he had one of the best candidates. Still, it was an avant-garde deal in many ways, not the least of which was financial. Because of the standard contract system, it was unheard of for actors to simultaneously sign with more than one studio for more than one picture, and everyone in the business *except* Vincent and Grant felt the risk was too great. Grant's take was, in fact, just the opposite; he felt he had nothing to lose and everything to gain by making this daring attempt to resurrect his stalled career. As far as Vincent was concerned, Grant had the talent and looks to become Hollywood's number one leading man. And if he succeeded, Vincent knew, no one would care anymore about the multiple-contract deal.

To complete the transition from contract player to freelance actor, Grant resigned from the studio-controlled Academy, which did not look favorably upon actors signing contracts with two studios at the same time. It was something he was delighted to do.

THE PLOT OF *WHEN YOU'RE IN LOVE* involves a "wealthy tramp artist" (played by Grant, in a role that once again echoed his idol Chaplin's great screen persona), a characterization often evoked by studios during the 1930s to romanticize the grim reality of the Depression. For a fee, the tramp marries a Mexican entertainer (Grace Moore, at the time one of Columbia's biggest female stars) to bring her legally into the country. Once they cross the border, they part, only to meet again later on and realize they are, after all, truly in love. Fade to gold.

Or so Cohn hoped. He made the picture to break out Robert Riskin, for several years Frank Capra's screenwriting partner on a series of enormously popular (and populist) movies that had helped keep the studio in business. After the success of Capra's 1936 *Mr. Deeds Goes to Town*, Riskin, believing his writing collaborator/director had always gotten too much of the credit for their films, was eager to branch out on his own (a move that, not surprisingly, caused a lifelong rift between him and the egomaniacal Capra).

Unfortunately, the Riskin/Capra magic could not be generated by Riskin without Capra, and despite a few glowing reviews — such as *Time* magazine's, which declared, "Following the pattern of *It Happened One Night* and *Mr. Deeds Goes to Town*, in which Director Capra established Clark Gable and Gary Cooper as comedians, Director Riskin herein does the same thing for Cary Grant" — Grant's first film as a freelance actor flopped badly and became another in an increasingly long line of his pictures that failed to make back their costs. While his four-picture deals with Columbia and RKO were technically solid, he knew that without a hit, they could very well become the last films he would ever make in America.

Grant then went directly into Rowland V. Lee's *The Toast of New York* at RKO, but despite a sharp script by Dudley Nichols, top costars Edward Arnold and Jack Oakie, and leading lady Frances Farmer, this bloodless biography of robber-baron Jim Fisk, effectively denatured by the Hays Office, featured Grant shoehorned into yet another standard-issue tuxedo romance.

Nevertheless, Grant wanted to properly celebrate his freedom from Paramount and his deliverance into the Hollywood nouveau riche. To do so, he asked Scott to cohost a series of parties at the beach house, a place where previously very few "outside" celebrities had been invited. For the next several months, they turned the place into a weekend salon filled with actors, actresses, writers, directors, the San Simeon set, and dozens of leading ladies and starlets from Grant's two new studios. Among the most frequent guests were Howard Hughes, playwright Moss Hart, Douglas Fairbanks Jr., Laurence Olivier (Larry O. to friends), and one of Grant's favorites, Noël Coward.

Grant and Scott quickly became the most gracious and charming hosts in Malibu. Grant's dazzling charm was the talk of the town, and his understated but barbed commentary about everything from Cohn's addiction to sturgeon to the lack of panties worn by Jean Harlow during the shooting of *Suzy* kept everyone in stitches, while Scott kept the champagne flowing. Caviar was consumed by the bucketful. Coward, a well-known homosexual, usually stayed over at the beach house on party nights, and his flamboyant, silk-robed presence always started the beach set buzzing with good-natured comments like "The queen has returned to her colony."

Coward was actually one of very few allowed to stay overnight, and whenever he did so he loved to play tricks on his two hosts, especially Grant, the more sensitive and therefore vulnerable of the two. Coward was aware that

Grant had costarred with some of the most famous women in Hollywood, and that it would therefore be difficult to "throw" him with star quality; there was, however, one he knew who would bring Grant to his knees. After arranging for her to come by the house, Coward called Grant at the studio and informed him that Greta Garbo was in Malibu and wanted to meet him. Garbo happened to be a friend of Dorothy Lamour, who, despite his newly-wed status, had lately been "romantically linked" with Scott, and was eager to see his and Grant's bachelor lair that she had heard so much about. Coward knew that Garbo had been an idol of Grant's since his Broadway-matinee-idol days. One time back then, Grant had once confessed to Coward that he had spotted the actress at the Astor Hotel on Forty-fifth Street and silently and carefully followed her all the way back to her own hotel, unable to work up enough courage to walk up to her and introduce himself.

Grant went dry-mouthed as he hung up the phone, and headed directly for his car. When he got to the house, he was greeted by Coward, who had a mischievous grin on his face as he made the formal introductions. At first Grant was too stunned to speak. At last he stuck out his hand and said, "Oh, Miss Garbo, I'm so happy you met me!"

Howard Hughes, on the other hand, was someone Grant, from their first meeting, felt extremely comfortable around. Hughes, like Grant, had a profound mistrust for the film industry. His mania for total control rivaled that of Chaplin without the accompanying artistic genius or business acumen. Like Chaplin, he loved women, and he loved the fact that they loved Grant. Beautiful bathing-suited babes were never scarce around the weekend soirées — young juicy girls with thick red lips, blue eyes, and hopeful breasts who were there because of Grant, and upon whom Hughes feasted like a frog on crickets.

One of the first things Grant did with his newly enriched bank account was to add a second, outdoor pool to the beach house that was only twenty-five feet from the sands of the Pacific. Oceanside pools were Hollywood's latest status symbol, and Grant insisted to Scott, an Olympic-level swimmer, that they had to have one. It quickly became a magnet for girls in bathing suits. One of the women Hughes swept off the Grant/Scott poolside was Ginger Rogers, at the time one of RKO's most popular screen "princesses." This produced a slightly awkward situation for Grant, who had been caught in the middle of Hughes's increasingly strained relationship with Katharine Hepburn, both of whom he considered his friends. Moreover he had a secret crush on Rogers himself from the time he had been introduced to her while visiting the set of *Roberta*, the musical starring Rogers, Fred Astaire, Irene Dunne, and Scott.

Still, as far as Grant was concerned, he was not going to make any moral judgments about Hughes's behavior, especially so soon after the sudden, shocking death of his first great discovery and former lover Jean Harlow (Grant's costar in *Suzy*) at the age of twenty-six, after complications from uremic poisoning. If anything, he wanted to be there for Hughes, and therefore wore his unrequited love for Rogers as a badge of friendship.

Despite his new attempts at sociability, Grant much preferred solitude and found something close to it with, of all people, the otherwise flamboyant Hughes. Like Grant, Hughes was a man of few words, perhaps due to the shyness he had developed growing up in the shadow of his empire-founding father, whose early death left an emotional void that Hughes would have trouble filling for the rest of his life. Grant admired Hughes's extraordinary physical and social advantages—his tall, muscular physique and handsome face, his inherited wealth, and his resistance to socializing in crowds larger than the number of fingers he had on one hand. Scott, on the other hand, was always up for a good time, a quick laugh, cocktails at five, parties that lasted until dawn, early-morning swims, long luxurious sunbaths, and this-will-fix-everything massages. Grant much preferred going to bed early, getting up early, reading the paper with a cup of coffee by the pool, listening to classical music on the radio, and on afternoons when he wasn't working, reclining on a canvas lounge on the sand with his feet hanging over either side being lapped by the cool incoming saltwater tide.

Not long after they met, whenever they were both free Grant and Hughes would spend afternoons that sometimes lasted until the evening sitting silently together in Hughes's massive mahogany den while he studied blueprints for his various self-designed airplanes, and Grant smoked a cigarette, sipped a scotch, read a book. As Grant later remembered, "Howard was the most restful man I have ever been around. We could sit for hours together and never say a word." According to Hughes's housekeeper, Beatrice Dowler, whenever the two dined together, most often only a few sentences were spoken between them during the entire meal.

But when they did speak about something important, it was usually Hughes giving advice, and Grant listening respectfully to what he had to say—mostly about women. To Hughes, who was likely unaware of Grant's homosexual desires—he either didn't know or didn't want to know—Grant seemed, if anything, too much in awe of women to see through what they were "selling" men and calling it love. Hughes often told Grant that he was a sucker for what he called "women's moneymakers."

As they got closer, Hughes continued to enthrall Grant with the thrill of flying. Although he had no desire to get behind the stick himself, Grant was impressed by Hughes's virile hobby and was gratified to have a friend who actually lived the kind of adventurous life, filled with women, danger, and excitement, that he, Grant, only portrayed onscreen. With Hughes, no twitching flicker separated fantasy from reality.

When, early in 1937, Hughes announced that he was going to fly his H-1 *Winged Bullet*, as he called it, out of Burbank nonstop to Newark, Grant, along with the rest of the country, held his breath while following the entire escapade on radio and was greatly relieved when Hughes safely landed seven hours, twenty-eight minutes, and twenty-five seconds after takeoff, establishing an aviation record that would last for many years. This was the flight that made Hughes an American flying folk hero, nearly as popular as one of his own idols, all-American aviator Charles "Lucky" Lindbergh, whose 1927 solo flight from New York to Paris had brought flying into the forefront of the world's consciousness. On his return trip, Hughes stopped in Washington, D.C., where President Roosevelt greeted him at the White House and awarded him the Harmon International Trophy. When he arrived in Los Angeles, Grant threw a huge party for Hughes at the famed Trocadero nightspot on Sunset Boulevard.

Noticeably absent was the fellow who had introduced the two, Randolph Scott. Indeed, the more time Grant spent with Hughes, the less he saw of Scott. It was an odd juxtaposition: Scott had always been the wealthier of the two and the more sociable, and although Grant had gotten married first, Scott was the one who had made marriage work by finding a wealthy woman who conveniently happened to live two thousand miles away. He very much embodied what Hughes had been trying to explain to him about women, "love," and "playing it smart." And while Scott was not a complainer and never openly fought with Grant, he was extremely judgmental, especially about Grant's "folly" with Cherrill, something that had left a scar on the relationship between the two men.

Hughes's friendship also gave Grant perspective on the intensity of his sometimes smothering relationship with Scott, which now seemed at times more like a marriage than . . . whatever it was that neither could exactly define. Even during the very occasional visits by Scott's wife, who would always ask why Grant was still there, the answer to that question was never discussed between the two men.

ONE MORNING WHILE GRANT WAS sunning himself by the pool, his next-door neighbor, legendary comic film director Hal Roach, dropped by for a noontime swim. The two had become good friends, and Grant had given Roach a standing offer to come by anytime he felt like going for a dip.

Roach, like Mack Sennett, had been a successful producer of silent comedy, but unlike Sennett, he had been able to continue delivering funny movies that talked. Of all the forms of filmmaking, comedy was the most profoundly changed by the advent of sound: the emphasis necessarily had to shift from the extraordinary visual hysterics of Chaplin, Buster Keaton, Harold Lloyd, Laurel and Hardy, and the other silent greats, sometimes for better and far more often for worse, to rapid-fire verbal humor. Among the most successful to make the transition were Laurel and Hardy, both of whom found voices that not only matched their silent-stare and arm-waving reactions but actually deepened the humor of their characters, so much so that in 1932 *The Music Box* (MGM) won the "Short Subject" Oscar for Roach and the comedy team. Now, a year after his second Academy Award,* eager to move into feature films, and searching for a new feature property to produce, Roach had come across the popular Thorne Smith novel *Topper*, which he believed contained all the elements necessary to make a hit movie: a simple but funny plot, great characters, henpecked husbands, spirited wives, and ghosts. When

---

*Roach won again in 1936 for Best Comedy (One Reel) Live Action Short Subject, for *Bored of Education*, starring the Our Gang kids.

George and Marion Kerby, high-flying socialites at home in tuxes and with Tiffany, are unexpectedly killed in a car accident, they return as sometimes visible, sometimes invisible apparitions. They then set about to help George's wealthy but submissive banker partner find liberation from the short leash of his well-meaning but bossy wife. Having made a number of ghost stories in both the silent and the sound eras with Laurel and Hardy, Roach knew they were surefire laugh-getters that showed what the screen could do that the stage couldn't.

That morning while having a dip in Grant's pool, Roach casually talked up his new project and pretended to suddenly be "struck" by the notion of casting Grant as George Kerby, the film's young romantic lead. Of course the whole thing had been planned, Grant knew it, and Roach knew he knew it. Amused by the unsubtlety of the charade, Grant laughed off the notion as part of the gag, but when Roach persisted, he gracefully declined the offer. His agent, he claimed, would never allow him to play it for anything below his new asking price, $50,000 a picture, which was far more, he believed, than Roach—who had come up in the era of five-dollar-a-day performers in short subjects whose entire budgets were often less than Grant's asking price— would ever agree to.

Undaunted, Roach raised the subject with Grant whenever he saw him, ignoring all suggestions to call Vincent and instead appealing to the friend-ship factor. Grant liked Roach and admired his films a great deal, particularly his silent comedies, so as a favor to him, he decided that if Roach agreed to make a percentage deal and the film could be done quickly enough, then he would say yes. Roach agreed and quickly hired director Norman Z. McLeod to direct *Topper*, a move that both surprised and bothered Grant. He had worked for McLeod before, in the Paramount ensemble production of *Alice in Wonderland*, and did not have fond memories of the experience. There was, in fact, little about that film that Grant had liked. He had hoped that Roach would hire someone more contemporary, someone with a greater flair for the patented Roach style of physical comedy.

In truth, McLeod had a terrific flair for it, having directed one of the best of the Paramount Marx Brothers features, *Monkey Business* (1931), a movie that captured them at their anarchic best. Moreover, he had worked with

Roach before and, despite Grant's concerns, knew exactly what his producer wanted — speed, energy, and razor-sharp timing for a comedy about ghosts — and that is precisely what he delivered.

In truth, the real reason Grant had said yes to Roach had less to do with friendship than with ambition. Having finally won professional independence, more than ever he wanted to play comedy. As he reflected later on, "For years I had begged Paramount to let me do something besides straight romantic leads. I said I ought to be doing light comedy. They wouldn't listen. When my contract was up, and they offered to renew, I said, 'Does choice of roles go with it?' and they said no. So I didn't sign . . . The first [comedy] I did as a freelance was *Topper*."

During filming, Roach came up with what he thought was a great plot twist, but Grant flatly refused to go along. It simply didn't fit into his long-range formulation for what he perceived as the "new Cary Grant." Roach had decided midproduction that he wanted to turn the film into a satire of marriage by having the Kerbys retake their vows after their death and reemerge as ghosts. Then, if George Kerby still wanted Marion as his wife, he would have to pursue her all over again. Grant steadfastly rejected the idea, as he had promised himself after working with Mae West; if Constance Bennett's character wanted him, if *any* female character onscreen wanted him, from now on *she* was going to have to do the pursuing.

Roach, unaware of the reasons for Grant's refusal to woo Bennett onscreen, thought it incomprehensible. Men chasing women was the very stuff of comedy, a reflection of the way the world really was. After thinking about it awhile, he finally concluded that Grant's real reason could be explained in two words: Ginger Rogers. Oblivious to Grant's sexual orientation, and to his reluctance to compete with Howard Hughes for Rogers's affections, Roach concluded that Grant's pursuit of her must not be going well, otherwise he would have had her by now, and that he didn't want to risk losing her altogether by chasing another woman, even if only in a movie. Ironically, the inspired lunacy of this logic was far more original and amusing than anything Roach came up with for the final scenario of *Topper*.

One aspect of the film that did intrigue Grant was Norman McLeod's use of cartoon sketches to show his actors how he wanted them to *look* in a scene (as opposed to how he wanted them to *act*). The comedy of physical action was something Grant wanted to learn more about. McLeod used his sketches to show facial expressions, body positions, and overall mise-en-scène he wanted within each frame. Grant studied them until he felt he had the character McLeod was after clearly in his head. With the director's help, he experimented with the range of physical comedy he was capable of, not merely to heighten the Cary Grant screen persona but to fundamentally redefine it.

Grant's next challenge in this project was less creative than commercial. Roach wanted Grant to share top billing with his costar, Constance Bennett, which he was reluctant to agree to. Billing (then as now) translated into money in Hollywood, and one of the primary reasons Grant had ventured out on his own was that he no longer wanted to play the second-fiddle, after-credit foil to Paramount's top female stars. But again, as a personal favor to Roach, he acquiesced.

Roach's first choice to play Cosmo Topper had been W. C. Fields, another former vaudevillian whom Grant very much admired and was looking forward to working with. When Fields turned the role down, Roach gave it instead to Roland Young. Ironically, earlier in his career Grant had played supporting roles in a number of Young's starring movies, when Paramount had believed Young was going to be Hollywood's next great leading man. Grant's part was by far the better one, but it still bothered him that, according to the credits, the title character belonged to Young.

Topper was released on July 16, 1937, and to the delight of both Roach and Grant, it was a huge success and captured the summertime imagination of audiences. It went on to be the second-highest-grossing film of the year, a giant career leap for Grant as well as a solid financial investment that paid off in huge dollar dividends. It was by far the most popular and best Cary Grant film to date, but before the year was over, Grant would surpass his work in *Topper* in every way.

BY THE TIME IT OPENED, Grant had formed a chaste passion for yet another Hollywood starlet, this time the young and beautiful Phyllis Brooks, whom he had met one weekend early in the shooting of *Topper*.

That Friday evening he had driven with Ginger Rogers up the coast to San Simeon for one of the weekend tennis celebrity tournaments that Hearst loved to hold on his castle grounds. Grant's natural athleticism put him among the front ranks of Hollywood's players, second only to Chaplin, who had far less natural ability but played with much greater ferocity. Rounding out the weekend, as always, was a full roster of events, including horse riding, lavish dinners in the unimaginably ornate dining room, and feature-length movies screened in the castle's modern, fully equipped screening room. This weekend, as always, was hosted by William Randolph Hearst and Marion Davies. Grant adored being in the company of Hearst and Davies, and they liked him as well, particularly Hearst. Grant was among the very few Hollywood celebrities equally welcomed at San Simeon and at the still-very-much-married Hearst's Sands Point mansion in New York, where the eastern intellectual elite were the favored privileged guests.

Grant got a kick out of the dramatic predinner cocktail entrance Hearst always made, alone and just before Davies; they would meet in the dining room and greet each other in beautiful formal wear, as Davies stretched out her hand for Hearst to kiss. He appreciated and respected their eccentric ways, such as their rigid alcohol policy (other than cocktails and wine), which Hearst enforced in deference to Davies's dislike for alcohol, something Grant and most of the other guests who liked to drink got around by stopping at David Niven's room before dinner and sharing the secret stash he always brought with him and kept hidden under his Richelieu guest bed.

This weekend's lush gathering was attended by dozens of Hollywood's most glamorous figures, including Chaplin, whom Grant finally got to meet, Tyrone Power, and his date for the weekend, Phyllis Brooks, "Brooksie" to her friends. Of all the guests at the affair, none caught Grant's eye more than the gorgeous young ingenue. Although he said nothing to her the entire weekend, after he left he could not forget her.

Phyllis Steiller (Brooks's real name) was a transplanted midwestern beauty who had come to Hollywood with the hope of parlaying her face and body into a film career. She had a naturally easy manner about her, a quick giggle, and a habit of running her hand through her hair before tossing it back. She also loved to swear like a sailor. In many ways, her personality, good looks, and salty manner resembled Carole Lombard's, which was how she managed to land a player development contract in 1934 at Universal. When it didn't happen for her there, she was let go; RKO picked up her contract, put her in a number of B movies, didn't renew her, and she landed next at Fox. By this time she was a now-and-again starlet, one of a number of pretty if nameless faces that could light up a screen like a sparkler on the Fourth of July, only to quickly burn out and be forgotten.

She was soon relegated to candy duty, assigned by studio execs to attend openings with their unattached male stars. Everyone welcomed her frequent presence at these events, even the cynical hatpin-in-the-rear gossips who smirked at any woman with a handsome Hollywood bachelor if there was no word of marriage lingering in the air. Louella Parsons in particular was especially fond of Brooks and never failed to write glowing passages whenever the beautiful young blonde showed up at a premiere.

Brooks was a natural night owl whose favorite haunt also happened to be Grant's, the Sunset Strip's Trocadero, where Hollywood's male motion picture royalty (and their current ladies-in-waiting) knew they could count on being effectively sheltered from the civilians forever seeking autographs, and the freelance photographers restricted to the front entrance in the hopes of catching a salable shot of the latest screen idol. It was at the Troc one night that Grant caught his next glimpse of the striking Brooks, on the arm of her agent, Walter Kane, who wore her like an expensive bauble he was looking to sell to the highest bidder with a movie deal thrown in.

That evening, Eleanor French, a friend of both Grant's and Brooks's, was at the Trocadero. A café club singer Grant knew from his theater days in New York, French had come out to the coast to vacation. He had always enjoyed her witty manner and the way she tilted her head to one side and smiled as she told her favorite off-color joke. When Grant asked her if he knew the young woman sharing a table with Kane, French smiled, said of course, and took him over and made the introduction.

As the night came to a close, Brooks insisted they all get together again sometime soon, and Grant, without hesitating, said his friend Randolph Scott was returning from a brief vacation in Virginia to begin work on his new film, *Last of the Mohicans*, and wouldn't it be sweet if they threw a welcome-home party in his honor. Brooks readily agreed, and the idea was sealed with the clank of three empty glasses.

What seemed like a happy coincidence was, in fact, anything but. Brooks had recognized Grant that night as soon as he had walked into the club. At the time she still had quite a crush on Tyrone Power but knew nothing could come of it because of the iron lock that ice-skating star Sonja Henie had on his emotions. (Henie happened to be out of the country when Brooks accompanied Power to San Simeon.) An eligible bachelor was her prey, and as far as she could tell, none was more eligible than the one actor she had met who was single and even more handsome than Tyrone Power—Cary Grant. Knowing her girlfriend Eleanor was coming out for a visit, that she knew Grant, and that he liked to frequent the Troc, she had worked out an elaborate (and unnecessary) plan of introduction, apparently unaware that Grant had noticed her as well that weekend at San Simeon. When he ended the evening by inviting them both to help throw a party to welcome home Scott, Brooks was, to say the least, elated.

Brooks was soon dating Grant on a regular basis, and within weeks was referring to him as "the love of her life."

13

"The great majority of screwball comedies save marriage for the final fade-out or even beyond. Screwball comedies are therefore generally comedies of courtship . . . . Cary Grant and Irene Dunne romp through a series of slapstick situations that would have given pause to Laurel and Hardy."

—ANDREW SARRIS

The surprising commercial success of *Topper* added luminosity to Cary Grant's screen image and bigger box office clout to his name, so much that Harry Cohn wanted him back at work on his next film as soon as possible, in a project he had already green-lighted, a comedy to be directed by Leo McCarey called *The Awful Truth*. Cohn decided to pair Grant with Irene Dunne, an extremely pretty southern-born actress who had come from nowhere a few years earlier to strike it big with a Best Actress Oscar nomination for her performance in Wesley Ruggles's *Cimarron* (1931). Cohn had recently signed her away from RKO for a long-term contract and wanted to put her to work right away. *The Awful Truth*, her twenty-third film, was the latest entry into the extremely popular, if ultimately short-lived, subgenre of comedy known as "screwball," which emerged during the great 1930s economic (and emotional) Depression. It was Grant's twenty-ninth film, and the one that would finally propel him to superstardom.

SCREWBALL IS A PARTICULARLY apt term for a certain type of movie that, like the baseball pitch of the same name, travels a fast but unpredictable path before somehow managing to cross the plate for a perfect strike. The dialogue is sometimes delivered as fast as two hundred words a minute, and oftentimes the meaning of a character's lines is submerged by the rhythm of its delivery, to the point that the delivery itself becomes the meaning.

Another defining element of screwball is the relationship between its male and female leads. They are almost always young, rich, unattached or separated, at once hopelessly attracted to each other and facing a particularly zany path on the road to true and lasting love. By the early 1930s the censorship of the Hays Office had helped to make a joke out of cinematic eroticism: the unfunny punch line of marriage always loomed at the final fade-out, the government-sanctioned metaphor for the end of guileless romance. As film historian Andrew Sarris points out, "Frustration [in screwball comedy] arises inevitably from a situation in which the censors have removed the sex from the sex comedies." Perhaps that is why children almost never appear in screwball, lest they replace the often childlike (but rarely childish) behavior of the adult romantic leads.

As a staple of Hollywood for much of the second half of the 1930s, screwball comedies excelled both at satisfying the censors and at getting a rise out of audiences by teasing them with beautiful women who were in turn teasing their costars. And who better to depict the victim of this female scheming than the actor who did not like his characters to pursue women?

The Awful Truth, based on a 1922 Broadway play by Arthur Richman, had already been filmed twice by the recently bankrupt Pathé Studios. Harry Cohn believed in recycling "sure things," as he liked to call remakes, because he thought it gave his pictures "better odds." When he acquired the rights to all of Pathé Studios' properties (for a onetime payout of $35,000), he found *The Awful Truth* among them and immediately commissioned an updated version of the 1929 Marshall Neilan film of the same name that he could make on the cheap.

From the outset Cohn wanted Leo McCarey to direct. McCarey had first teamed Stan Laurel with Oliver Hardy (a credit that is usually and wrongfully given to Hal Roach). After supervising, writing, and directing many of the best comedy duo's silent comedies, he then made a splash in sound pictures while a contract director at Paramount, with his 1933 direction of the Marx Brothers' *Duck Soup* and Charles Laughton's 1935 *Ruggles of Red Gap*. Despite the success of both movies, McCarey languished for several years through a series of undistinguished Paramount assignments, including *Belle of the Nineties* (1934) that starred an already-fading Mae West, and a failed attempt at resurrecting Harold Lloyd's career with *The Milky Way* (1936). McCarey finally scored another hit with what was, for him, a major stylistic departure, the unsettling Depression-era family tragedy *Make Way for Tomorrow* (1937), the personal favorite of all his movies, which restored some critical luster to his career. But it was too little, too late: McCarey was handed his unconditional release by Paramount at approximately the same time Grant decided not to renew with the studio.

Cohn, meanwhile, thought McCarey's comic talents had been misused and overlooked and immediately signed him as a possible replacement for Frank Capra, who was threatening to walk out on Cohn and Columbia. Having brought prestige and several Academy Awards to the studio, Capra demanded a hefty raise from Cohn, who refused to renegotiate Capra's long-term contract. Instead, he offered McCarey a bare-bones $100,000 a year. Desperately in need of cash, McCarey accepted and signed on to Columbia.

During the Laurel and Hardy phase of his career, McCarey used Oliver "Babe" Hardy as his onscreen alter ego—it was always Ollie, and never Stanley, who looked directly at the audience to comment on his own predicaments. But in real life McCarey was far more suave, sophisticated, and good-looking, with a degree in law and a witty sense of humor. He was, in brief, the real-life model for the comedic persona he was about to help Cary Grant refine in *The Awful Truth*.

After reading the original Pathé script, McCarey promptly threw it in the trash and, with the help of his friend and sometime freelance collaborator, Viña Delmar, rewrote it from beginning to end. In the McCarey-Delmar version, the story becomes one of marital deception and misconception that goes wildly out of control. A major breakdown in communication between a husband and wife leads to a breakup of their marriage, which sparks a series of schemes and tricks as each tries to win the other back without admitting that that is what they truly want, until one final, romantic reunion allows love to conquer (and clarify) all.

The Awful Truth is the epitome of screwball, what film critic Stanley Cavell described as "a comedy of *remarriage*." No one seeing the film ever doubts that Grant and Dunne will eventually wind up together (that the ball will cross the plate for a strike); the comedy comes from the crazy pathway they each take to get there. Jerry Warriner (Grant), in a story line McCarey and Delmar more or less lifted from Laurel and Hardy's *Sons of the Desert,* tells his wife, Lucy (Irene Dunne), that he is going on vacation to Florida, when what he really intends to do is remain in New York. To ensure the success of his marital deception, he takes sun-lamp treatments to make his fake vacation seem more convincing. When he finally returns home, he is surprised to find that Lucy is not there waiting for him like the good little wife. In fact, she is out and about, enjoying the company of her handsome but lecherous voice teacher, Armand Duvalle (Alexander D'Arcy). Upon her return, Lucy is surprised to see Jerry's tan, since the weather reports out of Florida had been all rain. Soon each Warriner becomes convinced the other is a liar and a cheater (and in fact either or both may have been, as the truth, whatever it is, remains purposefully ambiguous). Communication continues to break down between the two until they decide that divorce is the only answer. After a nasty court proceeding, Lucy wins custody of their beloved pet dog, Mr. Smith (played by Asta of *Thin Man* fame), while Jerry retains limited visiting rights.

With the terms of their divorce settled, Jerry wastes no time resuming the bachelor life. To make Lucy jealous (although he won't admit it to himself), he begins dating one of his former flames, saucy nightclub entertainer Dixie Belle Lee (Joyce Compton). Lucy, meanwhile, becomes involved with extremely wealthy but extremely dull oil heir Daniel Leeson (Ralph Bellamy), realizes she still loves Jerry, and prior to the finalization of her divorce, asks Armand to help her salvage whatever is left of her marriage.

Even as she is explaining the situation to Armand, Jerry shows up unexpectedly to make amends with his wife. Lucy, caught off-guard by his arrival, hastily stashes Armand in the bedroom. Soon Leeson arrives, and Jerry is given the hide-'em-in-the-boudoir treatment, where a slapdash tumult erupts and Jerry leaves, angrier than ever. To complicate matters still further, Jerry then becomes engaged to socialite Barbara Vance (Molly Lamont). To try to stop the marriage from happening, Lucy shows up at a dinner party Barbara's parents are throwing, pretends she is Jerry's sister, and proceeds to get rip-roaring drunk (on ginger ale). Jerry takes her outside to try to sober her up and winds up driving to their mountain cabin, where they finally unravel all their romantic misunderstandings and, presumably, live happily (if not nec-essarily ever) after.

During the making of *The Awful Truth*, Cohn had not bothered to assign an office to McCarey—he didn't believe directors needed such extrava-gances—so the director was forced to do the majority of his daily rewrites by hand in the front seat of his car, with Delmar sitting next to him on the pas-senger side, scribbling down pages of dialogue in pencil. Then after trying out that day's pages, they kept what worked with the actors and rewrote what didn't for the next day's shoot.

It was a directing style Cary Grant loathed. He was not a spontaneous actor; the "magic" didn't happen for him when the camera rolled. He pre-ferred to work from a completed script and rehearse his fixed lines with the other cast members over and over again until he had nailed every detail of his verbal and physical performance in advance, "freezing" it before a single foot of film ever passed through the camera's lens. This was Grant's standard method; with no formal acting training it was the only way he knew to approach a role.

Because Grant's pre-set approach was so radically different from McCarey's essentially improvisational style, it didn't take long for the two to clash and for Grant to start becoming emotionally unwound. His overall anxiety level soared, and he was noticeably on edge with the other actors.

To complicate matters further, Grant developed his by now familiar leading-lady crush on Dunne, whose projection of wholesome integrity made her wrong for the part of Lucy Warriner but an ideal candidate for one of Grant's chaste love-objects-from-afar. These infatuations were always the same—equal parts Leach and Grant, blended into whatever character was being cooked up. Besides whatever emotional tic they may have satisfied, these attractions also provided Grant with a valuable, if neurotic, focal point, the foundation for what came across as a smooth and sophisticated screen style.

Unlike Grant, his character was a womanizer, and while the written script left it purposely vague as to whether he actually committed adultery (so as not to rouse the Hays Office), his performance left little doubt that he had. This was something Grant found difficult to connect to, especially while in crush mode. Indeed, his infatuation with Dunne led him to believe that anyone lucky enough to be married to a woman like her (or Lucy Warriner), having blown it would not be able to get over it so easily, least of all by dating other women. So Grant at first felt no affinity for the kind of physical screwball comedy that McCarey's style demanded. He believed it substituted physical motion for emotional depth. His idea of film comedy was more Chaplinesque — humor as a reflection of tragedy, laughter happening between tears. To Grant, screwball's limits lay in the way it drove audiences to tears of laughter, in the absence of any intimations of tragedy that might otherwise deepen the story.

His insecurities and objections were not eased by McCarey's often rambling daily descriptions of what each day's scenes were supposed to be about; they only added to Grant's anger and confusion. On the first day of actual filming, someone handed him a series of notes handwritten on scraps of brown paper bag. Grant, as he read what McCarey wanted to get from him that day, thought the director was joking. And when none of the routines seemed to work, McCarey simply told his actors to make something up that sounded funny. Grant was appalled, but said nothing and did the best he could, believing things had to get better as the shoot developed.*

When the same thing happened the next day, however, Grant turned on his heels, left the set, and went directly to Cohn's office to register his dissatisfaction. Cohn, who had no patience for temperamental and what he considered vastly overpaid actors — which meant all actors, as far as he was concerned — brushed him off by growling at him to go back, do his job, and for chrissake stop acting like a little old lady.

The next day Grant returned to Cohn's office and politely offered to switch roles with Ralph Bellamy and play the smaller, supporting part of the

---

*Interestingly, it was out of these improvisations that Grant came up with one of the best lines of dialogue in the film. When Jerry shows up unexpectedly to visit his dog, Dunne opens the door and says, "Well, if it isn't my ex!" No one could come up with a line for Grant, and when McCarey told him to make one up, without missing a beat he said in his best deadpan manner, "The judge says this is my day to see the dog."

rich oil heir, a character for which he claimed he was much better suited. Bellamy, he assured Cohn, was willing to trade places. Cohn asked him to please get lost.

The day after that Grant went back again to Cohn, but this time before he said anything, he handed him a neatly typed eight-page memorandum that he, Grant, had stayed up the whole night working on and that outlined exactly what he believed was wrong with the picture (the total lack of comedy, the absence of a completed script, McCarey's unstructured, improvisational style of direction). Along with the note, Grant offered Cohn $5,000 in cash as a bribe to be taken off the picture, on top of which he promised to star in another picture for Columbia—*any* other picture—for *free*. Cohn refused the money and once again told him to go back to work.

McCarey was infuriated when he heard what Grant had done (and for years told anyone who asked that when he showed Grant's note to Asta, the dog bit him). From that day on, except for giving him specific directions, he refused to talk to his star for the remainder of the shoot and, except for when they worked together, for the rest of his life. At one point, McCarey later claimed, he became so angered by Grant's attitude that *he* went to Cohn and offered to *double* Grant's offer to $10,000 if Cohn would *fire* the actor.

Yet despite, or perhaps because of, the friction between director and star, the performance McCarey got from Grant was nothing less than astonishing. It not only redefined Cary Grant's image as a leading man, it helped alter the public's notion of what a leading man in film was supposed to be.

Prior to *The Awful Truth*, a romantic male who was at once charming, intelligent, romantic, sensitive, witty, sexy, rascally, and as beautiful as a leading lady simply did not exist in American movies. Hollywood's first generation of leading men were, with rare exceptions, courtly Europeans with sculpted mustaches and slicked-back hair such as Ronald Colman; elderly leches like Adolphe Menjou, devilish hedonists like Rudolph Valentino, or all-American cowboys like Tom Mix.

As talkies became the standard, this image shifted more toward all-American image of the WASP, largely humorless rural hunks—Gary Cooper, Clark Gable, young Jimmy Stewart, and to a lesser degree Henry Fonda and John Wayne. Cooper and Stewart in particular specialized in the duped hick steeped in and therefore redeemed by his own moral self-righteousness.

Others, like the urbane William Powell as Nick Charles in the *Thin Man* series (1934–47) and the cartoonishly insane John Barrymore in Howard Hawks's *Twentieth Century* (1934), were a combination of the older, mustachioed European sophisticates and arrested (and extended) American adolescents, where intellect and wit replaced rather than led to any real sexual sparks.

In *The Awful Truth*, Cary Grant's Warriner was handsome, sexy, and urbane, with just a whiff of British sophistication, and not a hint of two-fistedness to foul the funny air. His charismatic performance was, despite McCarey's methods, part Chaplin heartbreak — a wounded heart that must rise above the hurt — and part Keaton, imbued with an extraordinary physical grace that is at once attractive, elegant, and expansive. Ironically, McCarey's comedic skills and film smarts helped Grant, in spite of his resistant stance, merge his individual characteristics into a wholly realized character. As Jerry Warriner, his good looks were not just those of another pretty face but a personal come-hither invitation to stop by and look around, all the way to the inside of his soul.

With McCarey's assured direction, Grant had finally found a way to use physical humor to portray the essential humanity of Jerry Warriner. Grant's catlike physicality, which had brought him to the brink of lugubriousness in his earlier leading-heel roles, now translated into a youthful, rhythmic prance fueled by the high energy of light comedy. A bend of his knee became the equivalent of a punch line. A lifting of his palms expressed a lifetime's skepticism. A tilting of his head suggested a turning of the other cheek. Critic Andrew Britton pointed out, in one of the most insightful explanations of Grant's enormous appeal in *The Awful Truth*, that his performance was "remarkable for the extent to which characteristics assigned by those [traditional gender] roles to women could be presented as being desirable and attractive in a man."

The film also caused a sensation for its inspired and at the time postmodernist depiction of women. As portrayed by Dunne, Lucy is an attractive, intelligent *equal*, able to hold her own in the eternal battle of the sexes. Dunne's brilliantly lunatic performance set the stylistic stage for such later comic film actresses as Judy Holliday and Audrey Hepburn, and in TV comedy the antics of Lucille Ball, Carol Burnett, and Gilda Radner.

In the film's unforgettable last scene, in their cabin hideaway, McCarey brilliantly reconciles his characters' relationship by resolving their emotional crisis. In a reconciling two-shot, McCarey shows Lucy in bed, a quilt covering her legs, her chin resting softly in her right palm, her face lit with the beauty of forgiveness, watching her man go through a visual cacophony of facial expressions and body movements — brow furrowed, eyes wide and damp, mouth and throat locked in gulp, his right hand cupped and pointed up. The unspoken reconnection between them provides the audience with a privileged and breathtaking moment of pure requited love.

WHEN *THE AWFUL TRUTH* premiered on October 21, 1937, at New York City's famed Radio City Music Hall (the first of twenty-eight Cary Grant movies that would open there, a record never broken), the critical and popular reaction was rightly unanimous in declaring it the best film of the year, if not the entire decade. Among the most enthusiastic reviews was the one that appeared in *The New York Times*, which called it "an unapologetic return to the fundamentals of comedy [that] seems original and daring!"

In less than a month, *The Awful Truth* earned its costs back and then some, surpassing the half-million-dollar profit mark while still in its first-run release. It would go on to become one of Columbia's all-time box office smashes. Thanks to Vincent, Grant's cut of the film included 10 percent of the gross on top of his contract fee, a deal that would, at the end of the film's initial domestic theatrical run (prior to rereleases, foreign distribution, and eventual television and video rights), put more than a half-million dollars into Cary Grant's pocket.

In one of the most spectacular career leaps in the history of Hollywood, Grant had gone from a position of relative unimportance only two years earlier, when he had received less than 1 percent of the annual votes cast in the Motion Picture Herald Poll (at the time the most popular and respected pre–*Entertainment Tonight* listing), to one of the top five male box office attractions of 1937. His inspired performance, the first to give the world a glimpse of the comic persona of "Cary Grant," put him in the pantheon alongside Gary Cooper, Clark Gable, Paul Muni, and Spencer Tracy.

At a still-youthful-looking thirty-three, Grant had already lived a lifetime (by Hollywood's standards) of being miscast—"resplendent but characterless, even a trace languid, outrageously attractive if vaguely ill at ease—a slightly wilted sheik or a slightly fleshy cow-eyed leading man with a pretty-boy killer looks," as Pauline Kael later observed. Indeed, after nearly a decade spent as a vaudevillian acrobat, another as a moderately successful but undistinguished Broadway leading and song-and-dance man, and an uninspired run as a humorless foil to the most glamorous leading ladies in Hollywood, he had, at last, discovered a director—or more accurately, he was discovered by a director, Leo McCarey—who helped him make the transition into the sophisticated, handsome, witty, and urbane leading man the world would come to know and love as Cary Grant. Suddenly, women were swooning over his handsome face and physique while men tried to comb their hair the way he did and put metal screws to their chins trying to drill themselves a Cary Grant cleft. Everyone, it seemed, had gone crazy over him.

Everyone, that is, except Cary Grant. While he gratefully accepted the accolades for his performance in *The Awful Truth,* he confided to close friends that he still intensely disliked the movie and especially his part in it. Indeed, no one was more surprised than he was by its success, mostly because he had no idea where the great performance he had given in it had come from. He was amused but not cheered by everyone's assumption that he was in real life the same affable persona he was in the film—the superbly handsome comic rascal, everyone's perfect fantasy.

In truth, he still had no clear image of who he really was. Whenever he saw himself onscreen, it was like looking at a gigantic mirror whose reflection was familiar, but one he could not quite identify with or relate to. The person up there, the idealized and romanticized character whose every move was dictated by an unseen director, whose every clever word and turn of phrase were put into his mouth by an unseen screenwriter, and who was lit and photographed by unseen experts who knew just how to make his skin glossy, his eyes bright, his hair shiny, his chin granite—that manufactured character, he believed, was more handsome and funny and clever and wise than he could ever be in real life, more smoothly graceful and impossibly svelte than *any man could ever be.* That was the man everybody adored—*that* was "Cary Grant."

Back on his own real-life side of the glass, however, he could see all the shortcomings with crystal clarity. Without a producer, without a costar, and without a script, he didn't need a director to tell him what to do; he needed a god to show him who he was.

And sure enough, one was on his way, a fellow Brit who would know exactly how to redeem Cary Grant from the beautiful distortion of his own blinding starlight.

PART SIX

ENTER HITCHCOCK

PREVIOUS PAGE: *Cary and Hitch, Hollywood's oddest couple, here having lunch on location in France, on the set of* To Catch a Thief *(1955). Each looked at the other and saw the reflection of his inner self, reflections that lit up and set the silver screen on fire throughout their four-picture, eighteen-year collaboration.* (MacFadden Publishing/CORBIS)

14

"Cary Grant represents a man we know."

—ALFRED HITCHCOCK

Whenever Randolph Scott was away, either visiting his wife Marion duPont in Virginia or working on location on a film, Grant spent his evenings dancing at the Trocadero with "the Brooks." After the success of *The Awful Truth*, Grant was riding high, and his newfound fame and fortune helped, at least for the moment, to bring him out of his normally reclusive shell, as did his blossoming romance with Brooks. For her part, she fully expected an offer of marriage from Grant, one she would unhesitatingly accept, even if he stipulated that she had to give up her film career. In truth, it wouldn't be much of a sacrifice, as she didn't have much of a career beyond a steady stream of B movies, the dubious highlight of which was a couple of Charlie Chan flicks. For her, the only part that really mattered was that of Mrs. Cary Grant. The problem was that Grant had no intention of ever getting married again, and to gently discourage Brooks from going down that path, he insisted she keep looking for more movie work and promised to help her find better roles.

EVEN BEFORE *The Awful Truth* had completed its initial theatrical run, Grant signed on to do the radio adaptation. In the absence of television, video, DVD, or cable, except for the very occasional rerelease, once a film ended its theatrical run, both domestically and overseas (where American movies remained unerringly popular), network radio adaptations provided its only significant additional source of funds.

When Irene Dunne proved unavailable, Claudette Colbert took over as Lucy, and Grant arranged to have Brooks replace Joyce Compton in the supporting role of Dixie. They recorded the radio version shortly after the completion of the film for the Lux Radio Theater, a series on which Grant had by now become a regular. (The ongoing theatrical popularity of the film contractually forced Lux to delay its broadcast until sometime after the film was taken out of theaters to prevent moviegoers from listening to it "free" on the radio. Because of the film's unusually long theatrical run, the radio version wasn't aired until September 11, 1939, almost two years after the movie's initial release.)

Grant also saw to it that Brooks got a small role in Allan Dwan's 1938 remake of Kate Douglas Wiggin's novel *Rebecca of Sunnybrook Farm*, the rights to which producer Darryl F. Zanuck had purchased specifically for child star Shirley Temple. Coincidentally (it appeared), Randolph Scott was also cast in the film, as Tony, the radio producer who discovers little Rebecca's singing talents.

This awkward miscasting did nothing to help Scott's floundering career. After spending years appearing in beside-the-point Paramount films, he had finally scored as Hawkeye in George Seitz's 1936 film version of James Fenimore Cooper's *The Last of the Mohicans*. But when Zukor could or would not find a suitable follow-up film for him, Scott took it as a sign that his days at the studio were numbered. Shortly afterward, along with dozens of other contract players, he was cut, a move that surprised no one. What was surprising was how quickly Zanuck signed Scott to a long-term contract with 20th Century–Fox, assuring the actor that he would soon be cast in "quality" roles. As it happened, this sudden change happened precisely at the same time Marion duPont sold her shares in Paramount and made a cash purchase of a significant amount of stock in 20th Century–Fox, enough to give her an all-but-controlling interest in the studio.

Zanuck, meanwhile, as a "gesture of friendship" to Scott—who in turn was trying to help out Grant—managed to find a place for Brooks in the film.

Zanuck's motives weren't entirely altruistic. He knew full well about Scott's close relationship with Grant, as did everyone in the industry, and he hoped his gesture would impress the suddenly very desirable star enough to make him want to join his best friend and Brooks as a permanent part of the Fox family.

For his part, Grant was delighted that "the Brooks" was at last working on a big film, hoping it would keep her mind off the marriage awhile longer. Not that it made much difference: he had lately grown tired of "sharing," and while she was occupied with the movie, for company he quietly began to socialize with other actresses, among them the pretty young bottle blonde Jean Rogers, whose main claim to fame had been playing Dale Arden opposite Olympic swimmer-turned-actor Buster Crabbe in the amazingly popular *Flash Gordon* Saturday morning serial.

Grant's attraction to Rogers, like all his relationships with starlets, lacked a measurable lust factor, but he was genuinely amused by her bright and outgoing manner. She was a great talker, and he loved her hilarious stories about the making of the good-natured if totally ridiculous *Flash Gordon* episodes, particularly about the limited acting abilities of Crabbe, in real life a very good friend of Scott's.

As it happened, Grant had first met Rogers through Scott, while Scott was making Rouben Mamoulian's *High, Wide, and Handsome* at Paramount before his contract expired. Scott's costar was Dorothy Lamour, and as the two principals were paired romantically onscreen, the studio manufactured one of its publicity "romances" between them. (Rumors of their ongoing liaison lingered for years, but as Lamour confirmed years later, it was purely a product of the studio's PR department.) On her arranged dates with Scott, Lamour often brought along her good friend Rogers to accompany the ever-present Grant whenever Brooks wasn't available.

WHILE SCOTT WAS AWAY SHOOTING location scenes for *Rebecca of Sunnybrook Farm,* Grant began to think about moving out of the beach house for good. Both he and Scott had solid careers, which meant, among other things, that they had almost no opportunity to spend significant time alone together, as one or the other seemed always off making a movie.

Besides, Grant now had lots of money, so there was no longer any possible financial reason, if there ever had been, to share a house. (While no one in the business ever bought that excuse, it still gave them a cover for the general public.)

Grant turned to Howard Hughes for advice, and Hughes, without hesitation, told him it was time to make the break with Scott. What did he need it for, Hughes asked, given the constant rumors and the trouble it caused.

Grant had to agree. Scott was and always would be his soulmate, but something had changed, and it wasn't just their careers, although fame had certainly become a wedge between them. The closeness was gone now, the private laughter, the intimate feeling that they were a team, two against the world. Grant missed that with Scott since he'd gotten married and knew it would never again be like it once was.

WHEN HUGHES'S FRIEND DIRECTOR Howard Hawks was looking for someone to costar opposite Hughes's on-again, off-again lover Katharine Hepburn for a new project at Columbia, he suggested to Hawks that he consider Grant for the role.

Despite each of their many other romances, Hughes was still interested in Hepburn. He had still not reached his long-term goal of owning a major Hollywood studio, and he believed his best way to achieve that was by riding to power on Hepburn's Academy Awarded back. As for her, she had plans, as well. Visions of career independence required the kind of funds Howard Hughes could deliver. In that sense they were birds of a feather.

The picture was *Bringing Up Baby*, a last-minute project for Hawks after his planned version of *Gunga Din* for RKO had unexpectedly fallen through. After working on the *Gunga Din* script with Ben Hecht and Charles MacArthur, and later on with his good friend (and fellow industry union activist) Academy Award screenwriter Dudley Nichols,* Hawks had gotten MGM to agree to loan out Robert Montgomery and Spencer Tracy to play two of the three British soldiers. He then put all his remaining chips on acquiring the services of Clark Gable for the third but came up empty.

*He won Best Screenplay for John Ford's *The Informer* in 1935.

Louis B. Mayer's MGM, still in chaos after the early, unexpected, shocking death of its "boy wonder" head of production, Irving Thalberg, at the age of thirty-seven, was not about to lend out its biggest star to a rival studio.

Hawks had counted on his friendship with Thalberg that dated all the way back to the early 1920s, when they were both starting out in motion pictures. After Thalberg's passing the new head of RKO, Sam Briskin (a former production head at Columbia and another longtime friend of Hawks), shelved the Gable-less *Gunga Din* and urged Hawks, who had made what everyone considered the seminal screwball, *Twentieth Century* (1934), to find a comedy instead, something without a lot of expensive action sequences that he could quickly put into production.

If Hawks was disappointed, he didn't show it. Known for his tight-lipped, nonconfrontational style, he dutifully dipped into RKO's pool of potential properties and found a script in the studio's reading department, with an attached report that called its dialogue "hilarious and the possibilities of comic situations limitless." The story, *Bringing Up Baby*, by writer Hagar Wilde, had first appeared in the April 10, 1937, issue of *Collier's* magazine. After one reading, Hawks chose to make a movie out of it because, he said later on, it had made him laugh out loud. Briskin then had RKO buy the rights for the negotiated sum of $1,004.

In typical screwball fashion, the "plot" of *Bringing Up Baby* is thread-thin and hopelessly entangled: a convoluted role-reversal romance in which the female character chases the male, who appears oblivious to her feminine charms and increasingly bold sexual overtures. David Huxley, a shy, intellectual paleontologist, becomes the object of a heated sexual pursuit by Susan Vance, a rich society girl who, unbeknownst to him, has an aunt ready to give a million-dollar endowment to the museum where he works, an endowment he desperately needs to finish his life's work—the restoration of a gigantic dinosaur's skeleton. The day before he is to marry his iceberg assistant, David meets Susan, who falls in lust with him at first sight. Their relationship takes them down the zany screwball path to true love after another star turn by Asta the dog, who steals a crucial and priceless dinosaur bone (the "intercostal clavicle" that David needs to complete his hall-size reconstruction), the desperate attempt that follows to recover it, a couple of symbolic leopards (one domesticated, one wild) roaming throughout the

Connecticut farm where much of the film takes place, the most jovial jail-up in the history of motion pictures, and an ending that literally pulls the entire film together by the tips of its fingers.

While *Bringing Up Baby* was being turned into a screenplay by Dudley Nichols, Hawks began casting. His first choice to play Susan, the rich young niece, was easy: he wanted Carole Lombard, who had done such a magnificent job for him in *Twentieth Century*. But strictly for economic reasons, RKO's Pandro Berman, in charge of casting for the studio, insisted that Katharine Hepburn star in the film. (Berman had just been put in charge of the studio's A pictures after a disheveled RKO's financial situation worsened, forcing Briskin to resign midway through *Bringing Up Baby*'s production.) Despite her uneven box office record, the Academy Award winner still had three films left on her contract with RKO, and Berman (at the private urging of Howard Hughes, who stayed in the background so as to avoid clashing with his friend Hawks) still believed that with the right roles, costars, and directors she could become the studio's biggest star.

Having to use Hepburn presented a series of unforeseen problems for Hawks, mainly involving the cost of making the film. Originally budgeted at half a million dollars, that figure was revised upward to $750,000 to cover Hepburn's guaranteed salary. She received $72,000 up front (with large bonuses if the film went beyond its original shooting schedule), 5 percent of the gross between $600,000 and $750,000, 7.5 percent up to $1,000,000, and a then unheard-of 11 percent of the gross from there to eternity. Because of these provisions, Hawks would have to make up the money in production and shoot at a very economical pace — meaning fast, something he did not like to do.

More difficult was the casting of the male lead, a standard-issue milque-toast who, despite his boring scientific preoccupation, had somehow to give off enough sustained sexual heat to make it believable that Susan would so feverishly and relentlessly pursue him. Hollywood had no shortage of actors who had perfected meekness onscreen, most notably Harold Lloyd, the bespectacled screen comedian who, of the three great silent clowns (Chaplin and Keaton being the other two), had made the most successful transition to sound. Hawks was interested in Lloyd for the part, but Berman said no, RKO was not going to put Hepburn into a romantic comedy opposite Harold Lloyd, a milquetoast yes, a leading man most definitely no.

Ronald Colman was someone else Hawks liked, but Berman rejected him as well. Robert Montgomery, Fredric March, and a young and upcoming Ray Milland all got the green light from Berman, but all turned the part down because none of these A-list stars was willing to risk his paycheck working for a studio whose finances were as shaky as RKO's.

Then, at Hughes's suggestion, Hawks began to look seriously at Cary Grant, especially when he discovered that Grant had a nonexclusive four-picture deal with RKO but had yet to shoot a single foot of film there. The more Hawks thought about it, the more he liked the idea. At a meeting attended by Grant, Frank Vincent, Hawks, Berman, Briskin, and Nichols, Vincent insisted that Grant, if he took the part, had to get $75,000, as well as bonuses that matched all of Hepburn's. The demand infuriated Briskin for its sheer outrageousness — he well knew that Grant's RKO four-picture deal was for an agreed-upon $50,000 per film. But Vincent was prepared to have his client walk, and Berman wanted the already seriously delayed production to begin as soon as possible, so before everyone left the room, Berman offered Grant the part on the terms he wanted, and Grant accepted.

Vincent knew what he was doing. He had indeed negotiated Grant's four-picture deal with RKO at $50,000 per picture, but that was *before* his smashing success in *The Awful Truth*. Now that Grant was a top star, he wanted, and got, what he had originally asked for — and what Briskin had turned down — at the time of the original contract: $75,000 a picture. It was lost on no one that this made Grant the higher paid of the film's two stars.

The meeting appeared to settle everything, except for one last detail. That night Grant told Vincent that he had not yet decided to take the picture. The always unflappable Vincent said fine and told Grant to take his time deciding what he wanted to do. Grant then spent several days alone at the beach house in a total funk, avoiding calls from everyone while he wrestled with himself over whether he *could* play the part well enough to sustain the kind of success he had had with *The Awful Truth*. He still believed his performance as Jerry Warriner had been either a fluke, a lucky confluence, or a collaborative jackpot. Any way he looked at it, it was something he could take no real credit for (and never did), and he was afraid to make a movie that was too stylistically similar in which his performance would not be as good.

Two full weeks passed without a commitment from Grant, until the soft-spoken Hawks persuaded the actor to do the film by promising to personally guide his performance every step of the way. Hawks then suggested to Grant that he look at some of the films of Harold Lloyd. Grant did and was so taken with the comedian's style of acting that he actually copied it, almost gesture for gesture, in putting together his interpretation of David Huxley, down to thick black horn-rimmed glasses, one of Lloyd's cinematic trademarks.

Filming of *Bringing Up Baby* began September 23, 1937. Although she was a highly trained stage actress, Hepburn had had little experience playing comedy, and like Grant relied heavily on Hawks for guidance. His one demand was that both his stars deliver their lines at top speed. With Hepburn running full steam — she had most of the dialogue — and Grant wearing large framed glasses that all but hid his face, Berman was disappointed with the early rushes and demanded "more glamour" from both stars.

Despite her energy and speedy recitations, Hepburn was having difficulty finding the comic rhythm of her character. To help her, Hawks hired Walter Catlett, a veteran vaudeville comic who had spent years with the Ziegfeld Follies in New York, to try to get Hepburn to stop "acting" funny and start *being* funny, by playing the scene's logical flow, such as it might be, and allowing the laughs to come from the audience's recognition of the sheer silliness of the situations.

At the same time, Grant, again to the surprise of no one more than himself, excelled in the role of Huxley, due in large measure to endless meetings, not with Hawks, but with Hughes, who patiently and meticulously helped Grant discover every nuance of his character's part. With Hughes's encouragement, Grant came up with many of the most famous set pieces of the film, which he would bring to the set early and rehearse before the perennially late Hawks showed up. Among them is the scene in which Grant, dressed in a woman's bathrobe, responds to the question of why by declaring, with all the proper exasperation, "I've gone gay all of a sudden!"

The famous torn-tuxedo routine, which led to the torn-dress sequence (where Grant's top hat covers Hepburn's rear end and she remarks, "Will you please stop doing that with your hat?" followed by their memorable "lock-step" out of the ballroom), was a comic bit that Grant came up with and later claimed was based on something he had actually seen at the Roxy Theater in New York City while sitting next to the head of the Metropolitan Museum and his wife. At one point the man stood up to allow the woman to go to the bathroom, only to discover his fly was open. As he attempted to close it, he caught her dress in the zipper, and the two had to "lock-step" their way to the manager's office for a pair of pliers to get themselves uncoupled. Hawks marveled at the bit and, risking the ire of the Hays Office, used it in the movie.

Another Grant-inspired moment happened when, during a take, Hepburn's heel broke. Grant whispered to her, "I was born on the side of a hill," a line that she immediately repeated. That scene also remained in the finished film.

The best moment of all, however, comes at the end, when Hepburn finds herself atop the delicate scaffolding, reaching for Grant. The power of this scene is enhanced by Grant's great physical prowess, which encouraged Hepburn to play the scene herself, in a single take, without a stunt double. Grant carefully rehearsed Hepburn's moves over and over, teaching her how to do the "circus grip" of the wrists he had learned as a boy and prepare her body for the big hoist. When Hepburn slips off the scaffold at the last minute, he grabs her by the wrist, and there she hangs suspended between the skeletal reconstruction below and the object of her deepest (and highest) affections above. It is an inspired moment, the uncertain dangling of mankind between the primitive past and the hopeful future, with the sanctity of life defined as mysteriously and magically as it is in the touch of Michelangelo's two fingertips atop the Sistine Chapel.* When Grant confidently hoists her to safety, it is a moment not only of comic triumph but of pure cinematic grace; Susan's physical rescue becomes a metaphor for both her and Huxley's emotional redemption.

DESPITE THE STUDIO'S DESIRE FOR Hawks to turn out a cheap quickie, *Bringing Up Baby* developed into a long and difficult film to shoot. It com-

---

*It is a moment that resonated throughout Grant's career, resurfacing seventeen years later in a visually similar but emotionally different tableau in Alfred Hitchcock's *To Catch a Thief,* and four years after that in his *North by Northwest.*

pleted production on January 6, 1938, forty days over its original fifty-one-day schedule, an overrun that pushed the budget to well over a million dollars. (The automatic salary increases resulted in Grant and Hepburn each receiving an additional $120,000.) Then, just before the film opened, RKO fell into receivership. Once more it was Howard Hughes who came to the rescue, hoping to make a killing by buying at a fraction of their production cost the negatives of it and nine other RKO films, then selling them as a package to the Loew's theater chain.

Although the film is now regarded as a classic of the genre and a favorite of Hepburn fans and Grant fans alike, when it opened on February 18 at Radio City Music Hall and other venues around the country, it received mixed reviews and did not do well at the box office. Its first-week gross at the Music Hall totaled a modest $70,000, and it was pulled after a single week, prompting *Variety* to note that "the Katharine Hepburn draw, as expressed in some quarters, isn't what it used to be." The film's total initial domestic gross came to just over $715,000 in the United States, with another $400,000 earned overseas.* It fell far short of Hughes's hopes, and its failure would have serious short-term consequences for everyone involved with the film, including Grant. Hawks's contract called for participation in the profits only when the film grossed $2 million, which it never reached (in theaters), and RKO, despite Hughes's bailout, because of the way his deal was structured, lost $365,000 in unrecouped production costs. Hawks suffered the additional indignity of being permanently removed from *Gunga Din* before RKO out-and-out fired him, citing numerous breaches of his contract. Hughes vigorously objected to the studio's action, accusing it of making Hawks the scapegoat for its financial disarray, and threatened to back Hawks in a major lawsuit. In response, the studio offered Hawks a termination fee of $40,000 to walk, which he reluctantly took because he needed the money.

The film's failure also caused Harry Brandt, who was then president of the Independent Theatre Owners of America — an organization of exhibitors that monitored stars' popularity in terms of how much their films earned — to quite famously point his angry finger at Hepburn and accuse her of being

---

Bringing Up Baby lost $350,000 in its initial domestic theatrical release, according to *Variety*. An American rerelease in 1941 earned it an additional $150,000.

"box office poison." (Far less remembered, amid all the myths surrounding Brandt's "damnation," was the fact that Hepburn had been clustered by him with several other female movie stars, none of whom had had a particularly good year at the box office. The "bottom ten" list, with Hepburn holding the number one spot, also included such "A" stars as Joan Crawford, Greta Garbo, Marlene Dietrich, Kay Francis, and five other lesser names, all to a greater or lesser degree victims of the public's changing taste.)

Pandro Berman's public reaction to Hepburn's humiliation was to express his and the studio's continuing loyalty to her by insisting her career was far from over. Privately, Berman offered her a chance to buy out the remainder of her contract or face termination. Hepburn then forked over $220,000 for the privilege of never making another movie at RKO.

Disappointment in the film's performance added to the insecurity Grant already felt about his acting career. He had no easy explanation for the film's ungraceful flop, an apparent miss so disastrous it would help put an end to the era of screwball comedy. Although he managed to avoid the critical and professional fallout that Hepburn suffered, Grant felt that he had damaged his career making *Bringing Up Baby*. Now more than ever, he believed he would be able to make movies only as long as his face stayed pristine and his waist appealingly slim.

15

"Only one actor was agile enough to fly alongside the young
Katharine Hepburn, and that was Cary Grant. In their great
comedies, *Bringing Up Baby, Holiday,* and *The Philadelphia
Story,* there was merely the perfect effervescence of two of
the screen's greatest actors giving comedy everything they
had, including a genuinely acrobatic intelligence."

—VERLYN KLINKENBORG

Cary Grant began 1938 with a full and happy house: Randolph Scott
was finished making his latest movie and was back at the beach, "the
Brooks" was home from her shoot, and his savings for the first time topped a
million dollars. Despite the failure of *Bringing Up Baby,* he had become a
familiar figure at all the regular show business stops he liked. On any given day
he could be seen taking a long lunch at the Hollywood-Brit contingent's
favorite pub, the Cock and Bull on Sunset, most often sharing a booth with
Howard Hughes, or having dinner at either the Brown Derby on Vine or the
venerable Musso's and Frank's on Hollywood Boulevard, or dancing with the
Brooks to big band music at the Troc deep into the night.

His increased visibility made him more accessible to the press. Whenever
he was asked by reporters about his wealth and fame, in the beginning at least
he tried to display a certain self-effacing if low-key charm, always reminding

whoever wanted to know that he never felt he had traveled all that far from the "brutal borders of poverty" and was always aware of the inherently transient nature of both fame and fortune. What he did try to conceal, without much success, was his slightly paranoid feeling that the government was now trying to rob him of nearly all his hard-earned cash. It was a subject that bothered him, but one he always tried to dismiss with a folksy "money isn't everything" approach.

"Sure," he told a reporter from *Liberty* magazine, "the government gets eighty-one cents out of every dollar I earn. But I'm one of the lucky stiffs who earn a lot of dollars, all with a Grant-marked nineteen cents in them. That's nice going! Now, people will say 'Oh poor So-and-So having to work as an extra! How sad!' What they don't say, perhaps don't remember, is that So-and-So was up there in the chips for a while. He had all that fun and more than the average guy ever gets, and certainly if he's a man at all he's got good memories stored up in him, got good laughs he can laugh over once again."

In reality, money was no laughing matter to Grant. There were those he trusted to help him make it, and others he looked to for ways to keep it. Frank Vincent, his agent, was in charge of making the deals, but Grant did not want him to be spread too thin or lose his focus on that primary function. And he certainly did not trust any of the women he was associated with. Ever since his divorce from Virginia Cherrill, the last thing he ever wanted anybody to know was how much money he really had.

Grant was even wary of Hughes, but for different reasons. He felt he did not know him well enough to take his advice on investments, even if Hughes had been willing to offer any, which he never did. In this poker game Hughes held his cards even closer to his vest than Grant, a quality the actor happened to admire but that also kept him from seeking anything in the way of financial advice. Grant couldn't help notice how often Hughes seemed to lose significant amounts of money on ventures he invested in.

That left Randolph Scott, whose expertise in what many thought were crackpot schemes—his uranium investments, for example—had left him wealthier than ever. Scott continually urged Grant to put his money to work, to let it grow, and not through the tortoise-slow interest the banks offered— and who could trust banks anyway in these uncertain times?—but in the hare-fast profits of bonds and securities. Scott especially loved foreign investments, to which the U.S. government tax collectors' reach was not quite as long. That made sense to Grant, and following Scott's lead, he invested nearly half a million dollars in Philippine-based bonds, believing that within a year that money would double.

It was an investment that would come back to haunt both Scott and Grant and hasten their coming split.

THAT FEBRUARY GRANT WENT BACK to Columbia to star in a new film that reunited him with George Cukor and Katharine Hepburn, all three of whom had worked on *Sylvia Scarlett*. Cohn had been eager to return Grant to the screen in another comedy, but with Irene Dunne playing opposite him. Cohn envisioned the winning couple from *The Awful Truth* in a remake of Philip Barry's 1928 Broadway hit, *Holiday*, which the studio had already filmed once before, in 1930, starring Ann Harding, Robert Ames, and Mary Astor.

Following *Sylvia Scarlett*, Cukor had gone on to direct *Camille* at MGM, starring the already-legendary Greta Garbo, the young and handsome Robert Taylor, and the venerable screen icon Lionel Barrymore. *Camille* confirmed Cukor's reputation as a "woman's director," both in his handling of difficult movie stars and in the huge appeal his films usually had to female audiences. He was still under contract to Selznick International Pictures (SIP), in anticipation of his directing the much-delayed film version of *Gone With the Wind*, waiting for production on the film version of the popular novel to begin. Two years had passed since *Camille*, during which time Cukor had turned down several plum SIP assignments, including 1937's *A Star Is Born*, which starred Fredric March and Janet Gaynor and won an Oscar for Best Screenplay for William Wellman and Robert Carson, and nominations for Selznick (Best Picture), William Wellman (Best Director), and both March and Gaynor. The other big picture Cukor turned down was 1938's *The Adventures of Tom Sawyer*, directed by Norman Taurog (although some uncredited scenes were in fact directed by Cukor as a personal favor to Selznick, who was dissatisfied with Taurog's work).

Early in 1938, when Cohn approached Selznick about the possibility of borrowing Cukor, Selznick quickly agreed. So far that year SIP had paid Cukor $155,000 for his services just for the month of January for some preliminary *Wind* research and location scouting in the South. That was why Selznick, who was always strapped for cash, agreed to loan Cukor to Cohn at the rate of $10,000 a week, to be split evenly, according to the terms of Cukor's contract, between the director and SIP.

While Cohn was delighted to have snagged Cukor, his glee was dampened when Cukor flat-out rejected doing another Grant/Dunne film, telling Cohn it felt too much like a sequel to McCarey's *The Awful Truth*, something he felt doing would be beneath his current level of success. He insisted on using Hepburn, telling Cohn he would not work with any other female star.

Cukor had his reasons for wanting Hepburn. For one thing, she was his first choice to play Scarlett O'Hara, something he was having trouble selling to Selznick, who didn't think she had the looks, the talent, or perhaps most important, the box office clout to merit the world's most coveted film role. Hepburn offered to take a relatively small salary of $80,000 for the role, but Selznick remained unconvinced. Instead, to cover all bets, he signed her to a $1,500-a-week option on her services for the film. This convinced Hepburn she was going to get the part, and because of it she delayed her stage production of *The Philadelphia Story*, a project she had commissioned from the same Philip Barry who had written the stage version of *Holiday*, using Howard Hughes's money to do so.*

Once he heard that Hepburn was in contention to play Scarlett, Cohn changed his tune and allowed Cukor to cast Hepburn and signed her at what he thought was a bargain payout to Selznick, unaware that Hepburn was already in the process of buying herself out of her deal with SIP. Had he played harder ball, Cohn would likely have gotten Hepburn for nothing. Instead, he happily paid her several thousand unnecessary dollars.

As for Dunne, when Cohn informed her she was not going to be in the picture he had supposedly promised her, she reportedly stayed home and cried the entire weekend. Despite having been nominated for Oscars in each of the previous two years (for Richard Boleslawski's *Theodora Goes Wild* in 1936 and *The Awful Truth* in 1937), she was summarily dismissed, at Cukor's

---

*Hughes actually put up 25 percent of the financing for the initial stage production, which came to approximately $100,000. The deal also included the film rights, which, at Hepburn's insistence, remained in her control.

insistence, for his favorite actress and close friend, the far less popular Hepburn.

THE PLOT OF *HOLIDAY* reprises the best element of *The Awful Truth*—the two protagonists' reluctance to admit the existence and ultimate power of mutual love—and its atmosphere anticipates the peculiar charm of *The Philadelphia Story*, with its eventual switching of partners that leads them to the big dance. Also like *The Philadelphia Story* would have, *Holiday* has a well-polished veneer that gives its dark tale of sibling rivalry an appealing sophistication—what Cukor's biographer Patrick McGilligan defined as playwright Barry's stock-in-trade "see-saw of wit and despair."

The screenplay adaptation was done by Sidney Buchman, a Columbia contract writer, and Donald Ogden Stewart, who had starred in the original Broadway production as Ned Seton, the alcoholic son of the Seton family, and whom Cohn wanted for the movie until Cukor said no. The director preferred Robert Benchley, the popular middle-aged humorist. The role eventually went to Lew Ayres, the star of Lewis Milestone's 1930 Oscar-winning Best Picture, *All Quiet on the Western Front*.

For the key role of Johnny Case, the fiancé of the rich and spoiled Julia Seton (played in the movie by Doris Nolan), Cukor's first choice remained Cary Grant.

SHOOTING ON *HOLIDAY* had begun on February 28, the same day *Bringing Up Baby* was released, and a week after the Academy Award nominations for the previous year were announced. *The Awful Truth* was nominated for Best Picture, Best Actress (Irene Dunne), Best Supporting Actor (Ralph Bellamy), Best Film Editing (Al Clark), and Best Director (Leo McCarey, who would become the only Oscar winner of the group). Conspicuously missing from the list was the name Cary Grant.

Despite his not being nominated, Grant, at Cohn's insistence, attended the Awards ceremony. At the time the Oscars were still little more than an industry banquet, held that year at the Biltmore Bowl of the Biltmore Hotel in downtown Los Angeles. The coolness Grant felt toward him that night was palpable. A large majority of the Academy's executive members still harbored a grudge against him for having successfully broken the hitherto ironclad contract system.

Even at this very early stage, Grant had few supporters in Hollywood. Most actors were unnerved by the thought of existing without a studio contract, and creatively those like McCarey had no professional reason to try to improve relations with him. In truth, with the exception of fellow rebels like Howard Hughes, very few wanted to openly align themselves with Grant on any issue. In his acceptance speech, McCarey, still annoyed with the actor and smarting over his firing by Zukor for *Make Way for Tomorrow*'s box office fizzle, was greeted warmly by the studio-studded audience. After being handed his Oscar, he said, "Thanks, but you gave it to me for the wrong picture."

Grant said nothing as the audience cheered and applauded, the smile on his face as stiff as the tails of his tuxedo.

HOLIDAY OPENED ON June 15, 1938, and proved a critical and commercial failure. If *Bringing Up Baby* suffered from a lack of character depth, *Holiday*'s problem was its excess. Talky, insular, cranky, and only spottily sublime— Cary Grant's somersaults are a metaphor for his shifting romantic focus from Julia to Linda—the film was less screwball than three-fingered curve ball, slow, steady, with a decided dip in delivery. *Holiday*'s end-of-the-world-so-let's-party message celebrating the nonmaterial joys of life was one of Hollywood's favorite Thirties "messages": the rich are unhappily trapped by their wealth, while the poor are free to love. But this message left late-Depression audiences more puzzled than charmed, and they were not at all charmed by Hepburn's strident throwback-style performance as Linda, Julia's somewhat cynical sister, whose role is to help Johnny (and the audience) come to the realization that in cynical families, the true cynic is the only romantic.

The reviews for *Holiday* were mixed. *The New York Times* noted that "Hepburn's intensity is apt to grate on a man, even on so sanguine a temperament as Cary Grant's Johnny Case." Otis Ferguson's *New Republic* review called the film "mechanical" and "shrill" and advised audiences to "save your money and yawn at home"—advice they heeded.

Cohn had come up with the tag line for the advertisements—"Is it true what they say about Hepburn—that she's Box Office Poison?"—and a more misguided sell would be hard to find. *Holiday* also proved a major factor not only in costing Hepburn the role of Scarlett in *Gone With the Wind* but in driving her once again out of Hollywood. After the picture's poor showing, she returned to the Broadway stage, where with Hughes's help she finally mounted *The Philadelphia Story* and set about to try once again to resurrect her moribund career.

On a more positive note, for Cary Grant, in every way except financially, *Holiday* was a personal triumph. He liked the film's downbeat romance (more realistic to him than the lunatic look at love in both *The Awful Truth* and *Bringing Up Baby*) and especially the fact that Johnny, as written, is something of a ruthless heartbreaker (miserable and conniving, according to McGilligan) whose darker desires and impulses are masked by the charm of his somersaulting wit. The way Grant played him he was indeed a "case," but a likable one.

Nonetheless, *Holiday* did nothing to alleviate Grant's fear that, despite his winning performance, he had somehow lost the upward momentum of his career. Like *Bringing Up Baby*, it was a financial flop, his second in a row after the spectacular success of *The Awful Truth*, and significantly, he had no one to blame for being in those films but himself, having chosen them as the free-lancer he wanted to be. While he himself had made out well, the hard fact was that his first two films for RKO and Columbia respectively had lost money for the studios. His personal fan mail now ran in the thousands every week, but he still could not sleep at night worrying about how long he could remain an employable actor in a town where the studios greeted his name with hostility rather than awards.

On June 27, just twelve days after *Holiday*'s dismal opening, Grant began working on *Gunga Din*. Even though Hawks had been fired from the production, Grant had no hesitation in signing on to what was now a George Stevens movie, seeing it strictly as a matter of survival—his own. Although Grant had never worked with Stevens, he had met him socially while making *Bringing Up Baby*—Hepburn had introduced them one night over dinner at a Hollywood restaurant—and Grant liked him. Another reason he wanted to appear in the two-hour "adaptation" of Kipling's epic poem glorifying British imperialism was his desire to work with Douglas Fairbanks Jr., whom he had personally approached to be in the film, and the hugely popular Victor McLaglen, who had won an Oscar in 1935 for his performance in John Ford's *The Informer*. Grant wanted an ensemble male cast for the film so that if it failed, there would be plenty of "glory" for everyone to go down in.

It is difficult to discern what, if anything, remained of Hawks's original concept for the film in Stevens's version of *Gunga Din*, which today looks like nothing so much as a glorified Saturday-morning TV action serial. One reason is the lack of women. Except for the barest of subplots involving Joan Fontaine and Ann Evers, there is an almost total absence of love interest in the film, replaced by the romance of war and the hard-to-avoid erotic Three Musketeers style of male bonding common to "buddy" action adventure films.

Gunga Din is one of the very few films in which Grant appears in a military uniform, and the only one in which he actually engages in hand-to-hand combat. The film was, for all intents and purposes, a thinly veiled attack on Hitler's Nazi war machine—the Fuehrer is represented in the film by Eduardo Ciannelli's evil Guru, leader of a malignant cult bent on wiping out the British forces. Even as *Gunga Din* was in production, Hitler was threatening England with mass invasion (and its leader, Winston Churchill, with swift execution). But Pearl Harbor was still more than three years away, and Hollywood, like the rest of the country, remained severely divided about whether America should enter the war. Grant, a British citizen whose politics today would be described as liberal, was always careful to keep his views to himself and may not have immediately seen the parallels between the soldiers in *Gunga Din* and the plight of the British people. (The film was not shown in England until 1946, after World War II ended.)* But while the British were building up their military, drafting anyone who wasn't wheelchair-bound, serving His Majesty in any way but on the screen was not something Grant was particularly eager to do. There were those who even

---

*Sometimes attributed to the interruption of wartime film distribution rather than government censorship.

suspected that Grant—like many other members of the unusually silent Beverly Hills colony of British acting expatriates, including Sir Cedric Hardwicke, David Niven, Merle Oberon, Christopher Isherwood, Ray Milland, Sir C. Aubrey Smith, and Boris Karloff—had so deeply entrenched himself in Hollywood's elite celebrity society that he did not want to give up his life of luxury to return home to go to war.

Angry articles began appearing in the British press that those actors who chose to stay in America to avoid conscription should be considered traitors. In some cases the accusations were uncalled for—many expat Malibu Brits were simply too old for military service. But, among those who were not, only David Niven (five years older than Grant) voluntarily chose to give up his Hollywood life and career—he joined the British army in 1939, when England formally declared war against the Axis forces.* The decision would take him away from Hollywood for six years and cost him untold millions in earnings. Grant was not eager to follow in Niven's footsteps, and that summer he quietly reactivated his lapsed application to become an American citizen.

Grant was not acting out of unfounded fear or paranoia. Earlier that year the British government had begun requesting his return and may have enlisted the assistance of the FBI to get him to come home (presumably to put on a uniform). Even before the completion of *Gunga Din*, which took 114 days to shoot, twice as long as originally scheduled, at a cost of nearly $2 million that made it the most expensive movie RKO had ever made, Grant had begun an elaborate chess game with the American and British governments to win the right to legally remain in the United States.

IN THE SUMMER OF 1938 America's attention was temporarily diverted from the gathering storm in Europe by Howard Hughes's around-the-world solo flight, a high-risk venture that nearly cost him his life. Upon his touchdown

---

*Although Leslie Howard was another Brit who made American movies and voluntarily returned to England to take part in the war, he was never considered a full-time Hollywood resident, spending as much time in America on Broadway as he did in the movies, and he particularly detested both the film *Gone With the Wind* and his role in it. His designated service in England during World War II was to star, direct, and produce anti-Nazi propaganda films. Howard was killed when his plane was mistaken for one carrying Churchill and was shot down in 1943 by the Germans.

in Pennsylvania on July 14, the free world celebrated, seeing his achievement at least in part as a demonstration of American strength, endurance, ingenuity, and commitment. A ticker-tape parade down Wall Street for Hughes was scheduled by New York's mayor, Fiorello La Guardia, and Grant, whom Hughes had invited to see it in person, received permission from Stevens to be absent from the set of *Gunga Din* for two days.

After celebrating privately in New York with Hughes following the parade, Grant flew directly to Lone Pine, California, the largest outdoor studio location site, where many of *Gunga Din*'s exteriors were being shot. Observers recalled that Grant appeared uneasy, distracted, and, according to at least one, openly worried. Less than a week later he asked Stevens for permission to return to New York, and again Stevens let him go.

A month later, still in Manhattan, Grant was invited by David O. Selznick to a private party at "21" to meet Alfred Hitchcock, who had specifically requested an audience with the one Hollywood actor he most wanted to meet. It was the director's first visit to America, and for the occasion Selznick threw a black-tie gala in his honor at the "21" club.

Grant asked Jean Rogers to accompany him, as he was no longer involved with Phyllis Brooks. That past May, just prior to the onset of production on *Gunga Din*, Grant had actually proposed to the actress, but only a few weeks later he called it off because, he told her, he "just couldn't go through with it." Both the engagement and the "disengagement" to Brooks made the gossip columns, and despite many requests, Grant refused to talk to the press about the situation. That did not stop Brooks from confiding to Louella Parsons that as far as she was concerned, the breakup, as she termed it, was caused by the difficulties of their separate show business careers.

That summer Brooks moved permanently to New York City, where she appeared in a series of Broadway plays and musicals. She did not hear from Grant all the time he was in Manhattan with Rogers.

SELZNICK HAD HAD HIS EYE on the already-legendary British director for several years, waiting for the right moment to make his move. *Murder!* (1930), *The Man Who Knew Too Much* (1934), *The 39 Steps* (1935), and *Sabotage* (1936) were among the relatively few foreign films to successfully cross the Atlantic and find a popular American audience. While Hollywood films continued to dominate Great Britain, few British movies other than Hitchcock's had made any significant box office breakthrough in the States. In truth, the rotund and reticent director was better known to Americans than many of the British actors and actresses who appeared in his films.

Hitchcock had his reasons for wanting to relocate to the States. Gaumont-British, headed by Michael Balcon, the film company for which he had made his most successful films, was about to go under, symptomatic of the disarray into which the entire British film industry had fallen, due primarily to the political and economic uncertainties brought about by the war. Hitchcock wanted to continue to make movies, even if it meant moving to Hollywood to do so.

At age thirty-five, young David O. Selznick was one of the most powerful independent filmmakers in Hollywood, an impressive accomplishment in the era of studio domination. After his father went bankrupt in 1923 trying to establish himself as an independent in the film business, Selznick went to work as a story editor for MGM. With great speed he moved from MGM to Paramount, working as an associate producer on a number of successful movies. In 1931 RKO made him vice president in charge of production, where he supervised some of that studio's finest movies, including Cukor's *A Bill of Divorcement* (1932) and *What Price Hollywood?* (1932), and Merian C. Cooper's classic *King Kong* (1933), the success of which firmly established Selznick as a major Hollywood power player. That same year, when young Irving Thalberg fell ill, Louis B. Mayer offered Selznick a substantial raise to return to MGM to help oversee the studio's production schedule. During the next four years Selznick ran shotgun over Cukor's *Dinner at Eight* (1933) and *David Copperfield* (1935), Clarence Brown's *Anna Karenina* (1935), and several other notable films. In 1936, when a still-frail Thalberg insisted he was well enough to return full time to the studio, rather than engage in a power struggle, Selznick resigned his position at MGM and set up his own independent production house, Selznick International Pictures.

Selznick first made overtures to Hitchcock in 1938, looking to sign the director to an exclusive services contract. Other studios were interested in Hitchcock as well, particularly RKO and MGM; the latter had made an offer to Hitchcock that would allow him to remain in London and produce four movies in two years at a set fee of $150,000, with completion bonuses built in for timely delivery. Selznick then got down to serious business. He maneuvered the Selznick-Joyce Agency, a successful house partnered by his brother Myron and Frank Joyce, to sign on as the director's American representatives. Myron then deftly rejected all other offers while David O. set up an elaborate wine-and-dine whirlwind campaign that included, on August 23, the private party at "21" where, as he promised he would, Selznick delivered Cary Grant to the feet of Alfred Hitchcock.

Film critic and historian Molly Haskell has astutely observed, "One of the marks of a great director is the ability to capture the side of an actor that has remained hidden, and Hitchcock was a genius at exposing the neurotic underside of a star's image." Indeed. To the rest of the world, Cary Grant had become what Leo McCarey had made him into and Howard Hawks had finessed: Hollywood's most sophisticated, urbane leading man, at once romantic and humorous; romantic *because* he was humorous.

To Hitchcock, however, Grant was something else again, something or *someone* the others had missed, or gotten wrong, precisely because they had been too easily seduced by his physical beauty and agile manner. Hitchcock's greatest cinematic achievement was his ability to take the interior subtext of a character and project it as his visible exterior, to show his subconscious desires by conscious behavior, to make visible the parts of a character's emotional clock that make him tick. Meeting Grant that night Hitchcock confirmed his long-held belief that no one had as yet "gotten" him. One look was all he needed to imagine what it would be like to see his twisted repressed inner self projected onto the screen in the tall, dark, and handsome body of Cary Grant, by having Grant play a romantic character who behaved as if his inner self was, like Hitchcock, repressively short, fat, and bald.

THE NEXT DAY GRANT sent Rogers to Los Angeles while he flew directly back to the set of *Gunga Din*, to begin what would turn into another six weeks of shooting. He planned to follow this picture with one by Hawks, to whom he felt he owed a film after appearing in *Gunga Din*. Grant had scheduled a six-week break between the end of one film and the start of the next and was looking forward to the time off.

In November, however, only one day after *Gunga Din* wrapped, Grant received official notification from the U.S. Attorney General that he was under investigation for his involvement in a million-dollar Philippine bond fraud. Shocked and confused, and before he had a chance to sort out exactly what was going on, he received another, stranger notice, ordering him to pack his bags immediately and book a flight for himself to London. Even as the American authorities were investigating him, the British government was summoning him for a top-secret security meeting "of the highest priority." His trip, he was informed, had been cleared by the FBI.

In London, after checking into his hotel, he went directly to the headquarters of the British military, where he was submitted to intense questioning for several days about his intentions, if any, to aid the war effort. Afterward, he was taken before senior British security coordinator Sir William Stephenson, who, he assumed, was going to forcibly conscript him right then and there. Instead, Sir William shocked him by urging him to return as soon as possible to the United States, where he would be far more useful if he kept his eyes and ears open and turned in anyone in his Hollywood circle whom he suspected of spying for the Nazis. During the meeting Lord Stephenson introduced Grant to Lord Lothian, the British ambassador to the United States, who also stressed the importance of Grant's immediately returning to Hollywood, where he could best serve His Majesty.

Instead, he went directly to Bristol to visit his mother. He had not seen Elsie in three years, and as long as he was in England, he decided to drive to the family home, where, to his dismay, his mother did not seem to recognize him. She called him Cary instead of Archie and treated him as if he were a visiting American celebrity. After a few days, he told her it was time for him to return to America. What he didn't tell her was that he had just received official notification from J. Edgar Hoover, the head of the FBI, informing him that he was not on vacation and that his presence was immediately required in Washington, D.C. The seesaw had resumed.

Rather than flying back, Grant booked passage aboard the *Normandie*, deliberately taking as much time as possible. He eventually did meet with Hoover, but unfortunately, according to the Bureau, the details of that meeting, along with the secret file Hoover kept on Grant, were either lost or (more likely) destroyed.

Back in Washington, he met up with Scott, both of whom were now scheduled to answer their subpoenas in the Philippine bond fraud case on December 11. On that day, Grant and Scott gave separate sworn testimony about everything they knew in the matter. During his interrogation, Grant vehemently denied any knowledge of or involvement with one William P. Buckner Jr., the alleged mastermind of the investment scheme, who, as it happened, was at that very moment being held in London for attempting to illegally launder large sums of cash.

The case took an even more bizarre turn when Buckner turned out to be the husband of movie actress Loretta Young, Grant's costar in *Born to Be Bad*. Grant and Young had become good friends and maintained a casual but ongoing friendship. While he admitted this to the authorities, he maintained that he had never met, or for that matter even heard of, Buckner.*

At this point Grant appeared to be in for it; at the very least he would have to testify in open court about his involvement in a major fraud case. But after making a single statement to the press as he stood on the steps of the Justice Department building, in which he declared that he was only a victim and that the photographers should take "the picture of another sucker," Grant was never called upon again, in any capacity, regarding the investigation. Nor was Randolph Scott. Any and all interest by the U.S. government in the two suddenly evaporated, and both were allowed to return to Hollywood.

Scott was relieved. Grant was furious. On a personal level, as far as he was concerned, the whole embarrassing episode was Scott's fault, and it put the final nail in the coffin of their relationship, already shaky even before this latest disastrous turn of seemingly unrelated events — whose connective tissue would in due time be all too clear to Grant.

There was, however, another factor that convinced Grant he and Scott were through. On his return trip to the States aboard the *Normandie*, Grant met the woman who was soon to be the second Mrs. Cary Grant.

---

*Other Philippine bond investors who were subpoenaed and denied any knowledge of either Buckner or his scheme included Bing Crosby and producer Joseph Schenck. Ronald Colman, through his attorney, admitted having known Buckner, and being approached by him, but had never invested in Philippine bonds.

16

"If you haven't seen Cary Grant, Jean Arthur, and Rita
Hayworth in Howard Hawks's romantic and exciting 1939
South American flying drama, *Only Angels Have Wings,*
you have not experienced one of the most vibrant, resonant,
and deeply entertaining movies ever made."

—PETER BOGDANOVICH

One evening while crossing the Atlantic aboard the *Normandie,* Cary
Grant was invited to have dinner at the captain's table, where he was
formally introduced to the Countess Haugwitz-Reventlow, also known as
Barbara Hutton, heir to the vast Woolworth fortune that had made her one of
the wealthiest women in the world. Grant was delighted during the dinner
when Hutton complimented him on his performance in *Holiday,* a film she
had just seen at the Venice Film Festival. He smiled politely, thanked her, finished his meal, and excused himself from the table.

Just before he went to bed, he placed a phone call to, of all people, Phyllis
Brooks and asked her to meet him at the pier when he disembarked. She was
surprised and delighted to hear from him. He said he wanted to see her once
more, before he had to be in Washington, D.C., to give testimony in the
Philippine bond fraud case.

Grant resumed seeing "the Brooks" and continued to send her mixed
messages about his intentions. One week he would want to end everything

for good; the next he was having prenuptial papers drawn up and asking her what type of ring she would like to wear as Mrs. Grant. Not surprisingly, his ambivalence toward Brooks made her a nervous wreck, so much so that on at least one occasion she was admitted to a hospital for "observation." Not long after she was released, Brooks gave a long, rambling interview to Louella Parsons, in which she detailed the difficulties of trying to have a romantic relationship with Grant. Parsons then printed a series of openly hostile columns aimed squarely at the actor, in which she hinted at her longstanding suspicions of his homosexuality, overlaid with what she considered his "extremely unfair" treatment of Brooks.

In retaliation, Grant did something most actors would have been afraid to do (or were specifically barred from doing by studio contract). He sued Parsons for slander, ending, at least for the moment, her constant and increasingly unbridled personal attacks on him.[*]

GUNGA DIN OPENED February 17, 1939, and was a box office winner from day one—it would go on to become the highest-grossing film that RKO had yet released. The heart of its appeal was later described by Pauline Kael, who called it "one of the most enjoyable nonsense-adventure movies of all time." Even with a severely curtailed foreign market due to the outbreak of war, the film managed to gross an astounding $3.8 million, twice its total production cost. It outgrossed all the other major Hollywood films released in 1939 except one—a year that many critics and film historians judge to be the greatest single year in the history of the movies. Among the films released in 1939 include Victor Fleming's one-two combination, *Gone With the Wind* and *The Wizard of Oz*, Ernst Lubitsch's *Ninotchka*, Sam Wood's British-made *Goodbye, Mr. Chips*, Frank Capra's *Mr. Smith Goes to Washington*, Edmund Goulding's *Dark Victory*, Leo McCarey's *Love Affair*, Lewis Milestone's version of John Steinbeck's *Of Mice and Men*, John Ford's *Stagecoach*, and William Wyler's *Wuthering Heights*.[†]

---

[*]The case was eventually settled out of court, the terms of which are unknown.

[†]These are box office comparisons for the year 1939 alone. *Gunga Din* opened in February, while *Gone With the Wind* opened in December. Eventually, *GWTW* would outgross *Gunga Din*.

The only film that made more money that year was Henry King's *Jesse James*, starring Henry Fonda in the title role and costarring Randolph Scott as U.S. Marshal Will Wright.

Not long afterward Grant began filming Hawks's *Only Angels Have Wings*, in which he was paired with Jean Arthur, coming off her highly praised performance in Frank Capra's *Mr. Smith Goes to Washington*. Grant would have much preferred to star in Hitchcock's second American film, *Foreign Correspondent*, an independent feature made for producer Walter Wanger.* Hitchcock had wanted Grant to be in the film as well, but couldn't get Cohn to postpone production of *Only Angels Have Wings*.†

In *Angels* Grant played a Lindbergh-like character combined with a real-life flier whom Hawks had known, who had once parachuted from a burning plane, and whose copilot died in the ensuing crash, after which his fellow fliers shunned him for the rest of his life. Hawks set his film in the Andes and made his heroes daredevil fliers who delivered freight cargo. Geoff Carter (Grant), the operator of one such high-danger operation, gets caught off guard in the middle of his romance with showgirl Bonnie Lee (Jean Arthur) by the surprise reappearance of his ex-wife, Judy (Rita Hayworth, in the role that made her a star), married now to Bat MacPherson (Richard Barthelmess).

Once more Grant's personal dictum of not chasing women became an integral part of his character, as he and Hawks transformed Carter's "stoicism" into a metaphor for the very type of reserved, nonswaggering macho heroism that young American servicemen would need after America's coming entry into World War II, so much so that the film's signature line of dialogue, "Where's Joe," would serve as a catchphrase for the wives and mothers of a

---

*Hitchcock had signed a seven-year multiple-film deal with Selznick. Upon completing *Rebecca*, the director was eager to stay in America, fearful of the worsening war situation back home. To keep him happy and occupied, Selznick agreed to a one-picture loan-out to Wanger, which would allow Selznick to continue to put all his energies into *Rebecca* and, more important to him, *Gone With the Wind*. In addition, Selznick was strapped for cash due to heavy gambling debts. Having Wanger make a picture with Hitchcock, in which Selznick would own a piece but have to put up no money, was the kind of deal he couldn't turn down.

†The lead in *Foreign Correspondent* eventually went to Joel McCrea, after Hitchcock tried unsuccessfully to get Cary Grant, then Clark Gable and Gary Cooper. Years later, Hitchcock said this about the casting of *Foreign Correspondent*: "I would have liked to have had bigger names . . . I always ended up with the next best—in this instance with Joel McCrea." The Hitchcock quote is from Spoto, *The Dark Side of Genius*, 239.

generation of wartime G.I. Joes. As Peter Bogdanovich rightly points out, this picture transformed Grant from light comedy into the front ranks of Hollywood leading he-men, the first successful action film in which he got the girl — or rather, the girl got him.

The film finished shooting on April 29, 1939, and was rush-released into theaters by Cohn, in need of fresh box office income, barely two weeks later. It became another hit for Grant and helped confirm his reputation as a star who could open "big" — the picture debuted in New York's Radio City Music Hall the same week the World's Fair opened and still managed a whopping $143,000 in its first ten days.

Finally, *Only Angels Have Wings* is notable for its place in pop culture as the one that gave impressionists the world over their famous multisyllabic, progressively louder "Jee-u-dee, JEE-U-DEE, *JEE-U-DEE!*" that stands to this day as the mandatory Cary Grant impersonation. Forever after, Grant good-naturedly pointed out to the end of his days that he never actually said "Jee-u-dee, JEE-U-DEE, *JEE-U-DEE!*"*

TAKING BARELY A MOMENT to breathe, Grant now shuttled back to RKO to begin *In Name Only*, a film originally planned as his fourth pairing with Katharine Hepburn. But Hepburn had since severed her ties with the studio and moved to New York to appear on Broadway in *The Philadelphia Story*. The role went instead to Carole Lombard, who had appeared once before with Grant in *Sinners in the Sun* in 1932, before both became big stars.

Lombard was now at the peak of her popularity, coming off a string of hit movies that had elevated her to the highest ranks of stardom and also exhausted her. She was not all that anxious to make *In Name Only*, having just married Clark Gable, with whom she had vowed to spend as much time as possible. She finally agreed to do the picture after Pandro Berman built it into a four-picture deal at the then-astonishing fee of $150,000 per picture,

---

*Grant recorded a promo for the Lux Radio Theater version of *Only Angels Have Wings* in which he actually did say, "Jee-u-dee, JEE-U-DEE, *JEE-U-DEE.*" Nevertheless, years later Grant told *Variety* that "I've looked at all my films and soundtracks and never said it. I never even worked with Judy [Garland]. I think it began with [comic] Larry Storch's imitation, and everyone else copied it, like 'You dirty rat' imitations of Cagney."

plus profit percentages, and top billing in the film's credits and advertising. When Grant heard about this, he angrily vowed not to appear in the movie. Berman, through Frank Vincent, then agreed to raise Grant's base fee to $100,000 but refused to give away any more percentages and could not get Lombard to budge on her top billing. After much waffling, Grant, at Vincent's urging, reluctantly agreed to go ahead with the film.

In Name Only was directed by John Cromwell, coming off his hit movie *Made for Each Other*, which he had made earlier that year for Selznick International Pictures, with Lombard and James Stewart in the starring roles. Cromwell was a veteran utility director with a dozen years under his belt, the highlight of which was *Of Human Bondage* (1934) with Bette Davis. Lombard liked Cromwell, and to accommodate her, Berman hired him to direct *In Name Only*, the type of melodrama known in its day as a "woman's picture."

A three-star vehicle for the story of a romantic triangle (Lombard, Grant, and Kay Francis), the film surprised and disappointed audiences expecting something a little less heavy from Grant and Lombard, who had, between them, made some of the fastest and funniest movies of the 1930s. Nonetheless, the film proved enough of a commercial hit to satisfy RKO. As for Grant, he remained totally indifferent to all aspects of the project except its hefty paycheck.

THAT FALL ENGLAND FORMALLY entered the war, and Grant moved once more to extend his U.S. residency. Having immersed himself in making three films in a row, he was also ready to move onto a more personal battlefield and deal with Randolph Scott.

Ironically, it was Scott who made the first official move toward the endgame. Telephoning Grant from the new location set he was on, Scott grimly asked for a powwow, and a few days later he flew to have dinner with Grant at the Brown Derby to discuss their relationship. It was a long, diffi-cult, and emotional evening, during which they hugged, cried, laughed, and agreed it was time for both of them to move on. Afterward they drove back to the beach in separate cars, walked together barefoot in the wet, cool sand, reminisced about the good times, and vowed to remain friends forever.

Forever turned out to be a week. The next Friday was when Grant and Scott had their most serious argument, one that friends insisted was the real breakup. In the end, for all their declarations of friendship and loyalty, it all came down to property. "They both wanted the beach house, that was the thing that broke them up for good," said one who was close to the situation. According to the agreement they had made when they moved in, the one who married first—Grant—was to surrender the house. Scott now insisted Grant honor this promise. Besides, he said, he had been the one who originally found the place, and most of the furniture belonged to him. None of that mattered to Grant, who told Scott in no uncertain terms that he was not giving up the place. To avoid going to court, which Grant threatened to do, Scott, who feared his career would suffer from a public trial more than his former lover's, reluctantly agreed to move out of the house.

THE FIRST WEEKS ALONE at the beach were difficult ones for Grant. With Brooks off on another shoot, he rattled around by himself, sitting for long periods of time in the one chair Scott had left behind for the living room, going for a swim by himself in the morning, having a cup of tea in the late afternoon, alone and completely miserable. He had not realized he was going to miss Scott as much as he did, and on more than one occasion thought of calling and begging him to move back, until Vincent called and asked Grant, as a personal favor, to allow Frederick Brisson, Vincent's agency's London representative visiting L.A., to stay at the beach house.

At first Grant believed Vincent might be trying to fix him up, and when he asked him if that was the case Vincent told him not to worry, that Brisson wasn't gay. In fact, Vincent *was* trying to play Cupid—by pairing Brisson not with Grant but with Rosalind Russell, Grant's costar in his next scheduled film, *His Girl Friday*, Howard Hawks's version of the 1928 Ben Hecht/Charles MacArthur stage hit *The Front Page*, about the goings-on inside a big city newsroom. Brisson had seen Russell in the movie version of *The Women* and had fallen hard for her. When Vincent found out she was going to costar with Grant, he started the wheels rolling.

While waiting for production on *His Girl Friday* to begin, Grant, Sir Cedric Hardwicke, and Laurence Olivier were all summoned to Washington,

D.C. The notice Grant received gave him the shivers. As part of the British colony of actors in Hollywood, he, along with dozens of others, had recently signed a public statement supporting the Allies and denouncing the Nazis. The idea had come from Hardwicke, after stepped-up rumblings from the British government were heard all the way in the canyons of Beverly Hills, that those Hollywood Brits who didn't return home to help the war effort could be considered deserters.

In Washington, at a meeting with British ambassador Lord Lothian, all three were sternly warned that their statement had come dangerously close to violating the United States' Neutrality Act, and that they should cease taking political sides. They were there to observe, not to be observed. Grant agreed, as did Hardwicke, but Olivier, sensing darker meanings in the ambassador's message, left the meeting, immediately called his wife, Vivien Leigh, and told her to have all their things packed by the time he returned to Los Angeles. Within a week they were both back in London. Not long afterward Noël Coward, another British entertainer living in Los Angeles, returned home. One by one the most notable British names in Hollywood announced their voluntary departure for their homeland, loudly declaring in the press as they did so their unfailing sense of loyalty. Many of those who stayed continued to openly take sides. Charlie Chaplin, whose 1940 film *The Great Dictator* clearly violated the Neutrality Act by directly attacking Hitler, faced the possibility of criminal charges from two countries.

Grant, unlike his idol, wanted no part of any more political statements and was eager to begin work on *His Girl Friday*, believing a harmless comedy could not possibly get him into trouble with anybody. Back at the beach he held a preproduction meeting with Russell and learned for the first time that while he had been away in Washington, she had broken up with her boyfriend, actor Jimmy Stewart, and had started seeing Brisson.

A year later, in October 1941, Grant would be the best man at their wedding.

17

"Cukor's strategy was to keep Cary Grant close to his actual self: charming but exasperating, a mite empty at the heart."

—PATRICK McGILLIGAN

By the time *His Girl Friday* was released on January 18, 1940, to great reviews and tremendous box office, Cary Grant had all but disappeared from Hollywood's glittery nighttime social scene. Following his acrimonious split from Scott, he had reverted to his hermit ways, spending most of his time alone at the beach, and rarely visiting the new house he had rented for himself in Beverly Hills.* He went out only for meals and had most of them alone, at Chasen's, in a red banquette in the rear, or at the Beverly Hills Hotel, or very occasionally at the Brown Derby, until he had to give that place up because of the relentless autograph-seekers. Everyone, it seemed to him, wanted his autograph, even if it were scribbled on a wet napkin, and he had come to resent it. He even went so far as to complain about what he called the "absurd practice" to Louella Parsons, with whom he had reconciled, and who continued to write about him, although in less sensationalistic ways, this time using one of her columns to put the world on notice

---

*The house was located at 10050 Cielo Drive. Years later, after having been rebuilt several times, the address would become the site of the 1969 Sharon Tate murders, done at the directive of Charles Manson. Through the years, completely unfounded rumors have confused the addresses and the eras, at times placing Grant there, earlier in the day of the grisly slaughters, for a sexual rendezvous with Tate's houseboy.

that should they be lucky enough to see Cary Grant in person, they should not dare to ask for his autograph.

A few months later Grant agreed to make the actual long-awaited follow-up to *The Awful Truth*, costarring Irene Dunne and directed by Leo McCarey. *My Favorite Wife* instantly became one of the most anticipated productions of the year—until McCarey got drunk and totaled his car in a collision on Sunset Boulevard that nearly killed him and caused RKO to consider canceling the film. McCarey recovered enough to supervise the production, with Garson Kanin taking over as director.

In *My Favorite Wife*, Nick (Cary Grant), whose wife Ellen (Dunne) has disappeared in a shipwreck, waits the mandatory seven years before going to court to have her declared legally dead so he can marry the new woman in his life, Bianca (Gail Patrick). Nick loves Bianca, but not with the same passion he did Ellen. She will, he believes, be an excellent replacement mother for his two young children. Just as Nick remarries, Ellen is miraculously rescued from the deserted island where she has been living and shows up, only to discover she has been declared officially dead and Nick has a new wife. To complicate things further, Nick discovers that Ellen survived on that deserted island with a hunky partner (played by, of all people, Randolph Scott). All of this gets sorted out in the last reel to everyone's satisfaction, and along the way some genuine laughs are dealt. But the real-life tension and chemistry between Grant and Scott supplied the vibrancy. As they vie for the affections of Irene Dunne, they priss and preen at each other, competitively show off their bodies, and then all but ride off into the sunset together.

By now Grant was arguably the biggest male star in Hollywood, while Scott was still essentially a B movie actor, and it was generally believed that Grant had done Scott a favor by arranging for him to appear in this film. In truth, Grant did it simply because he missed Scott and wanted to see him. During filming the two reportedly spent several nights together at the beach house.

There was talk among their friends that they might even be getting back together, but that wasn't what Grant had in mind. His loneliness was not eased by the temporary reprise with Scott, who left the beach house for good, again, when production on the film ended. Grant was looking for something more, something better, something that would move him to the front of the trolley car.

"Plenty of room up front" was the way Grant answered anyone these days who asked how things were going. Sometimes he added, "Step to the front of the car," a response that baffled most people. The car he was referring to was a streetcar, like the ones that still rode up and down Hollywood, Sunset, and Santa Monica Boulevards. He found them the ideal metaphor for what the relentless life of making movie after movie was when there was no one to come home to every night. The streetcars ran on circular tracks that started nowhere and always arrived at the same place, merry-go-round style. "There's only room for one car on the line, and so many passengers. The instant the car begins to move, the conductor takes up the chant, 'Move up front! Plenty of room up front!' At the next stop, when a new mob tries to scramble aboard, a handful of bruised, battered, and bedraggled actors get pushed off, landing with a hollow thud on the concrete of Oblivion Street!"

Clearly Cary Grant was ready to make some changes in his private life, even if he didn't have a clue as to what he wanted or how to go about finding it.

AS IT TURNED OUT, he wouldn't have to. Change found him, beginning in the spring of 1940 when—out of nowhere, or so it seemed at the time—Barbara Hutton appeared in Beverly Hills and immediately sought out the companionship of Cary Grant.

Hutton had gained a bizarre reputation as one of the so-called Beautiful People whom everyone loved to hate. Born in 1912, she had grown up with her name and pictures in the newspapers from the day she was five years old and her mother committed suicide, leaving little Hutton a one-third heir to her grandfather Frank Woolworth's estate; her share was estimated at the time to be in the $100 million range. Her father took personal charge of his daughter's inheritance and improved it by another $50 million, then predicted the collapse of Wall Street and got out of the market weeks before America was plunged into its Great Depression.

The Hutton name then became synonymous with greed and selfishness—

and that was before blond, blue-eyed, five-foot-two, eighty-five-pound Barbara met Prince Alexis Mdivani, a universally reviled fortune hunter whom the twenty-year-old Hutton, it was widely believed, paid $2 million to marry her. She tired of him three years later and paid him $1.5 million more for a non-contested divorce so she could marry Danish Count Haugwitz-Reventlow, reportedly paying *him* $1.5 million for *his* hand in marriage. In order to conform to Danish rules of royal heritage, Hutton had to renounce her American citizenship, which she did without a moment's hesitation.

Hutton's second marriage lasted little more than a year, just long enough for her to have a baby, after which she and the count legally separated. She then relocated to London, where she planned to raise her infant son, Lance Reventlow, until England's entry into World War II drove her back to the safety of the United States.

She bought a home in San Francisco and, at the suggestion of her friend the Countess Dorothy di Frasso, hired a public relations firm to try to improve her image. She made a series of huge donations to several charitable causes, including a much-publicized $100,000 gift to the Red Cross.

In 1940, while she was visiting di Frasso, who lived in Beverly Hills, the countess threw a large, celebrity-studded dinner in Hutton's honor at her home. One of the invitees Hutton had insisted on was that handsome actor she had met on her voyage to America a year earlier aboard the *Normandie*.

IT IS NOT DIFFICULT to understand Hutton's attraction to Grant. Less obvious but no less compelling is why he was so receptive to her very public (and well-publicized) pursuit. While the moviegoing public adored him, he felt stuck on that streetcar. At the age of thirty-six he had already "divorced" twice, counting Scott, a relationship that in many ways had been more of a marriage than the one to Cherrill. His desire for a lasting, meaningful partnership churned beneath the surface of his emotional aloofness. Because the risk of being hurt by love was so frightening to him, he kept a careful distance from everyone for whom he felt anything—his onscreen persona of non-pursuit a reflection of the way he personally kept himself safely out of intimacy's reach. Grant's unrealistic notions of romantic love were conveniently entwined with his unconsummated infatuations. After his disastrous marriage to Cherrill, the only women he was able to form long-term, meaningful relationships with were those wealthy enough for him to be certain they weren't after "Cash and Cary's" money or those to whom he wasn't sexually attracted, such as Phyllis Brooks, Jean Rogers, Katharine Hepburn, and Rosalind Russell. On those terms, Barbara Hutton was a perfect match.

There was all of that, and something else. Grant's relationship with Scott had always been highly competitive, as intense as any real sibling rivalry. In many ways, Scott was, to Grant, the embodiment of the older brother he was denied by the early death of John William Elias Leach. Grant was by far a bigger star than Scott. He was also better looking and in better shape. He had managed to keep the house they had both wanted. Scott, on the other hand, had more money, and an heiress wife. By marrying Barbara "Woolworth" Hutton, Grant knew, he could surpass his former lover and sibling substitute on both counts.

When Hutton made herself available to Grant, he began to see her but insisted her publicity firm not cover their relationship. He did not want to see their names together in print. If she was interested in publicity, Grant told her, she should find someone else. And, as for her high-end social life, he wasn't interested in that, either.

Grant had more than the fear of somehow being exploited by Hutton on his mind when he insisted on keeping their relationship a secret. The last thing he wanted was a confrontation with the always-volatile Brooks over the new woman in his life. He didn't see the need to hurt her or go through any unnecessary confrontations. He didn't have time for that, or for much of anything else, conveniently adding new movies to his schedule.

Although he was somewhat bored making them, besides serving as his emotional escape valve, he also feared that if he were out of work for too long, the government would no longer allow him to stay in the country on what was, after all, a glorified if strictly limited work permit. He had agreed to England's request to make patriotic movies, whatever they were supposed to be, and he couldn't very well do that if he were off on a beach somewhere in Mexico. For that matter, due to his residency permit restrictions, he couldn't even go to Mexico, any more than he could go to Dover,

Rome, Barcelona, or the French Riviera. The war was raging everywhere, it seemed, except in America. Around the world men his age were worried about catching a bullet between the eyes, while his biggest worry was landing a role in Hepburn's newest project, the film version of her hit Broadway play *The Philadelphia Story*.

In the spring of 1940, at Cohn's suggestion, and because it seemed sufficiently "patriotic," Grant accepted a role in Columbia's production of Frank Lloyd's *The Howards of Virginia*. Cohn believed the film would open Grant's range to an even wider variety of roles, but the film turned out to be one of the least successful of Grant's career. *The Howards of Virginia* was a favored project of Cohn, who had purchased the original novel on which it was based, a buckskin War of Independence drama entitled *The Tree of Liberty* by Elizabeth Page. He chose Frank Lloyd, who had won an Oscar for directing *Mutiny on the Bounty*, to produce and direct it.

The film was shot mostly on location in the recently restored "colony" of Williamsburg, Virginia (which John D. Rockefeller had paid for and now let Cohn use for free as a way to promote tourism). In the movie, a badly miscast, ponytailed Grant plays Matt Howard, a surveyor friend of Thomas Jefferson, who works for Fleetwood Peyton (Sir Cedric Hardwicke) and falls in love with his daughter Jane (Martha Scott). At Jefferson's encouragement, Howard enters politics, and when the Revolutionary War threatens to break out, he sides with the colonists and runs off to join the army, despite Jane's pleas not to get himself killed. He is joined by his two sons, one of whom he has been estranged from. They reconcile in the heat of battle and return home to the waiting arms of a tearful wife and mother.

The Howards of Virginia is notable for being the first film in which Grant played "age." Gray temples and grown sons were odd elements for the still-young actor, as were the strangeness of buckskin and muskets. Grant vamped through the film while he waited for production to begin on *The Philadelphia Story*.

To no one's surprise but Cohn's, *The Howards of Virginia* laid a turkey-sized egg at the box office and in so doing put an end to Grant's unbroken string of box office hits. No one wanted to see Grant with gray hair and grown children. Unlike his other "war" film, *Gunga Din*, in which Grant, Fairbanks, and McLaglen *were* children, this film lacked humor and irony, as well as any trace of Grant's patented brand of urban sophistication.

BARBARA HUTTON HAD BEEN PLANNING to move to Hawaii with her son, Lance, for the duration of the war, but once her relationship with Grant became more serious, she decided instead to rent a place in Beverly Hills, while he worked on the long-awaited production of *The Philadelphia Story*.

The Broadway version of the Philip Barry play, written especially for Katharine Hepburn, had been a huge hit, but Howard Hughes was having difficulty selling the film rights in Hollywood, where Hepburn — the toast of the Great White Way, having won the New York Drama Critics Circle Award for her performance — was still considered something of a stomach-lining irritant. The handsome New York show that opened in the spring of 1939 costarred Joseph Cotten as C. K. Dexter Haven, Tracy Lord's (Hepburn's) divorced first husband; Van Heflin as Macaulay Connor, the sardonic gossip columnist (Heflin claimed, as nearly everyone else in the original cast did, that Barry had specifically written the part for *him* — in Hepburn's case it was true, in Heflin's it wasn't); and Shirley Booth. While the casting was perfectly suited for New York audiences, it did nothing to enhance the prospect of a film. Selznick said he wanted it, but as a vehicle for Bette Davis. MGM wanted it for Joan Crawford. The only decent offer Hughes got was from Warner Bros., which was willing to pay Hughes $225,000 if it could cast its star Ann Sheridan in the lead. The bottom line was, every studio was interested in the play, but none wanted Hepburn, and there was no way Hepburn would let Hughes sell the rights without her. When independent moviemaker Samuel Goldwyn, who according to his biographer Scott Berg was "mad for the material," offered to put Gary Cooper in the starring role and get William Wyler to direct, Hepburn said no to him as well. She wanted George Cukor, and only George Cukor, to guide her through this film.

MGM's Louis B. Mayer finally put an offer on the table that she felt she could live with — $175,000 for the rights, and $75,000 for her to reprise her Broadway performance as Tracy Lord. The studio envisioned Clark Gable or Spencer Tracy (whom she had not yet met), or possibly even Robert Taylor, as the male lead, and Mayer wanted to feature Jimmy Stewart in a supporting role.

MGM hit its first brick wall when Gable, Tracy, and Taylor turned the film down. Each was running hot at the box office and did not want to take the risk of starring opposite "box office poison" Hepburn, and besides, none of them particularly liked the script. Gable in particular thought it was too wordy, and Tracy was much more interested in playing Dr. Jekyll and Mr. Hyde in Victor Fleming's upcoming production of the Robert Louis Stevenson classic.

Mayer then offered her Cary Grant, and Hepburn jumped. (Grant had agreed to make the film for Mayer if he got top billing over Hepburn and a bump in his usual salary to $137,500—double what Hepburn was getting.) She was eager to work with him again, not because their previous outings together had been so great, but because he was now indisputedly the hottest actor in Hollywood. If he gave her Grant, Mayer said, she would also have to take Stewart, which was fine with Hepburn. Most important to Hepburn, and what sealed the deal for her, Mayer okayed George Cukor to direct. Upon hearing the news, a disappointed Goldwyn sent Hepburn a wire at the Shubert Theater in New York, where she was still appearing in the show: "I am heartbroken and I hope what I have heard is not so."

Gary Cooper was upset about losing out to Grant and publicly complained that Grant was too pretty to play Dexter, that no one would believe Hepburn could ever throw him out. On the other hand, he said, he, Cooper, would have been perfect for the role.

With the casting in place, Hepburn ended the play's Broadway run in May 1940, and production on the film began that July in Hollywood. On the first day of shooting Grant's high salary was reported in the gossip columns. Grant immediately announced that he was donating his entire salary to the British War Relief Fund, a gesture for which he was grandly applauded.*

From the famous opening silent prologue, in which Tracy breaks Dexter's golf club over her knee as he is leaving her, and he retaliates by covering her face with his palm and shoving her backward through the front door, *The*

---

*According to the IRS, Grant's donation was actually $62,500, the amount he earned after taxes and after paying the cost of refurbishing Vincent's suite of offices—a reward for his work in securing Grant the film at such a high fee.

Philadelphia Story is simply one of the greatest sound comedies Hollywood has ever produced. It opened in December 1940 and broke box office records everywhere, including at Radio City Music Hall, where it beat the venue's previously all-time highest-grossing film, Walt Disney's *Snow White and the Seven Dwarfs* (1937).*

In many ways, *The Philadelphia Story* is really the last great film of the 1930s. With traces of slapstick, melodrama, verbal wit, and manners, it represented nothing so much as the last, innocent days of an America that faded into history in the wake of the December 7, 1941, Japanese attack on Pearl Harbor. Here is a wealthy family so self-absorbed and isolated from the outside world that the only hint of gathering clouds is those on the outside of the iced champagne glasses. The Lords' house, for all intents and purposes, exists in a place where time and space serve only to elongate comic situations and airily glide into happiness-ever-after. As Grant told one reporter, regarding what he considered the film's irresistible charm: "When I go to the movies I want to forget the dirty dishes in my sink, and what's on my mind. I want to forget my troubles, get out of myself. I want to laugh a little."

Everyone in the cast of *The Philadelphia Story* gave what many critics consider the best performances of their careers. Bosley Crowther, writing in *The New York Times*, said it "had just about everything that a blue-chip comedy should have, a witty romantic script derived by Donald Ogden Stewart out of Philip Barry's successful play, the flavor of high society elegance, in which the patrons inevitably luxuriate, and a splendid cast of performers."

The film went on to become the second-highest grosser of the year, just behind the Warner Bros. release of Howard Hawks's World War I reluctant-hero, sleeping-giant-awakened hagiographic look at the all-American boy at (the coming) war, *Sergeant York*—starring—Gary Cooper.

IN NOVEMBER, GRANT RETURNED TO Harry Cohn and Columbia to begin work on his third movie of 1941, the soapy *Penny Serenade,* to be helmed by *Gunga Din*'s George Stevens.

***The Philadelphia Story*'s total Radio City Music Hall take was in excess of $600,000—more than half the net earned from the play's entire Broadway run.*

What had attracted Grant to this project was the chance to work again with Irene Dunne, his favorite costar, in a serious drama rather than another screwball comedy. He told one reporter shortly after production began, "Irene and I sit here and worry a half-hour a day, regularly, about the people who are laughing already, in anticipation of another mad marital mix-up. Oh, they're going to get chances to laugh, but the concentration in this film is on human drama. There isn't any other man and there isn't any other woman. We're married, and the story is about the trials and tribulations of two ordinary people and the things that might happen in any marriage."

The title *Penny Serenade* refers to the records played by Julie Gardiner Adams (Dunne) as she prepares to separate from her husband, Roger Adams (Grant). In flashbacks, we see their courtship unfold. Adams is a newspaperman who meets and woos Gardiner, a music shop sales clerk. They fall in love, marry, and move to Japan, where Roger has a job as a news correspondent. Julie becomes pregnant but is caught in an earthquake that provokes a miscarriage. She is subsequently told she can never have children again, and so they decide to adopt a baby daughter. They struggle through six years of financial hardship, only to suffer the death of their adopted daughter just as they appear to have finally become solvent. The marriage is almost destroyed but is saved when the couple agree to adopt another child.

Grant let Stevens guide him through a part he could play with his eyes shut and his hands tied behind his back, until on January 25, 1941, he was informed on the set that five of his relatives on the Leach side — Mr. and Mrs. John Henry Leach, his uncle and aunt, and their daughter, son-in-law, and infant grandson — were all killed when a German bomb made a direct hit on Bristol. The news of their deaths unnerved him and produced a swell of guilt and remorse for having avoided returning to England, joining the army, and fighting the Germans. Grant, however, made no public comment about the incident and allowed no interruption in his filming schedule. Ironically, the real-life grief he was feeling gave his portrayal of Roger Adams a nontechnical reality that was eerily unlike anything Grant had ever done before or would do again in the movies.

During the closing days of shooting, the Academy Award nominations for the best films, direction, technical expertise, and performances of 1940 were announced. As expected, Hepburn was nominated for Best Actress for her portrayal of Tracy Lord in *The Philadelphia Story*. The shocker came with the Best Actor nominations: James Stewart got one for his portrayal of Macaulay Connor, but Cary Grant was once again overlooked. Because of it, Grant chose not to attend the Awards ceremony. Stewart did and won, as did screenwriter Donald Ogden Stewart for his adaptation of the Barry play.*

PENNY SERENADE OPENED April 24, 1941, to positive reviews, many of which singled out Grant's performance for special praise. Otis Ferguson, writing in *The New Republic*, said, "Cary Grant is thoroughly good, in some ways to the point of surprise, for there is not only that easy swing and hint of the devil in him, but faith and passion expressed, the character held together where it might so easily have fallen into the component parts of the too good, the silly, etc."

Grant was pleased with the critical response to his performance, but he was now looking ahead to his first really exciting project since *The Awful Truth*. At last his schedule and Alfred Hitchcock's were in sync, and Grant eagerly signed on to appear in the director's fourth American film, *Suspicion*.†

What particularly delighted him was the role of Johnnie Aysgarth, a different type of romantic lady-killer from the ones he was used to playing.

A murderous one.

The Philadelphia Story was nominated for six Oscars: Best Actor (J. Stewart), Best Actress (Hepburn), Best Supporting Actress (Ruth Hussey), Best Director (Cukor), Best Picture (Joseph Mankiewicz, producer), and Best Writing, Screenplay (D. O. Stewart).

†Hitchcock's first three American films were *Rebecca* (1939), *Foreign Correspondent* (1940), and *Mr. and Mrs. Smith* (1941).

18

"The consensus was that audiences would not want to be
told in the last few frames of film that as popular a personality
as Cary Grant was a murderer, doomed to exposure."

—ALFRED HITCHCOCK

T he chance to work with Alfred Hitchcock couldn't have come at a better time. After his bitter disappointment at being left out of the nominations for *The Philadelphia Story*, and the personal trauma he suffered during
the making of *Penny Serenade*, Grant had considered retiring from movies. He
had made his money and left his mark; he wondered why he should continue
to subject himself to the further humiliation of being rejected by the Academy.
What renewed his interest in film acting was the opportunity to work with
Hitchcock.

Production on *Suspicion*, which had begun on February 10, 1941, only
weeks after Grant had completed *Penny Serenade*, dragged along for five
months, while Hitchcock and David O. Selznick furiously clashed over the
fate of the character of Johnnie Aysgarth.

BY THE TIME HE BEGAN *Suspicion*, Hitchcock had come to regret his decision to sign with Selznick. From the start he had found himself battling with
Selznick over the script for *Rebecca*, something that caused him great con-

sternation, especially when Selznick won most of the story points he was fighting for. Because of it, despite the film's winning the 1940 Best Picture Oscar, Hitchcock would always consider it Selznick's picture. In his notebooks Hitchcock bitterly observed that *Rebecca* had taught him that Hollywood regarded the director as "a minor figure in a fast film industry made up of entrepreneurs who headed the studios."

As for Selznick, by the end of 1940, having won Best Picture two years in a row,* he was physically exhausted, creatively spent, and ironically, in serious need of immediate cash. Both films were expensive period pieces that endured heavy cost overruns and produced myriad problems, all of which pushed him into a debilitating addiction to Benzedrine that in turn fueled an already-out-of-control gambling habit. In 1940 Walter Wanger (who had made a series of successful films in the 1930s while under contract to Paramount, Columbia, and MGM, respectively)† had signed a new distribution deal with United Artists, borrowed Hitchcock from Selznick to direct *Foreign Correspondent*, and wanted him again to direct *Suspicion*, which he was about to produce for RKO. Despite the fact that Wanger was willing to pay Selznick $5,000 a week for Hitchcock's services while Selznick was only paying the director $2,500 a week, Hitchcock made no attempt to interfere with the deal. No matter what it cost him in dollars, he was as anxious to get away from Selznick as Selznick was to get away from him.

Suspicion was based on the 1932 British novel *Before the Fact* by Anthony Berkeley Cox (written under the pseudonym Francis Iles), which RKO had purchased in 1935. After several unsuccessful attempts to make a movie out of it, they shelved the project until Hitchcock and Wanger found the book gathering dust on the studio's shelves. The novel tells the story of Lina McLaidlaw Aysgarth (Joan Fontaine), a passive but wealthy woman overly attached to her husband, Johnnie (Grant), who she discovers is in fact an embezzler, has murdered his best friend, and is about to murder her.

---

*Best Picture Oscars go to the producer. Selznick won in 1939 for Fleming's *Gone With the Wind* and in 1940 for Hitchcock's *Rebecca*.

†Wanger productions included the Marx Brothers' *The Cocoanuts* (1929); Frank Capra's *The Bitter Tea of General Yen* (1933); Rouben Mamoulian's *Queen Christina*, starring Greta Garbo (1933); John Ford's *Stagecoach*, the film that made John Wayne a star (1939); Fritz Lang's *You Only Live Once* (1937); and William Dieterle's *Blockade* (1938).

Debilitated by her love for him, she cannot do anything to stop him, and, in the climactic scene, she calmly accepts a glass of milk from him that she knows is poisoned and dies.

This was fertile turf for Hitchcock, who loved the idea of making a movie about a woman so masochistically attached to her husband she would actually allow him to kill her. If, in fact, that was what he intended to do. Hitchcock's brilliant twist was to keep the audience guessing until the very end whether Aysgarth was really a murderer, or if the whole thing was only a figment of his wife's paranoid imagination.

If Hitchcock clearly envisioned the film in his mind, his studio-assigned producer, Harry Edington, did not. And when Hitchcock, who had vacillated over the ending of the film, decided Grant should turn out to be a killer, Edington said that was impossible because audiences would never accept Grant in that type of role. This impasse came two months into production and lasted until Hitchcock finally and reluctantly altered the script to make the woman the victim only of her own paranoid delusions.*

Filming then resumed, and for the next three months Fontaine became so unnerved by the director's relentless harping on her to "act crazy" that she developed an upset stomach that once again halted shooting. This delay stretched into a week and caused the entire project to once again come up for review at RKO, where, because of the vagueness of the shooting script, in which it still remained unclear as to whether Johnnie was a killer, the studio's board members considered canceling the whole project. One alternative solution was to cut from the completed footage all negative references to Johnnie's character and see what that would leave; the studio then produced an incomprehensible fifty-five-minute "happy" version of the film that horrified Hitchcock, who then assured the studio that he would finish the film the way they wanted. As a result, *Suspicion* ends with a wild car ride

---

*According to Hitchcock biographer Donald Spoto, while Hitchcock insisted later on that he never intended to alter the plot of the original novel, his memos to RKO in its archives suggest that from the start the director "wanted to make a film about a woman's fantasy life." It is likely that the purpose of those memos was to tell the studio what it wanted to hear, in order to get the film into production. A previous attempt by the studio to film *Suspicion*, as a star vehicle for Laurence Olivier, had been abandoned for the very same reason: the studio refused to have him play a killer.

down the side of a winding road, in which Johnnie at first seems to be trying to kill Lina but in reality is only trying to save her from falling out of her side to certain death.

Despite all the plot confusion, for the first time in his career, due in large part to Hitchcock's direction, Grant gave a performance almost entirely defined by his character's internal emotional life rather than his exterior features. Grant's Johnnie Aysgarth embodied Hitchcock's darkest projections of himself, as the director audaciously took one of the most popular actors in Hollywood and used his smooth veneer as a mask to drive the audience mad trying to figure out what was underneath it. As had every other of the major directors who'd helped mold Grant's onscreen persona as an extension of their own, Hitchcock, through his skilled and idiosyncratic use of the tools of his trade — close-ups, angularity, the rhythm of the montage against the composition of the mise-en-scène — was able to create rather than elicit a performance from Grant without what he considered the unnecessary instrusion of "acting." In Sternberg's hands, Grant had become the epitome of the sleazy ladies' man; McCarey's vision was someone with charm, wit, and the boundless energy of love-infused youth; to Hawks, Grant was the romantic, athletic adventurer; to Cukor, he was the adventuresome, interior romantic. It was Hitchcock who finally took Grant deeper, who used his insecurity as an actor (a reflection of his own very real repression) to create a personality whose criminal darkness was the perfect cover to protect the emotional defects of the charismatic performer, the complex but amiable surface of the character he played, and the masterful director who managed to at once put them all on dazzling display. As John Mosher correctly put it in his review for *The New Yorker,* "Cary Grant finds a new field for himself, the field of crime, the smiling villain, without heart or conscience. Crime lends color to his amiability."

For both star and director, their inspired collaboration on *Suspicion* became a virtuosic display of not only what they could do on film but what film can do best, the visual, or surface, display of one's soul by the behavioral display of one's private (secret, repressed, forbidden) thoughts and desires. This great Hitchcockian touch is what makes *Suspicion* so compelling. By allowing Grant to act out the subtext of his character — a man so enraged at his wife that he wants to kill her — he becomes, in Hitchcock's morally rigid world, an actual killer. And even more shocking, his wife becomes his coconspirator for her "role" in triggering such murderous thoughts.

Even with its denatured script and studio-imposed happy ending, *Suspicion* proved an unqualified box office success and joined the two previous films he made that year—*The Philadelphia Story* and *Penny Serenade*—on the list of top-five-grossing films of 1941.* The film's record-breaking Thanksgiving weekend opening took place at Radio City Music Hall (officially kicking off the 1941 holiday moviegoing season), and this time everyone in the business believed there was no way the Academy could deny Grant a long-overdue Oscar.

SHORTLY AFTER HE COMPLETED WORK on *Suspicion*, Grant, claiming exhaustion, opted out of his next scheduled picture, Edmund Goulding's big-screen version of the long-running Broadway hit *The Man Who Came to Dinner*, in which he was to play Sherman Whiteside. The role went instead to Monty Woolley, who had done it on Broadway. Then on the morning of August 18, 1941, without telling anyone except the government, which had given him a special exit and re-entry visa, Grant packed a few bags, got into his car, and quietly drove to Mexico City, where he checked into the Hotel Reforma for what he told his friends was to be a long and well-earned rest.

It lasted two days.

---

*Of the sixteen movies Grant made in his first five years as a freelancer, *Suspicion* came in at number three, grossing more than $400,000 in its initial theatrical release, RKO's highest-grossing movie of 1941. *The Philadelphia Story* opened in December 1940 and played in theaters well into 1941. Grant made a third film in 1941, *Arsenic and Old Lace*, which was not released until 1944.

19

"Cary Grant is a great comedian, a great light comedian. He's very good-looking, but he's also very funny. That makes a devastating combination, and that's why he's been a star so long."

—FRANK CAPRA

Shortly after Grant arrived in Mexico City, Barbara Hutton flew down to be with him, bringing with her the happy news that her divorce from Count Reventlow was finalized. Before they had signed off on their financial agreement, the count had been detained in Denmark by the Nazi occupiers and supposedly, under "threat of death," been forced to collaborate with them on certain "matters of security." One of the "rewards" for his cooperation was his captors' promise that he would be allowed to sign his divorce papers, receive his money from Hutton, hand most of it over to them, and be released.

Grant and Hutton stayed together in Mexico through Labor Day, after which they returned, separately, to Los Angeles, where Hutton wrote to the Nazi officials in Denmark asking for written proof that her divorce from Reventlow was indeed finalized. That correspondence was copied without her knowledge and given to the American government. All during this time Hutton was unaware that she was the target of a secret FBI investigation and under constant surveillance by someone able to track her every move.

That someone was Cary Grant.

BY 1941, AT THE END of nearly a decade of nonstop filmmaking in which he appeared in forty features, Grant desperately looked to slow down the pace. After the highly satisfying but intense experience he had making *Suspicion*, he wanted to choose his next projects more carefully to see if he could maintain the quality of acting Hitchcock had gotten out of him.

Unfortunately, he was unable to do so. Shortly after returning to Hollywood, Grant met with Frank Capra, once Columbia Pictures' hottest director, who had finally made good on his threat to leave Cohn and moved to Warner Bros., where he was about to make the screen version of the long-running Broadway comedy *Arsenic and Old Lace*. Over lunch Capra told Grant that he was the only actor who could do justice to the role of Mortimer Brewster. The director was as good a salesman as he was a filmmaker. He had already offered the part to Bob Hope, who was eager to do it but couldn't get Paramount to agree to a loan-out. Capra had also approached Jack Benny, who said no, and even Ronald Reagan, who turned the part down, before Grant agreed to do it.

Production on *Arsenic and Old Lace* began that October. The plot of the movie centers on theater critic Mortimer's engagement to Elaine Harper (Priscilla Lane), which triggers mayhem, murder, and other assorted bits of craziness by his murderous aunts and deranged uncle, leading him to believe any children he will have will inherit his family's madness. The fast-paced farce continues until the final moments, when Mortimer discovers he was actually adopted and can therefore marry Elaine without fear of her giving birth to another generation of lunatics.

As it turned out, Grant did not at all enjoy working with Capra, and in the years that followed, whenever asked, he always described his portrayal of Mortimer as his least favorite film performance. Although he liked Capra personally—"a dear, dear man"—he felt the film "was not my kind of humor . . . too much hysterical shouting and extremely broad double takes." In truth he hated everything about the production. He thought the sets were wrong, too dark and stagy, the supporting cast—except for Jean Adair, for whom he had a special affection—too theatrical (both Josephine Hull and Adair, who played Mortimer's aunts, were borrowed by Capra for filming during their vacation from the still-running Broadway production), and the comedy bits too forced. According to screenwriter Julius Epstein, Capra was aware of the film's problems and meant to fix them with reshoots and editing. That plan changed when the Japanese attacked Pearl Harbor that December 7, and Capra abruptly left Hollywood to join the Signal Corps. Grant then donated his entire $160,000 salary to the United Service Organization, the British War Relief, and the Red Cross.*

Two unexpected events happened during the shoot that deeply affected Grant. The first reached all the way back to when young Archie Leach was touring with the Pender troupe; he had come down with rheumatic fever in Rochester, New York, and for several weeks was confined to his rooming-house bed, alone for most of the day. Jean Adair happened to be appearing at the same vaudeville house, heard about the boy whose only relatives lived in England, and made it a point to bring him flowers and fresh fruit every day until he recovered. When Capra introduced him to the actress on the first day of shooting, Grant immediately recognized her and asked if she did him. Of course, she replied, she had seen all his movies. When he told her he was that young acrobat who had taken ill in Rochester, she suddenly smiled, threw her arms around him, and pulled him close to her. While she didn't remember him by name (he was still Archie Leach at the time), she told him she thought there was something familiar about him.

The second event was Grant's unexpected reunion with his onetime roommate and companion Orry-Kelly, who by sheer coincidence happened to be the costume designer on *Arsenic and Old Lace*. Grant and Orry-Kelly spent a long evening together reminiscing about "the old days" and afterward promised to stay in touch.

They didn't.

---

*The film was withheld from release until 1944, when the original Broadway production finally closed. A clause in the contract between the producers and Warners prevented the film from opening until the show's stage run ended. That was fine with Grant, who hoped the film would somehow just disappear.

In January 1942, back at Columbia, Grant made *The Talk of the Town*, produced and directed by George Stevens, an altogether forgettable film about a small-town love triangle that costarred Jean Arthur and Ronald Colman.* Just before shooting began, in the wake of America's entrance into World War II, the thirty-eight-year-old Grant—who was still not an American citizen and therefore ineligible for the draft—decided to do volunteer work for the Hollywood Victory Committee, where he helped organize bond rallies and celebrity hospital tours and hosted several stateside performances for servicemen.

That February, Grant was nominated for Best Actor for his performance in *Penny Serenade*. The other nominees were Walter Huston in William Dieterle's *All That Money Can Buy* (aka *The Devil and Daniel Webster*), Robert Montgomery in Alexander Hall's *Here Comes Mr. Jordan*, Orson Welles in his Mercury Players production of *Citizen Kane*, and Gary Cooper in Howard Hawks's *Sergeant York*. The race was really between Grant, considered the favorite, and Cooper.

The Academy dinner, hosted by Bob Hope, was held on February 26, 1942, at the Biltmore Hotel in downtown Los Angeles. Grant attended with Hutton and sat quietly through the progression of awards, until James Stewart, winner of the Best Oscar the year before, was introduced by Rosalind Russell to award both the Best Supporting Actor and Best Actor. After announcing that the Best Supporting Actor went to Donald Crisp for *How Green Was My Valley*, Stewart opened the envelope for Best Actor and, staring at the name for several seconds, looked up and let a wide grin cross his face as he announced Cooper's name. The room broke into cheers, and Cooper received a standing ovation as he walked to the microphone. In his familiar halting, wet-lipped style, he leaned over and said, "It was Sergeant Alvin York who won this award." That brought on another round of applause.

---

*This was the only film Colman and Grant made together. At a studio screening of the film, Grant and Barbara Hutton arrived fifteen minutes late, and Hutton insisted on having the film restarted. This led to angry words between Colman and Grant and caused a rift that never completely healed. Source: William Frye, interview by the author.

Joan Fontaine then won Best Actress for her performance in *Suspicion*.

Backstage, after congratulating Fontaine, a gracious Cary Grant took Hutton's hand and left the ceremonies, skipping all the parties, and went home. In the car he turned to Hutton and said that this was the last Academy Awards he was ever going to attend.

J. EDGAR HOOVER BELIEVED THAT Barbara Hutton was funneling significant amounts of money to the Nazis, via her second husband, in return for their continued guarantee of his safety. In June, when production wrapped on *The Talk of the Town*, another secret meeting took place in Washington between Grant and Hoover. Within two days of his return to Beverly Hills, Grant asked Hutton to marry him as soon as possible. She agreed, and a day later Frank Vincent, at Grant's insistence, had a prenuptial agreement drawn up that said should he and Hutton divorce, he would not get any of Hutton's money (which was mostly held in secret Swiss accounts) and she would not get any of his. The notion of the prenup likely came not from Grant or Vincent but from Hoover, who, in order to protect Grant from any future complications, did not want his finances to be connected to Hutton's. Within days, despite all the previous delays, Grant's application for citizenship was suddenly expedited, and on June 26, 1942, at the age of thirty-eight, Archibald Alec Leach found himself taking the oath of allegiance from Federal Judge Paul J. McCormick in Los Angeles, after which he was officially a citizen of the United States. Later that same day he legally changed his name to Cary Grant.

On July 7, Hutton, her girlfriend Madeleine Hazeltine, and eleven members of the Hutton personal staff caravaned from Beverly Hills to Frank Vincent's mountainside getaway just outside Lake Arrowhead for her wedding to be held that day. To ensure that no one in the press would discover what was about to happen, Vincent was somehow able to obtain two marriage licenses with both names left blank.

To further throw everyone off track, a few days before, Grant had begun filming Leo McCarey's *Once Upon a Honeymoon*, a zealous bit of wartime nonsense that he had reluctantly agreed to star in for RKO at the request of the FBI, which had "asked" Grant to make an explicitly anti-Nazi film. Barely a week into the shoot, Grant asked for and received a two-day leave.

On the morning of July 7, 1942, he drove to Lake Arrowhead, stopping on his way to buy flowers from a Beverly Hills shop, and arrived at Vincent's by noon. Less than an hour later a six-minute wedding ceremony took place, conducted by the local Lutheran reverend. Grant's only witness besides Vincent was his male secretary, Frank Horn. Notably absent were Randolph Scott, Howard Hughes, and any members of the Malibu Brit colony. That night the newlyweds returned to Beverly Hills, and the next morning Grant decided to enlist.

He took and passed an army physical and on August 4 was notified by the Adjutant General's Office that he was to report on September 15 for official induction. However, without any explanation, at the time or for the rest of his life, Grant never showed up, and nothing was ever again mentioned about his "enlistment" by anyone in or out of the government. Three months later, on December 11, his eligibility was mysteriously changed from 1A to 1H by the Selective Service. The only official reference to all this is buried in an internal RKO memorandum that reads as follows:

> Washington suggests that they would like to have Cary Grant's name on their list of people who from time to time might do some temporary service. In each instance, if called upon, he will have an opportunity to say "yes" or "no" to whatever job is proposed and it is not at all certain that they will call upon him in any case. We understand that the type of work that he might be called upon to do would not be of the sort that would require him to drop out of whatever other activities he may be engaged in and the fact that he was doing the work would be publicized.

The studio source of this extraordinary document remains cloudy, but the source from "Washington" is, without question, J. Edgar Hoover. It assumes all responsibility for Grant's nonspecified "temporary service" in an unnamed organization and concludes with a promise of "publicity" that was standard FBI code for a Bureau coverup by way of media misdirection. In effect, the

FBI had put the studio on notice that Grant was to be made available whenever they wanted him.* This marked a dramatic shift in Grant's political activities, a far cry from the days when Hoover had personally warned Grant that he was in danger of violating the Neutrality Act (something, of course, that lost all meaning when America formally declared war on Japan, Germany, and the rest of the Axis powers).

Immediately after getting married, Grant went right back to making movies. He finished the aptly named *Once Upon a Honeymoon* and followed it with H. C. Potter's equally fortuitously titled *Mr. Lucky*, in which he looked absolutely shimmering as a handsome, roguish, *draft-dodging* gambler hustling the moneyed set aboard a cruise ship, only to be redeemed in the last reel by finding true love and renouncing his evil ways. The character was an unusual one for Grant to play and ventured almost beyond the limit of what an audience would accept from him. Manny Farber, writing in *The New Republic*, described the film, and Grant's performance in it, as "interesting, like a bad salad with an intelligent dressing."

With *Mr. Lucky* in the RKO can, Grant waited for his next assignment while the war raged on. In May 1943 he made a brief appearance at a Hollywood War Bond Drive, where Jack Warner buttonholed him and asked him to please play the starring role in *Destination Tokyo*. After the government's initial neutrality warning, and until he had been granted full U.S. citizenship, Grant had steadfastly refused to appear on film in any military uniform. He did not want to be seen as a foreign visitor portraying American heroes, fearing it might offend too many people and result in his somehow being asked to leave the country. With all of that resolved, however, he was more than willing to appear in Warner's picture.

To acquire Grant's services, Warner had to go through Columbia, where Grant had extended his nonexclusive contract. Columbia agreed to the loan-out in return for the services of Warner star Humphrey Bogart for *Sahara* (a role Grant had turned down), clearing the way for Grant to star in *Destination Tokyo* (in a role previously rejected by Gary Cooper).

---

*The author has been shown much of Barbara Hutton's FBI file and examined related files, tax returns, and court documents referred to in this chapter.

Directed and cowritten by Delmer Daves and Albert Maltz, based on an original story by Steve Fisher that appeared in *Liberty* magazine, and made with the full cooperation of the U.S. Navy, *Destination Tokyo* tells the story of an American torpedo submarine's daring and highly dangerous spy mission into the heart of Tokyo Bay. In the climax of the film the submarine sinks several Japanese warships, miraculously escapes from screen-shaking depth charges, and returns home to San Francisco.

Six weeks of filming began in September 1943 on a Burbank set that the studio built to the exact physical specifications of the interior of a naval submarine. The actors were directed to project the quiet authority of men on a mission. They talk in the hushed whispers of the righteous and acknowledge each other's bravery with smiles of pride and recognition. The only woman in *Destination Tokyo* is Faye Emerson, who was hardly even in the film until the end, when, home at last, the heroic Captain Cassidy (Grant) is reunited with his wife and child at the military dock. The film ends with their warm embrace — the implied reason "why men fight."

Grant enhanced his excellent performance by having thirty duplicate uniforms on hand at all times so he would always look immaculate onscreen — the epitome of the sleeves-rolled-up, handsome, manly, gallant American he envisioned his character to be.

Destination Tokyo was critically well received and proved to be a box office smash when it opened on New Year's Day 1944, two weeks before Grant's fortieth birthday. According to *Newsweek*, "Even moviegoers who have developed a severe allergy for service pictures should find *Destination Tokyo* among the superior films of the war . . . Cary Grant gives one of the soundest performances of his career; and John Garfield, William Prince, Dane Clark, and the rest of the all-male cast are always credible either as ordinary human beings or extraordinary heroes."

Because filming on *Destination Tokyo* had dragged on well beyond its original six-week schedule, Grant was forced to shoot his sequences at the Warner lot during the day, then scuttle back to Columbia Pictures, where he had already begun work on his next film. Alexander Hall's *Once Upon a Time*, costarring Janet Blair and the venerable James Gleason, was a fluffy life-on-Broadway comedy about, of all things, a caterpillar who stands upright and dances whenever he hears the song "Yes Sir, That's My Baby." *Harvey*esque in its concept—no one can see the caterpillar except Jerry Flynn (Grant)—the story, originally written and produced for the radio, was one of the more glaring miscues of Grant's prime career.

The overlapping production on the two films resulted in Grant's often staying overnight at the studio and sleeping in his dressing room—something that understandably displeased his bride, Hutton, who resented her husband's frequent absences. Increasingly during their first year of marriage, while Grant stayed either at the studio or alone at their rented house, Hutton attended lavish parties without him, thrown mostly by her transplanted European friends of questionable title (and apparently little money, as she usually paid for everything, something the always-parsimonious Grant resented). Alone at the rented house one night, Grant—who liked to be in bed by eleven when he was working, wearing only the tops of his pajamas, a cup of hot tea on the night-table, and reading a good book—had been completely captivated by *None But the Lonely Heart*, a novel by Richard Llewellyn, whose previous work, *How Green Was My Valley*, had been made into a spectacular movie by John Ford.

None But the Lonely Heart is set in poverty-stricken London in the days leading up to World War II. The hero, Ernie Mott, still not completely over the death of his father in the last war, works in his mother's secondhand store to help her get by. At one point he becomes so desperate for money that he joins a band of thieves and is nearly caught. When he finally gets home, he is shocked to find that his mother has been arrested for trafficking in stolen goods. He soon learns the reason for her action: she is dying of cancer and wants to make sure she leaves something behind for him. She dies in his arms in prison, and Ernie promises himself a better life.

Grant told RKO he was interested in the book, and Charles Koerner, the new head of the studio, immediately secured the rights to it with a preemptive bid of $60,000 and then agreed to Grant's $150,000 asking price plus 10 percent of the profits to star in it.

Clifford Odets, the Broadway playwright who had gained great fame (but not a lot of money) dramatizing the plight of the working class (*Waiting for Lefty, Awake and Sing!, Golden Boy*), was looking for a fat paycheck before being drafted into the army. He asked his agent to find him something quick and lucrative in Hollywood, and RKO responded by hiring him to adapt *None But the Lonely Heart* for the screen.

He actually began working on the script before Grant's deal was finalized and was shocked when he found out that the forty-year-old actor had been signed to play Ernie Mott, who was only nineteen in the novel and still living with his mother. Odets tried several different ways to make the disparity work, until he came up with a story that aged the boy and made the mother slightly younger, retaining the elements of their character in a more believable mold. Grant, who had also been concerned about the age factor, felt that Odets's screenplay so perfectly captured the essence of both the story and the characters that he called Koerner and insisted that Odets be hired to direct the movie, as well.

Not wanting to rock any boats, Koerner quickly agreed, which is how it came to be that the young Philadelphia-born and New York–based playwright, one of the founders of the Group Theater, who had never before set foot in Hollywood or directed so much as a foot of film, was hired to helm a big-budget movie on its journey from page to screen.

During production, Grant and Odets became good friends, and Odets helped Grant connect the film's dramatic high points to the touchstones of his own early life, particularly his relationship with his mother and the hardships of life in working-class London. Part apologia, part autobiography, part shrine to Elsie, and part social criticism, the film remained one of Grant's personal favorites.*

In an increasingly politically polarized 1940s Hollywood, however, the presence of the openly left-wing Odets, a onetime member of the American Communist Party, enraged the industry's powerful conservative faction. Odets became one of the first targets of the notorious Motion Picture Alliance for the Preservation of American Ideals (MPA), founded by right-wing extremists Walt Disney, William Randolph Hearst, and director Sam

---

*At the 1970 Academy presentation ceremony in which he received his Honorary Oscar, *None But the Lonely Heart* was the only film from which Grant insisted Mike Nichols include a clip in his pre-award montage.

Wood (and later headed by John Wayne).* The Alliance actively encouraged J. Edgar Hoover to launch an intensive "investigation into Communist infiltration of the motion picture industry." The FBI's 1944 investigation was a prelude to the postwar witch-hunts to come.

One of the first things the FBI did was to examine in detail the content of Hollywood's wartime films, and they singled out five as "among the industry's worst, i.e., most pro-Communist offerings to date": Herbert J. Biberman's *The Master Race*, which he also wrote; *Citizen Tom Paine*; H. C. Potter's *Mr. Lucky*; Delmer Daves's *Destination Tokyo*; and Odets's *None But the Lonely Heart*.† Amazingly, of the five movies the Bureau cited, three starred Cary Grant. A Bureau memo then stated that the following Hollywood celebrities had "known Communist connections": Lucille Ball, Ira Gershwin, John Garfield, Walter Huston, and Cary Grant. Grant's "known Communist connection," according to the FBI, was Clifford Odets. Later on, in 1947, during the first round of House Un-American Activities Committee (HUAC) hearings (brought to Hollywood at the urging of the MPA), Lela Rogers (the avenging mother of Ginger Rogers), who had been hired by RKO to serve as its resident "expert" on Communist infiltration, testified before the Committee that in her opinion *None But the Lonely Heart*'s despair and hopelessness were nothing more than Communist propaganda, citing as her proof the single line in the screenplay where Ernie Mott's mother tells him she is not going to get him to work in the secondhand store so he can squeeze pennies out of the little people poorer than he is.

She also cited *Destination Tokyo* for a single line of dialogue. Albert Maltz, who had written the film's screenplay (and would go on to become one of the so-called Hollywood 10 during the 1950s round of HUAC investigations), has Captain Cassidy (Grant) say after his submarine is almost blown up by an enemy bomb that was stamped "Made in the USA," "Appeasement has come home to roost, men." While the meaning of the line

*Odets joined the American Communist Party in 1934, a year before he gained fame as the author of the extremely successful, if overtly political, *Waiting for Lefty*.

†The author has been unable to find a listing of any film released in the 1930s or 1940s under the title *Citizen Tom Paine*.

seems clear enough—an ironic comment on the sale of American munitions overseas before the war—it somehow came to be interpreted by Rogers and the committee as Communist propaganda. John Garfield, Grant's costar in the film, was eventually called to testify at the second HUAC hearings, denied he was ever a Communist, and was subsequently blacklisted, as was Maltz. Unable to find work, Garfield turned increasingly to drink and died prematurely of a heart attack in 1952, at the age of thirty-nine.*

Yet Cary Grant—whose name and movies turned up repeatedly in these FBI's investigations; who starred in three of the five movies cited by the FBI's investigation into Communist infiltration; who was close friends with several of those later called before HUAC and accused of being Communists; who had avoided military service first in England and later in America; who refused to appear in any patriotic movies before being granted citizenship; who married a woman who had once renounced her American citizenship to marry a suspected Nazi sympathizer whose closest friends were either known or suspected Nazis or Nazi sympathizers—remained completely untouched and unsullied by both the FBI and the HUAC.

After an examination of existing files of others and related sources, the only logical and unavoidable conclusion is that Grant was protected by the one man in Washington with the power to do so—J. Edgar Hoover—most likely as part of a deal made with the FBI and the British government. This "deal" allowed Grant to avoid prosecution for the Philippine bond scandal, kept him out of wartime service in both Britain and America, allowed him suddenly to switch citizenship (making possible his marriage to Hutton and better access to the accountability of her money), and kept the HUAC hounds from nipping at his especially tempting heels. Grant's part of it—and what had made him so angry after that initial call from the British War Office—was his forced agreement to serve as one of Hoover's domestic "volunteer" spies. There can be little doubt that Cary Grant was a special agent or contact for the FBI assigned prior to and during the war to spy on Barbara Hutton.

---

*Odets somehow escaped the wrath of HUAC and went on to write several more screenplays, most notably Alexander Mackendrick's *Sweet Smell of Success* (with Ernest Lehman). His close friendship with Grant may have been part of the reason.

Given Hoover's known methods of intimidation and persuasion — which included threats of prosecution and/or exposure of the private sexual practices of those whose services he wanted, and Grant was clearly vulnerable on both counts — it is not difficult to see how effective Hoover's exercise of power, or more accurately, his abuse of it, could be.

Except for one incident, there is little evidence that Grant actually did anything for the Bureau, other than supplying information about Hutton's finances. She had an ongoing "friendship" with one Carlos Vejarnano Cassina. Grant, a bit jealous, believed Cassina was pretending to be romantically interested in Hutton to get to her money, and he was soon arrested by the FBI as a Nazi spy. When taken into custody, a personal letter of recommendation was found in his coat from Hutton for a highly sensitive defense job that Cassina was trying to get. After keeping him under surveillance for months, the FBI had known just when to pounce. Grant had been present the day Hutton handed Cassina the letter.*

IN 1944, AFTER FINISHING WORK ON *None But the Lonely Heart,* Grant looked forward to the return of Hutton's only son, Lance, who had been away for six months in New York visiting his father, the count. Reventlow had suddenly been released by the Nazi authorities in Denmark, flown directly to New York City, remarried, and settled into life in a luxurious Park Avenue apartment, all without any visible means of support. Grant was genuinely fond of the boy and enjoyed playing ball with him and taking him around Hollywood to see the sights. That July, when Lance arrived in Pacific Palisades, he was dropped off by representatives of the count, who delivered a message to his ex-wife that he intended to seek full custody of their son.

One week later Lance disappeared. Fearing he had been kidnapped, Grant called the police, and a frantic search ensued. Police swimmers searched the shallow coastal waters in case the boy had accidentally drowned. A day later Grant and Hutton received word from the count that his men had taken the boy and secretly transported him to Canada, out of the clutches of his ex-wife and beyond the reach of American law.

*Cassina was eventually acquitted of all charges.

The strain of the kidnapping finally brought Grant's already-shaky marriage to an end. Hutton had railed at him about it for weeks, blaming Grant for "pushing" her ex-husband to take her son away, referring to the fact that the count had managed to get an injunction preventing Grant from being alone with the boy because, the document claimed, Lance had told him that Grant persistently used "foul language." It was a provocative charge that could easily explode into something much uglier for Grant should the courts ever decide to bring charges of child abuse against him.

By early August Grant had had enough. One night he quietly packed his bags, left the house without saying a word, and moved into a temporary apartment in Beverly Hills he had secretly rented the week before.

The next day an angry Hutton announced to the press that she and Grant had separated. Furthermore, she wanted to make clear, she was the one who had decided to end the marriage, not her husband, and there was "no chance of reconciliation."

In February 1945, after several months thinking it over, Grant filed for divorce, finalized at a single fifteen-minute hearing held later that summer, during which it was agreed that because of their prenuptial agreement, neither party would receive any money from the other. Hutton insisted that Grant keep the many expensive gifts she had lavished on him, a trove that included several hundred thousand dollars' worth of diamond watches, cufflinks, and other assorted jewelry. When the judge asked her why she thought her husband was filing for divorce, she paused for a few seconds and then, with a smirk on her face, said that they did not share the same circle of friends.

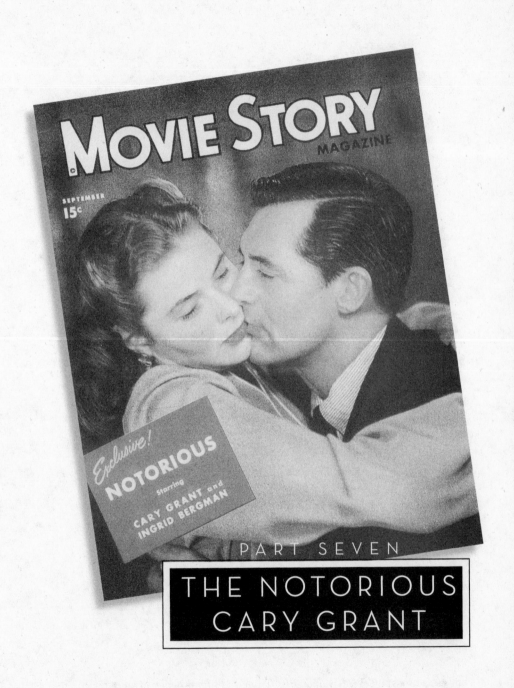

PART SEVEN

THE NOTORIOUS CARY GRANT

PREVIOUS PAGE: *Cover boy and girl—Grant and Ingrid Bergman grace the cover* of Movie Story *magazine to promote the release of Alfred Hitchcock's 1946 classic,* Notorious. *(Rebel Road Collection)*

20

"I can't portray Bing Crosby: I'm Cary Grant. I'm myself in that role. The most difficult thing is to be yourself—especially when you know it's going to be seen immediately by 300 million people."

—CARY GRANT

In February 1945 Cary Grant was nominated for Best Actor by the Motion Picture Academy for his performance as Ernie Mott in *None But the Lonely Heart*. It was his second nomination, his forty-sixth film. He believed he had no chance to win, not only because of the Academy's longstanding hostility toward him, but also because the film had opened to mixed reviews and done poorly at the box office, and Hollywood was loath to give awards to actors whose movies lost money. Unwilling to give the Academy yet another chance to snub him, Grant kept his promise to himself and passed up the chance to sit at a table for hours with a smile fixed on his face until the time came for him to applaud when someone else's name was announced from the podium.

His instinct proved correct. At the ceremony Bing Crosby was awarded the coveted gold statuette for his portrayal of Father Chuck O'Malley in Leo McCarey's *Going My Way*. The Academy then underscored its snubbing of Grant by awarding a Best Supporting Actress Oscar to Ethel Barrymore, Best Original Score Oscars to composers C. Bakaleinikoff and Hanns Eisler, and a Best Editing Oscar to Roland Gross, in recognition of their work on *None But the Lonely Heart.*

For the rest of the year, a bitter Grant rejected all scripts offered to him for his consideration and reverted to his postmarital love-lost rejection/depression/remorse cycle, not all that different from what he had put himself through following his divorce from Virginia Cherrill. When he found out that Hutton had taken up residence at the Mark Hopkins Hotel in San Francisco, he tried to reach her there, but no matter how many times he called — and on certain days it was as many as a dozen — she refused to come to the phone. When that didn't work, he sent flowers with all sorts of expensive presents attached, none of which managed to evoke from Hutton a call or even a thank-you card. When at last he did manage to catch her on the telephone, she was friendly but cold. Nevertheless, just hearing her voice made him believe they were going to get back together, and a suddenly-happy Grant confidently told his friends they were reconciling.

They were not. While Hutton still considered herself a friend of her ex-husband ("How could anyone really stay angry at such a lovely man," she told one of the gossips), she remained firm in her conviction that their marriage was history. To get that message hammered into Grant's handsome head, Hutton used Louella Parsons as her personal messenger. She took to having frequent chats with the columnist, knowing Parsons's column was the surest way to send her ex-husband missives. When he could no longer stand it, Grant traveled to San Francisco and waited for Hutton in her hotel's lobby until she came down. She was surprised to see him but remained cordial. They talked and even had a drink, and Hutton told him once again that the time had come for both of them to move on. The next day Parsons ran another item from Hutton: "Cary was the husband I loved most, he was so sweet, so gentle, it didn't work out. But I loved him." Grant took that as a hopeful sign.

Not long afterward, Hutton moved to Tangier, where she planned to live out the rest of her days. Upon hearing the news of her departure, Grant holed up in his apartment and for weeks did nothing but fumble around from room to room, according to friends, crying at night and drinking himself into fitful sleep.

It was the persistent Frank Vincent who, that spring, finally broke through Grant's black cloud and convinced him the time had come to reenter the world of the living. For openers, he insisted Grant move out of his dark and depressing apartment and into a real home. He found Grant a spacious six-room split-level above Hollywood in the lavish, star-studded Beverly Hills.

Despite an ongoing housing shortage, Vincent had no problem jumping to the front of the long line of buyers wanting the house, because it happened to belong to Howard Hughes, who had purchased it with the intention of living there with Katharine Hepburn upon her triumphant return to Hollywood following the success of *The Philadelphia Story*. Although the two actually did spend a little time in the house, the interior paint had barely dried before Hepburn left Hughes for good, having fallen in love with Spencer Tracy. The house then sat empty until the summer of 1945, when Hughes finally put it on the market. Vincent quickly gobbled it up for Grant (taking the discount Hughes offered for cash).

In the fall of 1946, as the Hills of Beverly were beginning to give up their warm summer breezes for the slicker spicy cool that blew through the storied canyons, Grant finally moved his relatively few pieces of functional furniture out of his small apartment and into his spacious new home.

Harry Cohn, meanwhile, was growing increasingly impatient with his sullen, reclusive star and wanted him to make the one movie left on his contract. As it happened, Jack Warner, whose studio had scored a major hit with *Destination Tokyo*, was also interested in using Grant again, whose postwar value had skyrocketed. Many of the biggest male stars who had gone off to war had returned with the wear from their emotional and physical battles etched into their once-smooth faces.

Two of the biggest, Clark Gable and James Stewart, had joined the armed forces as perfect physical specimens, only to come back looking rugged and creased and, in Stewart's case, with far less hair on his head. Gable, arguably the single biggest male star of the 1930s, had suffered more than most, beginning with the untimely, horrible death of his beautiful wife Carole Lombard; he had spent the rest of the war in uniform, as if to atone for somehow being personally responsible for the war bond plane crash that had killed her and her mother. As a result, his once-mischievous grin had flattened into a permanent leathered fret, and the new gray brushstrokes around his temples put even more distance between this Gable and the roguish prewar Rhett Butler. Stewart, too, had acquired some roughness around his edges; his eyes now reflected a haunted look. Besides Gable and Stewart, dozens of other A-listers had newly "matured" in one way or another, including Tyrone Power, Robert Taylor, and after four long years in the British service, David Niven.

There was no getting around the fact that few of Hollywood's male stars, such as Henry Fonda and Bob Hope, looked as good as they had before the war (and none looked as good as Grant did, before *or* after). At forty-two years old, Grant could easily play ten years younger on the big screen. Jack Warner believed that Grant's physical perfection made him the last of his generation's leading men who could still deliver a romantic picture into big profit. That was why he put out feelers to Columbia about the possibility of purchasing the rights to Grant's last unmade film he owed the studio. He had a specific project in mind for Grant and took Frank Vincent to lunch to discuss it.

Vincent listened patiently, then said simply that it didn't make any difference whether Columbia said yes or no—Grant was not ready to resume making motion pictures and might not ever be, and the best thing Warner could do was wait. In time, he might be able to get Grant without having to go through Columbia.

That sounded like nonsense to Warner, who thought it had to be some kind of bargaining ploy. The next week, ignoring Vincent's advice, he arranged a meeting with Harry Cohn, and the day before it took place, he called Vincent and suggested he be there for it. To Warner's surprise, Vincent showed up with Grant, who was beautifully tailored, well tanned, smiling, and bright-eyed. Vincent had told Grant about the meeting, and was surprised to hear him say he wanted to go. Grant told Vincent he respected both men, they had been very good to him, and while he had absolutely no interest in making any more movies, he felt obliged to at least show them the respect of listening to their offers.

Grant's mindset abruptly changed when Warner revealed to him the picture he had in mind—a musical biography of Cole Porter that he wanted to call *Night and Day*, with Grant starring as the great composer.

It was a temptation Grant couldn't resist. In addition to his stated feelings to Vincent of moral obligation to his friends, his decision to attend the meeting most likely meant his emotional cycle had finally turned and he was ready to go back to work. The Cole Porter biopic sounded to him like the perfect picture with which to make a triumphant return to film.

He was right. A biographical movie often was the highlight of an actor's career. In the seventeen years of the Academy's existence prior to the release of *Night and Day*, biopics had brought Oscars to an impressive roster of stars, including George Arliss for *Disraeli* (1929), Charles Laughton for *The Private Life of Henry VIII* (1933), Paul Muni for *The Story of Louis Pasteur* (1936), Spencer Tracy for Father Flanagan in *Boys Town* (1938), Gary Cooper for *Sergeant York* (1941), James Cagney for George M. Cohan in *Yankee Doodle Dandy* (1942), and Jennifer Jones for *The Song of Bernadette* (1943).*

The elusive Oscar was still very much on Grant's mind. The very nature of both the business he was in and the person he was, and the fact that each was such a defining element of the other, meant that a part of him still des-

---

*Academy Award winners in biographical roles after *Night and Day* include Best Actors: Maximilian Schell as Hans Rolfe in *Judgment at Nuremberg* (1961), Paul Scofield as Sir Thomas More, *A Man for All Seasons* (1966), George C. Scott, *Patton* (1970), Gene Hackman as Jimmy "Popeye" Doyle, *The French Connection* (1971), Robert De Niro as Jake La Motta in *Raging Bull* (1980), Ben Kingsley, *Gandhi* (1982), F. Murray Abraham as Salieri, *Amadeus* (1984), Daniel Day-Lewis as Christy Brown, *My Left Foot* (1989), Jeremy Irons as Claus von Bülow, *Reversal of Fortune* (1990), Geoffrey Rush as David Helfgott, *Shine* (1996); Best Actresses: Anne Bancroft as Annie Sullivan, *The Miracle Worker* (1962), Katharine Hepburn as Eleanor of Aquitaine, *The Lion in Winter* (1968), Barbra Streisand as Fanny Brice, *Funny Girl* (1968), Sally Field, *Norma Rae* (1979), Sissy Spacek as Loretta Lynn, *Coal Miner's Daughter* (1980), Hilary Swank as Brandon Teena, *Boys Don't Cry* (1999), and Julia Roberts as *Erin Brockovich* (2000). Several actors won biographical Supporting Oscars, such as Joseph Schildkraut, *The Life of Emile Zola* (1937), Walter Brennan as Judge Roy Bean, *The Westerner* (1940), Anthony Quinn as Paul Gauguin, *Lust for Life* (1956), Shelley Winters, *The Diary of Anne Frank* (1959), Patty Duke as Helen Keller, *The Miracle Worker* (1962), Estelle Parsons, *Bonnie and Clyde* (1967), Jason Robards as Ben Bradlee, *All the President's Men* (1976), Robards again as Dashiell Hammett, *Julia* (1977), Vanessa Redgrave, *Julia* (1977), Maureen Stapleton as Emma Goldman, *Reds* (1981), Haing S. Ngor as Dith Pran, *The Killing Fields* (1984), Brenda Fricker as Mrs. Brown, *My Left Foot* (1989), Martin Landau as Bela Lugosi, *Ed Wood* (1994), Judi Dench as Queen Elizabeth I, *Shakespeare in Love* (1998), Marcia Gay Harden as Lee Krasner, *Pollock* (2000), Jim Broadbent as John Bayley, *Iris* (2001), and Jennifer Connelly as Alicia Nash, *A Beautiful Mind* (2001).

perately wanted to win one, if for no other reason than to be able to wave its golden ass in the faces of those studio heads dedicated to seeing that he never got the chance to do so. Comedy hadn't done it for him; neither had romance or drama. Perhaps, he figured, biography was the way to go.

The notion of playing the flamboyant Cole Porter, a social acquaintance of his for many years but not a particularly close friend, held enormous appeal to Grant. Porter had been, during Grant's Broadway years, a manneristic (rather than a physical) role model; one reason why it had amused him when the small, gnomish, physically impaired, and owl-eyed composer, asked by the press who, in a perfect world, he could see playing him onscreen, had replied without hesitation, "Why, Cary Grant, of course!"

Negotiating with Jack Warner, Porter expressed concern over what "facts" might actually be included in a film about his life. He would agree to sell the rights to his story only if the script excluded certain "touchy" elements of his real life. These included the composer's excessive drinking, his well-known homosexual lifestyle, and his marriage-for-appearance-and-bankbook to the older and extremely wealthy divorcée Linda Lee Thomas. And, of course, the price had to be right.

Night and Day had been a pet project of Jack Warner since 1943, although when he first had the idea of making a movie about Cole Porter, he knew very little about the songwriter's life. One night, not long after the Warners biopic *Yankee Doodle Dandy*, directed by Michael Curtiz, had opened to rave reviews and great business, Warner was having dinner with songwriter Irving Berlin, during which the subject somehow turned to Cole Porter. Berlin told Warner about the famous horseback-riding accident that had crippled Porter. The idea of making a movie with a physically impaired hero, at a time when wounded soldiers were starting to return to the States, appealed to Warner, who was still looking for the right project to mark the twentieth anniversary of *The Jazz Singer*, the film his studio had made that had ushered in the era of talking pictures.

Before *Night and Day*, Warner had gone into production on another songwriter bio, *Rhapsody in Blue*, a big-budget star-studded bonanza about the life of George Gershwin. The problem with the picture was that its lead, Robert Alda, wasn't a big enough star or strong enough to outshine his supporting players. The film was a hit, but not the smash Warner was looking for, and he was still searching for the right subject to commemorate *The Jazz Singer* when he had dinner with Berlin and shortly after decided to turn Cole Porter's life into a movie.

Warner paid Porter $300,000 for the rights to his life, a deal in which Porter would have total script and cast approval and retain the final choice of which of up to thirty-five of his songs would be included in the film. Warner then went after Cary Grant, the only star he believed could do justice to the role. He offered Grant $100,000 up front, plus a percentage. In addition, he bought out the contract for Grant's last film that he owed Columbia.

WHILE GRANT WAITED FOR Warner to come up with a script that Porter approved, he remained at his new, still barely furnished Beverly Hills house, where he spent much of his time reading mystical self-help books, of which he had become a fan, occasionally venturing out at the behest of Howard Hughes.

One evening Hughes, enmeshed in negotiations to take control of the perpetually money-losing RKO, needed a place to hold a top-secret meeting with Dore Schary—privacy never an easy thing to secure in Hollywood. Tipsters all over town grew rich reporting to the gossips the whereabouts of stars and their supposedly secret goings-on, while the owners of celebrity hangouts such as the Trocadero, Ciro's, the Brown Derby, and Chasen's regularly serviced the gossips in return for a mention in their columns.

The one place Hughes knew to be absolutely impenetrable to the press was his former home, Grant's present one. As Billy Wilder once wryly observed, "I know of not one single soul—nobody—who has been inside Cary Grant's house in the last ten years." Grant's reclusiveness made it the place of choice for Hughes's most important meetings, as well as his many secret sexual rendezvous with young starlets. Hughes, who shunned being the target of scandalous rumor as if it were a communicable disease, knew Grant was one of the few people in Hollywood he could trust unconditionally. Grant, as well, considered Hughes one of his best and most loyal friends, and whenever he wanted to use his former house, Grant was more than accommodating, to the extent of leaving all the bathrooms the way the six-foot-four Hughes had had them custom-built, with extra-large toilets, show-ers, bathtubs, and beds to suit his lengthy frame.

The night of the meeting Schary arrived a few minutes late and saw Hughes's automobile already parked in the driveway. Upon being let in by Grant himself, who answered his own door—he no longer employed full-time live-in help and even kept his part-time cook's food budget to one hundred dollars, preferring cold turkey sandwiches made in the afternoon to elaborately prepared evening meals—Schary, who had never been to Grant's home before, was surprised by what he saw, or more accurately, what he didn't see, inside of the home of one of the wealthiest stars in Hollywood. Aside from a few framed seascapes, notable for their lack of human figures, and a studio daybed in the living room still unmade, its blankets in a bunch, "there wasn't a paper, a cigarette, a flower, a match, a picture, a magazine—there was nothing except two chairs and the sofa. The only sign of life was Hughes, who appeared from a side room in which I caught a glimpse of a woman hooking up her bra before the door closed."

The woman Schary saw was Linda Darnell, one of several actresses Hughes was chasing at the time, among them Swedish-born actress Ingrid Bergman, red hot since winning the 1944 Best Actress Oscar for her role as the victim in George Cukor's *Gaslight*. Bergman accepted an invitation from Hughes to travel with him to New York City one weekend, as long as they had a twenty-four-hour chaperone. Every straight actor in Hollywood (and more than one well-known lesbian actress) was after Bergman, despite the fact she was married at the time to Swedish doctor Peter Lindstrom, the father of her seven-year-old child. None of that mattered to Hughes. As far as he was concerned, her fame, her fortune, and the fact that she was a Swedish beauty made the luscious, tall, high-nosed actress irresistible.

After much convincing, Grant told Hughes he'd chaperone, provided he could bring a suitable traveling companion to make the reason for his pres-ence a bit less obvious. Grant then asked Irene Mayer Selznick if she'd like to accompany him, and she quickly agreed. Grant and Selznick had been friends since his theatrical days in New York City, when he was an actor and she was a producer, and Grant still considered her one of his closest and most trusted confidantes. At the time Selznick and her husband were having difficulties in their marriage, and Grant thought the trip might take her mind off her troubles for a few days. He was right; they both had a ball watching Hughes fall flat on his face trying to woo Bergman. All four spent at least one night together in the upstairs room of "21" eating peanut butter and jelly sandwiches, Grant's choice, chased with expensive iced champagne. The only thing Hughes got out of it was a sticky tongue.

That Monday, Grant and Selznick took an early commercial flight back to L.A., while Hughes insisted that Bergman fly with him later in the day. When they arrived a few minutes late at check-in, Bergman discovered that not only had the seats Hughes insisted he had reserved been given away, but all the seats on every L.A.-bound flight scheduled for that day had been sold. She didn't know it at the time, but Hughes had purchased them all so that they would have to fly home in his private plane, which happened to be fully fueled, on the runway, and cleared for takeoff. "It was all very flattering," Bergman said later, "and I imagine some women would have been very impressed."

Unfortunately for Hughes, she wasn't one of them. She found his attempts at seduction laughable (and, not surprisingly, she found Grant far more attractive). Upon their arrival back in Los Angeles, Hughes dropped off Bergman and went directly to the home of Linda Darnell and apologized for the "pressing business" that had necessitated his sudden trip to New York that weekend.

WHEN JACK WARNER FELT he had a workable Cole Porter script, delivered to him by a team of screenwriters that included Charles Hoffman, Leo Townsend, William Bowers, and Jack Moffitt, he hired Porter's close friend and Broadway veteran Arthur Schwartz to produce the movie, and Monty Woolley, another member of Porter's tight circle, to serve as technical adviser (he also played himself in the film). To direct, Warner chose Michael Curtiz, a selection that made no one happy except Warner, who had him under salaried contract. Curtiz, a solid journeyman director, had an old-world temperament and histrionic methods that made him extremely unpopular among actors, despite his roster of impressive movies that included *Angels* with *Dirty Faces* (1938), for which he was nominated for Best Director, *Yankee Doodle Dandy* (1942), for which he was again nominated, and *Casablanca* (1942), which finally brought him the coveted Oscar.

Production on *Night and Day* began in the fall of 1945. Grant, in a foul mood and still lingering in post-Hutton melancholia, was in no mood for Curtiz's high-booted whip-cracking, and soon the two were going at it, in an on-set feud that became the talk of Hollywood.

For Grant, however, the real problem wasn't Curtiz but the gnawing fear that once again he had chosen a project that, rather than propelling him forward, was merely spinning his wheels.

Night and Day was released July 2, 1946, its world premiere held at Radio City Music Hall. Despite generally lukewarm reviews by skeptical critics, who knew better than to accept this version of Cole Porter's life as anything but Hollywood fantasy, everyone loved Grant's acting and even his campy singing in a memorable rendition of "You're the Top." Whenever Porter was asked how he felt about it, he insisted he loved the film as well, but he was always quick to qualify his opinion with the disclaimer that there wasn't a word of truth in it.

Audiences didn't seem to mind the film's extended flight of fancy, and to Grant's surprise and Warner's delight, *Night and Day* became the hit of the summer, grossing more than $14 million in its initial domestic theatrical release, more than justifying the huge amount of money Warner had spent to make it. Indeed, he had spared no expense, insisting that the picture be shot in beautiful three-strip Technicolor — Grant's first color feature film — and the incandescence it added to Grant's face astonished audiences, most of whom had previously seen Grant only in glossy black and white.*

Having once more proven his alchemical ability to turn leaden celluloid into box office gold, Grant decided to leave the motion picture business on a high note, and this time he meant forever.

---

*Grant had actually appeared onscreen in color once before. In 1935, MGM released a twenty-minute color short, *Pirate Party on Catalina Isle*, that featured several cameo appearances, including a very brief shot of Cary Grant sitting at a table with Randolph Scott, listening to Buddy Rogers and his band. The film was directed by Louis Lewyn. Grant was in it because, at the time, he was on loan to MGM for *Suzy*, and the studio wanted to take advantage of his availability. Grant agreed to do the short on condition that Scott appear in it as well. After its brief initial release, it was rarely screened again in theaters.

Hollywood's quintessential leading man.

Courtesy of the private collection of the Virginia Cherrill Estate

Rebel Road Collection

A rare photograph of a young Archie Leach (seventh from left) touring with the Penders on the Keith vaudeville circuit, just shy of his eighteenth birthday.

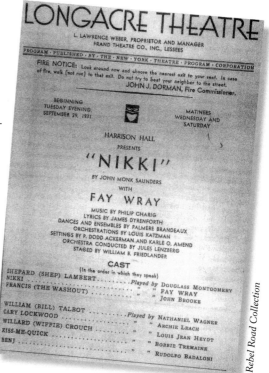

Rebel Road Collection

Twenty-six-year-old Archie Leach on Broadway in the Shubert production of *A Wonderful Night* (1930), opposite Mary McCoy.

The title page of the program for Archie Leach's last Broadway show prior to his moving to Hollywood. The star of the show, Fay Wray, would suggest he keep the first name of his character, "Cary," when he switched to making movies. "Grant" was suggested by Paramount's publicity department.

LONGACRE THEATRE

L. LAWRENCE WEBER, PROPRIETOR AND MANAGER
FRAND THEATRE CO., INC., LESSEES

PROGRAM · PUBLISHED · BY · THE · NEW · YORK · THEATRE · PROGRAM · CORPORATION

FIRE NOTICE: Look around now and choose the nearest exit to your seat. In case of fire, walk (not run) to that exit. Do not try to beat your neighbor to the street.
JOHN J. DORMAN, Fire Commissioner.

BEGINNING
TUESDAY EVENING,
SEPTEMBER 29, 1931

MATINEES
WEDNESDAY AND
SATURDAY

HARRISON HALL
PRESENTS

"NIKKI"

BY JOHN MONK SAUNDERS
WITH

FAY WRAY

MUSIC BY PHILIP CHARIG
LYRICS BY JAMES DYRENFORTH
DANCES AND ENSEMBLES BY PALMÈRE BRANDEAUX
ORCHESTRATIONS BY LOUIS KATZMAN
SETTINGS BY P. DODD ACKERMAN AND KARLE O. AMEND
ORCHESTRA CONDUCTED BY JULES LENZBERG
STAGED BY WILLIAM B. FRIEDLANDER

CAST
(In the order in which they speak)

SHEPARD (SHEP) LAMBERT .... Played by DOUGLASS MONTGOMERY
NIKKI .... " FAY WRAY
FRANCIS (THE WASHOUT) .... " JOHN BROOKE
WILLIAM (BILL) TALBOT ....
CARY LOCKWOOD .... Played by NATHANIEL WAGNER
WILLARD (WIFFIE) CROUCH .... " ARCHIE LEACH
KISS-ME-QUICK .... " LOUIS JEAN HEYDT
BENJ .... " BOBBIE TREMAINE
                                  " RUDOLFO BADALONI

Rebel Road Collection

Cary Grant was signed by Paramount in 1932 as a substitute for Rudolph Valentino, whose sudden, early death left a void in the studio's roster of European-style leading men.

Courtesy of the private collection of the Virginia Cherrill Estate

Paramount Publix publicity photo of Cary Grant holding his pet Sealyham terrier, "Archie Leach," circa 1932.

Courtesy of the private collection of the Virginia Cherrill Estate

Courtesy of the Academy of Motion Picture Arts and Sciences

Together wherever they went. Virginia Cherrill did not appreciate Randolph Scott's having so much of a physical presence in her marriage to Cary Grant. The three are seen here shortly after Cherrill and Grant's wedding, winter 1934.

Bettmann/CORBIS

To offset the persistent rumors of Grant's homosexuality, nervous Paramount executives were always eager to have their star photographed with as many beautiful women as possible. Here he is seen with the finalists of the studio's 1935 "Starlet Most Likely to Succeed" contest: Ann Sheridan, Grace Bradley, Katherine DeMille, Gail Patrick, Wendy Barrie, and the winner, Gertrude Michael.
Underwood & Underwood/CORBIS

Opposite, below: Randolph Scott and Cary Grant keeping in shape at their home gymnasium, circa 1935.

Grant attending a Hollywood party in 1937 with *The Awful Truth* costar Irene Dunne (left) and Fay Wray, a good friend from his Broadway years.

Hulton-Deutsch Collection/CORBIS

Howard Hawks, Grant with Harold Lloyd–type glasses, and Katharine Hepburn, during the making of *Bringing Up Baby* (1938). Now regarded as a highlight of the screwball era, the film was not an immediate hit with audiences. In it, Grant perfected his persona of the man pursued, rather than the pursuer.

Courtesy of the Academy of Motion Picture Arts and Sciences

AP Wide World Photos

Divorced from Cherrill for several years and prior to his 1942 marriage to
Woolworth heiress Barbara Hutton, Cary Grant and Randolph Scott continued
to be seen together in public, despite persistent rumors regarding the sexual
nature of their relationship. Seen here at one of their favorite pastimes, the
Friday-night fight in Los Angeles, 1940.

Bettmann/CORBIS

On June 26, 1942, Cary
Grant finally becomes a
U.S. citizen, amid lingering
rumors of draft-dodging and
undercover work for the FBI.
He refused to appear in any
American movies wearing a
military uniform until he was
a fully legalized citizen.
Although he insisted he
wanted to join the American
military, he never did.

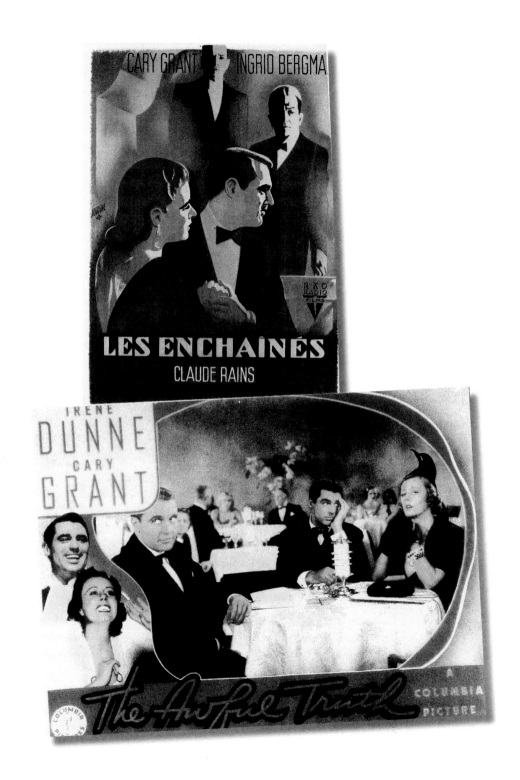

Cary Grant films as conceived by the three directors who most vividly shaped and influenced his comedic and dramatic screen personalities: Leo McCarey (*The Awful Truth*), Howard Hawks (*Bringing Up Baby*), and Alfred Hitchcock (*Suspicion* and *Notorious*).

Cary Grant and Barbara Hutton on their wedding day, July 7, 1942, at the Lake Arrowhead home of his agent, Frank Vincent.

Courtesy of the Academy of Motion Picture Arts and Sciences

AP Wide World Photos

January 17, 1947, five days after they are reported missing and feared dead in a Hughes-piloted plane that was assumed to have crashed, Howard Hughes and Grant show up very much alive in Mexico City visiting the president of that country. Left to right: Hughes; A. C. Blumenthal, nightclub and hotel operator; Mexican President Miguel Alemán; Grant; Rogelio de la Selva, secretary to the president; and Francisco Busch de Parada, a friend of the president.

Bettmann/CORBIS

On July 16, 1951, at the 94th ceremony in front of Hollywood's legendary Grauman's Chinese Theatre, Cary Grant signs the slab containing imprints of his hands and footprints. "Always follow your dreams," he tells the enthusiastic crowd.

AP Wide World Photos

During the climax of Alfred Hitchcock's *North by Northwest* (1959), rescue becomes redemption, Grant/Hitchcock style. In a scene repeated many times throughout Grant's career, he reaches for the lady, in this instance Eva Marie Saint, and lifts her to a safer and higher place.

Cary Grant, Sophia Loren, and Frank Sinatra at a preview screening of *The Pride and the Passion*, June 1957. Both men had crushes on Loren during the making of the film. Grant's claim that he and Loren were madly in love and going to marry was described by his friend, producer William Frye, as "just some sort of daydream that he made up."

Bettmann/CORBIS

Bettmann/CORBIS

Cary Grant surrounded by his heirs apparent in 1962: Rock Hudson, Marlon Brando (during the filming of *The Ugly American*), and Gregory Peck.

Bettmann/CORBIS

Cary Grant in 1976, near the East River, New York City, on a walkway made from the stone and brick rubble of the World War II bombing of his hometown, Bristol, England.

On March 12, 1968, Cary Grant was involved in a car accident in Queens, New York, en route to Kennedy Airport to return to Los Angeles and his divorce hearings. He was accompanied by 23-year-old Gratia von Furstenburg, whose presence in the limo Grant feared would hurt his chances for joint custody of his daughter, Jennifer. The chauffeur suffered serious head injuries, von Furstenberg a broken leg and collarbone, and Grant cuts and bruises. Photographs of the injured and apparently disoriented Grant appeared on front pages all over the world.

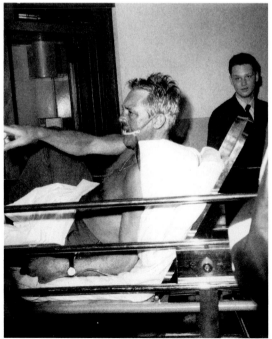

AP Wide World Photos

AP Wide World Photos

In the summer of 1977, 73-year-old Cary Grant accompanies his 11-year-old daughter to one of his favorite pastimes, watching the Los Angeles Dodgers play at home.

AP Wide World Photos

Two months before his death, Cary Grant and his fifth wife, Barbara, make a rare public appearance to attend a party for friend Clint Eastwood, in September 1986.

An unused ticket for the show Grant did not live to perform. He died that night after suffering a stroke during rehearsals.

ADLER THEATRE
DAVENPORT IOWA
SATURDAY 8:30 P M
"A CONVERSATION WITH CARY GRANT"
Presented By

NOV. 29 1986

December 1, 1986: News of Grant's death is flashed around the world in front-page headlines.

MANHATTAN ★★★ RACING FINAL

DAILY NEWS

NEW YORK'S PICTURE NEWSPAPER®

Monday, December 1, 1986

35¢

CARY GRANT DEAD AT 82

Film great had stroke

Stories begin on page 4;
His career in pictures in centerfold

CARY GRANT IN 1982

GRANT'S WIVES were (l. to r.) Virginia Cherrill (1934-35), Barbara Hutton (1942-45), Betsy Drake (1949-62), Dyan Cannon (1965-68) and Barbara Harris (1981).

The New York Daily News

21

"*Notorious* resumes the general visual key of *Suspicion* with Cary Grant common to both films, like the theme of domestic poisoning . . . To [the former's] single-minded study in undeserved paranoia, *Notorious* counterpoints an undeserved contempt."

—RAYMOND DURGNAT

This time forever lasted all of two weeks, before Grant eagerly agreed to appear in *Notorious*, the film that would reunite him with Alfred Hitchcock. The director had to wait in line for another chance to use Grant, having wanted him for *Shadow of a Doubt* (1943) to play the murderous Charlie, a role that went instead to Joseph Cotten, and for *Spellbound* (1945) as the psychotic John Ballantine, whom Gregory Peck eventually played, neither of which role would have met with the audience's approval.

Hitchcock first began to think about *Notorious* as early as 1943, when he had a notion to make a movie about a woman "carefully trained and coached into a gigantic confidence trick which might involve her marrying some man . . . the training of such a woman would be as elaborate as the training of a Mata Hari." It would become a movie about a man whose control over a woman also makes him her victim, to the point of testing her loyalty by forcing her to marry his rival and then inconsolably suffering over it when she does—cinematic manna to both Hitchcock and Grant.

By early 1945 Hitchcock had developed and clarified the theme of the film. During lunch at Chasen's, he told William Dozier, a producer at RKO, that the film was going to be about sexual enslavement. After listening to a breakdown of the plot, Dozier took it directly to Selznick, who was eager to get the play-or-pay Hitchcock back into production, even if he, Selznick, was too busy to supervise the making of the film itself. At the time Selznick was in preproduction on *Duel in the Sun*, a postwar western eroto-epic ("Lust in the Dust!") that starred Gregory Peck (whose spectacular performance in Hitchcock's *Spellbound* had resulted in his being hailed as the "new" Cary Grant). Selznick was also more than a little preoccupied with *Duel*'s female lead, the comely Jennifer Jones, who happened to be his paramour and eventually the second Mrs. Selznick. (Grant was relieved that Selznick wasn't going to be around very much: he didn't want to be caught between his professional obligations to Selznick and his personal friendship with his wife, who was, at the time, suffering from Selznick's public romancing of the much younger and far more beautiful Jones.)

Selznick's involvement with *Duel* stalled the commencement of production on *Notorious*, something that did not bother Hitchcock all that much. He was happy to collect his $7,000-a-week paycheck while he waited for *Notorious* to get the green light, and he used the time to work on the script, whose first draft, written by *Spellbound* screenwriter Ben Hecht, had fallen far short of what Hitchcock envisioned. At Grant's suggestion, the director called in Clifford Odets to rewrite the script, but he soon quit when Hitchcock insisted he add additional "love scene" dialogue between Devlin and Alicia while she is lying in bed, about to die from poison.

To solve the problem of his split loyalties (to his two films, not his two women), Selznick sold off *Notorious* as a completely self-contained package to RKO for $800,000 plus 50 percent of the eventual net, leaving him, after all preproduction expenses (including salaries), with an instant profit of $500,000. It wasn't that difficult a choice; *Duel in the Sun* was his obsessive love letter to Jones, while his difficulties with Hitchcock had made him reluctant to work again with the director. To ensure that Hitchcock would not be offended by the deal or try to do anything that might kill it, Selznick offered him guaranteed star billing—"An Alfred Hitchcock Production,

Directed by Alfred Hitchcock."* In the parlance and value system of Hollywood, that meant creative control, something the director craved. But true to form, Selznick managed to keep an active hand in virtually every step of the production of *Notorious*, particularly with the still-unfinished script, constantly pushing Hitchcock to build up Grant's part. In the early versions of the screenplay, in a pivotal scene, Alicia goes to the wine cellar alone and discovers her husband's "secret"; Devlin is thus absent from one of the most important scenes in the film. At the end of several early versions, Alicia dies in Devlin's arms, even as her husband, Sebastian, is planning, with his Nazi cronies, to expand their sphere of evil. Selznick's stubborn insistence that the film must have a "happy ending" forced Hitchcock to restructure the entire story.†

Selznick also dictated that the role of Sebastian's mother, Madame Sebastian, become more central to the sexual aspect of the doppelgänger struggle between Devlin and Sebastian, as Devlin's bitter rage at Alicia gradually turns to love, even as Sebastian's love for her turns to murderous rage. In this sense, thanks to Selznick, the Devlin-Alicia-Sebastian triangle becomes infinitely more complex by the increased presence of the fourth member of this bizarre couple-swap, Madame Sebastian. Selznick's story instincts apparently triggered Hitchcock's wealth of Oedipal fantasies, which run rampant through the film, as Madame's fierce jealousy of Alicia inspires her sadistic plan to kill her while forcing her guilt-ridden son to help her do it.

NOTORIOUS OPENS IN MIAMI during the last months of World War II. The night following the conviction of her father as a Nazi spy, we discover Alicia (Ingrid Bergman) at a party, where she is celebrating by getting drunk. Also

---

*Hitchcock was the producer of *Suspicion*, although onscreen credit went to Harry E. Edington.

†Everyone, it seemed, wanted in on the making of this film, even Grant's former "associate," J. Edgar Hoover, from whom permission was needed to officially incorporate the FBI into the story. Hoover, Hollywood wannabe that he was, in response to Selznick's request, wrote him the following memo: "The film might subject the FBI and you [Selznick] to criticism on the grounds of morality," referring to the sexual nature of Alicia's character. "Why not make [her] an impersonator of the real Alicia Huberman? Since the ersatz Alicia would presumably not be an American citizen, the real Alicia would emerge from the scheme with her patriotism — and her virginity — intact."

at the party is undercover agent T. R. Devlin (Cary Grant), who has been assigned to simultaneously seduce and recruit her. The self-absorbed Devlin soon becomes conflicted about his attraction to Alicia, aware of her family background and reputation as a hard-drinking, "fast-living" (sexually loose) woman.

In each of the four films Hitchcock made with Cary Grant, there is a dangerous car ride that serves to cleverly thrust the plot forward. In *Notorious* it takes place when, early on, even though Alicia is drunk, Devlin lets her take the wheel. She drives fast and recklessly—life is cheap and expendable to the both of them. She starts to speed. He warns her she is going sixty. She pushes hard on the pedal and takes them to eighty, looking to go even faster when she is pulled over by a motorcycle cop. Just as she is about to be arrested, Devlin takes control of the situation, pulls rank, and the policeman backs off. Having barely escaped a bad situation, Alicia wants to remain in the driver's seat. In response, Devlin slaps her into submission, then shoves her over to the passenger side and takes the wheel. For the rest of the film, they will struggle over which of them is really in the driver's seat.

On orders from the Bureau, Devlin assigns her the job of spying on Alex Sebastian (Claude Rains), the head of a Nazi Party cell located in Brazil, to find out what secret weapon the group is harboring. Alicia does her job a little too well; against the advice of his sadistic, possessive, and jealous mother (Leopoldine Konstantin), Sebastian proposes marriage, and in a move that surprises, infuriates, and embitters Devlin (in that order) but one that he is not in a position to oppose, she accepts. At a postwedding reception to which Devlin has been invited by Alicia, they find their way down to Sebastian's wine cellar, where they discover a secret stash of uranium ore (or something) hidden in specially marked champagne bottles. When Devlin realizes that Sebastian is spying on them, he suddenly grabs Alicia and kisses her to throw Sebastian off. It doesn't work. To his horror, Sebastian realizes he is married to an American agent. Totally humiliated, he listens to his mother, and together they begin to slowly poison Alicia to death. Just before she succumbs, Devlin, sensing she is in great danger, boldly goes to Sebastian's house, where he rescues her and in so doing sends Sebastian and his mother to their certain death at the hands of their vicious fellow Nazis.

Although filled with intrigue, espionage, murder, sex, and betrayal, to Hitchcock the film was essentially a love story. Devlin's Mephistophelean character is enraged at Alicia for being a drunk and a slut, and at himself for being attracted to her. To punish her and protect himself, he becomes her pimp by turning her into a prostitute, all in the name of duty to country. She chooses to marry Sebastian partly out of her own fury—she wants Devlin to prevent it, and he doesn't. She then taunts Devlin by showing him the power of her own sadistic tendencies: the ability to seduce powerful, if damaged, men and enjoy it. The sexual merry-go-round then shifts into high gear: Devlin loves Alicia but gives her to Sebastian; Alicia loves Devlin but gives herself to Sebastian; Sebastian is hopelessly slave-locked in forbidden boy-love with his mother while at the same time jealous of Devlin.

This crazy carousel apparently carried over to real life. Those close to the action believed that during production Hitchcock had fallen deeply and hopelessly in love with Ingrid Bergman; what Hitchcock dared not try in real life, he could act out and control vicariously through the actions of his characters. As Hitchcock directed Grant, so did Devlin direct Alicia.

At times, it is difficult to tell if Grant is playing Devlin, or Devlin is playing Grant, especially when so much of Devlin's behavior to this point in the film mirrors Grant's in real life, at least some of which Hitchcock must have been aware of and that he may have used as a way, for the sake of the character, to try to connect Grant to his own darker side. Devlin works for a national security bureau; Grant had been involved with the FBI. Devlin slaps the woman he loves; Grant had been accused by Virginia Cherrill of slapping her. Devlin falls in love with a woman who has strong emotional and family ties to Nazis; Grant's second wife was suspected of being friendly with several Nazis.

Notorious is filled with scenes that rank among the most famous set pieces of both Grant's and Hitchcock's careers, including the famous kissing scene between Devlin and Alicia, interrupted and therefore extended by incidental dialogue and even a phone call (critic Andrew Sarris described it as "a kissing sequence that made 1946 Radio City Music Hall audiences gasp"); cinematographer Ted Tetzlaff's beautifully paced and razor-blade precision shot that begins at the top of the stairs and steadily zooms in to a close-up of Alicia's fist, offering a glimpse of the all-important key to the wine cellar that she has stolen from her husband; the quick-zooms into the faces of Sebastian and his mother at the moment of Alicia's realization that they are in the process of killing her; the fantastic wine cellar lipless kiss that she and Devlin "fake" to try to mislead Sebastian.

Finally, the entire film is held together onscreen by what must be ranked among the best performances of the decade—Claude Rains's tortured mama's boy, Leopoldine Konstantin's dragon mother murderess, Ingrid Bergman's lusty leggy nymphomaniac, and Cary Grant's matinee-idol hero/Satan.

Notorious was not only a huge commercial success, it provided Grant with a crucial career leap. His performance as Devlin proved once and for all that he could successfully portray charming, heroic, romantic characters that had both darkness and depth, even while dressed in his requisite tux (which he donned for the reception scene). Prior to this film, his comic turns in *The Awful Truth*, *Bringing Up Baby*, and *The Philadelphia Story* had heightened his reputation as a fine comic actor, even as critics tended to dismiss his more serious roles as too offbeat, such as Ernie Mott in *None But the Lonely Heart*, or as mere personality poses, like Captain Cassidy in *Destination Tokyo*. Ironically, by allowing Hitchcock to cast him in a role that was emotionally truer to any that he had played in the past, he was newly hailed for his ability to "act" by playing against type. As he had done in *Suspicion*, Hitchcock understood that the best way to "direct" Grant was to shine the spotlight precisely on the dark side.

SHORTLY AFTER COMPLETING THE FILM, Grant decided to take a week off and travel to England. With the war over, he was at last able to reunite with Elsie, who seemed to have regained some of her mental faculties. Shortly after his arrival, she took him on a shopping spree through Bristol (where he was all but mobbed), then back at the house bawled him out for divorcing Hutton. Meanwhile, Grant once more tried to persuade her to return to Los Angeles with him. Once more she refused.

Back in the States, he filled his calendar with social activities, one of which was a Fourth of July party where he ran into Jimmy Stewart, who had recently returned from nearly four years of active wartime duty. Stewart had been the first major American movie star to enlist, joining the Air Force eight months before the Japanese bombed Pearl Harbor. Grant congratulated him for his heroic exploits and wished him well in his new "comeback" picture, Frank Capra's *It's a Wonderful Life* (a film originally conceived by Capra and purchased by RKO as a vehicle for Grant). The following day he was off to New York with Ingrid Bergman and Alfred Hitchcock on a publicity junket for the highly anticipated Radio City Music Hall world premiere of *Notorious* on July 22, 1946. RKO had chosen to kick off its summer season with the film's glittering black-tie opening, where Grant and Bergman fairly shimmered in the spotlighted night.

The film broke the opening-week box office record at Radio City (previously broken the year before by *Night and Day*). Audiences gasped and critics raved at Hitchcock's newest sex-and-spy thriller. *The New York Times* declared the film "just about as thrilling as they come, with an intensity of warm emotional appeal." Herman Rich Isaacs, writing in *Theater Arts* magazine, lauded Grant for "bringing glamour and sultry vitality to the lead." But it was James Agee, film critic for *The Nation*, who most accurately caught the pitch of Hitchcock's moody meditation, singling out Grant's "precisely cultivated, clipped puzzled-idealist brutality."

Notorious grossed more than a million dollars for RKO in its initial domestic theatrical release, placing it among the biggest hits of the year. Grant's second consecutive multimillion-dollar-grossing film decisively returned him to the position in Hollywood he most enjoyed.

Being on top.

THE DAY AFTER THE OPENING Grant received a call in his studio-provided suite at the Warwick Hotel from Howard Hughes, who was in town and preparing to fly back to Los Angeles. Hughes asked Grant if he, Hitchcock, and of course Ingrid Bergman would all like to make the trip home with him in his private plane. Bergman accepted, Hitchcock said no. The director was well aware of Hughes's daredevil flights and was too afraid to fly with him. Always cautious and highly superstitious, once Grant and Bergman canceled their commercial reservations, Hitchcock, who had been booked on the same flight, canceled his as well and instead booked himself, his wife Alma, and their daughter Pat on a cross-country excursion by rail.

Mechanical problems caused Hughes to postpone his takeoff several times, and for the next two nights, while technicians worked on the plane's engines, Grant and Hughes drank themselves into pleasant stupors at the Warwick's dimly lit bar. When they finally did take off, Hughes decided to change his flight pattern and made several unscheduled "pit stops" along the way. The flight took two days to complete, with the result that the tortoiselike Hitchcock arrived in Los Angeles before the airborne Hughes, Grant, and Bergman.

A few days later, while testing his experimental XF-11 military plane, engine trouble forced Hughes to crash-land over Beverly Hills, barely missing a neighborhood of upscale Beverly Hills residences. Hughes was rushed to the hospital, where doctors fought to keep him alive. The only person he let into his room who wasn't on staff was Grant, who sat with him in silent support for days at a time.

NOT LONG AFTER HUGHES RECOVERED, Grant began work on his next film, a light comedy for Selznick called *The Bachelor and the Bobby-Soxer*, directed by Irving Reis, produced by Dore Schary, and written by then-unknown screenwriter Sidney Sheldon. As if to accentuate his approaching middle age, he let himself be cast opposite the suddenly voluptuous Shirley Temple, who had set off a generation of middle-aged men into cold sweats while still a toddler and now came on like gangbusters, thrusting her ample bosom at Grant's bespectacled high school teacher every chance she got. In the film, her emerging teenage hormones are fueled by the (mostly imagined) competition for Grant from her older sister (Myrna Loy). Although Grant was more than twice Temple's age, he looked better next to her than to Loy, who was only one year younger than Grant but looked to be at least five years his senior.

The film reflected Hollywood's recognition of the emerging teenage market that was changing the demographic makeup of the postwar moviegoing audience. The new faces in the audience were attracted to a different style of acting onscreen, a blend of bravado over having won World War II and the gnawing paranoia about the emergence of superpower Communism, reflected in the tender but twisted new faces of Marlon Brando and Montgomery Clift. Brando had shaken up Broadway with his incendiary performance as Stanley Kowalski in Elia Kazan's 1947 stage production of Tennessee Williams's *A Streetcar Named Desire*, Fred Zinnemann's 1950 film *The Men*, and Kazan's 1951 cinematic reprise of *Streetcar*. Clift, another stage-trained actor, made his motion picture debut in Zinnemann's *The Search* (1948) but made his neurotic presence felt a year later in Hawks's *Red River* as John Wayne's surrogate son, one more symbolic passing of Hollywood's postwar torch.

As for "old Cary Grant," who thought the country needed some comic post-war relief with movies like *The Bachelor and the Bobby-Soxer*, he couldn't quite understand what this new style of acting was all about. To him, the up-and-coming breed of movie stars seemed generally unkempt, indistinguishable from one another, and awfully hard to hear. As if on cue, Hitchcock proposed to Grant that they make a new film of Shakespeare's *Hamlet*, a project Grant had considered for a long time before rejecting it, fearing he wouldn't be able to master the proper British accent. Besides, he told Hitchcock, in the current youth-oriented atmosphere of Hollywood, he was far too old to play the Danish prince.

And then real-life tragedy suddenly interrupted everything in Grant's life when Frank Vincent, having just turned sixty-one, dropped dead of a heart attack. Grant was shocked when he heard the news, disappeared from sight for a week, and went on a bender that showed no signs of letting up. Worried friends tried to intervene, but the only person he would see was Hughes, who suggested the two of them get out of Hollywood for a while. Having just finished modifying his latest airship, the *Constellation*, a World War II B-23 bomber, into a passenger prototype for his new airline, TWA, he was about to fly it to New York and convinced Grant to come along for the ride.

They arrived in the city on January 8, and after two days of making the rounds, they were ready to fly back to L.A. Sometime during the night of

January 11, 1947, while flying over the Rocky Mountains, the plane lost radio contact and disappeared from radar screens. When it failed to arrive at an appointed stopover in Amarillo, Texas, word quickly spread that the plane had gone down somewhere over the Rockies, and that both Hughes and Grant had been killed in the crash.

22

⌈∙∙∙∙⌉

"I'd been flying for a lot longer than he had. I wasn't terribly
fond of riding as a passenger in planes piloted by Hughes,
because I didn't think he was a great flyer."

—HOWARD HAWKS

The January 12 morning editions of newspapers across the country
screamed the terrible news in giant front-page headlines:

CARY GRANT AND HOWARD HUGHES
KILLED IN PLANE CRASH!

While the world awaited the discovery of the wreck, Hollywood gussied
itself up for the biggest public funeral it had ever produced, bigger than the
one for Carole Lombard, bigger than the one for Will Rogers, bigger even
than what New York gave Valentino.

Meanwhile, after sleeping late into the morning, Grant and Hughes
awoke in a hotel in Guadalajara, oblivious that the world was in mourning
for them. They ordered breakfast in their room, relaxed, cleaned themselves
up, and went to the airport, which is where they first discovered they were
supposed to be dead. Having intended to go to Mexico City, they returned
instead to Los Angeles.

Upon landing, they were besieged at the airport by hundreds of reporters from all over the world, who treated the two as ghostly heroes who had some-how managed to find their way back from the far side of the River Styx. After refusing to make any comments, Grant finally cleared up some of the mys-tery by telling Hedda Hopper, "All we did was to change plans in the course of our flight. Howard doesn't like to get embroiled with crowds; neither do I. So when we landed at El Paso, Howard rolled out to a dark part of the air field, and we sat in the plane drinking coffee while awaiting our clearance to proceed on to Mexico City. When we discovered the weather there was so bad, we went to Guadalajara instead. The next morning someone spotted us and said, 'Didn't you fellows know that you're in the headlines? You're sup-posed to be lost.' Howard and I laughed. Being lost suited us fine. We figured for as long as nobody knew where we were, we could live in peace."

Although he would never admit it to his friend, high-flying with the macho, reckless Hughes through the boundless skies had always frightened as much as it excited Grant. Now, however, the notion that they could actu-ally both have been killed in the wake of Vincent's death was what finally sobered him up. Ironically, his own "death" had resurrected his desire to live.

A FEW WEEKS LATER Grant placed an ad in the trades to announce that he would, from this point on, represent himself in all negotiations, with the assis-tance of his longtime lawyer and good friend, Stanley Fox, and that he had sold off all his remaining interests in Frank Vincent's talent agency.*

Grant's announcement attracted the attention of Jules Stein, who was in the process of rebuilding his Music Corporation of America from a small agency that specialized in booking local bands into "the octopus," the "General Motors of Hollywood," two still-used nicknames for what was to become the most powerful entertainment conglomerate in Hollywood, MCA Universal-International. Stein quickly convinced Grant that he would be far better off with professional representation and, to ensure his continued

*Fox quietly arranged for Grant to purchase Vincent's home at 9966 Beverly Grove from his widow, who no longer had any use for the enormous French-farm-style spread. Grant had always loved the whitewood and brick one-level unit, located high in the Beverly Hills with sweeping views of the city and ocean, and couldn't bear the thought of strangers living there. He continued to live at his other house and made 9966 into something of a shrine, leaving it exactly as Vincent had when he died.

independence, offered him a deal he couldn't refuse. He promised he would negotiate all of Grant's future pictures so that the rights to the negatives would revert to him after seven years. Stein, always ahead of the industry curve, believed television was the future of Hollywood and that the need for programming would send the networks to the studio's film libraries. This stroke of genius on Stein's part would eventually make Grant one of the wealthiest men in all of Hollywood.

But it still wasn't enough for him. Grant wanted their arrangement to be nonexclusive, for each individual contract that Stein set up was to be subject to final approval by Grant and Stanley Fox, who was to be included at the negotiating stage of all deals, for which he would receive half the agency's 10 percent commission. It was the only nonexclusive representation pact that Stein ever agreed to. He then assigned up-and-coming talent agent Lew Wasserman to personally handle Grant, whose first deal under MCA's guidance was the starring role in Samuel Goldwyn's highly anticipated *The Bishop's Wife*.

The notion of starring in a pseudo-religious/angel/spirit film appealed to Grant, who believed the genre was a particularly good one for actors, especially during the lucrative Christmas season, which immediately preceded the announcement of Oscar nominations when the holiday films were freshest in the minds of the voters. Robert Montgomery had earned an Oscar nomination for his role as a premature ghost in the heaven-on-earth comedy *Here Comes Mr. Jordan* (1941); Jennifer Jones had won an Oscar for playing Bernadette in *The Song of Bernadette* (1943); Lubitsch had been nominated for his direction of *Heaven Can Wait* (1943), which featured Laird Cregar as the devil; and Bing Crosby's performance as a godlike priest in *Going My Way* (1944) had brought him an Oscar, along with one for its director, Leo McCarey (the year Grant received his second nomination, for *None But the Lonely Heart*). Although not an Oscar contender, Henry Travers as the angel Clarence all but stole Capra's *It's a Wonderful Life* (1946). Grant's own *Topper*, in which he played a happy-go-lucky ghost, was one of his earliest hits.

Grant had originally intended his next picture to be the George Cukor/Garson Kanin film *A Double Life*, about the tortured existence of a popular actor, but at Wasserman's urging he changed his mind at the last minute and opted for Henry Koster's *The Bishop's Wife*, once Goldwyn made it clear he was willing to pay whatever it would take to get him. Before Wasserman was through, Goldwyn agreed to an astonishing $500,000, by far the most Grant had ever earned up front for a single movie.

It was enough to compensate Grant for a role and a script he wasn't all that crazy about. Written by Leonardo Bercovici, *The Bishop's Wife* concerns the tribulations of Bishop Henry Brougham (David Niven) and his singular and increasingly desperate attempts to raise money from his wealthy parishioners for a new cathedral, ignoring everything and everyone else to do so, including Julia (Loretta Young), his beautiful wife. His prayers are literally answered when Dudley (Grant), an angel from heaven, arrives and swiftly restores the priorities to everyone's life, including Henry's, by flirting with neglected Julia. When their relationship threatens to turn real, Dudley moves the rest of his miracles along rather swiftly to get Henry his cathedral. Then, with great personal regret, Dudley disappears, taking the memory of his brief visitation with him.

Niven was first approached to be in the film, for what he assumed was the role of Dudley, who is a handsome charmer, a romancer, and steadfastly angelic, while Henry is, throughout, humorless, stiff, unromantic, and unpleasant; his conversion from self-righteousness to self-awareness is the essential theme of the picture. When Niven, whose career had not yet regained its prewar momentum, complained about the role he was given, Goldwyn threatened to fire him.

Things became even more complicated when Grant expressed his dissatisfaction with *his* role, told Goldwyn he thought Dudley was "a rather conceited, impudent, high-handed magician," and didn't see what he could possibly do with him. He was equally dissatisfied with Henry Koster, the director whom Goldwyn had settled upon after firing William Seiter and failing to convince William Wyler to take the film. Seiter's dismissal caused the film to be shut down for six weeks, until Koster, best remembered for a series of Deanna Durbin movies, was in place and ready to resume shooting. The Wyler/Seiter/Koster debacle bothered Grant, as did the choice of Loretta Young, with whom Grant had worked in 1934 in *Born to Be Bad*. He had always considered her overly vain, and the bond fraud incident with her husband didn't help matters any.

Grant's overall frustration with the slow progress of the film took the form of daily battles with Koster. He remained dissatisfied with everything the director did, from the placement of his camera to the pace of the comedy sequences. Things became even more tense on the set when Grant and Young openly clashed over the blocking of their love scene, when Young refused to be shot from the left. Grant became completely fed up and then refused to be shot from *his* left side. As a result, Koster had to shoot the scene with the actors talking to each other while they stared out a window, both their right profiles in plain view.

An increasingly frustrated and disappointed Goldwyn showed Koster's final cut of the film to Billy Wilder, with an offer of $25,000 to "fix it," which upset Grant, who had no use for this director either. Wilder made some suggestions and Koster reshot a few scenes, but it was clear to everyone that the film remained flawed. Nevertheless, largely on the strength of Grant's box office appeal, *The Bishop's Wife* opened to positive reviews and was nominated for a Best Picture Oscar.*

GRANT'S NEXT FILM, *Mr. Blandings Builds His Dream House*, was not scheduled to go into production until that fall. Grant, who had turned forty-three that January, decided to spend the summer in England and meet with Alexander Korda about the possibility of starring in a film called *The Devil's Delight*, in which Carol Reed would direct. Grant was interested in playing the title role—the devil—in what he thought might be a neat turn after Dudley the angel. He also wanted to travel the British countryside by automobile with his new best friend, sixty-six-year-old British sometime playwright and full-time eccentric Freddie Lonsdale (author of *The Last of Mrs. Cheyney*), whom he had met while Lonsdale was visiting Hollywood.

In London, Korda and his wife, actress Merle Oberon, from whom he was officially separated but with whom he was still friendly, took Grant to see all the new shows playing at the West End. One of them, *Deep Are the Roots*, was an American import. During the performance a featured player happened to catch his eye. Her name was Betsy Drake, a tall, blond, cute twenty-

---

*It lost to Elia Kazan's *Gentlemen's Agreement*, starring Gregory Peck, who was also nominated for his performance but lost—to Ronald Colman, in the leading role Grant had turned down in *A Double Life*.

three-year-old American actress making her British debut in the play. He made a mental note to find out more about her when he got back to the States.

As it turned out, he didn't have to wait quite that long. The last week in September Grant and Lonsdale boarded the *Queen Elizabeth* at Southampton, bound for America. Postwar summers in England had become the new fancy for many of Hollywood's Brit-born stars, and several had booked passage back to the U.S. on this voyage of the *Queen Elizabeth*. Besides Grant and Lonsdale, among the entertainment heavyweights who had commandeered first-class accommodations were fifteen-year-old movie star Elizabeth Taylor and her mother; Oberon; financier and art collector Jock Whitney; and Betsy Drake, traveling in unusually comfortable fashion for a still largely unknown actress.

Drake was the daughter of hotelier Carlos Drake, a writer whose family had built the Drake and Blackstone hotels in Chicago. She was born in Paris in 1923, while her father was living his "Lost Generation" novelist dream, and returned to America at the age of six with her parents, after the 1929 stock market crash forced Carlos Drake to return to Chicago to attend to family business matters. At the age of seventeen, Betsy quit school and moved to New York to make a life for herself as an actress. Her striking looks soon landed her a contract as a Conover model. She eventually found work on Broadway in a series of plays and in 1946 was signed to a film contract by Hal Wallis, who flew her to Los Angeles for a screen test, which she failed. She then returned to New York and auditioned for and won her role in the British production of *Deep Are the Roots*.

Now, aboard the *Queen Elizabeth*, she was approached by Merle Oberon, whom Grant had sent as an envoy to arrange a formal introduction. Oberon invited Drake to have lunch at the captain's table, which was where she first met Grant. The two talked for the rest of the day, and for most of the night atop the deck, and the next day they met again and resumed their ongoing verbal marathon. Grant was, by now, totally smitten. He liked everything about her, from the unusual way she spoke, with the slightest trace of a French accent cut with a noticable, and to Grant adorable, lateral lisp, to the stylish way she dressed—little high collars, princess-style coats, flared skirts, white cuffs, and white gloves. He was equally enthralled by her passion for the Eastern philosophy of Taoism and the power of hypnotism.

By the time the ship docked in New York's harbor, Grant was convinced he was in love with Drake, nineteen years his junior. With much reluctance, after spending a week with Drake in New York, he had to leave her behind, but not before making her promise to visit him in Los Angeles, where he was scheduled to begin work on H. C. Potter's *Mr. Blandings Builds His Dream House.*

The film was a light and sophisticated comedy in which Grant played a Manhattan executive who moves his family out of the crowded city and into their own "dream house" in the suburbs. David O. Selznick had bought the best-selling novel by Eric Hodgins as a property for Grant and Myrna Loy to star in, a follow-up of sorts to *The Bachelor and the Bobby-Soxer.* Selznick hoped the pairing of Grant and Loy might blossom into a series of films, similar to Loy's earlier run in the *Thin Man* series opposite the debonair William Powell, which had recently ended its lucrative five-picture, twelve-year run.

If Grant was still uneasy working for Selznick because of his much-publicized engagement to Jennifer Jones, he went ahead with the picture at least in part to promote Drake's acting career. When production on *Mr. Blandings* was completed, Drake came to Los Angeles in January 1948 to celebrate Grant's forty-fourth birthday. For the occasion, he moved into the larger 9966 Beverly Grove house so Drake could have her own bedroom. Nevertheless, for all practical purposes, although neither one officially said as much to the other, they were now living together.

Grant began setting up appointments for Drake, first with Ray Stark, a hungry talent agent who agreed to take on Drake as a client.* Grant also met with Selznick and Dore Schary, the new head of production at RKO, to convince them, as he had Stark, that it was in their best interests to sign his young "protégée." Selznick then worked out an unusual arrangement with Schary, to "share" Drake. It didn't hurt matters any that Howard Hughes had finally gained a controlling interest in RKO and was, for all practical purposes, Schary's boss.

Not long afterward Schary began production on *Every Girl Should Be Married,* starring Cary Grant as Dr. Madison Brown, a bachelor pediatrician who is relentlessly pursued by Anabel Sims, a sales clerk working in the chil-

---

*Stark would go on to become a highly successful film producer.

dren's clothing section of a large department store. Brown resists with everything he has, but at the end, when he can no longer hold her off, he succumbs to Anabel's "charms," and they go off together into the matrimonial
sunset. It is supposed to be a comedy.

Schary had wanted Barbara Bel Geddes to play Anabel, but he was over-
ridden by Hughes, who gave the part instead to the studio's newest acquisition—Betsy Drake. Grant knew that acting on screen with Drake was a risky
proposition. People were going to say that she had gotten the part only
because she was his girlfriend, and they would be right. Drake, however,
believed just the opposite, and she told Hedda Hopper so. If everyone
thought she had gotten her big break because of Grant, she explained in an
interview with the columnist, then they were very wrong about her *and* Cary.
A better way to look at it, she suggested, was that Grant had simply made it
possible for them to share a creative experience with their real-life chemistry
out there for all the public to see.

The film turned out to be a positive experience for both Grant and Drake;
the only downside was that Hughes insisted on becoming actively involved
in every aspect of its production, with the result that Schary abruptly resigned
from RKO. Hughes then allowed Grant to rewrite much of the script, and
even to instruct director Don Hartman in how to shoot several scenes, so as
to shift much of the film's visual emphasis from his character to Drake's.

When the film was completed, Grant felt the time had come to introduce
his new love to his mother.

PART EIGHT

MARRIAGE AND OTHER MONUMENTS

PREVIOUS PAGE: *A shockingly thin Cary Grant, still recovering from the infectious hepatitis he contracted in England during the making of* I Was a Male War Bride *(1949), is greeted upon his return to the States by future wife, Betsy Drake. At the time, Grant was 45 years old and Drake was 26. (AP Wide World Photos)*

23

"I've been called the longest lasting young man about town.
It's ridiculous for a man in his fifties, but then until thirty-
five a man is often a self-centered idiot. After thirty-five he
should begin to make more sense. Sufficient kicks in the
rear over the years do make a difference."

—CARY GRANT

On August 26, 1948, Cary Grant and Betsy Drake left together for Germany, where Grant had agreed to star in Howard Hawks's post-war military comedy, *I Was a Male War Bride*. Grant had agreed to star in the film only after much cajoling from Hawks, who had signed a new four-picture deal at 20th Century–Fox and was, a decade later, finally in a position to do a follow-up of sorts to *Bringing Up Baby*.

After World War II, many European countries froze all foreign assets, including $24 million of 20th Century–Fox's money. That left the studio little choice but to go to where its money was and make movies there. *I Was a Male War Bride* was one of twenty-four such productions the studio scheduled to be shot on location in Europe in the late 1940s. Hawks, who had just completed principle photography for the one and only independent film of his career, the classic western *Red River*, seized the opportunity to make the German-based comedy. To get Grant to say yes, Hawks agreed to the ever-parsimonious actor's insistence that Betsy Drake accompany him on the entire overseas shoot, all her expenses paid by the studio out of the film's budget, including a visit by the both of them to Bristol so he could introduce her to Elsie.

Howard Hughes was not happy about Hawks's getting Grant to be in his film. He had wanted Grant to continue working at RKO, but for both professional and personal reasons, Grant had declined all of Hughes's offers. For one thing, the intensity of their friendship suffered by what Grant felt was Hughes's overbearing and unfair interference during the making of *Every Girl Should Be Married*. Grant considered Schary a good friend as well, and although he did not say anything at the time, he did not appreciate having to watch him be bullied by Hughes.

Moreover, a growing postwar political schism was dividing Hollywood's Left and Right. And while Hughes was a staunch conservative, active in the HUAC machinations, Grant remained resolutely liberal and was particularly outraged that Hollywood's powerful, fanatical right-wing forces, to which Hughes was completely committed, had Charlie Chaplin at the top of their hit list.

THE CHARLES LEDERER, Leonard Spigelgass, and Hagar Wilde script for *I Was a Male War Bride* was based on the best-selling autobiographical novel by Henri Rochard, which recounted the trouble he had run into as a French-born soldier trying to marry an American woman. Military marriages between occupying soldiers and native civilians were popular throughout the 1940s and 1950s and the subject of several postwar movies, including *Sayonara*, Joshua Logan's grim Academy Award–winning 1957 film adaptation of James Michener's best-selling novel. In *I Was a Male War Bride*, the subject was treated much more lightly, as the title character, played by Grant, winds up sneaking aboard a U.S.-bound transport by dressing as a female officer, something Grant found unbelievably funny, having grown up in the world of British music hall humor, where "going drag" was a longtime staple of Saturday-night skits. In fact, most people tend to remember *I Was a Male War Bride* as a film that Grant spent entirely in drag, although he actually spends less than ten minutes in a dress, near the end of the film, and does so quite unconvincingly. The essential plot contrivance of *I Was a Male War Bride* has Captain Henri Rochard (Grant, playing a "suave French captain" without the slightest hint of any accent other than his usual light Bristol see-saw) in love with American WAC officer Lieutenant Catherine Gates (Ann Sheridan), who also happens to be his assistant. They go through a tumultuous courtship that ends in matrimony but leaves the couple no chance to consummate their union. It is postwar Europe, and Captain Rochard, a French citizen, cannot accompany his American-born wife to the United States unless he enters under the newly restrictive immigration policies, whose only military exemption is the category of "war bride." At this point, he disguises himself as a civilian woman.

GRANT'S FIRST STOP on the way to Germany was London, where he met up with Hawks for preliminary rehearsals at Shepperton Studios. The first time Grant put on a dress, he performed a drag show for the director, exaggerating all his disguised character's feminine gestures. Hawks didn't think it was at all funny and advised Grant to play the character as straight as possible. Being an obvious straight male in disguise, as opposed to a gay man in a skirt, became the key to Grant's finding the humor in his character.

For the duration of the stopover, Grant, Drake, Hawks, and Sheridan were all put up at a luxurious apartment complex in Grosvenor Square, but even so it was difficult for Grant to ignore the postwar miasma that had settled upon bombed-out London, accentuated by endless fog and drizzle. Because of the heavy rehearsal schedule he did not have time to take Drake to Bristol, and Hawks had to assure him that he would be able to return to England during a break in the production schedule.

The next stop was Heidelberg, where actual filming began on September 28, 1948. Hawks shot his location exteriors first, preparing his actors to be ready to do their scenes at certain designated hours to catch the best light. This was Grant's first time shooting on the European mainland, and he was not used to the weather or the harsh postwar conditions. It was cold, the skies were gray, and meals were served up on tin plates. He especially did not appreciate having to use the same bathroom as Sheridan. Only Drake seemed to enjoy the whole thing and treated it as an adventure. She loved the idea of "roughing it," as she put it, and even volunteered to help prepare the company's meals.

On weekends Grant and Drake flew either to Switzerland or to France, where they would live like royalty for two days before returning to the harsh environs of Heidelberg.

PRODUCTION SHIFTED BACK to London that December, and Grant planned to take Drake to Bristol his first free weekend. Unfortunately, shortly after they arrived, Sheridan came down with pleurisy, made worse by the relentless British winter, the fiercest the country had seen in twenty years. Grant had to remain on seven-day call to accommodate the improvised shooting schedule that now changed daily, and as a result he had to once again postpone taking Betsy to meet Elsie.

Two weeks later Sheridan had recovered enough for Grant to film his one remaining scene with her, after which he was scheduled to drive with Drake to Bristol. Before they could leave, however, Grant came down with a severe headache, his temperature spiked, and he began coughing. Hawks sent him back to his hotel early to get some much-needed rest. By two A.M. Grant had turned yellow. He was rushed to the hospital, where he was diagnosed with infectious hepatitis, complicated by jaundice, a potentially lethal combination that landed him in the intensive care ward.

He remained there for four weeks, during which time he dropped forty pounds. At one point his doctors told a nearly hysterical Drake to prepare herself for the worst, that Grant had less than a 10 percent chance of surviving. The problem, they explained to her, was the damage that years of hard drinking had done to his liver.

Grant's otherwise superb physical conditioning is what saved him. Upon his release from the hospital, he was ordered to remain in bed and was taken to a small suite in London's Mayfair Hotel. The only nurse he would allow to care for him was Drake, who stayed by his side around the clock and served his every need.

With production on the film once again shut down, the rest of the cast and crew, including Hawks, returned to the States. Two weeks later, after helping Grant move into Pamela Churchill's luxurious Mayfair flat that he had sublet, Drake left for Hollywood at his insistence to begin working on a new film, *Dancing in the Dark*, which he had helped her get.

Grant, alone with a new private nurse who was a complete stranger, lapsed into the worst depression of his life and, he later admitted to friends, thought seriously about suicide.

In January 1949, four months after his his initial attack and well on the road to recovery, Grant was finally well enough to go home. An elated Drake, still in the United States working on her film, arranged for his return to Los Angeles via the Dutch ship *Dalerdijk*. She chose that vessel because it was specially equipped for long-distance medical treatment. The *Dalerdijk* left Antwerp on March 10, with Grant aboard in a private suite that doubled as his personal infirmary. Unusually rough waters and bad weather made his confinement all that much more lonely an affair. Bedridden for the voyage, he suffered the entire two weeks it took for the ship to cross the Atlantic, pass through the Panama Canal, and eventually up the southern waters of the Pacific to Los Angeles Harbor.

In the meantime Hawks finished as much of the picture as he could and rescheduled the rest of Grant's scenes to be shot at the Fox studios. One scene in the movie has Grant driving through a haystack on a motorcycle. Only the first part of the scene had been completed before he took sick. Later on, while looking at the rushes, Hawks wryly commented that it looked as if "Cary came out [the other side] weighing twenty pounds less."

Production on the film took an unusually long and grueling eight months, with a budget that had skyrocketed to over $2 million due to all the unforeseen delays. And, because of his illness, Drake never got to meet Elsie, the whole reason Grant had taken the movie.

In December 1948, during production of *I Was a Male War Bride*, *Every Girl Should Be Married* was released and received a lukewarm critical reception. *Time* magazine said of it, "Newcomer Betsy Drake seems to have studied, but not learned, the tricks and inflections of the early Hepburn. Her exaggerated grimaces supply one solid laugh—when hero Grant mimics them cruelly and accurately. In the past, Cary Grant has shown a talent for quietly underplaying comedy. In this picture, he has trouble finding comedy to play."

Despite a respectable box office, Drake felt humiliated by her uniformly poor reviews and began to think about returning to New York and the live stage. Grant would have none of it. Still weak and underweight, he insisted he needed her by his side and promised to get her more film work. The only way to win over the critics, he told her, was by making good movies—hopefully ones they could appear in together.

Grant kept his word and used his influence at Fox to get Drake cast in the starring role of a film version of the 1931 stage musical *The Bandwagon* by Howard Dietz and Arthur Schwartz. The film, renamed *Dancing in the Dark* during production, was directed by Irving Reis (who had been fired from *The Bachelor and the Bobby-Soxer* because Grant disliked his work). The producer of the film was George Jessel, a good friend of Reis who, as a result of the bad blood between Reis and Grant, determined to make the shooting as unpleasant as possible for Drake, after the studio forced her, at Grant's "urging," into the role originally intended for June Haver.

Dancing in the Dark opened shortly after Grant's return to Los Angeles in the spring of 1949 to scathing reviews, many of which once again focused on Drake. To keep her from directly packing her bags and boarding a plane back to the East Coast, Grant arranged for her to appear with him on the Lux Radio version of *Every Girl Should Be Married*. The show was broadcast June 27, and proved so popular (like every show Grant did on the radio) that it was repeated April 17 the following year, and afterward Grant agreed to do a radio serial based on *Mr. Blandings Builds His Dream House*, costarring Betsy Drake as his wife. He had been able to get the radio serial rights from Selznick, who always needed money, and Howard Hughes, who put up the money to buy them.*

Broadcasting was a medium Grant felt particularly comfortable in. According to his producer, William Frye, "He was very meticulous, exact, charming, funny, and sweet. Difficult, too, but I found working with him a lesson in professionalism. He would go over the scripts word for word, and if

---

*Hughes, eager to return to Grant's good graces, was more than happy to provide the funding.

there was one that affected the character's point of view, he would insist that we change it to make it better."

This proved to be not as easy as it sounds. The show's principal writers, Jerome Lawrence and Robert E. Lee (who would later go on to write several Broadway shows, including *Inherit the Wind*, and numerous television serial dramas), made it difficult for Grant to change so much as a single word. Not long after production began, he stopped speaking to them and they to him. "One problem with the show," Frye recalled later on, "was that Betsy, a lovable actress onscreen, had problems in radio because she had a slight stammer, and that held production up for hours on end because she needed special editing and reediting."

Another thing Grant did to keep Drake with him was to bring up the subject of marriage.

That stopped Drake packing for good.

IN JUNE 1949 WORD FROM "unnamed sources" began appearing in the Hollywood gossip columns that Grant and Drake were secretly engaged. This produced a burst of fan hysteria and media frenzy that made the forty-five-year-old Grant and his twenty-six-year-old bride-to-be the number one subject on everyone's lips. It actually wasn't until July that Grant officially proposed to Drake, but his continuing health problems, related to a slower-than-expected full recovery, forced them to leave open the date of their marriage. Grant spent much of the remainder of the summer undergoing tests at Johns Hopkins Hospital in Baltimore, including the most comprehensive physical checkup he had ever had, to make sure nothing was lurking in his system that might be the reason for his inability to completely shake the lingering effects of his recent illness.

To his and Drake's relief, he emerged with a clean bill of health, although he did receive a warning to cut down on his drinking and give up smoking, neither of which he did. Satisfied that he was in good enough condition to get married, he and Drake secretly set the date.

I Was a Male War Bride opened on September 2, 1949, and Grant and Drake attended the gala New York premiere together. If the making of the film had been unexpectedly difficult for Grant, standing at the back of the Roxy Theater (where it had been moved from Radio City due to scheduling conflicts caused by its delayed opening), he felt completely gratified as he listened to the black-tie audience roar with approval several times throughout the screening. At the party afterward Grant was asked by a reporter from *The New York Times* for his reaction. "Having just seen the picture," he said, "I was amazed how the audiences laughed themselves sick . . . I honestly feel it's the best comedy I've ever done."

The film's first run lasted through October and grossed more than $4.5 million, making it by far 20th Century–Fox's biggest hit of 1949, its most successful comedy, and the third-biggest Hollywood release of the year by any studio, in a virtual tie with Anatole Litvak's Academy Award–winning *The Snake Pit*, and surpassed only by Henry Levin's lavish musical *Jolson Sings Again* and Elia Kazan's racially controversial *Pinky*. *I Was a Male War Bride* would eventually rank as the third most successful film of Howard Hawks's entire oeuvre, just behind *Sergeant York* and *Red River*. It not only restored his reputation as a bankable Hollywood director, it allowed the forty-five-year-old Grant to close out the 1940s on a note of high professional achievement and unprecedented popularity.

As the day of their wedding — December 25 — approached, to ensure privacy Grant called upon the ultimate expert at it, who was, once again, happy to help. Howard Hughes handled all the details. On Christmas morning the billionaire personally picked Grant and Drake up in his car, drove to the airport, and then flew them all to Phoenix in one of his private planes to a small hacienda owned by a friend of his, real estate baron Sterling Hebbard. There, a brief, nonreligious ceremony was performed by Methodist minister Reverend Stanley H. Smith. Hughes served as Grant's best man; Drake had no maid of honor. Immediately following the ceremony Hughes flew them both back to L.A. and then drove them home, where waiting for Drake was her wedding present from Grant, delivered by one of Hughes's trusted assistants while they were gone: a white poodle that she immediately named Suzie. As he carried her over the threshold, Drake told Grant she couldn't be happier.

The press, effectively locked out of the whole affair, managed to get a story out of Grant's wedding to Drake anyway by wondering if he, like so many others in show business, was being love-laced by something queer in the American air. As one of the most tumultuous decades in American history came to a close and Hollywood was sinking into political turmoil, the rich and famous, not only in Tinseltown but in Washington and New York as well, were suddenly marrying each other in a frenzy unseen since the last, giddy days of the Roaring Twenties. What's more, the older the groom, the younger the bride. Besides the hitching of 45-year-old Grant and 26-year-old Drake, that December no less than the Vice President of the United States, 71-year-old Alben Barkley, married a 38-year-old St. Louis widow; 59-year-old William O'Dwyer, mayor of the City of New York, married a 33-year-old ex-model; Tyrone Power, 35, married Linda Christian, 24; 41-year-old Jimmy Stewart married 31-year-old Gloria Hatrick; 45-year-old Greer Garson remarried, this time to 58-year-old cattle baron E. E. (Buddy) Fogelson; 39-year-old ice-skating sensation Sonja Henie married for the second time thrice-married New York blueblood 55-year-old Winthrop Gardner Jr.; the King of Hollywood, 48-year-old Clark Gable, married his fourth wife, 39-year-old Douglas Fairbanks's widow Lady Sylvia Ashley; and 47-year-old David O. Selznick, his divorce from Irene official, finally married 30-year-old Jennifer Jones.

But of all of them, it was the Grant/Drake marriage that dominated the headlines. The morning of December 26, the day after their hushed-up wedding, the front page of the *Los Angeles Examiner*, in a headline worthy of the start of the next world war, screamed out the news that "CARY GRANT, BETSY DRAKE ELOPE IN HUGHES' PLANE."

It was the spinsterish Hedda Hopper, herself rumored to be hopelessly in love with Grant, whom she routinely dubbed "the handsomest leading man in Hollywood," who got in the last, slightly cynical but still insightful word on Grant's marriage to Drake. Quoting screenwriter Lenore Coffee, she put it this way in her concluding column of the month, the year, and the decade: "When a man of forty falls in love with a girl of twenty, it isn't her youth he is seeking but his own."

24

"Selectivity always suggests art and, in the case of the very
few stars who achieve the magnitude of Cary Grant, art of
a very high and subtle order. Indeed the evidence both of
our eyes and of such testimony on the point that the star
himself has offered, suggests that Grant went further than
most in that the screen character he created, starting some
time in the mid-1930s, drew on almost nothing from his
autobiography, his characters created almost entirely out
of his fantasies of what he would like to have been from
the start, what he longed to become in the end."

—RICHARD SCHICKEL

Cary Grant was feeling youthful and benevolent. His third marriage
had reinvigorated his spirit and given him the feeling that he was
once more solidly in control of his career and his life; and of Betsy as well. They
did everything they could together and seemed to enjoy each other's company
more than anyone or anything else. Early in 1950, with neither of them committed to making a movie, Drake suggested they board a tramp steamer and
travel around the world. Grant rejected that idea, his last trip home from
England having eliminated any lingering romanticism he had about the open

seas. Instead, he introduced Drake to one of his favorite pastimes, the daytime races at Hollywood Park. Grant loved horses and often described their physical motion as an act of pure elegance. And he loved betting on them, although throughout his life he remained strictly a two-dollar man. What he loved was the action of the race, the stable smell of the horses, the sunshine he basked in along with the rest of the crowd, always flecked with the faces of some of the biggest Hollywood stars, who met at the specially reserved part of the park on a daily basis to lunch, talk, drink, eat, flirt, date, hustle, and occasionally even bet on a horse or two.

That spring Grant signed on to make one or two more movies, strictly to help out those he cared about, including Drake, after which he planned to formally announce his retirement and take his wife on their long-overdue journey to Bristol. He agreed to play a brain surgeon in *Crisis*, Dore Schary's first film at MGM, where the writer/director had landed after Hughes forced him out of RKO. Grant knew that his appearing in the movie was the kind of hit insurance Schary needed to commercially revitalize his career, even if the script was less than spectacular, which it decidedly was.

In *Crisis*, the directing debut of Richard Brooks, brain surgeon Dr. Eugene Ferguson (Grant) and his wife Helen (Paula Raymond) are kidnapped while visiting an unnamed South American country. His captors force him to operate on dictator Raoul Farrago (José Ferrer), and they warn him that if their leader dies, so will Ferguson and his wife. The good doctor operates and saves Farrago's life; a revolution then breaks out, and Farrago is killed, during which the Fergusons are rescued and set free.

Despite his good intentions, *Crisis* was a poor choice for Grant's first film of the 1950s. It was cheaply made; its poor production values and black and white cinematography made it look more like an episode of an early action-adventure TV series than a big-screen movie. Grant, still underweight from his illness, looked gaunt and noticeably older than he had in *I Was a Male War Bride*. For the first time he let his close-cropped hair show substantial gray around the temples. Still, his haggard appearance fit the overall character, and with Grant's name above the title, *Crisis* was successful enough to accomplish what he had wanted it to, which was to firmly establish Schary at MGM. The film also gave Brooks his first hit, for which he was grateful to his star. Brooks and Grant became good friends during the making of the film and remained so for the rest of Grant's life. On numerous occasions Brooks would ask him for his opinion on scripts. It is a little-known fact that Grant was one of the better script-doctors in Hollywood, able to break down a film into its component parts and analyze characters as well as the personal style of any producer or director he had ever worked with.

During the making of the film, Grant, way ahead of his time, had strongly urged Schary to see to it that all the South American roles in the film were played by authentic Latin actors, which resulted in the casting of José Ferrer, Ramon Novarro (the original Ben-Hur of silent films), Gilbert Roland, Vicente Gómez, and a dozen others. At least part of Grant's heightened awareness in this area came from Drake, who had taken it upon herself to educate the already liberal Grant in the unfair ways of Hollywood typecasting. At a time when Hollywood was drawing ever-deepening political lines in the sand and demanding to know which side someone was on, Grant, with Drake proudly by his side and urging him on, stepped up publicly to the left.

While Grant was starring in *Crisis*, Drake appeared in Warner Bros.' *Pretty Baby*, a role she got due to Grant's quiet insistence to Jack Warner that he use her in the film. *Pretty Baby* was a nondescript comedy costarring Dennis Morgan and Zachary Scott, two contract leftovers from the war years, when actors in Hollywood were scarce and anything that moved in pants, stood over five foot five, and had a military deferment qualified as leading-man material.

Grant next agreed to appear in *People Will Talk* for Joseph L. Mankiewicz, a Fox film produced by Darryl F. Zanuck. It was Mankiewicz's first film after his dazzling *All About Eve* (1950), for which he won two Oscars — Best Director and Best Screenplay (and two the year before for *A Letter to Three Wives*).* Based on a German play by Curt Goetz that Mankiewicz adapted, *People Will Talk* depicts the growing paranoia at the heart of the McCarthy era. Grant plays another doctor, Noah Praetorius, with a "mysterious" background who teaches at a university. He comes under an

*The double back-to-back awards made Mankiewicz the only person in Hollywood to ever win four major-category Oscars in two successive years.

administrative investigation led by Professor Elwell (Hume Cronyn), during which he marries Deborah Higgins (Jeanne Crain), a single pregnant young woman, to save her from committing suicide. Afterward he is exonerated from whatever it was the committee thought he might have been guilty of.

The script played better than it sounds and reflected Mankiewicz's style of multilayered story lines. Despite Grant's gem of a performance, remembered mostly for the final shot of the film showing him ecstatically conducting a symphony orchestra, the film did not find an audience. After its poor opening, it disappeared quickly from the screen (and has rarely been seen since). At about the same time, *Pretty Baby* opened and also flopped at the box office, after which Grant and Drake decided to take a break from Hollywood and spend some time in Palm Springs. While there, Grant was visited by another old friend who had fallen on hard times and needed his help to resuscitate his career.

Even though Grant had not exactly set the world on fire so far in the 1950s, dozens of scripts continued to come his way. One in particular was hand-delivered to him in the desert by visiting neighbor George Cukor, who had a film he felt was perfect for the actor. Grant had already heard about the script at the track, where producer Sid Luft had brought it with him every day for weeks, trying to convince Grant to at least read it, which he had steadfastly refused to do.

The screenplay, by Cukor's old friend, Broadway playwright Moss Hart, was an updated musical adaptation of the original William Wellman/Robert Carson screenplay for the 1937 *A Star Is Born*, which had starred Fredric March and Janet Gaynor. This dark-side fable of the film industry was a modern retelling of Shaw's *Pygmalion*. The original film was loosely based on the life of actor John Gilbert, one of Hollywood's greatest silent movie stars, whose career was destroyed by the industry's switch to sound, for which Gilbert's voice was not suited. While on top, Gilbert had married a young actress, Virginia Bruce, whose star did indeed rise as his fell. The movie also had elements of B. P. Schulberg's struggles at Paramount, the sudden early deaths of Rudolph Valentino and Irving Thalberg, and the alcoholism and tragic decline of John Barrymore. *A Star Is Born* was one of the highest-grossing films of 1937 and won writing Oscars for Wellman and Carson,

Academy nominations for March, Gaynor, Wellman (director), and David O. Selznick (producer), and an honorary award to W. Howard Greene for his innovative use of color photography.

Selznick had always wanted to remake the film, but after SIP, awash in debt, was dissolved in 1951, the project seemed out of reach. He eventually traded the rights to it to Warner Bros. in exchange for $25,000 and the film rights to Hemingway's *A Farewell to Arms*. Jack Warner had been eager to acquire the project and turn it into a musical vehicle for Judy Garland. Once he had control of the property, he hired Hart to do the rewrite and chose Cukor to direct.

Cukor managed to convince Grant to keep an open mind long enough to at least read the screenplay. If he read it and still refused, Cukor said, he would never bring it up again. Under those terms, the next night at Cukor's nearby desert home, Grant read aloud the part of Norman Maine, with Cukor doing all the others. It took several hours to get through, and when they were finished, Cukor smiled and said to Grant, "This is the part you were born to play!"

"Of course," Grant agreed. "That is why I won't."

His primary reason for turning down *A Star Is Born* had to do with the obvious similarity of the script to his own life, something he had always carefully managed to avoid onscreen. The character of Norman Maine is an older leading man; so now was Grant. Maine is married to a much younger, talented actress, who is unknown at the time they wed but is a star by the time the film ends; Grant was married to the much-younger Betsy Drake, whose career he was mentoring, even as he felt himself edging toward retirement. Maine is a cold, narcissistic, self-involved actor with a serious drinking problem; Grant was considered by many in Hollywood to be too aloof and narcissistic, and while he wasn't an alcoholic, at least not by the definition of the day, he definitely drank too much.

The script, then, provided a direct bridge to his inner self without the essential redemptive resolution that Hitchcock had managed to bring to the characters Grant played in both *Suspicion* and *Notorious*. In these films Hitchcock had taken him and the audience to the brink and then, at the last possible moment, brought them back to the safety of literal solid footing and moral redemption. In *A Star Is Born*, Maine commits suicide.

Having said his piece, the evening came to an end, and Grant left. For the rest of his life Cukor never forgave him for turning him down. He felt at the very least, Grant owed him something for having cast him first in *Sylvia Scarlett* and then in *Holiday* and *The Philadelphia Story*. (James Mason eventually played the role of Norman Maine, opposite Judy Garland, both of whom were nominated for Oscars for their performances in the film's 1954 release, one of the highest-grossing films of that year.)*

INSTEAD, GRANT NEXT CHOSE to do a film version of Cervantes's *Don Quixote* for Warners, but the project never even made it to the script stage. One former studio executive described it as "one of those periodically increasing episodes after he married Drake when he enjoyed the thought of chasing windmills." When it fell through, Jack Warner convinced him to costar with Drake in something called *Room for One More*, a domestic can't-miss comedy that would also complete the studio's two-picture obligation to her.

Directed by Norman Taurog, *Room for One More* concerns the plight of "Poppy" Rose (Grant), a struggling civil servant, and the unrealistic generosity of his "goofy" wife Anna (Drake), who takes to bringing home orphaned pets and child misfits unwanted by their own families. Inevitably, the cranky Grant, who complains they can't afford to be so benevolent, sees the errors of his ways and not only saves the lives of the children (one boy becomes an Eagle Scout) but gets back in touch with his inner, better self. Released in January 1952, it had been held back until after the Christmas season, a sure sign of how little Warner Bros. thought of its box office potential. And although Drake received the best notices of her career—the *Hollywood Reporter* review called her "superb"—for a genuinely funny and charming performance, she would not make another picture for five years.

Apparently neither Grant nor Drake was the least bit concerned about the film's failure. Grant in particular insisted to everyone that he couldn't care less; the only role that interested him now was playing the student to Betsy Drake's one-on-one tutor in the art of self-hypnosis, which he hoped would

---

*The film was nominated for a total of six awards. Mason lost Best Actor to Marlon Brando in Elia Kazan's *On the Waterfront*, and Garland lost Best Actress to Grace Kelly in George Seaton's *The Country Girl*.

help him give up smoking. They went so far as to have no-smoking weekends. As for making films, Grant steadfastly maintained that he had once and for all retired, the reason being, as he told a reporter from the *Star Weekly*, a Hollywood fanzine, "Heavy romance on the screen should be played by young people, not middle-aged actors."

No sooner had Grant convinced everyone that his filmmaking days were over than he signed on with Howard Hawks to star in *Monkey Business*, a fountain-of-youth comedy with a terrific script by the veteran team of Ben Hecht, I.A.L. Diamond, and Charles Lederer, two of whom had worked with Hawks or Grant before.*

What attracted Grant to the film was precisely what had kept him away from *A Star Is Born*. Both films deal with essentially the same theme — the "perils" of aging — but they handle it in completely opposite stylistic ways. *Monkey Business* concerns the experiments of an aging all-my-joints-ache research chemist, Dr. Barnaby Fulton (Grant), who stumbles upon the formula for eternal youth that causes him to become sexually responsive to his secretary, Lois Laurel (rising-starlet Marilyn Monroe), much to the consternation of Mrs. Fulton (Ginger Rogers, in one of her brightest and most relaxed performances).

The film portended future youth mix-up comedies like Penny Marshall's *Big* (1988) starring Tom Hanks (an actor who many thought might become his generation's Cary Grant). Grant's performance is pure delight; his athletic abilities come into clever play when he takes the drug and turns into a gangling, superfit teenage lover-boy. Under Hawks's clever and speedy direction, the film manages to celebrate middle age by defining it in terms of mature love, inevitability preferable to the energetic emptiness of adolescent passion. It also spoofs Grant's longstanding refusal to chase women in his films. Only when he is under the influence of the youth drug does he pursue Monroe. When he recovers, he reverts to his mature, i.e., passive, married and happy self.

The film also put Hollywood on notice that its next reigning sex goddess

---

*Hecht had written much of *Notorious* and the Grant/Russell version of *His Girl Friday*; Lederer had collaborated with Hecht on *His Girl Friday* and had written *I Was a Male War Bride*.

was as troubled as she was talented. In her few brief scenes, Monroe flashed her delectable beautiful-but-dumb-blonde character's thighs in a way that could make dead male audiences sit up and take notice. For her part, Monroe all but stole the female spotlight from the aging, staid, if equally unnaturally blond, Ginger Rogers. As perfect as Monroe appeared onscreen, however, on the set she had been a completely different story.

During filming, front-page headlines revealed that as a teenager Monroe had posed nude for a calendar to make money after her mother was committed to an insane asylum. Monroe had a near breakdown when the story was revealed. While most of the others involved with the film were angered by her seemingly erratic behavior, Grant, however, felt empathetic toward her. Both "news flashes" were familiar touchstones for Grant, who had done time as a male escort—something he was never comfortable talking about—and had also suffered through the twisted tangle of his own mother's early fate. When Monroe was briefly hospitalized for "nerves" during production, the production company released a cover story to the press that she had had a sudden attack of appendicitis. Meanwhile, Hawks wanted to fire her over the delay that her "illness" caused, until Grant persuaded him to keep her on the film. Monroe's future in Hollywood owed a debt to the compassion of Cary Grant, at a time when she was considered to be just one more dumb blonde in an industry that purchased them twelve at a time for ten cents a pack. Had she been fired at this early juncture, she would most likely not have been given another chance in Hollywood.

Still, not everyone appreciated Grant's concern for the young starlet. Joe DiMaggio, the Yankee slugger, had just begun to date Monroe, and one time she had invited him to come to the set to watch her work. When he showed up, studio publicity photographer Roy Craft was promptly dispatched to take DiMaggio's picture with her and the film's star, Cary Grant. The next day the photo appeared in a slightly altered version in nearly every newspaper in the country. In the original version Monroe is seen with a smile as wide as the Hollywood Freeway, and Grant showing a lot of teeth as well. Only DiMaggio seems ill at ease. In the published version, Grant, at DiMaggio's insistence, was carefully cropped out.

Monkey Business opened on September 15, 1952, to surprisingly good reviews. John L. Scott, in the *Los Angeles Times*, thought the film hilarious:

"Ever catch a film comedy that made you double up with laughter even though you knew it was silly, ridiculous, and even preposterous? It's a pleasure to report that *Monkey Business*, starring Cary Grant, Ginger Rogers, and Charles Coburn, is just such a movie." Despite its generally favorable critical reception, however, the film did not do well, prompting Grant to look to make one more. Because his last three, *People Will Talk*, *Room for One More*, and *Monkey Business*, had all failed at the box office, he didn't want to retire on a triple down note.

In his search for a surefire hit movie to go out on, he turned once more to Dore Schary (now firmly ensconced at MGM) and screenwriter Sidney Sheldon (who had written *The Bachelor and the Bobby-Soxer* and was now directing as well as writing) to develop a comedy for him. They came up with something they called *Dream Wife*, a film about a businessman, Clemson Reade (Grant), married to a State Department official, Effie (Deborah Kerr), who is too preoccupied with her position to pay any attention to him. He decides to leave her for a Bukistani woman he meets, schooled in the art of "pleasing men." Princess Tarji (Betta St. John) comes to the United States but learns the ways of American female emancipation (such as it was in the early 1950s) from who else but Effie. In the end it all works out—Clem returns to his wife, and everyone lives happily ever after.

Except for introducing Deborah Kerr into Grant's world of leading women, the film was yet another creative, critical, and financial disappointment, and Grant believed it was the handwriting on the wall he would not, after all, be able to erase. To his way of thinking, in an industry and art form that revered youth, he could no longer lay claim to be the ultimate Hollywood pretty boy. He worried that his long bout with hepatitis had irrevocably pushed him past his full physical bloom of just six years earlier, when his star had shone so brightly in *Notorious*. The intervening seasons had drawn his face taut and had made the veins stick out in his thick neck. His hair, once shiny black, had taken on the cool gray tones of salt and pepper. He feared the industry now considered him a has-been, and that many of the old guard were more than eager to celebrate his professional passing with the shouted epitaph of good riddance.

He was not completely wrong. Despite his enduring reputation as

Hollywood's eternal golden boy with the Midas touch, by the early '50s the reality was that Cary Grant was no longer that much in demand. His glorious acting career had been reduced by the unavoidable trivialization that comes with the crime of aging in L.A. The only award he was even considered for these days came from Igor Cassini ("Cholly Knickerbocker" to his syndicated newspaper column readers) for "Best-Dressed Actor" of 1952 (Irene Dunne won for best-dressed actress). Ever the gentleman, when interviewed on the subject he smiled to hide his humiliation and obligingly explained in earnest detail that the secret of his good looks was really his clothes—custom-made suits and shirts—and advised men who wanted to emulate him to never wear suspenders, belts, or garters but instead to go with hidden waist-tabs to keep their pants up and straight. Not exactly the acceptance speech he had long envisioned delivering on Oscar night.

Late in 1952 Grant and Drake slowly began their reemergence from Palm Springs into Hollywood's social scene. They had been appearing in a radio series based on *Mr. Blandings Builds His Dream House*, and one night they invited the show's producer, William Frye, to a black-tie dinner at Perino's, which many considered to be the best restaurant in L.A. That night Grant was reminded of the age difference between himself and Drake, which he had assumed nobody cared about. As Frye remembered, "Cary was being very mysterious, and all he would tell me was that he would let me know at the right time what we were going to do after. Well, it was quite a guest list—Cary, Betsy, Leslie Caron and actor Richard Anderson, and my date was the daughter of Sharman Douglas, the ambassador to Great Britain. I arrived at Cary's house, and we all went down to the restaurant in a limo. Cary sat in the front, and Richard and I sat on the jumpseats, with the women in the regular back.

"The dinner was fabulous, all pre-ordered, the way Cary always arranged, and after, we got back in the limo, and were taken to the little Biltmore Theater to see one of the most remarkable 'comebacks' in show business history, the closing night of Mae West's one-woman show. What can I say, she moved like she had a motor attached to her, all gyrations under flashing lights, etc. After, Cary took us backstage to say hello to her.

"And there she was, in the dressing room, still in costume, rhinestones, feathers, a great big hat, and a cane in her hand. She had positioned herself near an electric fan so that the feathers would move a certain way. She looked like she had been wound up. 'Cary, baby,' she said to him, with a big smile on her face, 'come and see mama!'

"'I want you to meet my wife, Betsy,' Grant said. Mae looked at her for several seconds and said, 'Well, where in the world did you find this one?'"

A few weeks later Grant canceled the radio series when two writers on the show filed a lawsuit to recover $25,250 in monies they claimed they were owed for scripts written that were never produced. Having done thirty-nine episodes, Grant was bored and wanted out. He quickly settled and the show went off the air.

The majority of films coming out of the new, postwar Hollywood—torn by its own political paranoia fed by the vengeful HUAC and beaten into submission via self-flagellation—were reflective exercises in doom and gloom, tic-tac-tortured visions filled with beautiful young zombie antiheroes, the slouching Brandos, the mad-eyed Clifts. Mainstream Hollywood film had turned fully in the direction of Kazan's Method acting, a world in which Grant felt supremely uncomfortable. He decided to finally and officially announce to the world that he had irrevocably retired from motion pictures. "It was the period of blue jeans, the dope addicts, the Method," he would say later on, "and nobody cared about comedy at all."

Early in February 1953, a month after his forty-ninth birthday, Grant held a press conference to formally announce his retirement and used the opportunity to speak out in defense of Charlie Chaplin. The State Department had just revoked Chaplin's visa for suspected Communist involvement while the great comedian was vacationing overseas—not long after Howard Hughes had refused, for political reasons, to exhibit Chaplin's latest film, *Limelight*, despite a longstanding agreement the screen legend had with RKO theaters in place years before Hughes had acquired the chain. Grant was enraged by all this and wanted the world to know that he supported Chaplin and was adamantly against the blacklist, even if it meant speaking out against Howard Hughes.

In an extraordinarily brave statement, a display of courage all too scarce in the Hollywood of the early 1950s, Grant, after saying he would make no more movies and that he and his wife were about to embark on an extended vacation, told the gathering of reporters, "[Chaplin] has given great pleasure to millions of people, and I hope he returns to Hollywood. Personally, I don't think he is a Communist, but whatever his political affiliations, they are secondary to the fact that he is a great entertainer." After a pause he added in a low but firm voice, "We should not go off the deep end." The silence of the crowd of reporters hung like wet laundry on a windless day, as they wrote down the words of this star of the first magnitude who, until now, had survived in Hollywood by always managing, in public at least, to stay above the public political fray.

Having said his piece, Grant bid the reporters farewell, after which he and Drake took a slow boat to China.

25

"The results of living in reality are more satisfying than living in unreality. Larry Olivier said, 'An actor spends his life being somebody he is not. We are not ourselves. We are the product of the writers, directors, and producers.' I find reality more interesting."

—CARY GRANT

For the next several months, Cary Grant and his wife, Betsy Drake, traveled in glorious simplicity around the world, seeing the sights and seeking out the various religious, mystical, and psychological figures who were far more important to them than any heads of state. If it had been up to Grant, they would have lived like this for the rest of their lives.

While in the Far East, they toured Hong Kong and Tokyo, where, without publicity representatives, press, sponsors, or TV crews, they spent several days visiting American soldiers wounded in the Korean conflict and hospitalized in Japan. After doing the same in Singapore, Grant chose Tangier as their next destination because, he told Drake, he wanted to visit his ex-wife, Barbara Hutton; he missed her son, Lance, whom he hoped to spend some time with. Drake said she didn't mind at all.

During the visit a surprisingly friendly Hutton offered to finance an independent movie for Grant, the subject of which could be of his choosing, as long as it was shot entirely in Tangier. It was an offer he found tempting but ultimately turned down. His mood then took a nosedive when Hutton told him she planned to marry international playboy Porfirio Rubirosa.*

Grant and Drake left Tangier, and while working their way through France, their eventual destination being England and Bristol, Grant received a telegram from Dore Schary asking about the possibility of his returning immediately to Hollywood to film a sequel to the as-yet-to-open *Dream Wife*. By this time Grant, still depressed over his visit to Hutton, was more than ready to cancel the rest of the "endless honeymoon" and the promised, long-delayed meeting between his wife and his mother. He informed Schary via return telegram that he and Drake would arrive back in Los Angeles by March 20, after which he would be delighted to discuss the new project.

The film that had lured him back to America and out of retirement was tentatively titled *The Honeymoon Is Over*.

NO SOONER HAD THEY ARRIVED in Hollywood, even before meeting with Schary, than the emotionally seesawing Grant wanted to leave again. This time he purchased a spacious Mexican adobe-style vacation villa in Palm Springs that he intended to make his and Drake's permanent residence. The outdoor patio had what he referred to as the "conference table," a large area with a tamarisk tree in the center of it, around which Grant could read scripts and Drake could read, write, and paint. The daily desert routine they estab-lished — what Drake called their excursion into the art of living in simplic-ity — was to get up early, ride across the desert to see the sun rise, then return to the house and prepare a breakfast of coffee, eggs, and bacon. Most days Grant spent at least an hour swimming. He hadn't done regular laps since his days living at the beach house with Randolph Scott, and now he could feel his body starting to tighten up and return to the superb physical condi-tion he had kept it in for so many years. Often at night they would take long rides to see the sunset, cook steaks and vegetables under the desert moon, and finish off pastries or pies especially prepared by their cook, one of only two part-time staffers they employed. Drake occasionally played her guitar

*Hutton married Rubirosa later that year. The marriage lasted seventy-three days and cost Hutton the $2 million she paid him for agreeing to an uncontested divorce.

and sang for Grant and in her private moments continued her spiritual studies. On nights when he couldn't sleep, he let her practice hypnotism on him.
And, at least once every two weeks, he liked to take her on the three-hour
drive to Las Vegas, not to gamble, which he had no interest in, but to see the
live shows. (His itinerary was always arranged for, and his hotel suite comped,
by Hughes.) Grant loved the town's live nightclub entertainment, as it
reminded him of his early days in live vaudeville.

He eventually got around to reading Schary's script, which had been
delivered by messenger and sat on a table in the living room for weeks without being opened. He got through about half of it before rejecting the
intended sequel to *Dream Wife*. The reason, he told Schary, was that it just
wasn't funny.

AS THE WEEKS AND MONTHS PASSED, Grant continued to get offered major
movies that, for one reason or another, he rejected, much to Drake's delight,
who preferred he stay at home with her and explore the adventure of their
private life together. Among those films he turned down during this period
were William Wyler's *Roman Holiday* (1953), opposite Audrey Hepburn.
The role eventually went to Gregory Peck and won three Oscars. Selznick
had wanted Grant for the leading role in his filmed version of F. Scott
Fitzgerald's celebrated novel *Tender Is the Night*, opposite Jennifer Jones.
Grant had actually wanted to do this one, but turned it down out of loyalty
to Irene Selznick: he knew he would not feel comfortable acting with Jones.
The film was shelved, and ten years later Fox made it, directed by Henry
King, with Jason Robards playing Dick Diver, and Jennifer Jones playing his
wife, Nicole.

Warner then approached Grant about the remake of *Don Quixote* he had
for so long wanted to appear in, with Cantinflas, the Mexican comic star, playing Sancho Panza. Grant considered it for a while, then turned it down. David
Lean wanted him for *The Bridge on the River Kwai* (1957); the role he rejected
eventually went to William Holden, and the movie won seven Academy
Awards, including Best Picture. He also turned down the lead in Billy Wilder's
Sabrina (1954), which went to Humphrey Bogart (opposite Hepburn and

William Holden), and the Sky Masterson role in Joseph L. Mankiewicz's *Guys and Dolls* (1955), a role that Marlon Brando wound up playing.

During all of this, there was one project he wanted MCA to purchase for him. While in New York, he had seen the Broadway play *Bell, Book and Candle*, a light comedy about a man who unwittingly falls in love with a beautiful witch. Grant saw it as the perfect vehicle for himself and Drake. However, when he went to Jules Stein to have a package put together, he discovered that MCA had already bought it for James Stewart, who, Stein told him, was Lew Wasserman's favorite client. This angered Grant so much that he considered dropping Wasserman from his team of agents.

The only director able to lure Grant out of his second retirement was the one man whose movies and methods still stimulated and intrigued him, and for whom he believed he had done his best work. When Alfred Hitchcock asked to come to Palm Springs for a visit with a new script for Grant to consider, over Drake's somewhat muted advice to say no before it was too late, Grant told Hitchcock he would love to have him and his wife as his and Betsy's guests.

Drake was quiet but firm about her not wanting Grant to return to film. Their life together in the desert was, as far as she was concerned, nothing short of idyllic. Why, Drake wondered aloud, would he possibly want to give it up? She certainly didn't. Besides, they had each agreed to stay away from films in order to spend as much time together as possible. Wasn't that still enough for him?

The answer was no. Even though Grant had been strongly tempted by at least two projects, Wyler's *Roman Holiday* and Lean's *The Bridge on the River Kwai*, he had turned down all film offers for the sake of his marriage. But that was about to change with the arrival of Alfred Hitchcock, who showed up in the hundred-plus-degree desert in his familiar black suit, white shirt, and tie, carrying a revised script under his arm that would prove irresistible to Grant.

LIKE GRANT, HITCHCOCK had gone through a series of highs and lows after *Notorious*, scoring a bull's-eye with that one, hitting less well with its follow-up, *The Paradine Case* (1947), which starred Gregory Peck in the last of the Hitchcock/Selznick joint ventures. He then all but lost his audience with the experimental *Rope* (1948, made for Transatlantic Pictures, an American-British independent film production company), an excercise in single-take moviemaking, the story loosely based on the infamous Leopold-Loeb murder case, that starred Jimmy Stewart and Farley Granger. He followed it with another disappointment, *Under Capricorn* (1949), then with the murder mystery *Stage Fright* (1950, Warner–First National), which proved a split victory, getting a thumbs-up from the critics, but a thumbs-down from audiences. It wasn't until *Strangers on a Train* (1951, Warner–First National) that Hitchcock regained his magic touch. The film was a spectacular success on every level, bolstered with a (first-draft) screenplay by the great Raymond Chandler and featuring Farley Granger and Robert Walker Jr. in the best performances of their careers. It was this film that restored the lost luster to Hitchcock's career.

He then went down again with *I Confess* (1953, Warner–First National), which featured a miscast Montgomery Clift in the leading role as a priest who witnesses a murder, then came back strong with his highly popular version of the London and Broadway stage smash *Dial M For Murder* (1954, Warner–First National, originally shot in 3-D but widely released in flat screen when the fad quickly faded). Audiences loved *Dial M for Murder*, especially the alluring presence of its female star, Grace Kelly. Hitchcock followed that one with his first film under his new multiple-picture deal at Paramount, the awesome *Rear Window* (1954), which finally and irrevocably placed him in the top rank of movie directors. Hitchcock wanted something equally terrific to follow it, a feature that would keep him in the critical and financial stratosphere. That film, he believed, was *To Catch a Thief*, and as far as he was concerned, only Cary Grant could do justice to the role of the handsome catlike reformed jewel thief who manages to steal Grace Kelly's heart.

TO HITCHCOCK'S DELIGHT, Grant loved the brilliant John Michael Hayes screenplay adaptation of the original David Dodge novel. Hitchcock had discovered it in Paramount's archive of unmade properties, where it had been shelved when the studio deemed it unmakable. Before he left the desert, Hitchcock had a commitment from Grant to star in it.

Not long after, Hitchcock announced that he had signed the astonishingly beautiful Grace Kelly to costar in the film. Kelly, of *High Noon*, *Dial M for Murder*, and *Rear Window*, had become one the most sought-after actresses in Hollywood. While filming *Rear Window*, the always repressed Hitchcock, as he did with most of his blond leading ladies, had fallen completely in love with her and couldn't wait to pair her up with his favorite cinematic doppelgänger, Cary Grant. The fact that when production started Grant had just turned fifty while Kelly was just twenty-five only deepened Hitchcock's desire to see them romantically entangled on the big screen.

In *To Catch a Thief*, John Robie (Grant) is an especially agile jewel thief with the reputation of one of the best cat burglars in all the world before he proclaims himself both retired and reformed. He seemingly has the ability to leap over time itself into the passion of his own remembered youth after he meets the luscious heiress Frances Stevens (Grace Kelly), who, while vacationing on the Riviera with her mother Jessie Stevens (Jessie Royce Landis),* volunteers to be the lure to help "catch" the thief and, along the way, romantically catches Robie.

In one scene, showing off her jewel necklace, Frances all but thrusts her gorgeous, supple, sparkling breasts into Robie's mouth, holding them up from below (as close as the censors would allow), while murmuring to him with wet lips and laser eyes, "If you really want to see the fireworks, it's better with the lights off . . . I have a feeling that tonight you're going to see some of the Riviera's most fascinating sights . . . look . . . hold them . . . ever have a better offer on your plate?"

To which Robie replies, "You know just as well as I do this necklace is imitation."

Frances replies, "Well, I'm not!"

Robie cannot resist, they draw together in the darkness to kiss, and the camera cuts to the fireworks. In Hitchcock's view, Robie's greatest heist is the

---

*Four years later, Landis played Grant's mother in *North by Northwest*. In real life, she was a year younger than Grant.

precious gem that is Frances's youth, the imagined conquest done by proxy, via Grant's Robie, because it is a theft in which Frances ultimately "catches" Robie in the Hitchcockian snare of dangerous, beautiful, slightly masochistic love.

Although Robie (robber?) insists he is retired, having repented for his crimes by doing service for the French underground during World War II, he nevertheless becomes the chief suspect when a series of jewel thefts takes place. Everyone in law enforcement believes he is the cat burglar. When he denies it, the authorities enlist him to catch the real cat burglar. In order to prove his innocence, he must, in effect, "become" the cat burglar in order to catch him. His stirred romantic attraction to Frances lures him back into the world of his passionate youth, with all its lawless and sexual abandon. In the end, Robie catches the real cat burglar, who happens to be a young woman, the daughter of one of his former colleagues.

While Grant threw himself enthusiastically into the part, Drake was less than thrilled that her husband would be doing love scenes with Grace Kelly, who, she'd heard, had a habit of sleeping with her leading men. When she told Grant of her concern before he left the States, his reply was to laugh — that was one thing she didn't have to worry about, he said. Drake likely did not understand the full implications and therefore could not accept his answer. Thus began an argument that would continue between her and Grant throughout the making of the film. By the time the two set sail in May 1954 for the Côte d'Azur, where the film was to be shot, they were barely speaking to each other.

Drake's uneasy presence in France may have actually helped Grant connect his performance to the real-life focus he needed to play Robie. In the film, the so-called cat burglar insists he is retired, something the authorities have trouble believing. In real life, Grant had twice announced his retirement from film yet was making another one. In the film, Robie is attracted to Frances, a beautiful blonde half his age. In real life, Grant had married a beautiful blonde half his age. In the film, Robie, in order to prove his innocence, must go back and participate in one last robbery in order to catch the real thief. In real life, Grant came out of retirement to make one last movie to prove he was still a star of the first rank. Onscreen, the result of all this "doubling" would be a triumph. In reality, the consequences of that triumph would prove disastrous.

The by-now obligatory Grant/Hitchcock car scene happens when Kelly (eerily, on the very same road that, years later, would lead to her death) drives Grant down the famous long and winding Three Corniches along the Côte d'Azur. They are on their way to the picnic grounds (where she will offer him a choice of breast or thigh from her basket of goodies). It is the young, somewhat reckless and sexually aggressive Frances who is steering (leading, luring) Robie. He is content to let her do the driving for now, but we correctly sense it will be Grant in the driver's seat by the film's end. In a scene that recalls the one with Hepburn in *Bringing Up Baby* and that antic- ipates the one with Eva Marie Saint in *North by Northwest*, Grant holds the "real" cat burglar by her wrists while he dangles her from a rooftop to force a confession out of her.

DURING THE FILMING, Grant and Drake stayed at the famed Hotel du Cap for the entire shoot, while the rest of the cast and crew were housed at the Carlton, in Cannes (except for Kelly, who stayed with her lover, Oleg Cassini, in a private villa). Most evenings Grant and Drake joined Kelly and Cassini and the Hitchcocks for dinner at one or another of the many small candlelit restaurants along the hillsides of southern France. On weekends they would all go sailing. Grant hoped that Drake and Kelly would form a friendship that would defuse his wife's jealous fears.

It did not happen. Instead, Drake's dissatisfaction with her husband grew with what she perceived to be his increasingly amorous mood — not toward her but Kelly. Whether it was Grant's ritual leading-lady infatuation — the only acting "method" he ever relied upon (and a fetish he shared with Hitchcock) — or simply the fact that he felt more at home, more real, more in control, and therefore more comfortable with Kelly (an idealized version of Drake), the onscreen heat he generated with her was undeniable, palpable enough to enlist Drake into the artistic if neurotic jamboree of screen-to-life criss-crossing that was so much a part of any Grant/Hitchcock collaboration.

By the time the film was finished and Grant and Drake returned to the idyllic surroundings of the desert, both knew things had irrevocably changed between them. As far as Drake was concerned, she had lost parts of her husband to Kelly, Hitchcock, and the one lover she could never successfully compete with — "Cary Grant." For his part, Grant found that he had nothing left to say to or teach Drake, or worse, to learn from her. Their moment, he knew, had passed. Alone together, he had been something of a father figure to Drake, the child he had never had; in her thirties now, she was too old to sit on Daddy's knee, while Grant, in his fifties, for the first time felt too old to want to keep on bouncing her there.

26

"I had a theme in most of my movies—to take a fellow who seemed to dress rather well, who was moderately well-educated and sophisticated and should know his way around, and put him in a series of ridiculous and untenable situations. How is he going to get out of that? *To Catch a Thief* and *North by Northwest* come quickest to mind. The attraction then to the audience is this: If it can happen to him, it can happen to me. And the fact that it's happening to me and not to them is their relief. I tried to be myself on screen. I learned it was the most difficult thing to do. That's exposure of one's self. The hardest thing is to be yourself in front of 30 million people. By contrast, it is much easier to hide behind a character."

—CARY GRANT

To *Catch a Thief* did not open for almost a year after shooting was completed, because Hitchcock had to work on his new TV series while editing the film. It was finally released in August 1955, a month before the official fall season, an indication of Paramount's lack of faith in the film's commercial viability, even as it touted Grant's "comeback." The obvious age difference between Grant and Kelly was a concern to the studio's executives, who remained unsure if audiences would buy it. Besides, no one at Paramount could figure out the film's plot. "Was he really the cat burglar, or wasn't he?" became the question most asked after the screenings, even though the film had a fairly unambiguous ending. If the Paramount crowd couldn't stay with it until the end, the studio executives wondered, could audiences?

Grant personally attended the lavish "world premiere" at New York's Paramount Theater—a theater he had performed in as a young man when it was a legitimate playhouse some thirty years earlier. Despite all the fanfare and promotion, the film received mixed reviews: "*To Catch a Thief* is not the thriller it could have been," wrote the *Hollywood Citizen-News*; "What else can I tell you? The dialogue is so bad that Cary looks embarrassed to be saying it," opined *The Saturday Review*. In defiance of all the doubts, however, *To Catch a Thief* went on to become the biggest hit of the first half of the 1950s. It also reenergized Grant's desire to make motion pictures, even if it meant the end of his marriage to Betsy Drake. As far as he was concerned, that love ship had already sailed.

EAGER AS HE WAS to get in front of a camera again, another year passed before Grant chose his next film. It was not for any lack of desire on his part, or a shortage of scripts. He just wanted to wait, to see if *To Catch a Thief* was his resurrection and not his epitaph. Once the film proved it had legs, he proceeded carefully, so as not to halt the momentum of his comeback. While in search of the right script, he was interviewed by *Pix* magazine about the secret of his longevity. A smiling Grant sang a new tune now about his seemingly ageless place in the ever-changing world of film. "The movies are like the steel business," he told the interviewer. "An actor should be good at any stage and last forever."

Among the offerings he turned down during this period was Otto Preminger's *Bonjour Tristesse*. Preminger thought Grant perfect for the role of the father of waiflike Audrey Hepburn (with whom he would costar eight years later as her lover in Stanley Donen's *Charade*). Thanks, Grant said, but no thanks.* Fox wanted him for the lead in *Can-Can*. He said no again, and Frank Sinatra got the part. He thought about making a movie of Thomas Mann's *Joseph and His Brethren* and wanted Clifford Odets to write and direct it. When that fell through, Grant asked Odets to consider writing instead the story of a brigadier general who commits suicide, after which it is revealed he had led several different, secret lives. It, too, went nowhere. Columbia then proposed a musical version of *It Happened One Night*. Grant said yes if they would somehow retool the script into a remake of *His Girl Friday*, in which he could star again with Grace Kelly. "I can be ready in ten minutes," Grant told them. Not surprisingly, that project quickly died. Perhaps strangest of all was the offer made to him by Mae West, who wanted to redo *She Done Him Wrong*. Sorry, he politely told her.

Even Mike Todd, the grand impresario of motion pictures and the flamboyant husband of Elizabeth Taylor, sought Grant's services, to star in his lavishly planned film version of Jules Verne's *Around the World in Eighty Days*. The film's gimmick was to have every major star in Hollywood play a cameo role—precisely why Grant did not take part. He was never one to share the screen with too many other stars, afraid he would get lost in the crowd and wind up appearing smaller than life. The film would eventually be made with David Niven in the lead and win the Best Picture Oscar of 1956.

While Grant waited for exactly the right film, his relationship with Drake continued to deteriorate. They decided to sleep in separate beds, then in separate houses. The gossips somehow picked up on it, and as the couple quietly passed their fifth anniversary, rumors flew that the marriage was in trouble. Whispers of Grant's homosexuality resurfaced, augmented by those who claimed Drake was gay, as well. The highly idiosyncratic nature of their marriage added fuel to these rumors, however unfounded they might have been. For the most part, Grant took his return to the gossip columns as a sign that he had also returned to prominence.

The picture Grant finally chose as his follow-up to *To Catch a Thief* was Stanley Kramer's $4 million costume picture set in the Napoleonic Wars, *The Pride and the Passion*, based on C. S. Forester's novel *The Gun*. (Forester, at

*The roles eventually went to David Niven and Jean Seberg.

Kramer's urging, personally asked Grant to honor him by being in the film version of his novel.) In keeping with his often-puzzling and ultimately self-destructive pattern, it would prove the worst of all possible choices.

The Pride and the Passion's main character is a Spanish cannon, one that British naval officer Anthony (Grant) must prevent from falling into the hands of the French. Along the way Anthony meets Miguel (Frank Sinatra), a leader of the Spanish guerrilla forces, who wants to take the cannon to Ávila and use it to run the French out of the city. They join forces against their common enemy, even as they compete for the affections of Juana, a female guerrilla fighter, played by Sophia Loren at the height of her cinematic low-cut peasant glory.

It is not all that difficult to understand what Grant was attracted to in this costume drama, his first since the disastrous *The Howards of Virginia* some fifteen years earlier. For one thing, it was to be shot in Spain, and Grant, eager to put some physical distance between himself and Drake, looked forward to going on location by himself this time. For another, he was eager to work both with Academy Award–winning producer-director Stanley Kramer and with Sinatra, who was red hot since winning an Oscar in 1954 for his role in *From Here to Eternity*. As far as Grant was concerned, the picture was a can't-miss.

Grant had costar approval on the film and had wanted Ava Gardner, now living in Spain, to play opposite him, until Sinatra, who was going through an ugly separation and divorce from the actress, made that choice a practical impossibility. Grant then made overtures to Grace Kelly, now Princess Grace; she reluctantly turned the film down, having agreed to give up movies for the prince. His third choice was one suggested by Stanley Kramer, who had wanted Sophia Loren from the start; her paramour, Italian filmmaker Carlo Ponti, was pressing Kramer to give Loren her first English-speaking role. With Grant's quiet approval, Kramer offered Loren a one-time-only, take-it-or-leave-it $200,000 to make the film. She took it, in what she called "the easiest decision I ever had to make."

Grant waited until just before he left for Spain to tell Drake that she was not going with him, and then called his friend producer William Frye to ask him to "take care of her while I'm gone." An angry and insecure Drake warned him that he had better not do anything on set that he would later be sorry for. She had heard too many stories, mostly from him, about his leading-lady infatuations, and she wasn't about to sit by and allow Loren to take him away from her. Not that she would have minded all that much if Grant never came back. It was, by this time, more a question of public humiliation than private heartbreak. Not to worry, he told her.

Shooting began April 20, 1956, in Segovia. By the end of the first week, Grant had fallen hopelessly in love with Sophia Loren.

To COMPLICATE MATTERS FURTHER, so had Frank Sinatra, although he would deny it for the rest of his days. His jealousy over the twenty-two-year-old Loren's preference for Grant, thirty years her senior and ten years older than Sinatra (and Ponti), led him to do something no one else had ever dared around the romantic-leading-man idol. He openly ridiculed Grant's sexuality, always referring to him on the set as "Mother Cary." If there was any logic to this strategy, it didn't work. Although Loren did not speak English very well, she knew that Sinatra was picking on Grant, and after one particularly difficult day of shooting, she had had enough of it and did what Grant wouldn't, or couldn't. She rebuffed Sinatra's pettiness by calling him out in front of the entire cast and crew and labeling him "an Italian son of a bitch."

To Sinatra, still smoldering with rage over his breakup with Gardner, this was the last straw. He could not wait to get out of "Windmillville," as he referred to Segovia, and actually left the production before he had completed his scenes (he later finished them in Hollywood), forcing Grant to talk to a suit on a hanger in remaining scenes together.

Grant, meanwhile, increasingly sought Loren's company on location and at the end of the day would have long, rambling, confessional talks with her that stretched from the early evening into the next day's sunrise, talks in English, a language she barely understood at the time. They were constantly together on set, which started a rumor that somehow made it all the way back to Hollywood. In a flash, Drake, after reading about Grant and Loren in one of the columns, boarded a flight bound for Spain.

What didn't hit the columns—at least not at first (and when it eventually did, he vehemently denied it)—was the fact that even before Drake's arrival in Segovia, Grant had proposed marriage to Loren, promising he could obtain a "quickie" divorce from Drake. Loren's reaction was not the one he had hoped for. She returned his proposal with a reminder to him of her commitment to Ponti.*

Once in Spain, Drake assured Grant that she was there only because she missed him and made no reference to the headlines his "affair" was making back in the States. After only two weeks, however, she had had enough. She simply couldn't stand the hangdog look Grant got on his face whenever Loren was around. If that was the way he wanted it, fine, she thought, and via long-distance telephone broke her moratorium on appearing in films by accepting an offer made by Frank Tashlin to appear in his upcoming comedy, *Will Success Spoil Rock Hunter?* Hoping this might bother Grant enough for him to ask her to give up the picture and stay, she was dismayed when he wished her the best of luck with the movie. The next day she booked herself first-class passage back to the States aboard the flagship of a fleet of luxury Italian liners, the *Andrea Doria*.

The *Andrea Doria* set sail from Genoa on July 17, 1956, to make its fifty-first crossing of the Atlantic to New York. The next day Drake boarded at the ship's first stop, the port of Naples. Grant, claiming a full day's shooting schedule, did not take her to the pier to see her off

A week later, at precisely 11:10 P.M. on the night of July 25, a dark and foggy night, the worst peacetime disaster at sea since the sinking of the *Titanic* took place sixty miles from Nantucket Island, Massachusetts. Only hours away from docking in New York, the *Andrea Doria* collided with the smaller Swedish cruise ship, the SS *Stockholm*. As the *Andrea Doria* began to sink barely a half hour after the crash, its more than 1,197 passengers and

---

*To the press, Grant continually denied not only that he had proposed but that they had had a relationship at all. His standard response to any direct inquiry was "Where do all these rumors start?" Or "As I remember it, Sophia was in love with Frank Sinatra." True enough, although that was a reference to the film, not real life. Years later, in 1979, Loren, with her coauthor A. E. Hotchner, wrote about the circumstances of Grant's pursuit in her autobiography. In 1980 Loren's memoir was made into a TV movie, and Grant unsuccessfully sued to have himself and his experience with Loren during *The Pride and the Passion* eliminated from the script. When the film aired, Grant's only public comment was "I can't believe that anyone would exploit an old friendship like this." Privately, it was a completely different story. To begin with, Grant had been personally approached by Loren during the writing of her memoirs to help her remember certain details, to have some input, to which he flatly refused. According to Loren, in *People* magazine (March 24, 1980): "He was part of my life. I loved him dearly, so I rang him and said, 'I can't leave you out.' He told me, 'I still love you and trust you, so anything you write is fine with me.'" Grant also told his close friends that he was in love with Loren and indeed planned to marry her, and that he saw this happening when they were reunited a year later in Melville Shavelson's *Houseboat*.

crew scrambled for places on the lifeboats and dropped into the sea like ice cubes into highballs. Miraculously, out of the total of more than seventeen hundred people aboard both ships, only forty-six died, mostly from the force of the initial collision.

Among the *Andrea Doria*'s survivors was Betsy Drake, although more than $200,000 worth of jewelry that she had taken with her to Spain to wear for Grant, all of it gifts from him, and a manuscript of a book she was working on went down with the ship. Her being aboard became a big story within a bigger story and made headlines on its own. For Drake, the worst part of the entire experience was that Grant did not immediately drop everything and fly to be by her side. He couldn't, he told her by phone, because his departure would shut down production on a very expensive shoot.

He neglected to add that he was, at the moment, busy trying to convince Loren to marry him.

To let him know she had arrived safely back at their home in Los Angeles, she sent Grant a one-line telegram that said simply, FROM YOUR SAFE AND SOUND WIFE.

"WE FELL IN LOVE," Loren admitted in her unusually frank autobiography. "Slowly, as our relationship grew and his trust in me grew, he came to realize that trust and vulnerability went hand in hand; when his trust was strong enough, he no longer bothered with his mask. And I was just as open and trusting with him. He told me about his early life, and I told him about mine, and we found a bond in their emotional similarities. We saw each other every night; we dined in romantic little restaurants on craggy hilltops to the accompaniment of flamenco guitars, drank the good Spanish wine and laughed and were serious and confessional and conspiratorial . . .

"But I was also in love with Carlo . . . and now here was Cary Grant, ready to renounce everything for me. Wanting me with no strings attached . . . Cary talked about getting married. With every passing day, he said, he was surer that we belonged together, that finally he had found someone to whom he could commit himself and to hell with being vulnerable."

Vulnerable she was, but not indecisive. Loren owed her career to Ponti and was not prepared to leave him to marry Grant, no matter how much she may have loved her costar. When the long shoot was finished and her romantic but chaste affair with Grant about to end, she felt relief that she was due in Greece to start filming Jean Negulesco's *Boy on a Dolphin*. Ponti, still married to someone else at the time (a situation that made everything even more complicated for the devoutly Catholic Loren), was well aware of the situation with Grant and wanted to get her as far away from him as he could. He had arranged for Loren to leave immediately with him for Greece, with production set to begin the day after her work on *The Pride and the Passion* ended.

After seven long, eventful, and ultimately heartbreaking months in Spain, Grant at last returned home with nothing to say to anybody, least of all Drake, about his "affair" with Loren. Instead, he seemed to have found a renewed sense of commitment to his wife, happy that she had survived her ordeal at sea and grateful she was apparently willing to have him back.

Drake was indeed happy to see him, but if he was not willing to acknowledge the undeniable distance he had put between them, she was. Soon enough their separate residences did not seem nearly far enough apart for her. Drake, in the middle of filming *Will Success Spoil Rock Hunter?*, was grateful to be involved in something that took up so much of her time.

During the making of the film, she increased her studies of and participation in hypnosis, in the hope she might find relief from the post-traumatic depression she had fallen into after the accident. Eventually she sought treatment from Dr. Mortimer Hartman, one of the early experimenters with lysergic acid diethylamide 25, otherwise known as LSD.

With his wife away now for so much of the time, and still smitten with Loren, Grant found himself in the grip of a new bout of loneliness. To get himself out of it, he plunged himself back into the only cure he knew, the welcome-wagon world of moviemaking. In 1957 he made four movies in quick succession, all the while secretly obsessing over how to get his Italian beauty to marry him.

27

"Nobody doesn't like Cary Grant. He's a Hollywood
monument, and nobody wants to tamper with that . . .
he survived the end of his own career in a manner that
will probably never happen again."

—WARREN HOGE

In February 1957 Cary Grant, despite having released one film in three
years, was nevertheless riding high in the popularity polls, placing third
among the top ten actors of that year.* *An Affair to Remember,* his new project,
was the first of a two-movie deal he had made with producer Jerry Wald that
was in turn part of Wald's new multipicture deal at 20th Century–Fox. The
film was a remake of Leo McCarey's 1939 weeper *Love Affair,* which had
costarred one of early sound cinema's great European lovers, Charles Boyer,
and a favorite costar of Grant's, Irene Dunne. Wald, one of the new wave of
hotshot hustling independents (widely believed to have been the prototype for
Budd Schulberg's Hollywood novel, *What Makes Sammy Run?*), offered
McCarey a chance to remake his own film, modernized by color and widescreen cinematography, on the condition that he sign Cary Grant to play the
male lead.

*In a poll conducted by *Popularity,* the top ten were, in order, Rock Hudson, William Holden, Cary
Grant, Frank Sinatra, Gary Cooper, Marlon Brando, James Stewart, Burt Lancaster, Glenn Ford, and
Yul Brynner. Clark Gable and John Wayne placed eleventh and twelfth.

McCarey, who had not found his way back to Grant's list of favored directors, knew that Grant never wanted to play a role that someone else had orig-
inated. Still, he made the obligatory approach, figuring that once Grant
turned him down, he could then go back to Wald and try to come up with a
viable alternative. To McCarey's surprise, Grant immediately accepted, and
Wald green-lighted the film.

An Affair to Remember was essentially the same story that it had been in
the first version, and for that matter the same story told with minor variations
a thousand times over since the beginning of film. Boy meets girl, boy loses
girl, boy gets girl (give or take a few years). In this version, Nick Ferrante
(Grant) is engaged to Lois Clark (Neva Patterson), a wealthy heiress whom
he does not love. On board a cruise bound for America from his adopted
home of Naples, he meets Terry McKay (Deborah Kerr), who is about to
marry Kenneth Bradley (Richard Denning). Nick and Terry fall in love but
agree they must honor their previous commitments. They wistfully plan to
meet again in the future, to see what if anything has happened in their lives.
On that fateful day Terry is hit by a taxi and paralyzed from the waist down.
When she doesn't keep the appointment, Nick tracks her down, declares his
love, and doesn't care that she's "crippled." They go off happily together into
the sunset of their lives.

What set McCarey's remake apart from the dozens of other weepies
released that year was the great chemistry between the film's two stars. At fifty-
three, Grant seemed preternaturally handsome, with an onscreen persona
that projected refinement, sophistication, maturity, and an enormous capacity to love and be loved. Opposite the thirty-one-year-old Kerr, the charming,
urbane, witty side of Grant came on display, a side that Hollywood had lately
seen too little of. Onscreen their relationship was mannered, restrained, articulate, and civilized, and yet it projected plenty of widescreen heat. Under
McCarey's sharp direction, the film hit a vital nerve with female audiences,
whose collective longing for Grant was perfectly personified by the non-
threatening warmth of Deborah Kerr.

IF GRANT'S SCREEN IMAGE seemed more flawless than ever, it served as the
perfect mask behind which he could take refuge from the difficulties he was

having in his private life. For one thing, while he was making *An Affair to Remember*, Sophia Loren and Carlo Ponti arrived in Hollywood and were staying at the Beverly Hills Hotel as Ponti negotiated a multiple-picture deal for Loren with Paramount. As soon as he found out, Grant began sending flowers every day, not caring about Ponti and oblivious to Drake's deepening depression over her husband's being still so obviously smitten. For her part, Loren did not discourage Grant's mannered advances and quite likely used them as the catalyst to get what she really wanted, a wedding ring from Ponti that could only come if he was granted a divorce from the Vatican. Loren had begun to suspect Ponti was using his first marriage as a convenient excuse and fought his complacency with her supposed "love" for Grant.

During production on *Affair*, one of the cameramen shooting a close-up of Grant noticed a lump on his forehead. Grant said it was a permanent bruise he had acquired during his USO tours, when he had to wear a steel helmet that didn't fit right. The studio insisted he have it looked at, and after a battery of tests it was diagnosed as a benign tumor. He arranged to have it removed upon completion of production and before the start of his next film, another Wald project, Stanley Donen's *Kiss Them for Me*.

Two days before the surgery Grant made a surprise appearance at the March 1957 Academy Awards, his first in sixteen years. The only reason he attended was that his good friend, Ingrid Bergman, who had been nominated for Best Actress of 1956 for her performance in *Anastasia*, had asked him if he would accept for her if she won. Bergman was still in "exile" in Europe for having committed the crime of falling in love with married Italian director Roberto Rossellini during the filming of *Stromboli* in 1949, and having his baby out of wedlock. When the scandal broke into the national headlines, Bergman, who was still married to her husband and who only two years earlier had been riding high from a decade starring in several successful Hollywood movies, including Michael Curtiz's *Casablanca* and Alfred Hitchcock's *Notorious*, found herself unable to find work. The lockout lasted eight years, until 1957, when her long relationship with Rossellini finally came to an end. That same year she was "forgiven" by the Academy and nominated for the British film production of Anatole Litvak's *Anastasia*. Grant was one of the very few stars who had stood by Bergman throughout her ordeal and publicly announced that it would be his honor to represent her at the Oscar ceremony.

Grant relished the chance to embarrass the Academy's old guard, and the night Bergman's name was called, he walked proudly to the podium on the stage of the Pantages Theater and said into the microphone in a soft but commanding tone, "Dear Ingrid, wherever you are in the world, we, your friends, want to congratulate you, and may you be as happy as we are for you."

The next day Grant entered Cedars of Lebanon Hospital. He had a phobia about surgery and dreaded submitting to a doctor's scalpel, which he feared might permanently damage his face. Drake offered to hypnotize him, to calm him in preparation for the difficult procedure, and, to her surprise, he agreed. Shortly after, Grant gave this account of the actual surgery: "I'd taken advice about [the tumor] once from the great British plastic surgeon, Sir Archibald MacIndoe. He told me it would take about a month to remove. I couldn't afford the time. I had Betsy hypnotize me before the operation. She emphasized that I had to stay calm and even enjoy the operation. I did just that. The surgeon used a local anesthetic. He might have been cutting my hair for all I cared. It [healed] with no scar."

Drake attributed his quick recovery to the hypnosis and, thus encouraged, urged him to follow her lead again and enter psychoanalysis. At the relatively late age of fifty-three, in an attempt to save his marriage, for the first time in his life Grant agreed to see a shrink.

As GRANT COMPLETED THE FILMING of his next movie, *Kiss Them for Me*, both *The Pride and the Passion* and *An Affair to Remember* opened; the former proved another major box office disappointment for Grant, while the latter was among the biggest hits of 1957. The message from the public seemed clear. They preferred the modern, urbane, and romantic Grant rather than the costumed, exotic, and rural one.

With his third film of the year already in the can, he was ready to start a fourth, Melville Shavelson's *Houseboat*, a light comedy that takes place aboard wealthy widower Tom Winters's (Grant's) houseboat, where a relationship with his maid, Cinzia Zaccardi (Sophia Loren), blossoms into true love amid a gaggle of children. Grant had committed to making the film before *The Pride and the Passion*, and it had been intended as a costarring vehicle with Betsy Drake. But, while in Spain, Grant had secretly arranged with Ponti's approval for Drake to be replaced in the lead by Sophia Loren.

With production about to begin, Grant believed the time was right for him to make his big move on the Italian sex goddess. Unfortunately, it did not work out the way he had hoped. As a result, Grant vented his frustration and anger on Shavelson, who had to listen to him carp over the smallest of details. In reality, what upset Grant was that Loren showed up every day for shooting with Ponti attached to her side, especially after he learned — through Louella Parsons's column, no less — that one weekend during production Ponti slipped away with Loren, obtained a quickie Mexican divorce, and married her.

Upon their return, at the end of that day's shooting, Grant kissed a beaming Loren on the cheek, shook a giggling Ponti's hand, and wished them both much happiness and health. The next day, in a beautifully fitting tux, Grant "married" a luminous Loren in the film's climactic wedding scene, while Ponti stood just off camera, intently watching every move both of them made.

Later that night, alone and tipsy, Grant parked himself in his favorite booth at the back of Chasen's, pissing and moaning out loud that he had "lost Sophia forever." To at least one friend, producer Bill Frye, the loss, like the romance, took place mostly in Grant's tortured imagination. "It was all just some sort of extended daydream that he made up," Frye said. "Sophia Loren was never his to lose. It was just another one of his crazy romantic fantasies that could have had no other ending."

The day after that, Grant returned to the special, experimental therapy his wife had introduced him to, and was given his thirtieth consecutive weekly hit of LSD 25.

28

"In *North by Northwest* during the scene on Mount Rushmore,
I wanted Cary Grant to hide in Lincoln's nostril and then
have a fit of sneezing. The Parks Commission of the Department of Interior was rather upset at this thought. I argued
until one of their number asked me how I would like it if they
had Lincoln play the scene in Cary Grant's nose. I saw their
point at once."

—ALFRED HITCHCOCK

Cary Grant had begun his supervised use of LSD shortly after completing *An Affair to Remember,* at the recommendation of Drs.
Mortimer A. Hartman and Arthur Chandler, two Beverly Hills psychiatrists
pioneering the use of psychedelics as a way to medically enhance the benefits
of traditional psychotherapy in the treatment of depression. They had performed a series of physical and psychological tests on Grant that he had submitted to at Drake's urging and afterward decided Grant was a prime candidate
for their still-experimental treatment. One Saturday morning early in 1957,
Grant took acid for the first time at Hartman and Chandler's Psychiatric
Institute of Beverly Hills, together with approximately one hundred other
patients, as he would continue to do so for the next three years. Although he
has always gotten the most (and mostly unwanted) notoriety for it, Grant was

by no means the only celebrity to participate in these LSD-laced sessions. The hundreds of other "name" experimenters working with the institute at the time included writers Anaïs Nin and Aldous Huxley, actor Jack Nicholson, actress Rita Moreno, comedian Lord Buckley, screenwriter Gavin Lambert, and musician André Previn.

Grant's doctors had come to the conclusion that he was suffering from "prolonged emotional detachment" and had used acting as the way to try to "reattach" to his inner emotional self. Of all the directors Grant had worked with, only Hitchcock had succeeded in at least defining the parameters of that dark passageway, but movies were movies, and at the end of every film, Cary Grant always parted ways with "Cary Grant." Only by taking acid was he finally able to achieve a meeting of mutually shared minds, bodies, and emotions.

In his "autobiography" Grant touched lightly on some of his feelings regarding his experiences with LSD. He talked of the hallucinations the drug induced. He described them as dreams that relaxed the conscious controls he had imposed on himself, controls that were, he had come to realize, the result of a lifetime of neuroses that had prevented the truthful revelations from emerging. When he took acid, he said, these revelations were finally able to connect him to himself.

During Grant's supervised sessions, he described in far more detail the hallucinations as they were taking place, pathways to his subconscious that were then analyzed by his doctors. For the entire three years, Grant kept a diary of his reactions to the drug. In it, he said he learned "to accept the responsibility for my own actions, and to blame myself and no one else for circumstances of my own creating. I learned that no one else was keeping me unhappy but me; that I could whip myself better than any other guy in the joint . . . I learned that everything is, or becomes, its own opposite . . . I learned that my dear parents, products of *their* parents, could know no better than they knew, and began to remember them only for the most useful, the best, the wisest of their teachings. They gave me my life and my body, the promising combination of the two and my initial strength; they endowed me with an inquisitive mind . . . it takes a long time for happiness to break through either to the individual or nations . . . as a philosopher once said, you cannot judge the day until the night. Since it is for me evening, or at least teatime, I can now look back and assess the day. In 1932, I sat in that Paramount studio office, took up the pen and wrote for the first time, 'Cary Grant.' And that's who, it seems, I am."

At one point he described what he saw as his "rebirth," which he attributed to LSD: "I passed through changing seas of horrifying and happy sights, through a montage of intense hate and love, a mosaic of past impressions assembling and reassembling: through terrifying depths of dark despair replaced by glorious heavenlike religious symbolisms.

"I was noting the growing intensity of light in the room and at short intervals as I shut my eyes, visions appeared to me. I seemed to be in a world of healthy, chubby little babies' legs and diapers, and smeared blood, a sort of general menstrual activity taking place. It did not repel me as such thoughts used to . . .

"When I first began experimentation, the drug seemed to loosen deeper fears, as sleep does a nightmare. I had horrifying experiences as participant and spectator, but, with each session, became happier, both while experiencing the drug and in periods between . . . I feel better and feel certain there is curative power in the drug itself."

There can be no question that taking LSD profoundly changed every aspect of Grant's personal and professional life. With the start in November 1957 of his next film, *Indiscreet*, he began, for the first time, what he knew would be the real process of retirement, not just from the movies but from the make-believe world that he inhabited in the guise of a legend. He was ready, at last, for the "teatime" of his life, a civilized world in which he could actually live in real time as a wholly realized, emotionally connected human being.

That same month fifty-three-year-old Cary Grant was named in a national poll as "Hollywood's Most Attractive Man."

INDISCREET WAS THE SECOND FILM Grant made for producer/director Stanley Donen, the first being *Kiss Them for Me*, where the two first met. When it was finished, they formed an independent production company called Grandon. Their goal was to independently produce a series of films that they owned from the outset, and then acquire a distribution deal with one of the major studios—in effect, reversing the by now all-but-extinct autonomous Hollywood studio system. Rather than working for one of the majors, they would make the film themselves (funded by banks), which meant hiring the director, star, and producer, paying all production costs, including prints, obtaining distribution, and retaining full ownership of the final product. One of Grant's stipulations was that his deal with Donen be nonexclusive, so that if he wished, he could make movies outside Grandon; and he insisted on having total script approval, to ensure that no more *The Pride and the Passion* debacles would befall him. For *Indiscreet*, Grandon paid Grant $300,000 up front and a brand-new Rolls-Royce to be purchased and left for him in England, for his exclusive use whenever he was there.

Donen and Grant had acquired the property while it was still running on Broadway under its original name, *Kind Sir*, with Charles Boyer and Mary Martin in the leads. It was a sophisticated "older couple" comedy staple of the Broadway theater party crowd, which tended to skew older. Grant and Donen then hired *Kind Sir*'s playwright, Norman Krasna, to "modernize" (heat up) the film version by making both leads ten years younger. To costar, Grant chose his dear friend Ingrid Bergman. Donen then changed the name of the film to *Indiscreet*, a sexually suggestive title that in more ways than one echoed the single-worded *Notorious* that Grant and Bergman had costarred in twelve years earlier.*

Because Bergman was still living in London, Grant had the script's locale switched from New York to England. This excited him for several reasons. The first was that he would get the chance to visit his mother, now in her

---

*According to critic Steven Cohan, "*Indiscreet* clearly functions as a reference to the earlier pairing of a younger and more sexually tense Grant and Bergman in *Notorious*; the comparison between these two films is historically revealing, not the least for understanding how 1940s notoriety can be transmuted into 1950s indiscretion. In *Notorious*, Bergman appears to confirm every one of Grant's suspicions about the duplicity of women, which he himself motivates since he is the one who repeatedly places her in that 'notorious,' not to say dangerous position of espionage and promiscuity . . . as others have said, the film indicates a dark, sadistic streak in the Cary Grant persona, especially since his manipulation of Bergman is in large part motivated by his character's desire to punish her active sexuality. By contrast, *Indiscreet* was made after Bergman's return to Hollywood's good graces and a second Oscar; though he does not marry her, this Grant is overly concerned with preserving her reputation."

eighties, and to do so without Drake, whom he no longer had any interest in introducing to Elsie.

Ever since they had begun taking LSD, Drake had shown a greater desire to revitalize their relationship; the drug produced the exact opposite reaction in Grant. Under the influence, he had slowly come to realize that all three of his choices of wives had been wrong, disastrously so, and for one overwhelming reason: none of them had ever expressed the least desire to have his children. In his mid-fifties now, with mortality creeping into his thoughts and with LSD helping him to reconcile the issue of his connection to his own inner self, for the first time the notion of extending his own life through a child had become not just a desire but a priority. The unsolvable problem for Grant with Drake was that even if she suddenly decided that motherhood was for her, which she had not, this was not the woman Grant wanted to bear his offspring. That was a gift that would have to wait for a woman who better fit his new revised bill of requirements.

In *Indiscreet*, Anne Kalman (Bergman), a star of the West End, decides to take some time off and rest. Her older sister, Margaret Munson (Phyllis Calvert), and her husband, Alfred (Cecil Parker), who works for NATO, arrive in London to attend a dinner in honor of Philip Adams (Grant), an international financial expert. Anne meets Philip at the dinner, and they begin a courtship, during which he informs her that he is married, although separated from his wife, and is having difficulty obtaining a divorce. They agree to remain just friends. In fact, Philip is lying; he has never been married and has used that excuse to keep from losing his cherished confirmed-bachelor lifestyle. Anne finds out and decides to make Philip jealous — an unnecessary strategy, as he has already decided to take the plunge with her. The couple then go into a boy-gets-girl, boy-loses-girl (when Philip finds her with her chauffeur, as she has planned), and then boy-gets-girl-for-better-or-worse, as the film ends.

It is easy to see why Grant was attracted to this script, and how it was tailored for him from the original play, about two middle-aged loners trying desperately to make a connection, into a more conventional, 1950s-style battle of the sexes, centered on the male's reluctance to be "captured" and the female's increasingly desperate desire to "get married." Philip lies, and deceptions are accepted as normal male defensive play in the service of freedom (bachelorhood), while Anne's lying and deceptions are taken as a gender defect, otherwise known as feminine wiles. In the end, the man succumbs to marriage, rather than celebrating winning his life's love.

The similarities to Grant's and Bergman's real-life issues were hard to miss and purposefully emphasized to play on Grant's problems with Drake and his recent "affair" with Loren. In the film, Philip's ambivalence toward marriage — which, as in most films, is a metaphor for sexual intimacy — is writ large. Also, he is Roman Catholic and uses that as one of his excuses for not being able to easily obtain a Church-sanctioned divorce — a virtual copy of Ponti's long-standing excuse for not marrying Loren. In the film, Grant's charm, good looks, and enormous integrity, as always, lead him to do the right thing, to satisfy the audience's desire to see him happily married. As for Bergman, her longtime scandalous affair with Rossellini is reflected in Anne's willingness to romance a seemingly married man, also happily reconciled in the film to please the paying crowd.

Most important, the chemistry of the Grant-Bergman pairing was nothing less than inspired, not only recalling the dynamics of *Notorious* but reflecting Grant's feeling that Bergman had been a victim of scandal. His acceptance of her as his leading lady helped make her acceptable to the audiences, and *Indiscreet* signaled the end of her years of self-imposed exile from Hollywood; such was the power of "Cary Grant."*

During the British shoot, Betsy Drake decided to fly over and spend Christmas with her husband. They went with Bergman to Italy for Christmas Day, after which Grant and Drake joined Prince Rainier and Princess Grace aboard Aristotle Onassis's yacht in the Mediterranean, where they stayed until January 1. Just before returning to the set for the final month of shooting, Grant left Drake in London to do some shopping, while he went alone to Bristol to visit his mother.

Elsie, in her eighties now and suffering from increasing memory lapses,

---

*Bergman's next film, Mark Robson's *The Inn of the Sixth Happiness* (1958), was her first American production made for a major studio — 20th Century–Fox — in ten years, since her appearance in Lewis Milestone's *Arch of Triumph*. *Under Capricorn*, made by Alfred Hitchcock in 1949, was a British production, and *Stromboli*, the film that caused her exile, was wholly Italian, shot in 1949.

had difficulty more than ever recognizing Grant, something he found extremely upsetting and hard to accept.

FILMING ENDED ON *Indiscreet* in February 1958, and the film was rushed into release by May, distributed by arrangement with Warner Bros., in order for Grandon to start to quickly earn back some of its investment.* Just as the film opened, Grant and Drake took a holiday junket to Moscow organized by producer Sam Spiegel. Upon their return to London, Grant was met by a reporter at the airport who asked why he would visit a Communist country. With a slight squint in his eyes, an offended Grant testily told the reporter, "I don't care what kind of government they have in Russia, I never felt so free in my life."

It was an unfortunate choice of words, as Grant was referring to his own state of mind, not to the benefits of the system of government. Nevertheless, Hedda Hopper—still hanging on as one of the most persistent of right-wing extremist William Randolph Hearst's political harridans—wrote in her column that if Grant loved the Red life so much, he ought to move to Moscow. Grant tried to respond by explaining to another reporter that when he said "free," he meant not being hounded by autograph-seekers, but the minor tempest did not completely go away, and despite the waning HUAC hysteria, many in Hollywood still considered Grant too far to the left for his own good.

UPON HIS RETURN to New York, Grant continued to march to the beat of his own drummer. In a famous story that has been told many times, Grant, while staying with Drake in separate suites at the Plaza Hotel, always ordered two English muffins for breakfast, split into four halves. One day only three arrived. In a fury, he called room service to find out why. He was told that an efficiency expert had determined that most people eat only three, and that if the hotel held one quarter back, they could gain a full extra order of English muffins for every four orders.

---

*This explains why it came out before *Houseboat*, which was actually made before *Indiscreet* but was not released by Paramount until November 1958, as its big holiday film.

Grant blew a Humphrey Bogart *Caine Mutiny* gasket. He placed a call to the president of the Hilton chain (which at the time owned the Plaza Hotel) and vowed to start an "English Muffin Lovers Society" to "protect the rights of English-muffin lovers everywhere!" The next day he found four halves of his English muffins included in his morning order.

BACK IN HOLLYWOOD, while planning his next film with Stanley Donen, Grant was offered the leading role in the screen version of Vladimir Nabokov's *Lolita*, to be directed by Stanley Kubrick. He angrily turned it down, describing the film as nothing more than a "degenerate" project. The role was then offered to Olivier, who also turned it down. It eventually went to James Mason, who gave one of the great performances of his career in a movie that has attained classic stature.

Grant instead chose to play the lead in Alfred Hitchcock's next venture, *North by Northwest*, a film that Grant could not wait to make. After reading the script, he knew the main character was one he could completely identify with, and understood why Hitchcock had told him he was the only one who could do complete justice to the role.

As usual, Hitchcock had gotten it exactly right.

29

"I've heard the fag rumor for years. Look at it this way. I've always tried to dress well. I've had some success in life. I've enjoyed my success and I include in that success some relationships with very special women. If someone wants to say I'm gay, what can I do? I think it's probably said about every man who's been known to do well with women. I don't let that sort of thing bother me. What matters to me is that I know who I am."

—CARY GRANT

n 1957, as the next to last of a multiple-picture deal with Paramount (*Psycho* would be the last), Alfred Hitchcock had made *Vertigo*, the most personal movie of his career. Although many consider it among his best work, *Vertigo* was something of a box office disappointment and would not gain its rightful reputation as a classic for many years to come.* It starred James Stewart, one of the two screen alter egos Hitchcock most preferred, the other, of course, being Cary Grant. If Grant is unthinkable driven to immobility as the tem-

---

*It was not, however, the disaster many people think. It cost $2.5 million to make and grossed $3.2 million in its initial domestic release, nearly a million-dollar profit. Nevertheless, it disappointed the studio bottom-liners because it made only half as much profit as *Rear Window*, Hitchcock's biggest money-maker for Paramount.

porarily insane hero gone mad over the haunting image of costar Kim Novak, Stewart remains likewise impossible to conceive as the athletic, unflappable, seemingly invulnerable Roger O. Thornhill, the "hero," for lack of a better term, of *North by Northwest*.*

To ensure a better deal for his next series of films, Hitchcock signed with Lew Wasserman, who had conceived Hitchcock's TV show, which was by now one of the biggest hits in MCA-Universal's TV roster. Hitchcock wanted to make an out-and-out mainstream hit and knew that Cary Grant's enormous star power was the best guarantee he could get. Wasserman made a one-picture deal for Hitchcock at MGM to serve as a bridge until a new multiple-picture deal at Universal could be worked out. He paired Hitchcock with Ernest Lehman, the successful screenwriter (*Sweet Smell of Success, Somebody Up There Likes Me, The King and I*, and *Sabrina* are a few of his better-known movies), at the time under contract to MGM.

Hitchcock and Lehman already knew each other well. They had first met during the filming of *Rear Window*, a film that so impressed Lehman that when the opportunity came to work with Hitchcock, he jumped at it. During the making of *Vertigo*, Hitchcock had come across a novel by Hammond Innes called *The Wreck of the Mary Deare* that for a while he considered filming. Lehman had done a first draft for the film that Hitchcock liked but ultimately decided it was not a subject he wished to take on. Hitchcock still wanted very much to work with Lehman and instructed him to try to come up with a script that would fit Cary Grant as well as one of his custom-made suits. Lehman then began working on something he called *In a Northerly Direction*, later on *Breathless*, before it had its final title, suggested by MGM story editor Kenneth MacKenna: *North by Northwest*.

The story of the film, described by Donald Spoto as "a superbly paced comic thriller about mistaken identity, political depravity, sexual blackmail, and ubiquitous role-playing," was a self-homage to Hitchcock's favorite film format, an emotional criss-cross over the physical landscape of a hero and his girlfriend thrown together by something that resembles, in Hitchcock's

---

*Stewart desperately wanted to star in *North by Northwest*, but from the start Hitchcock had his sights set on Grant. Rather than coming right out and telling him so, he diplomatically waited until Stewart began work on *Bell, Book and Candle*, a film he was contracted to do, and then told the actor that he was sorry, it was his (Hitchcock's) loss, and wished him well.

world, the religion of fate. The director had used this landscape scenario several times before, in *The 39 Steps*, *The Lady Vanishes*, *Young and Innocent*, and *Saboteur* and with some variation in *Strangers on a Train*, *Vertigo*, and *To Catch a Thief*.

Hitchcock offered Grant $450,000 up front, a full one-third more than his normal asking fee, 10 percent of the gross profits on all earnings over $8 million, plus an extra $5,000 a day seven weeks after the contract was signed, no matter what unforeseen delays might take place. Those seven weeks quickly came and went before a single foot of film was shot, which raised Grant's actual salary closer to $750,000.

Having signed Grant, the rest of the casting went smoothly, once it became clear to Grant that Hitchcock was not going to be able to get Sophia Loren as his costar. Hitchcock had initially agreed with him that their pairing would work for the film, but Ponti said no. He had had enough of Grant and absolutely refused to let his new wife appear with him again. MGM pushed for its contract star Cyd Charisse, but she left Hitchcock cold. He preferred blond beauty Eva Marie Saint, a Grace Kelly look-alike who had won a Best Supporting Actress Oscar for her work on Elia Kazan's *On the Waterfront* (1954). If Grant could not have his obsessive desires met, Hitchcock could satisfy his own. He saw in Saint, who had played mostly working-class women onscreen (*Waterfront*, *A Hatful of Rain* [1957]), something glamorous and mysterious that made her the perfect romantic lure to ensnare Grant into her world of sex and spy games.

Filming on *North by Northwest* took place on locations across the country, beginning in New York at United Nations Plaza, the first of the film's many monuments that spread the canvas of the screen, from New York to Chicago, to South Dakota, and finally to California. The interior of the Plaza Hotel, the CIT Building at 650 Madison Avenue, Grand Central Terminal, the Phipps estate in Old Westbury, Midwest cornfields, and Rapid City's Mount Rushmore—all showed off the physical beauty of the rolling American landscape that became, in Hitchcock's view, a metaphor for the beauty of endless freedom, both the country's and the leading characters' quest to defend it.

The story centers on an innocent man who is caught in a web of deceit and intrigue, then is drawn into it until, through a series of increasingly bizarre misadventures, he turns into the very man he has been mistaken for and falls in love with a beautiful woman far guiltier than she appears to be. Roger O. Thornhill (Grant) is kidnapped by foreign spies who mistake him for the CIA operative George Kaplan. Thornhill narrowly escapes death when he is forced to drink a bottle of bourbon, then is put behind the wheel of a car at the top of a winding road. This time, in *North by Northwest*, the mandatory car scene is played early on, with a comedic tone rather than a suspenseful one, primarily because no one would ever believe Hitchcock would kill his star this early in the film.* Instead, the car ride signals the beginning of a far more precarious journey to self-discovery, personal freedom (from the clutches of a domineering mother and two previous wives who left him "because they thought I led too dull a life"), and ultimately romantic redemption in the beautiful guise of Eve Kendall (Eva Marie Saint). Ingeniously, Hitchcock (and Lehman) have Thornhill chase himself, in his pursuit of "Kaplan," across the country.

Unknown to him, Thornhill has been misidentified by the enemy as a CIA operative who doesn't actually exist, a creation of the agency to throw the "bad guys" off the trail of the real counterspy they have embedded in their evil midst. After Thornhill is set up as the assassin of a UN representative, he goes on the run, fleeing from the authorities while pursuing the "real" Kaplan. Complicating matters, he becomes involved with a beautiful blonde on a train, Eve Kendall, who as it turns out is not only the lover of the enemy ringleader, Vandamm (James Mason), but also the secret CIA operative whom "Kaplan" was created to protect. Somehow along the way, between several of the film's best-remembered set pieces—Thornhill doing battle with a low-flying crop-duster, his ingenious escape from the auction, his faked "murder" by Eve at the base of the presidential monuments—he is at last let in on the various subterfuges by CIA chief (and Hitchcock surrogate) "the Professor" (Leo G. Carroll). Thornhill eventually tracks Eve to the cliffhanger home of Vandamm, which sets up the film's glorious climax. Thornhill literally scales the angular side of the house like a human spider, gets inside, and overhears Vandamm and Leonard, his second-in-command (Martin Landau), planning

---

*Hitchcock would have the last laugh when he turned that conventional assumption on its head two years later, in *Psycho*.

Eve's murder. The scene culminates in both Thornhill and Eve dangling off the face of Mount Rushmore, where he rescues her by grasping her wrist and seemingly pulling her back to safety. The camera cuts from a close-up of Grant to one of Saint and back to Grant, and this time a pull-back reveals the two on a train, traveling east, married, and in love. Once again, as with Hepburn in *Bringing Up Baby*, Grant's rescue of Saint is a redemption, an elevation from the pedestrian world of loners to the poetic landscape of lovers. The famous final shot of *North by Northwest* that always gets a laugh for its sexual metaphor—a train plunging into a tunnel—suggests something darker as well: a nearly religious ritual of the inevitably joyless sexual industrialization that is, in Hitchcock's world, the unhappily-ever-after of the dutifully, if no longer romantically, married.

The key to the film is Grant's duality, as Hitchcock allows Grant, in the guise of mama's boy Thornhill, to once again play his character's subtext as text, the subconscious as conscious, the unleashed id as ego. This makes the real "chase" of the film the repressed Thornhill's desire to invade and inhabit the adventurous, brave, physical, clever, aggressive, and finally romantic world of the idealized (and mythic) hero George Kaplan, the man Thornhill secretly (subconsciously) wishes he could be. The genius of Hitchcock lies in how he gets the audience as well as Thornhill to believe in the existence of George Kaplan, until by the end of the film, it is Kaplan who survives, while Roger Thornhill simply ceases to exist (although the final shot suggests that Kaplan may already be turning back into Thornhill).

Even as Hitchcock's cameras were rolling for *North by Northwest*, Grant's secret, ongoing LSD sessions had allowed him to turn his own pursuit inward, to make the vital connections between the persona of "Cary Grant" and the private Cary Grant. In that sense, the film celebrates as much as it reflects the success of that union and turns Hitchcock's orchestrated Thornhill-to-Kaplan into the most personal, revealing, moving, and ultimately profound screen performance of Grant's long and brilliant movie career.

DURING THE FILMING OF *North by Northwest*, Grant, fifty-four, and Drake, thirty-five, made public what had been a de facto reality for years: that they were officially separated and headed for divorce. On October 16, 1958, they issued a joint statement that said, "After careful consideration and long discussion, we have decided to live apart. We have had, and shall always have, the deepest respect for each other. But, alas, our marriage has not brought us the happiness we fully expected and mutually desired. So, since we have no children needful of our affections, it is consequently best that we separate for a while. There are no plans for divorce and we ask only that our statement be respected as being complete and our friends to be patient with, and understanding of, our decision."

Grant provided scant more information even to his closest friends, offering only the familiar litany of reasons he had given for his first two divorces: that he had become bored, that he wasn't suited to domestic life, and that he and Drake had simply run out of things to talk about.

In FEBRUARY 1959, one month after his fifty-fifth birthday, Grant, for the first time in his career, reached the top of *Box Office* magazine's annual popularity poll, as it named him the number one film star of 1958.* Six months later *North by Northwest* was released to critical and commercial success. It grossed $7 million in its initial domestic theatrical release, nearly twice what it cost to make, and would go on to become Hitchcock's highest-grossing film ever, as well as the third highest of Grant's career.

While Grant was in New York to attend the Radio City Music Hall opening of *North by Northwest,* an ugly and unsubstantiated story broke in newspapers across the country that detailed his former British chauffeur's revelations of having had a love affair with Grant. In the story, twenty-five-year-old Raymond Austin claimed that he expected to be named "the other man"—Grant's lover—in Drake's impending divorce action against him.

An outraged Grant immediately contacted his attorney, Stanley Fox, to issue an angry written denial. A month later Austin tried to commit suicide in London by taking an overdose of pills. Although he survived, it was the last anyone heard of him or his claim.

---

*Following him in order of selection were William Holden, Yul Brynner, Rock Hudson (the previous year's number one choice), Marlon Brando, Glenn Ford, Gary Cooper, Jerry Lewis, Frank Sinatra, Kirk Douglas, James Stewart, and Clark Gable.

As soon as his publicity obligations for *North by Northwest* were completed, Grant flew to Key West to begin production on his next picture, Blake Edwards's *Operation Petticoat*, a light sex comedy involving the crew of a submarine and the ship's unlikely cargo of female nurses during World War II. Granart was yet another company he had set up (with this-time-only partner Robert Arthur, through their jointly owned Granart Company Productions) to independently produce the picture. During filming Grant became close with costar Tony Curtis, one among many new Grants-in-waiting, whose career was sizzling after the success of *Some Like It Hot* and who was responsible for bringing *Operation Petticoat*, via Universal Pictures, to Grant. According to Curtis, "I was doing so swell those days that Universal asked me what kind of movie I wanted to make next, and I said, 'A service comedy about submarines.' They said, 'Fine, we'll get Jeff Chandler or Robert Taylor to play the captain.' I said, 'No, I want Cary Grant.' They got back to me later and said, 'Robert Taylor wants to play that part very much, and he'll give you five percent of his ten percent of the gross.' I said, 'No, I want Cary Grant.' That's what I wanted, and that's what I got."*

Grant jumped at the opportunity to work with Curtis. He loved the young actor's onscreen charisma and likely saw something of his younger self in the handsome, dark-haired romantic leading man. When they met, he was completely charmed by Curtis's humor as well. Grant told him he found his on-the-money impersonation the year before in Billy Wilder's *Some Like It Hot* absolutely hilarious. According to Curtis, "I never worked it deliberately as a Cary Grant imitation . . . [but] so much the better if the Cary voice makes it a little funnier for some people."

Grant always loved young female costars, believing they made him look younger when he played opposite them; in a similar fashion, he believed act-

---

*Other unsuccessful candidates for the title included TV star and Grant look-alike Craig Stevens, TV's *Peter Gunn*; TV star and Grant look-alike John Vivyan, TV's *Mr. Lucky*; and TV star and Grant look-alike, cleft-chinned David Janssen, star of *Richard Diamond, Private Detective* and later *The Fugitive*. Universal was hoping to talk Curtis out of Cary Grant because the film would have been much more profitable for them with any other actor in the role of the captain. When they acquiesced, it meant they also had to use Granart, Grant's production company, as the only distributor and therefore received a much smaller percent of the profits.

ing with Tony Curtis might make him more accessible to younger male and female audiences.

DURING FILMING AN INCIDENT OCCURRED between Grant and respected veteran Hollywood syndicated columnist Joe Hyams, who had, after years of trying, eventually got Grant to agree to a series of sit-down interviews.* Throughout his career, Grant had cultivated his dealings with the press into something of an art form, giving essentially the same interview every time he wanted to publicize a new movie: he was born in Bristol, he joined the Pender troupe, he traveled with them to New York, he got his taste in clothes from his father, he loved women, he loved acting, he loved life, he loved everything about life, he was grateful for all that he had been able to achieve in life, etc., etc., etc. This time, for some reason known only to Grant, he told Hyams things that he had never told any interviewer before. When he saw his words in print, they horrified him.

One likely theory of why Grant suddenly became so loose-lipped is that his sessions with LSD had given him a new sense of self-confidence—one of the first things he discussed with Hyams was how uplifting his experience with the drug had been. Up until this time he had always denied that he had ever so much as seen a psychiatrist, let alone been one of the early experimenters with LSD. According to Hyams, Grant readily confessed to him that "I hurt every woman I loved ... I was an utter fake ... a self-opinionated bore ... until one day, after weeks of treatment [with LSD], I did see the light ... now for the first time in my life, I am truly, deeply and honestly happy." These statements left Hyams open-mouthed with astonishment and sent him rushing for his typewriter.

However, before Hyams's series of articles based on the interviews appeared, another journalist, a Brit by the name of Lionel Crane, published an article in a London newspaper that contained virtually the same "revelations." Hyams was angered and puzzled by the timing, especially when, after interviewing Grant, he had received a phone call from the actor asking him

*Not to be confused with Charles Higham, one of Grant's unauthorized biographers.

as a personal favor not to print anything they had talked about, at least for the time being. Hyams, who had a reputation as a Hollywood insider who could be trusted, reluctantly agreed.

But once the Crane piece appeared, Hyams quickly published a two-part nationally syndicated article that quoted Grant's every last word concerning his psychiatric treatment, his acid-taking, his attitude toward women, and his lifetime of self-loathing. Needless to say, it caused a sensation that sent Grant into a rage. Without thinking the situation through, he publicly denied ever having been interviewed by Hyams, a claim Louella Parsons breathlessly repeated as gospel fact, without so much as making a single phone call to check with Hyams.

The journalist angrily rebutted both Grant and Parsons by publishing the details of the events that led up to the series of interviews, along with a photograph of himself conducting them with Grant taken at the Florida naval base during the shooting of *Operation Petticoat*. Hyams's rebuttal drew even more attention to the story, and a livid Grant, through Stanley Fox, threatened to sue him, the newspaper syndicate that distributed the articles, and the newspapers that carried them.

Hyams could not understand why Grant had so vehemently turned against him, until he learned that, shortly after Crane's piece appeared, the actor had sold the "complete and exclusive" story of his taking LSD to *Look* magazine for a substantial amount of money—a deal that, because of his interview, was now in danger of being canceled. Hyams then double-jumped Grant and sued him for slander to the tune of $500,000 for claiming that he had made up the entire interview and never met.

Grant panicked. He did not want to undergo a deposition, knowing full well that things might come out that were far worse than anything that had already appeared. To prevent that from happening, days before Grant's scheduled appearance before Hyams's lawyer, Stanley Fox offered the writer a generous settlement. He could ghostwrite Grant's "autobiography," with complete access to Grant, sell it for whatever he could get, and keep all the money it made. It was a deal that was too good to resist. Grant's only stipulation was that it could run only once, as a magazine piece, and never as a book. Hyams agreed, if Grant would allow the byline to read, "By Cary Grant as told to Joe Hyams."

The two then spent a great deal of time together taping discussions that were, for the most part, Grant's usual interview material. It gradually became clear to Hyams that this was going to be less an incisive, revelatory self-examination than a pleasant recounting by Grant of his well-trod, occasionally romanticized memories—"Cary Grant's" memoir, not Cary Grant's. Still, he told his stories in such a disarming way and included enough interesting material to make the rather fanciful "autobiography" alluring to *Ladies' Home Journal*, which bought it for an astonishing $125,000.

When Grant found out about how much Hyams was making, he angrily threatened to cancel the entire deal. Fox then called Hyams and suggested the writer give Grant a $22,000 Rolls-Royce as a gift. Hyams did the math and decided 20 percent was not a bad amount to pay to avoid any further legal fees. He purchased the car for Grant324 and had it delivered bearing the license plate CG-1.

There the whole curious affair should have ended, except it didn't. Hedda Hopper, who had been after Grant for years to let *her* write his life story, was so angered he had given the assignment instead to Hyams that she wrote a vicious letter, not to *Ladies' Home Journal* but to one of the editors of *Look* magazine, where Grant had made his own lucrative deal, in which she "outed" Grant, claiming that everyone in Hollywood knew his upcoming "autobiography" was nothing more than his cheap attempt to cover up the truth about his lifelong homosexuality. *Look* decided not to print Hopper's letter (which is reprinted in Charles Higham and Roy Moseley's hasty post-mortem Grant biography).

Instead, the magazine went ahead and ran its lengthy contracted LSD story, written by Laura Bergquist, entitled "The Curious Story Behind the New Cary Grant," in which Grant agreed to be interviewed and talked of his experiences in discovering the joys of taking LSD. Early on, Bergquist set the tone for the piece by quoting David Niven, who described Grant in a way no one in his circle had ever dared do before in public, alluding to all the quirks of Grant's personality, and even, very indirectly, to his homosexuality. "I've known Cary for twenty-five years," Niven said, "and he's the most truly mysterious friend I have. A spooky Celt really, not an Englishman at all. Must be some fey Welsh blood there someplace. Gets great crushes on people like the late Countess di Frasso, or ideas like hypnotism, then moves on. Has great depressions and then some great heights when he seems about to take off for outer space."

In the piece, Grant responded, "I am through with sadness. At last, I am close to happiness. After all these years, I'm rid of guilt complexes and fears." He then went on a reverie of rambling, sharing such interesting details with Bergquist as his new-found, post-acid ability to "think" himself thin without benefit of exercise or diet. At the end of the piece he addressed his feelings about acting and shared this startling revelation: "Acting isn't the most essential business in the world . . . Personally, I think I'm ready at last to have children. I'd like to have a whole brood cluttering around the dining room table. I think my relations with women will be different too. I used to love a woman with great passion, and we destroyed each other. Or I loved not at all, or in friendship. Now I'm ready to love on an equal level. If I can find a woman on whom I can exhaust all my thoughts, energies and emotions, and she loves me that way in return, we can live happily ever after." To this Bergquist insightfully concluded, "There are Hollywood skeptics who wonder if the 'new' Grant may not be the best character part he has ever played."

By comparison, Hyams's "autobiography" (which took two years to appear in the *Ladies' Home Journal*) was extremely tame, with most of the unsightly blemishes carefully airbrushed from Grant's life, like wrinkles from a publicity photo, in deference to the afterimage that still burned so brightly in the eyes of his legions of fans. Nevertheless, it became the "factual" reference point for so many of the lasting misconceptions surrounding the life of Cary Grant.

After her letter to *Look* magazine and the publication of his authorized autobiography, Grant never spoke to either Hopper or Hyams again.

Instead, as he moved into the 1960s, fifty-six-year-old Cary Grant preferred to look ahead, to a new life that, as far as he was concerned, was just beginning.

A DAUGHTER IS BORN

PART NINE

PREVIOUS PAGE: *Cary Grant, fourth wife Dyan Cannon, and Grant's only child, three-month-old Jennifer, in 1966, during the brief period of time the couple appeared to be happily married. (Bettmann/CORBIS)*

30

"I was a self-centered boor. I was masochistic and only thought I was happy. When I woke up and said, 'There must be something wrong with me,' I grew up. Because I never understood myself, how could I have hoped to understand anyone else? That's why I say that now I can truly give a woman love for the first time in my life, because I can understand her."

—CARY GRANT

At Drake's insistence, Grant tried a reconciliation that he knew couldn't possibly work. Even before he finished *North by Northwest,* Grant was preparing himself for his permanent exit from the marriage and once again rushed into the protective safety of another movie. Emotional separation had always been difficult, and nothing else in his life could occupy him so completely and take his mind off his personal woes as making movies. In his capacity as filmmaking "tycoon, bargaining with a mind like an IBM machine," and in a deal he negotiated on his own, Grant turned the tables on Universal Studios by insisting it guarantee Grandon 75 percent of the profits or 10 percent of the gross, whichever was greater, with a guarantee of $1 million up front and outright ownership of the negatives after seven years.

It was still a good deal for Universal, but a great one for Grant, who had become more actively involved in the financial planning of his motion pictures after he summarily dispatched Lew Wasserman and MCA. With the huge financial success of *North by Northwest*, the agency had begun to press him to move into television, something he had openly resisted ever since the little flickering box first began to appear in living rooms across the country. In his biography of Wasserman, Dennis McDougal describes how the Wasserman-Grant split happened: "The final outrage [after MCA's failure to acquire *Bell, Book and Candle* for Grant] came when Grant was summoned to appear at Wasserman's Beverly Hills office for a career discussion. There, several executives told Grant he ought to follow his triumphant appearance in *North by Northwest* by doing his own TV series. Grant immediately became hostile. He asked again whether they really believed that he should appear in television and MCA replied, 'Yes.' Grant asked who would produce the show and was told it would be MCA, of course. He stood up, scanned the roomful of Wasserman clones, all clad in dark suits, white shirts, and black ties, and said, 'Our contract is over as of now,' walked out and never returned."

Grant had every reason to be outraged. It was clear to him now that MCA was far less interested in prolonging his giant film career than reducing it to twenty-one black-and-white inches, in a medium where they would have complete control of the vehicle, the talent, the advertising, and the profits. Wasserman had done the same thing with Alfred Hitchcock in the mid-1950s, giving him a half-hour drama anthology series, then using it as a way to bolster Revue, Universal's TV unit. (The director, however, was smart enough to ensure that he would be allowed to continue to make movies and maintain creative control over the show's content as well as long-term ownership of all its episodes. Wasserman was not going to make that mistake again. Grant would not have been offered creative input, profit participation, or ownership.)

As always, Grant's timing was perfect. He left Wasserman and MCA just as the government was tightening its long-term investigation into the alleged monopolistic practices and mob influence at the powerful management and talent agency.*

---

*McDougal's account of Grant's exit from MCA was taken from an FBI audiotape of the meeting, made on November 4, 1960, without the knowledge of any of the participants.

RELEASED IN DECEMBER 1959, in time for the lucrative holiday season, *Operation Petticoat*, Grant's sixty-seventh film, became the most successful of his career. It outgrossed *North by Northwest* by more than $3 million and in doing so elevated Grant into the rarefied air (of the time) where independent producers of films that surpass the $10 million gross mark (in their initial domestic theatrical release) were few and far between. As producer and star of *Operation Petticoat*, he earned a personal net gain of $3 million, the most he had ever made from a single picture. A month after the film's opening, on the strength of his powerhouse box office, Cary Grant became the first star in film history to have his films gross more than $10 million *in a single theater*. He had already had a record twenty-four movies of his premiere at the cavernous 3,200-seat art deco Radio City Music Hall auditorium in the heart of New York City. *Operation Petticoat* pushed Grant's collective Music Hall gross over the $10 million milestone.

AS HE CROSSED THE MID-FIFTIES line on his life's journey, each tick of the biological clock sounded more and more like a soundtracked funereal bass. His continued regular weekly doses of LSD were the best reminders of who he really was and what he still needed to do, even as he sensed that time was running out to salvage his own childhood by creating his own child. In February 1961, just after his fifty-seventh birthday, Grant told an entertainment reporter from *The New York Times* that "there is no doubt that I am aging. My format of comedy is still the same as ever. I gravitate toward scripts that put me in an untenable position. Then the rest of the picture is spent in trying to squirm out of it. Naturally, I always get the girl in the end. It may appear old-fashioned. There seems to be a trend toward satirical comedy, like *The Apartment*. Perhaps it is because young writers today feel satirical living in a world that seems headed for destruction."*

---

*Billy Wilder, someone Grant was never particularly fond of, produced and directed *The Apartment* (1960), for which he won Best Picture, Best Director, and Best Screenplay (with I.A.L. Diamond) Oscars. The film also won for Art Direction–Set Direction and editing. Grant's reference is an obvious one. Wilder's black and white film is cynical, sexual, and edgy, while Grant's post-Hitchcock films were at Grant's directive colorful, positive, wholesome, and relaxed.

Grant's notion that his films could somehow save the world was a macro fantasy of fatherhood as wild and expansive as it was appealing to him. That month Grant quietly began spreading the word among friends that he was offering a bounty of a million dollars in cash for "the right woman willing to bear him a son." That bounty would be resurrected periodically for the rest of his life.

GRANT DECIDED TO COMPLETE ALL his outstanding film commitments to his own and Donen's film companies and take on no new projects. That winter he finally began work on *The Grass Is Greener*. The film was based on a successful British stage play by Hugh and Margaret Williams, shot on location in London and directed by Stanley Donen. Grant had insisted the film be shot there because he wanted to return to England. Thrifty as ever, he had found a project that would finance the entire trip without interfering with his nonmoviemaking affairs. *The Grass Is Greener* was, in that sense, the ideal project. With the exception of one or two scenes, it is essentially a one-set project; much of the action takes place in Lynley Hall, the stately mansion of Victor, Earl of Rhyall (Grant), who for financial reasons—he's flat broke—has opted to turn the place into a tourist attraction.

Grant cast Deborah Kerr to play his wife, Hilary, although she wasn't his first choice; the earthier Jean Simmons was. Simmons, however, was on the verge of divorce and because of it asked for and got the smaller role of Hilary's girlfriend, Hattie Durant. Donen recommended Robert Mitchum to play Charles Delacro, the wealthy young American who, while taking the tour, meets and falls in love with Kerr. In the key role of the butler, Grant dearly wanted Noël Coward, but Donen preferred Moray Watson, who had created the role onstage at the West End—the only original cast member to make the transition to film. Grant acquiesced.

The plot centers on Charles's efforts to woo Hilary away from Victor. The sex mess is treated in a veddy Briddish manner, meaning much civilized talk with little physical action, until the two men agree to resolve their differences in a duel. Victor is wounded, Hilary realizes she still loves him, and everyone lives happily ever after, including Charles, who somehow winds up with

Hattie (with whom Victor had faked a romance in the hopes it would make Hilary jealous and win her before any shots were fired).

Grant had, at one point, considered not being in the picture at all, and unofficially offered his part instead to Rex Harrison, who agreed to do it—until the death of his wife, Kay Kendall, forced him to drop out. To avoid an expensive delay, Grant then agreed to play the role after all, one he knew he could do with his eyes closed. Mitchum, on the other hand, stood out like an American sore thumb, cast against type in the guise of an articulate, understated wealthy American urbanite. Grant okayed Donen's choice of Mitchum because he had already starred in two films with each of *The Grass Is Greener*'s female costars, and thought their experience would produce a familiar chemistry well suited for this ensemble piece.*

As it happened, Grant felt early on that Mitchum's acting was too understated, and that because of it he, Grant, would be seen as overplaying his part. Mitchum saw things differently. He complained that his role was under*written*, consisting mostly of reactions like "Really?" and "Oh?" amid long stretches of dialogue from either Grant or Kerr. Moreover, Mitchum found Grant a bit old-man stodgy, both in the part and in real life, and he later told friends that he didn't appreciate Grant's "humor . . . sort of old music-hall jokes. 'What's that noise down there? They're holding an Elephant's Ball? Well, I wish they'd let go of it, I'm trying to get some sleep,'" adding somewhat facetiously, "I guess that was when he was coming off his LSD treatment."

Donen remembers the film as a milestone of sorts, marking the end of a certain type of sophisticated British comedy, before the antic humor of Peter Sellers arrived and dominated the English cinematic 1960s: "Cary played a titled Englishman, and [in several scenes] was wearing what an earl would wear at night in his country house—a dark green velvet smoking jacket. Halfway through making the picture, he got terrified. 'I don't want to be in a smoking jacket,' he said. He was afraid that by playing that kind of man he would lose people's interest. A certain sort of polish in films—the way people moved and spoke—vanished then. And it never came back."

---

*Mitchum starred with Jean Simmons in Otto Preminger's *Angel Face* (also known as *Murder Story*) (1952) and Lloyd Bacon's *She Couldn't Say No* (1954), and with Deborah Kerr in John Huston's *Heaven Knows, Mr. Allison* (1957) and Fred Zinnemann's *The Sundowners* (1960).

DURING FILMING, GRANT SPENT EVERY weekend in Bristol visiting his mother, for the first time enjoying the occasional flash of genuine wit that emerged from her diminished capacities without the overlay of guilt that had long plagued their relationship. Grant loved treating Elsie to shopping sprees in search of the antiques she loved to collect.

Less blissful was a visit he received from Drake, who, as part of yet another of her futile attempts to reconcile with Grant, flew to England to be with him for several weeks while he was shooting. During her stay she and Grant were invited by Princess Grace to go sailing with her and Prince Rainier off the shores of Monaco—something that caused the prince no little amount of consternation. Not only had he absolutely forbidden his wife to return to filmmaking, he didn't even like being reminded of that part of her life, which, as far as he was concerned, was, like all of Hollywood, cheap and tawdry (and threatening). No doubt he both envied and feared his imagined (and in some cases real) Hollywood rivals for Kelly's affections. He was especially jealous of Grant, who was much taller and far more fit than the pudgy prince, who could not get out of his head the images of the passionate kisses and sexual flirtation between Grant and his wife in *To Catch a Thief*. (He nevertheless screened the film frequently at the palace, when guests from America stayed with them, always by request. Of all her films, it remained the only one he refused to allow to be shown publicly in Monaco.)

According to one who was there, throughout Grant and Drake's visit "the prince did not hide his bad humor during their stay at the palace. He spoke to no one. He sulked . . . the princess, meanwhile, was cool—her usual attitude to her husband's moods."

For her part, Drake mistook the princess's coolness for well-founded jealousy and in turn became jealous herself. The resulting criss-crossing of tensions made everyone less comfortable than they otherwise might have been. Princess Grace and Grant both knew what was taking place and did their best to ignore their spouses' suspicions and just enjoy themselves.

This was the last official invitation to Monaco Grant would receive during the princess's lifetime.

⁕

THE GRASS IS GREENER opened in December 1960, and its comic conceits—that the British were essentially so superior to the Americans in the ways of civilized love that their marriages could survive a little harmless flirtation, while the boorish Americans, no matter how rich or refined, would chase anything in a skirt, single or married—laid a gigantic egg in the United States. Even Grant's most diehard female fans tended to stay away, not wanting to see their idol compromised by, of all men, the swarthy, bullying Robert Mitchum.

Because of it Grant took a bit of a financial bath, something at the time with which he simply could not be bothered. Instead, his focus returned once more to his pursuit of finding the proper soulmate as a wife and future mother. While he continued his search, he moved along briskly with his plan to eliminate all remaining film obligations. He soon began production on the decidedly all-American *That Touch of Mink*, in which he appears opposite Doris Day, the cross-eyed, freckled, lemon-haired eternal virgin of the American mid-twentieth-century cinema.

Grant plays the role of a suave and debonair millionaire ladies' man originally intended for Rock Hudson, Day's onscreen partner in the hugely successful sex(less) comedies *Pillow Talk* and *Lover Come Back*, both made at Universal. Day's husband, manager, and producer, Martin Melcher, felt that Hudson had gotten too much credit and Day too little for the previous films' successes, and as the Hudson characters were always described as "Cary Grant" types, he decided to go for the real thing.

Grant, meanwhile, since firing Wasserman, loathed the thought of doing any more business with Universal and turned Melcher down several times. Finally Stanley Fox came up with a workable plan good enough to convince Melcher's company, Arwin Productions, to bring in Grant as a partner and make Stanley Shapiro the film's screenwriter and coproducer, along with Grant and Melcher. It was the choice of Shapiro that finally convinced Grant to sign on. Shapiro, who came up with the original concept for *That Touch of Mink*, was also the screenwriter for *Operation Petticoat* and a cowriter of both *Pillow Talk* and *Lover Come Back*, all three of which were highly successful, big-profit pictures.

In *That Touch of Mink*, millionaire bachelor Philip Shayne (Grant) romances working girl Cathy Timberlake (Day). After a meet-cute in which Grant's Rolls-Royce accidentally douses Cathy's coat with mud, Philip, assisted by his ever-loyal manservant and moral adviser Roger (Gig Young), decides to romance Day every-American-woman's-fantasy style, which includes a visit to the dugout of the New York Yankees (Grant, a lifelong baseball fan, was thrilled to death to appear with Mickey Mantle, Roger Maris, and Yogi Berra in a scene shot on location at Yankee Stadium), a trip to Bermuda on everything but gossamer wings, and midnight top-of-the-world dinners at his penthouse, all of which gets him no closer to having sex with Cathy. Somehow this only makes him want her more. In the end, they get married.

The film, which borrowed heavily from Shapiro's previous Day comedy *Lover Come Back*, is a basic meat-and-potatoes middle-aged man meets girl, middle-aged man loses girl, middle-aged man gets chicken pox (and the girl who gives it to him). Audiences loved it and welcomed back the familiar "American" Cary Grant with open arms and wallets. The film opened at Radio City Music Hall on July 18, 1962, and earned more than $1 million in its initial domestic theatrical release. It went on to become the second-highest-grossing Cary Grant film of all time (just behind *Operation Petticoat*).

Although *That Touch of Mink* earned $4 million for Grant, personally he remained indifferent to the film and thought nothing about it other than it was one less he would ever have to make.*

THREE WEEKS LATER, on August 13, 1962, Drake, who had returned from a trip to England after not hearing from Grant even once the entire time she was gone, was convinced at last that their relationship could not be saved and sued for divorce on the grounds of mental cruelty.

According to court records, Drake's reasons for seeking the divorce included the fact that Grant "preferred watching television to talking to me.

---

*As part of his deal, Grant kept the beautiful wardrobe custom-designed for him to wear in the movie by Norman Norell and (an uncredited) Rosemary Odell.

He appeared bored. I became lonely, unhappy, miserable, and went into psychoanalysis. He told me he didn't want to be married. He showed no interest in any of my friends."

As was his custom, Grant made no public comment, other than the one-sentence comment that "Betsy was good for me." Drake's initial reaction to the press waiting outside the courtroom door after the one-day hearing (at which Grant did not testify) was done with dramatic flair: "I was always in love with him," she said, then paused, turned her head, and added, "and I still am."

Later on, pressed by Louella Parsons for more "exclusive" information, Betsy told the gossip, "I left Cary, but physically he'd left me long ago."

Drake received a generous settlement from Grant rumored to be more than $1 million in cash and a portion of the profits from all the films he had made during the nearly thirteen years they were married. Shortly thereafter she left show business, and his life, forever.

The swiftness and generosity of Grant's participation reflected his only remaining interest in his third wife: getting rid of her as soon as possible so he could continue to search for the woman truly worthy of being the mother of his child.

31

Q: How old Cary Grant?
A: Old Cary Grant fine. How you?

—CARY GRANT

After the divorce Grant reverted to his reclusive ways, this time to avoid the opinions of everyone in the press and at his favorite watering holes as to why his marriage to Betsy Drake had failed. As usual, everyone both in print and out got it wrong. The majority insisted on making Drake a victim, even though it was she who had, publicly at least, initiated the divorce and come out of the marriage financially secure for the rest of her life. Grant was peeved that instead of focusing on her new-found freedom and wealth, publications like *Time* magazine chided him for being able to buy his way out of every bad marriage, claiming he had so much money he could join NATO. Discussion of his Jack Benny–like cheapness, a favorite topic of the press, never failed to make him wince. *Time* concluded its piece by insinuating that "he also has virtually every nickel he has ever earned."

He took it as one more tired replay of the old "Cash and Cary" wisecracks that had plagued him ever since his second marriage to the heiress Hutton. It didn't help that he was, in truth, a notoriously stingy tipper, the surest way to turn any waiter into a press informant; or that he would give autographs only if the fan who requested one, even a child, paid him a twenty-five-cent fee, money he claimed he saved up and gave to charity but actually pocketed for himself; or that he only took two hundred dollars with him to the Hollywood Park Race Track, which he always jokingly referred to as "a day at the races," and he placed only two-dollar bets—"because," he loved to tell anyone who asked, "they won't take a dollar-fifty. I've tried."

Rather than continuing to read about himself every day in the gossip columns, Grant took to watching nightly series television, which is where he first laid eyes on actress Dyan Cannon. He was in bed early one Wednesday night, watching a 1961 TV series he liked called *Malibu Run,* which ran opposite NBC's *Wagon Train,* one of the top-rated shows in the country. Grant had no interest in the western, preferring Malibu to the old Chisholm Trail. This night he could not take his eyes off the young blond beauty guesting on the show. Dyan Cannon had been cast by the series producers off a Hollywood-produced daytime soap after they couldn't get Elizabeth Montgomery for the part.

After a few minutes Grant reached for his pad and made a note to call Stanley Fox and have him track Cannon down and offer her a part in his next film. The next day Fox found her agent, Adeline Gould, who told him that Cannon was, at the moment, making a picture in Rome. Fox said he wanted to set up a meeting between her and Grant "immediately," something Gould said could be arranged if Grant was willing to buy Cannon a round-trip first-class air ticket. Fox went to Grant, Grant said no, Fox went back to Gould, Gould said fine, Grant could see her when she returned. The fifty-eight-year-old actor then had to wait several weeks before a face-to-face meeting with the twenty-three-year-old Cannon could be arranged.

It finally happened at his small bungalow office at Universal. Even though Grant had left the company, every movie he had produced and starred in since *Operation Petticoat* was, by prior arrangement, distributed by Universal-International, which was also the distributor of his next film with Stanley Donen. Grant no longer cared who distributed his movies, or much about anything having to do with them. He had even closed down Grandon Productions (although he agreed to consider any acting parts on a film-to-film basis). Despite its enormous success, Grant no longer wanted to do anything except show up, say his lines, and go home. Donen then made a new deal with Universal that included Grant's continued use of a small office for both him and Grant—rent free, of course.

This is how Cannon remembers that first meeting with Grant: "I had just returned from Rome, where I had been subsisting on pasta and meatballs and having a glorious time. A very important Brazilian was in love with me . . . anyway, I went over to the Universal lot and my agent said, as long as we are here, let's go over and say hello to Cary Grant. Cary had seen me in a TV show and wanted me for a part in a movie. I said okay, and we spent about an hour and a half in his office. No mention of the picture he had wanted me for. And then when we walked out, I said to myself, I'm ready to die! I've met this gorgeous man, and if I die tonight my life is complete."

During the meeting Grant never brought up any film roles for Cannon, and after an hour and a half he cordially ended it. That night, however, he could not get the young and beautiful actress off his mind. The next day he called and asked her for a date. Cannon said yes, then called back and said no. He waited, then called, she said yes again, then called him back and said no. This went on until she finally agreed to have dinner with him. Cannon: "Cary called me the next day and we made a date, and I broke it. We made eight dates, and I broke them all. Something told me not to go. The ninth time he called me, two hours before we were to meet for lunch, and said, 'You may not know it, but I'm a very busy man. I'm shooting a film. We've made a date, why don't you just keep it?' So we had lunch, and when it was over, we shook hands, and I thought, well, I've had a dreamboat date with Cary Grant. The next day was for dinner, and he brought me home, and then outside the house I asked him to kiss me goodnight. I had never asked a man to do that. The next morning, at 8:15, my phone rang, and it was Cary saying he wanted me to turn on my radio to a station he wanted me to listen to. The program was called *Unity* and it was all about positive thinking. After that, every morning he would call me, and we'd listen to this program together. That's how it all began."

Born in Tacoma, Washington, Samille (after her grandfather Sam) Diane Friesen, the daughter of a Baptist insurance broker and a Jewish mother, began her show business career as a singer at the Seattle reform temple. The five-foot-five blonde, nicknamed "Frosty" by her friends, attended the University of Washington, took a course in drama, entered a pageant, and won the Miss West Seattle title. She dropped out after two years and moved to Hollywood to pursue a career as an actress. Her first jobs were as a showroom model, for which she earned $49.50 a week, and a beautician at Slenderella. In 1960, after going on hundreds of auditions, Samille was having lunch one day at Villa Frascati with two girlfriends when one of their boyfriends, assistant producer Mike Garrison, who happened to be producer Jerry Wald's assistant, promised to set up an audition for Samille with Wald.

Garrison kept his promise. Wald liked what he saw so much that he decided to invest in her future. He changed everything about her, even renaming her Cannon because he thought it sounded explosive, and got her her first real audition at 20th Century–Fox, for the title role in a planned upcoming *Harlow* bioflick. The audition did not go as well as either of them had hoped. Recalled Cannon, "I bombed right in front of Wald." (The movie was postponed until 1965, with the part eventually going to Carroll Baker.)

Wald continued to push Cannon, and soon she was getting dozens of small parts in TV shows and B movies, most notably as Dixie in Budd Boetticher's feature *The Rise and Fall of Legs Diamond*. Made and distributed by Warner Bros., the film disappeared quickly, but not before Cannon caught the eye of film critic Pauline Kael, who described her performance as "comic-pornographic." The mention by *The New Yorker*'s film critic was enough to launch Cannon into the middle-time, where she was treading career water until summoned by Grant to his office at Universal.

They started dating immediately. Later on, Cannon would tell interviewers that she quickly became "smitten" with Grant and before long took to staying overnight at the house on Beverly Grove, where she quickly became familiar with his two primary idiosyncrasies—the way he liked to watch TV all the time and how he constantly urged her to "dress down," to wear less makeup and perfume, which he said he disliked on women, and to let her hair "go natural."

All the while Grant was being pursued by Jack Warner, who had just paid an unprecedented $5.2 million for the rights to *My Fair Lady*, the smash Broadway musical by Lerner and Loewe. For such a prestigious (and expensive) production, Warner decided that neither Rex Harrison nor Julie Andrews, the show's original stars, was big enough. As far as he was concerned, only Cary Grant and Audrey Hepburn could ensure the film's financial success. To that end Warner approached Hepburn, offering her $1.1 million to play Eliza Doolittle. Hepburn, however, was hesitant to sign on, and with good reason. Julie Andrews had become a legitimate show business phenomenon because of *My Fair Lady*, and everyone had assumed she would repeat her performance in the movie. Warner's bypassing of Andrews caused an uproar, and because of it Grant was reluctant to try to replace Rex Harrison, who happened to be a good friend of his. After months of pursuit by Warner, Grant officially passed on Warner's $1.5 million offer, telling him, "No matter how good I am, I'll either be compared with Rex Harrison, and I don't think I'll be better than he is, or I'll be told I'm imitating him, which isn't good for him, or for me. And not only will I not do it, but if you don't hire Rex, I won't even go see it."

As was often the case, Grant had other, more private motives for turning down what would have likely been an Oscar-winning performance. To begin with, he still had an unusual British accent with cockney nuances that would have made him a laughingstock, as he naturally tended to sound closer to Eliza than Professor Higgins. Another reason was his longstanding refusal to play any part that too overtly reflected the circumstances of his real life. He was, at the moment, playing Higgins to Cannon's Eliza, mentoring her in everything from what she wore around the house to what roles she should play, who she should meet and be seen with, which parts she should take, and which she should turn down. The last thing he wanted to do was to attract any attention to the nature of their relationship, most notably the thirty-five-year difference in their ages, which he was sure everyone would misinterpret, or to have anyone interfere with the way he saw his relationship with Cannon—as a kind of dress rehearsal for fatherhood.

Rex Harrison went on to play Higgins, opposite Audrey Hepburn, and won the 1964 Best Actor Oscar.*

LATER THAT FALL Grant and Cannon flew to New York, where they checked into Grant's permanent suite at the Plaza. Cannon was scheduled to begin rehearsals for her Broadway debut in the comedy *The Fun Couple*, while Grant intended to work with the writers and Stanley Donen on

---

*A disapproving Academy denied Audrey Hepburn even a nomination for the role of Eliza. Ironically, the Best Actress Oscar that year was awarded to Julie Andrews for Disney's *Mary Poppins*.

Donen's *Charade*, a pseudo-Hitchcockian thriller based on Peter Stone's original *Redbook* magazine short story "The Unsuspecting Wife." Donen, with Grant's approval, had signed Audrey Hepburn as his costar, prior to her commencing work on *My Fair Lady*.

In *Charade*, young Regina Lampert (Hepburn) returns home to Paris after a brief holiday in the French Alps to find her home ransacked, her husband murdered, and a quarter-million dollars in stolen money missing. Peter Joshua (Grant), a mysterious middle-aged man she met on her trip, suddenly shows up and offers to help solve the mystery. Meanwhile, three former associates of the late Mr. Lambert who had been involved in the acquisition of the stolen money also show up wanting their share. It is not until the end of the film that the mystery of who is who and what is what is solved, allowing Grant and Hepburn to live, presumably, happily ever after.

After a few weeks in the city working with the writers, Grant, unhappy about having to leave Cannon, reluctantly took off for Paris, the film's shooting locale. She promised to join him for the holiday break in her rehearsal schedule. True to her word, the day after Christmas she took a red-eye to France and spent the next several days alone with Grant in his Paris hotel suite. That New Year's Eve she and Grant were the guests of Audrey Hepburn and her then-husband, Mel Ferrer, at the castle they owned on the outskirts of Paris, where they dined on baked potatoes smothered with sour cream and caviar and drank expensive French champagne until dawn. Both would later remember that week as one of the most romantic they ever spent together. Two days later, on January 2, Cannon flew back to the States to resume playing her role on Broadway, while Grant stayed on to continue work on the film.

During production Grant took a weekend off and traveled to Bristol, and this time he was able to convince Elsie, who had just turned ninety, to check into a nursing home, all expenses paid, after promising he would keep the house in her name should she ever want to return to it. Just before he left for Paris, she told him to dye his hair. It was too white, she said, and if he didn't do something about it, he'd never find a suitable girlfriend.

CHARADE OPENED AT Radio City Music Hall on Christmas Day 1963, the twenty-sixth Cary Grant picture to open there. Despite mixed reviews, the film took in more than $170,000 in its first week of release. Nevertheless, it was hard to avoid the age factor. Critic Andrew Sarris wrote the inevitable emperor-has-no-clothes review, in which he said that while the film had its moments and was "consistently better than ordinary without ever being extraordinary," it had "a plot that smelled of red herrings [and] the saddest news of the year is that Cary Dorian Grant is finally beginning to look his age."

Grant agreed. Watching himself onscreen in *Charade* convinced him that he was simply too old for the kind of movies audiences wanted to see him in, no matter how much they were willing to pay for that privilege.

Not long after, the "pluperfect leading man," as critic Charles Champlin described Grant, found himself at a Malibu party for Margot Fonteyn and Rudolf Nureyev, watching Shirley MacLaine frugging with Nureyev to a rock quartet in the host's living room. "I don't know," Grant said. "When I dance with a girl I like to hold her. That's the pleasure of it."

Cannon's career, meanwhile, had taken off. She went out on a nationwide tour of *How to Succeed in Business Without Really Trying* for much of that year and the next. To occupy his time waiting for her to return to Los Angeles, Grant, who had little outside interest in anything these days other then horse-racing, formed another new production company, Grandox, to produce one film to be distributed by Universal. What convinced him to return to the screen was the movie's concept. His seventy-first film, he believed, had all the qualities needed to bring him the big prize, an Academy Award. He couldn't resist one more run for the elusive golden child of his dreams.

The film was *Father Goose*, whose original screenplay by Frank Tarloff was, at Grant's insistence, rewritten by Peter Stone. The film concerns the wartime adventures of Walter Eckland (Grant), a grizzled South Pacific loner forced to become a reconnaissance spy for the U.S. government during the early days of World War II, as the Japanese army is advancing on the Allies' positions in the Pacific. Alone on an island, the cranky, boozy, unshaven Eckland finds himself the involuntary caretaker to Catherine Freneau (Leslie Caron), the very proper and (of course) single schoolmarm and her seven little girl students, all trapped with him after a bombing raid and forced to share his single recon hut. At first Eckland refuses to have anything to do with either Freneau or her children, but he gradually falls in love with her and them and at the film's climax performs a heroic rescue and saves the whole bunch with the promise of marriage to Freneau on the horizon. Familiar Hollywood moral of the story: a wife and children will turn a meaningless existence into one filled with meaning and joy.

Not surprisingly, the chance to play against type held great appeal to Grant. He was happy to shed the custom suit and perfect haircut of the suave über-urbanite in favor of the dirty, disheveled garments of a boozy old geezer (who somehow still manages to have the thirty-four-year-old Caron pursue and fall in love with him). All of it was carefully calculated by Grant to court Oscar.

If the Academy favored any one type of performance, it was one in which an actor went against image. Bing Crosby had done it when he switched from bebopster to priest in *Going My Way* (1944), Ray Milland did it by going sloppy drunk in *The Lost Weekend* (1945), José Ferrer did it disfiguring his face in *Cyrano de Bergerac* (1950), Humphrey Bogart did it going from suit-and-tie tough guy to unshaved alcoholic in *The African Queen* (1951), Gary Cooper did it playing over-the-hill in *High Noon* (1952), William Holden did it as a crewcut POW cynic in *Stalag 17* (1953), Marlon Brando did it as a punch-drunk fighter in *On the Waterfront* (1954), Ernest Borgnine did it as a mama's boy in *Marty* (1955), Yul Brynner did it being bald and barefoot in *The King and I* (1956), and Alec Guinness did it losing his mind building *The Bridge on the River Kwai* (1957).

Production on *Father Goose* began on April 9, 1964, and finished in time for the film to be released for a gala Christmas opening at the Music Hall, which Grant attended personally. While in New York he appeared at the fourteenth annual Chanukah Festival for Israel at Madison Square Garden. (Some Hollywood cynics derided this as Grant's attempt to win a few extra Jewish votes for the upcoming Oscars, apparently unaware of Grant's years of extensive work for several Jewish charity organizations.)

Father Goose was a smash holiday hit and continued Grant's streak of box office winners, grossing more than $6 million in its initial domestic theatrical release. It was, however, a bit of a financial disappointment to Grant, because it did $150,000 less than *Charade*, $2.5 million less than *That Touch of Mink*, and $3 million less than *Operation Petticoat*. He was still big box office, but the message he read in the diminishing returns was that his popular appeal was softening. Because of it, he became unusually accessible to the press, engineering and guiding his own campaign to win over the voters of the Academy.

His efforts seemed to pay off. Even before the film's big open, Hollywood was buzzing with Oscar talk for Grant's need-a-shave performance. In her column in the *Hollywood News*, syndicated gossip Sheilah Graham declared that, having seen an advance screening and getting him to do a rare sit-down, she was proud to announce that "Cary Grant's latest picture, *Father Goose*, is the very best of his whole career. And he plays it with dirty sneakers, shabby clothes, a beard and I was just about to say, no glamour, but that's not true. It's there and it always will be.

"I chatted with Cary during his twenty-four hours in New York after the preview of the picture and he corroborated something about success. It does not happen haphazardly. Every step is as carefully planned as those of an architect building a good house. I'll come to that in a minute.

"First of all I have to make a correction in my Academy Award prediction for the best actor of the year. I stated yesterday that Rex Harrison stood alone, far out in front [for *My Fair Lady*]. That isn't true anymore . . . In my crystal ball I see an Oscar for Mr. Grant."

Despite, or perhaps in defiance of, Grant's big push, the aging majority of Academy members had long memories of Grant, few of which were positive. That February when nominations for the 1964 Oscars were announced, *Father Goose*, despite Grant's concentrated PR campaign, was noticeably absent from most of the major categories, amid an unusually strong roster of films. The Best Picture nominations included Peter Glenville's *Becket*, Kubrick's *Dr. Strangelove: or, How I Learned to Stop Worrying and Love the Bomb*, Robert Stevenson's *Mary Poppins*, and Michael Cacoyannis's *Zorba the Greek*. Best Actor nods went to Richard Burton and Peter O'Toole (*Becket*), Anthony Quinn (*Zorba*), Peter Sellers (*Dr. Strangelove*), and the eventual winner, Rex Harrison.

Father Goose received three nominations, all in nonperformance categories — Best Writing, Story and Screenplay Written Directly for the Screen, which it won (S. H. Barnett, Frank Tarloff, and Peter Stone), Best Editing, which it lost to *Mary Poppins*, and Best Sound, which it lost to *My Fair Lady*.

According to close friends, Grant was crushed to have not even been nominated and vowed once again not to attend the Awards ceremony. Instead, he put all his efforts on dream child number two.

IN THE SUMMER OF 1965 Grant decided the time had come for him and Cannon, who had concluded her national tour of *How to Succeed*, to get married. Grant had proposed marriage several times in the three years they had been seeing each other, but Cannon had remained noncommittal. Then in June she quietly informed Grant that she was pregnant, prompting him to once more pop the question. This time she said yes, she would marry him, right then and there, before the weekend was over.

They obtained a marriage license at Godfield, a small desert town two hundred miles northwest of Las Vegas, where no press hounds lurked, then drove to Vegas. To ensure privacy, Grant once again called upon Howard Hughes to make the final arrangements. Hughes hired James Prennen, a local Las Vegas justice of the peace, to perform the top-secret ceremony at the Desert Inn, the Vegas hotel that Hughes now owned. Immediately afterward the sixty-one-year-old Grant whisked his twenty-eight-year-old bride to Bristol, England, via private plane provided by Hughes, to meet his mum.

While away, rumors of his "impending" marriage to Cannon began to appear in the American press. To avoid any unnecessary hounding, Grant chose Roderick Mann of the British *Sunday Graphic* (pointedly snubbing his cobiographer Joe Hyams, who had been trying to reach Grant for confirmation of the rumor spreading through Hollywood) to announce that he had indeed married Dyan Cannon. "I'm only telling you now because you asked me. So many people have been hinting that we were thinking about marrying, were about to marry, or were actually married — but nobody actually came right out and asked."

The story ran in the following Sunday's *Graphic* and immediately made headlines around the world.

When they returned to Los Angeles, Cannon revealed to the press that she was pregnant. That night Grant celebrated his wife's public announcement by taking her to a luxury box at Dodger Stadium, where the two dined on Dodger dogs, chips, and sodas while they root, root, rooted for the home team. Grant later told a friend he was never happier.

Unfortunately, the feeling would not last for very long.

32

"I don't like to see men of my age making love on the
screen . . . Being a father will make me more free than I
have ever been. It will be a great experience. I can't wait."

—CARY GRANT

As much as he claimed to be excited by the prospect of becoming a
father, something of the old, pre-acid Cary Grant remained terrified
at the thought; no scar, physical scrape, or emotional blow ever heals completely. Shortly after his wife announced to the world she was going to have his
baby, Grant suddenly signed on to make another movie, telling Cannon she
should stay home and rest while he was in Japan on location. When she
protested, telling him she was only in her first trimester and was perfectly capable of traveling with him, he would hear none of it. The last thing he wanted,
he said, was to in any way cause her to have a miscarriage, not at this stage of
his life. Besides, he told her, not winning an Oscar for *Father Goose* had taught
him a lesson. "Cary Grant" was dead. Therefore, why not kill him off for good?

Cannon must have wondered how her pregnancy had somehow become
all about his career.

AFTER TURNING DOWN A multimillion-dollar deal to play the lead in the
film version of the hit stage musical *The Music Man*, Grant formed Granley

Productions, with producer Sol C. Siegel, and signed on Columbia Pictures to serve as the distributor for his next film. The company then acquired the rights to a 1943 George Stevens wartime comedy, *The More the Merrier*, which had starred Joel McCrea and Jean Arthur and character actor Charles Coburn. In it, the chronic wartime housing shortage causes Coburn to wind up sharing Jean Arthur's apartment. He then splits his half with McCrea, the premise that sets up the comic unfoldings and the eventual romance between McCrea and Arthur, helped along by Coburn's gentle guidance. The film had been nominated for Best Picture and lost to *Casablanca*, but Coburn as the elder Cupid figure had walked away with the Best Supporting Oscar in an upset over the overwhelming favorite, Claude Rains, Bogart's foil in the fabled North African adventure romance. The role Grant now wanted was Coburn's, in a remake to be called *Walk, Don't Run*.

Whatever subconscious motivations may have been at work, Grant envisioned his seventy-second film, his last hurrah, as a farewell kiss to his audience. To ensure that this message wouldn't get lost, for the first time since his earliest days at Paramount when he lost Dietrich to Herbert Marshall in *Blonde Venus*, he would not get the girl — in this instance Samantha Eggar, a ravishing British redhead who had caused a sensation the year before as the gorgeous victim opposite Terence Stamp's schizo kidnapper in William Wyler's *The Collector*. Grant personally selected her to play the romantic lead. Jim Hutton, also cast by Grant, was a tall, slender, charming, and athletic actor in whom Grant saw a clear reflection of his younger self. Veteran non-boat-rocker Charles Walters (*Easter Parade*, *High Society*) was chosen by Siegel to direct.

The production was on location in Japan in time to shoot during the 1964 Summer Olympics, but problems slowed the filming down and kept Grant in Tokyo for nearly six months after the Games ended, allowing for only three brief trips back to the States. Not until late in February did Grant get to shoot his last scene in the movie and the last of his career. In it, he gets into a limo and instructs his driver to take him home to his wife and two children, "who are almost grown." Taking one last look through the window, the camera then pulls back and rises slowly as Grant, with all the majesty of a king, slowly rides off into his final cinematic sunset.

BACK HOME HE HAD BARELY unpacked when Dyan Cannon went into labor. On Saturday, February 26, 1966, Grant drove his wife to St. John's Hospital in Burbank, where just eighteen minutes later she gave birth to a four-pound, eight-ounce baby girl they named Jennifer Diane Grant.

A day later, Grant, still at the hospital, met with the gathering press corps and had this to say: "One does join in the stream of life with parenthood. There's an advantage to being older, wiser and more mature when you become a father for the first time, and there are disadvantages, too. A person can never fully understand a child until he understands himself."

From the moment of Jennifer's birth, Grant eagerly assumed the role of adoring father. He awoke promptly each morning at seven-thirty to kiss her good morning and supervise her feeding before leaving for the studio to work on the final edit of *Walk, Don't Run,* after which he rushed home to spend more time with the child he happily described to friends as "the most completely perfect baby in the world."

When Jennifer was barely three months old, Grant insisted that he and Cannon take her to Bristol, to meet Elsie. Fearful that his mother did not have much longer to live, he was determined that she meet her granddaughter.

In England, Grant doted on Jennifer and spent nearly all his time with Elsie. Years later Grant would recall the visit this way: "I was sitting up front in the car with the chauffeur, and [Elsie] was sitting behind with my cousin. Mother tapped me on the shoulder and said, 'Darling, you should do something about your hair.' I asked her what should I do about my hair, and she explained, 'Well, dear, it's so white. You should dye it. Everybody does these days.' 'But why should I,' I asked. 'Because it makes *me* look so old.'" Whenever she talked to Cannon, Elsie referred to her as Betsy.

Grant happily squired his mother and daughter around town, accepting the congratulations from the crowds that followed them wherever they went. Cannon, feeling a bit left out, asked Grant if he minded her going to London by herself for a few days. She was surprised when he told her no, she couldn't go, and shocked when he took away her keys to the car. When she asked why, he explained that the trip was being paid for by Columbia Pictures, in exchange for some personal appearances he was to make in connection with the upcoming release of *Walk, Don't Run*, and therefore she had to stay with him so as not to run up any unnecessary charges. Cannon could not believe what she was hearing. From then on, to pass the rest of her time in Bristol, she kept to herself, read a lot, walked through the town's many churches, and spent afternoons chatting with Grant's friendly relatives.

When at last they did get to London, it was for the studio's arranged press junket, which he had insisted Cannon accompany him on. When a reporter asked if he had any plans to star in a film with his wife, the question seemed to visibly annoy Grant, who responded that he thought he had made it clear to the world that *Walk, Don't Run* was his last movie. The rest of the press crew laughed out loud when Cannon nodded her head vigorously up and down in response to the same question, indicating that she very much wanted to make a movie with her husband. Grant did not appreciate the gesture and openily and angrily glared at her. The incident was reported as a "disagreement" in the next morning's papers.

GRANT WAS OPPOSED not only to continuing his own career but to Cannon's continuing hers, something that did not sit well with her. He didn't care. He insisted his wife be a stay-at-home mother and devote herself to the full-time job of raising their daughter. A few days later, speaking to a luncheon for Columbia executives attended by the British press, Grant, out of nowhere, suddenly changed the subject to marriage and declared that the institution was dying. By the year 2066—one hundred years from now, he emphasized—it would be outmoded. Why? Women were more in competition with men than ever before.

By the time they returned to Los Angeles, in October, Grant had become angry and bitter about Cannon's unwavering decision to keep acting, and she began to suspect that because of it her marriage to Grant might actually be in trouble. Ever since her head-shake joke at the London press conference, he had seemed a completely different person from the one she married. Now, whenever she tried to get his attention away from the baby, even for a moment, he become verbally abusive. A month later he locked her out of his bedroom and put a lock on the outside of hers to keep her in it at night. And when she insisted she was ready to go back to work, Grant threw a fit, angrily complaining that her proper place was at home taking care of Jennifer.

A few weeks later they attended the twenty-fifth wedding anniversary cel-ebration of Grant's old friends Rosalind Russell and Freddie Brisson, hosted by Frank Sinatra and his wife, Mia Farrow, at the Sands Hotel in Las Vegas. Cannon was startled when Grant suddenly and inexplicably broke down in tears, something Cannon found not only embarrassing but a sure sign that her husband had gone completely off the deep end. Later that day Grant took his friend Bill Frye aside and asked him to arrange a flight for him and his wife back to Los Angeles.

As soon as he and Cannon returned home, she packed her bags, took Jennifer, and left, she said, for an extended stay at her parents' home in Seattle. Grant was disturbed and frightened, and when he got Cannon on the phone he tried to get her to come back home by promising he would, after all, costar with her in a film. He already had a project picked out, he said, a script called *The Old Man and Me* that he had optioned a while back but never pursued.

Cannon would have none of it. A few weeks later, when she finally did return to Los Angeles, it was to a small rented apartment in Malibu. Not long afterward word of their separation reached the press. On August 22, 1967, just seventeen months after their wedding day, Cannon sued Grant for divorce on the grounds that he had treated her in "a cruel and inhuman manner." In her court papers she stated that the couple had been living apart since the previous December, which was technically true, as Grant had been in Japan during that period filming *Walk, Don't Run*. Cannon's suit estimated Grant's worth in excess of $10 million and demanded "reasonable support" for her and their baby daughter. Also in her papers Cannon stated that she had begun psychiatric treatment, presumably due to Grant's "cruel and inhu-man" treatment.

He was at first devastated. Losing his wife *and* his baby was too much for him. Then his rage kicked in. If Cannon wanted to leave, fine, but he was going to fight to keep Jennifer. He put together a powerhouse team of lawyers and filed a countersuit in which he described Cannon as an unfit mother and demanded sole custody of his daughter.

Against the advice of his legal team, Grant tried to call Cannon several times a day. At first she refused to talk to him, but after a while she responded, especially when he agreed to provide her with an interim allowance of $4,000 a month, which she desperately needed. By September they were seen together around town, at restaurants, at Dodger Stadium, in Las Vegas, always with baby Jennifer in tow. Things appeared better between them, but despite Grant's pleas that she come home, Cannon insisted on staying in her own apartment, and demanded that they both attend marriage counseling. Grant resented the suggestion, but agreed in order to keep seeing his wife and daughter. (But he never paid for the sessions. The doctor eventually sued him to collect $7,000 in uncollected bills.)

Even so, Cannon refused to rescind her suit for divorce. That November she left for New York to star on Broadway in *The Ninety Day Mistress* and took Jennifer with her. Grant found out about when she was going, followed her to the airport, and got himself booked on the same flight. In New York he booked a room at the Croydon, the same hotel where she was staying. This last move proved too much for her, and through her lawyers she advised him she was about to obtain a restraining order unless he checked out. Reluctantly Grant—who did not wish to go to another hotel, where he knew he would surely be hounded by the press—took up an invitation to stay with one of his old friends from Hollywood, Robert Taplinger, who had recently moved to New York to run a major public relations firm.

Taplinger, whom Grant had met on one of his earlier films, was a notorious ladies' man, best remembered for his torrid affair with Bette Davis. He now had a huge bachelor pad on East 49th Street, where, for business, he entertained clients every night. That did not bother Grant at all, who was grateful for all the familiar faces that came by. Another thing that Grant appreciated was the close tabs Taplinger could keep on Cannon. As a big-time PR executive, he was able to get advance warning on virtually every New York social and PR move Cannon made and happily passed them all along to Grant, who made it his business to show up at the same functions as his wife.

Taplinger, like many of Grant's friends, worried about his increasingly obsessive behavior toward Cannon and thought it might be good to distract him before he got in serious trouble for it. He began throwing small dinner parties in his friend's honor and made it a point to always include three or four young, single, and beautiful women, in the hope that one of them might catch Grant's eye.

One did.

Her name was Luisa Flynn, a tall, slim, dark-haired Argentine beauty who was living in New York to represent a British-based firm with ties to Argentina specializing in mergers and acquisitions. Among all the hopeful beauties who paraded in front of Grant like so many finalists in the Miss America pageant, only Flynn, a divorcée with a six-year-old child who had kept her married name, paid no attention at all to Grant. In her early thirties, her first impression of him was that, while he was extremely good-looking, he was also quite old. After he had introduced himself to her, she asked someone his real age. Told he was sixty-three, she dismissed any and all further thoughts about him.

Grant, however, took a liking to her and struck up conversations at subsequent Taplinger parties. Flynn later recalled the extreme bitterness that punctuated all his talks: "He struck me as an angry and bitter man, and said awful things about his wife, from whom he was separated at the time. He always had a drink in his hand, and I thought that was probably fueling the level of his anger."

There was something else Flynn noticed about Grant: he always mentioned Mae West. West had grown old and lonely, he said, and whenever he was in New York, where the aging onetime sex goddess was, he made it a point to visit her and talk about the old days. Flynn found that side of Grant endearing and thought to herself that West was far more suited to be his mother-surrogate than she.

As CANNON'S BROADWAY stay lengthened, Grant began to look for reasons to remain in New York. He signed on with Columbia Records to make a Christmas album of readings from classic material, with Peggy Lee singing backgrounds. Unfortunately, the recording sessions left him maudlin and melancholy, and he started calling Cannon again, daily, sometimes hourly, begging her to at least spend Christmas with him so that he wouldn't have to be alone over the holidays. She agreed, and they all had fun, but she still would not budge on her decision to pursue the divorce.

In January 1968 a disconsolate Grant returned to Los Angeles, but soon afterward began to commute weekends to New York to be near his wife and child. He always stayed with Taplinger, and whenever Flynn showed up tried to engage her in conversation.

To one of Taplinger's dinner parties, attended by such luminaries as Kirk and Anne Douglas, Aristotle Onassis and Maria Callas, Rosalind Russell and Freddie Brisson, Irene Mayer, and several of the upper echelon of international banking, Flynn decided to bring along her six-year-old son. Grant was immediately drawn to the boy and marveled at how physically beautiful he was. At one point Grant took Flynn aside and offered her a million dollars in cash to have his baby. Flynn brushed off the suggestion as a joke.

Also at the party that night were several film producers trying to get Grant to return to movies. More than one approached Flynn and asked her to use her influence, such as it was, to get him to consider their scripts. A famous French director said he would put up millions for the chance to work with Grant. Flynn merely directed them to the actor, made the appropriate introductions, and stayed as far away from the situation as possible, believing what Grant had told her so many times, that he had no intention of ever returning to film.

One other person he met while at one of Taplinger's soirées was Paul Blackman, the president and CEO of Fabergé. Blackman was a client of Taplinger who was assigned the job of finding celebrities to represent the company's products.

MARCH 20, 1968, was the date the Los Angeles Superior Court had set to begin hearing testimony in Cannon's suit for divorce. As the day approached, Grant grew more apprehensive. On March 12 a few New York friends of his got together and threw a dinner party at Delmonico's in his honor, to try to cheer him up prior to his leaving for the airport to catch an evening flight for Los Angeles. He planned to leave from the Manhattan restaurant and go directly to Kennedy Airport. One of his friends offered to send him in a limousine. Grant accepted. Gratia von Furstenberg, a young, good-looking woman in charge of special events at Delmonico's, went along for the ride to make sure a slightly inebriated Grant safely made it onto his flight.

The 1968 stretch Cadillac never made it to the airport, colliding with a truck on the Long Island Expressway. Ambulances quickly arrived with lights flashing and sirens screaming, then took Grant and Furstenberg to St. John's Queens Hospital, where he was treated for minor cuts and bruises, the worst being a nasty slash across his nose. Furstenberg suffered a broken leg and collarbone.

The accident couldn't have occurred at a worse time, and the presence in the limo of a pretty twenty-three-year-old, Grant knew, did nothing to help his upcoming court battle. The next morning his worst fears came true, when details of the accident, including the presence of Furstenberg in the limo, made front-page news across the country. Worse, everyone except Grant seemed to revel in their fifteen minutes of fame. A hospital spokesman told a hastily called press conference that his patient had only suffered surface wounds and that "Grant is as good-looking as he was yesterday. The only problem is that the nurses may kill him with kindness."

That same kindness wasn't extended to him by the Los Angeles Superior Court, which refused to delay the start of the hearing and warned Grant's lawyers they had better deliver their client on the twentieth as scheduled, or it would start without him. Grant chose to remain in the hospital.

During her extraordinary testimony, Cannon delivered a nightmarish account of her marriage to Grant. Grant had always claimed that his intake of LSD was limited to the hundred trips he had taken in the late 1950s and early 1960s before the drug was declared illegal, but she testified that he had secretly continued to use it on a regular basis and that during these "trips" he had at various times screamed at her, physically beaten her, and publicly humiliated her. He often tried to get her to go on LSD trips with him, she added. One time, she testified, she went to a party without his permission, and upon her return he gave her a hard spanking, laughing as he administered it. When she threatened to call the police, he told her the press would have a field day with it, so she didn't. Another time, while watching the Academy Awards, he got so upset with the winners that he "danced on the bed" and "went out of control." When she wanted to wear a dress that he felt was too short for the public to see her in, she testified, he took away her car keys and locked her in her room. One time while locked up she called her agent, and Grant picked up an extension phone to listen. "Addie," she claimed he said (referring to her agent, Adeline Gould), "stay out of my marriage. I'm going to break this girl. She's not going to leave until I break her." Gould was called upon to testify and confirmed this conversation. Cannon also testified that Grant accused her of having a sexual relationship with her psychiatrist.

One of Grant's witnesses was Dr. Sidney Palmer, an associate professor at the University of Southern California Medical School, who testified that Grant had come to him the previous September to have his emotional state evaluated in preparation for the divorce hearings. During their visits, Dr. Palmer said, Grant admitted that he was still taking LSD but only under strict medical supervision. "I found nothing irrational or incoherent about him," the doctor said. He added that Grant showed great concern for his daughter's welfare and had "deep love and affection" for Jennifer. "I found nothing indicating his behavior would be dangerous to a child."

Another witness for Grant, Dr. Judd Marmor, his psychiatrist for a brief period of time, testified under oath that Grant had told him that he had spanked his wife, but for "reasonable and adequate causes."

All the while, Grant convalesced in the hospital. Even before his lawyers conferred with him, he knew from the newspapers the damage that had been done. Some of Grant's friends suggested to the press that Cannon had set him up, that she had married him only to advance her own career, but this kind of unprovable speculation sounded defensive and gained scant attention alongside the sensational revelations of Cannon's sworn testimony. Grant had prepared a rebuttal statement to the court, but after her testimony, he quickly withdrew it.

On March 22, two days after the trial had begun, Dyan Cannon was granted a divorce from Cary Grant and was given custody of two-year-old Jennifer. Grant was allowed sixty days of visitation rights per year, a "reasonable" number of overnight visits, with a nurse or governess to be present for all extended visits. Presiding Judge Wenke noted in his decision that Grant's continued use of LSD had made him "irrational and hostile," but he also cited a stipulation — entered by the actor's attorneys and agreed to by

Cannon's, presumably with the understanding that the joint entry would prevent a long, drawn-out appeal—that Grant had not used LSD in the past twenty-four months. The Grant mystique evidently held some sway when the judge awarded Cannon the relatively modest sum of $2,000 a month child support and thirty-six months of alimony to begin at $2,500 a month and gradually decrease to $1,000, and use of the beach house. He followed his final words, "This is now over," with a single pound of the gavel.

The next day, a haggard-looking Grant checked out of the hospital, ashen and still heavily bandaged. He had no comment for the phalanx of press awaiting his discharge, other than to say that he hoped "to keep breathing in and out."

Later that day he flew back to Los Angeles aboard the private plane of George Barrie, owner and president of the Rayette-Fabergé Corporation. Barrie and Grant had spoken by phone several times after being introduced to each other in person by Blackman at one of Taplinger's parties. Barrie then offered to fly Grant back aboard his personal aircraft. Taplinger's introduction was no happy accident. He wanted Barrie to somehow convince Grant to join such other Fabergé luminaries as Joe Namath, Muhammad Ali, and Margaux Hemingway to pitch their company's products.

Taplinger had cannily put Barrie and Grant together, hoping their show business backgrounds might help put them in business together.* Born in New York City, Barrie fancied a career as a musician and during his early songwriting years supported himself by using his charismatic personality to sell hair-care products for a company called Rayette. By the '60s, he was half owner, created the Brut line of cosmetics for men, and came up with the idea of name endorsements as a way to sell the cologne. The formula worked, sales skyrocketed, and Brut became ubiquitous, with celebrities pitching it in numerous television ads and in magazines all over the world. Barrie then sold Brut to Fabergé for a reported $50 million and continued to run the promotional side of the company while writing songs for Hollywood movies.

---

*Barrie is generally acknowledged to have created the celebrity-endorsement method of selling products. His music career eventually paid off as well. He was a two-time Academy Award nominee, once in 1973, along with Sammy Cahn, for Best Original Song, "All That Love Went to Waste," from Melvin Frank's A Touch of Class (they lost to Marvin Hamlisch for "The Way We Were" from the picture of the same name), and again with Cahn in 1975 for "Now That We're in Love," from Whiffs (produced by Brut for 20th Century Fox. They lost again, this time to "I'm Easy" from Robert Altman's Nashville, music and lyrics by Keith Carradine).

During the flight, alone with Grant, Barrie proposed that the actor consider joining the board of Fabergé, a position that offered only a token annual salary of $15,000 (with stock options) but would require nothing more than the occasional personal appearance. As part of the deal, Fabergé would provide a permanent suite at the Warwick Hotel in New York, unlimited use of the corporate jet for business and personal reasons, limousines and drivers everywhere around the world, and any and all expenses incurred promoting Fabergé to be paid for by the company.

Barrie did not think he had much of a chance of getting the actor to accept the deal, but to his surprise, shortly after returning to L.A., he received a phone call from Grant saying he would love to be associated with the world-famous cosmetics firm as its "Good Will Ambassador." The next day Barrie formally announced Grant's assignment to Fabergé's board of directors. The day after that the company's stock rose two full points.

As Grant later told reporter Cindy Adams, he was delighted to represent Fabergé because "The use of my name doesn't harm the company and I'm permitted to do whatever I choose. They ask can I be someplace and I say yes or no. People flock to actors."*

The Fabergé deal gave Grant something to do with all the time he now had on his hands. Instead of making movies where he played rich, sophisticated tycoon bachelors, as in *That Touch of Mink*, he could now be that rich, sophisticated tycoon in real life. Shortly after he joined Fabergé, Grant accepted another, even more surprising corporate invitation, this time to become a full member of the board of directors at MGM. Even though for most of his professional life he had been considered an outsider to the studio system, he jumped at the offer because the package allowed for unlimited accommodations at the entertainment conglomerate's new hotel on the Las Vegas Strip. To celebrate Grant's assignment to the board, the studio named the main screening room at its Culver City headquarters the Cary Grant Theater.

---

*Grant gave up his apartment at the Plaza for the penthouse of the Warwick Hotel (which at one time belonged to Marion Davies), the same hotel where he had stayed early in his stage career. He was delighted to learn that the hotel's room service still delivered the same hot dogs he had subsisted on when he had first come to New York. He ate hot dogs for lunch and salmon steaks every night for dinner because he believed they were good for the lining of the stomach.

That same year he purchased his first stock in the Hollywood Park Race Track from his good friend, proprietor Marje Everett. The track had a storied history as the locale for the famous Hollywood Turf Club, formed in 1938 under the chairmanship of Jack Warner. Its six hundred original club members were a roster of 1930s greats, including Al Jolson, Raoul Walsh, Joan Blondell, Ronald Colman, Walt Disney, Bing Crosby, Sam Goldwyn, Darryl Zanuck, Ralph Bellamy, Hal Wallis, Anatole Litvak, and Mervyn LeRoy. It was LeRoy who had first brought Grant to the track and introduced him to the so-called Sport of Kings.*

For a while he considered moving back to London to stay with his mother for the rest of her life. He decided against it, however, when his lawyers told him the courts would never allow Jennifer to travel abroad with him. Instead he bought a new and bigger home on five acres of land in Beverly Hills that he designed himself, with Eastern, Hebrew, and Mediterranean-inspired interiors, to accommodate Jennifer on her overnight and every-other-weekend visits. He gave her the biggest bedroom and always made sure it was stocked with lots of toys and dolls.

He never altered the schedule of her visits or missed a single one. He made sure his duties at Fabergé and the other boards were all adjusted to work around his designated time with his daughter. Having learned his lesson from his auto accident in New York City, he stopped going out in public. He didn't want any overeager photographer taking his picture with some young woman who might be standing nearby, lest it somehow hurt his visitation rights. Instead, he visited friends in their homes, mostly for dinner parties, where he could be counted on to sit down at their piano and riff through some modern jazz. In January 1968, on the occasion of his sixty-fourth birthday, a few friends insisted on throwing a party for him. He agreed, as long as there was no cake, ceremony, or gifts. And, he insisted, after dinner he must be allowed to entertain by taking requests for songs he would then play and sing for everyone.

---

*In 1973, an aging Everett personally sold Grant enough additional stock to give him a controlling interest in the track and club, assured he would continue to keep the place running as it had for the past thirty years. Shortly afterward he was named to its board of directors as well.

ALSO IN 1968, GREGORY PECK was elected president of the Academy of Motion Picture Arts and Sciences. It was a milestone that signaled a new, younger, and more liberal generation of actors wresting control of the Academy from the fading, conservative old guard. One of the first things Peck did as president would previously have been unthinkable: at the request of Sammy Davis Jr., who claimed he was speaking for Hollywood's black community, he postponed the fortieth Oscar ceremonies for four days following the assassination of the Reverend Martin Luther King Jr.

That year Mike Nichols won Best Director for *The Graduate,* a film that confirmed Hollywood's tidal generational shift in movies and the leading men who starred in them. Dustin Hoffman became an overnight star for his portrayal of Benjamin Braddock, a 1960s malcontent who has an affair with his father's partner's wife and then falls in love with her daughter. Best Picture went to Norman Jewison's *In the Heat of the Night,* a decidedly liberal movie that dealt with racial prejudice in an explosive southern town.

Without question, the stars, the movies, the system that made them, and the people who went to see them were all for and of a new young, hip, rock-and-roll generation. Peck, wanting to right what he felt were some longstanding wrongs of the Academy, began lobbying for a lifetime achievement award for Cary Grant. His request would likely have been granted for the 1969 Awards had Grant's messy divorce not been played out in the media. Barely missing the required votes, Peck continued to press for the honor and, early in 1970, announced to the world that at that year's Academy Awards, the great Cary Grant would, at last, be given an Honorary Oscar "for his unique mastery of the art of screen acting with the respect and affection of his colleagues."

According to friends, news of the award reduced a grateful Cary Grant to tears.

PART TEN

INTO THAT GOOD NIGHT

PREVIOUS PAGE: *A gray-haired, contented Cary Grant at 80, along New York City's East River. (Bettmann/CORBIS)*

33

"Every one of my wives left me. I don't know why, maybe they got bored, tired of me. I don't know. Maybe I was making the mistake of thinking that each of my wives was my mother, that there would never be a replacement once she left...
I'm not at all proud of my marriage record, but I have wanted a family for years. I finally have this one child, and I will do whatever I can for her... It has taken me many years to learn that I was playing a different game entirely. My wives and I were never one, we were competing... My first wife accused me of being a homosexual. All the women except Betsy have accused me of being a homosexual. Virginia was just the first."

—CARY GRANT

In January 1973, two weeks short of her ninety-fifth birthday, just after high tea, Elsie Leach took an afternoon nap and passed away in her sleep at the nursing home in Clifton, England, where Grant had placed her. Beside her bed was a picture of her son Cary and one of her granddaughter Jennifer.

Grant received word of his mother's death en route to a board meeting of Western Airlines, the newest corporation he had joined. He had last seen Elsie only two weeks earlier, on one of his regular visits to Bristol.

He immediately boarded a private plane provided by George Barrie to attend her funeral. As he prepared to take off from Kennedy Airport, a few members of the press found him and asked for a reaction. Grant thought about it for a few seconds, then told them "she never smoked, never drank, and ate very lightly. She died in her sleep. There will be no services. I shall reunite her with my father in the Bristol cemetery. With the past now gone, I'll have the future ahead—with my daughter Jennifer." He made no other public comment regarding the passing of his mother.

Elsie's death triggered a bizarre reaction in Grant. He resumed calling Dyan Cannon every day. Cannon, who had since moved into the Malibu colony and was living with radio and TV personality Joey Reynolds, refused to take his calls. According to Reynolds, "I was there the night Mr. Grant called and announced that he was trying to buy the house next door. Dyan had a hissy fit, and it ruined a good pot high. She had made a record deal with a friend of mine from Motown and was singing to me on her bed when the call came. Grant was trying to harass her because she had, lately, been giving him a hard time on visitation."

Eventually Grant stopped calling. Not long afterward, he licensed the broadcast rights to six of his films to National Telefilm Associates, a TV film distribution company, for $2 million plus royalties. They included *Operation Petticoat, Indiscreet, That Touch of Mink, The Grass Is Greener, Father Goose,* and *Penny Serenade.* Grant later claimed he did it so he could watch them in private without having to screen them in the projection room of his home, because whenever he did, it greatly upset his daughter. "Jennifer once walked up to the screen and tried to slap Deborah Kerr. She kept telling her to 'stop kissing my daddy.'" Ironically, the medium Grant had always refused to appear on out of fear that it would dilute his moviegoing audience became the primary cultivator of a new generation of Cary Grant fans.

He occasionally leaked to the press that if something came along that interested him, he might return to making films, but he continued to reject any and all offers to do so. He turned down a million dollars from Warren Beatty to make a cameo appearance in *Heaven Can Wait,* and the lead in Joe Mankiewicz's film version of the hit play *Sleuth,* which went to Laurence Olivier (opposite cockney actor Michael Caine). MGM offered him the lead in an all-star-cast remake of *Grand Hotel.* He said no to that as well. He also turned down the chance to costar opposite Elizabeth Taylor in *Night Watch*. Even George Barrie tried to get him to star in the first film for Fabergé's new motion picture division, Brut Pictures' *A Touch of Class*, opposite Glenda Jackson, but after much wavering, Grant turned him down too, and the part was rewritten to suit the more youthful George Segal. "I'd have done it if I were fifty years younger," Grant later joked to *Variety*.

Director Peter Bogdanovich also tried to convince him to return to movies in his film homage to screwball comedy, *What's Up, Doc?* opposite Barbra Streisand. Grant said no, and that part went instead to Ryan O'Neal. Grant then told friends that the only roles he was suited for were old fellows in wheelchairs, and he had no desire to portray that type of character. Unfazed, yet another producer offered Grant $2 million in cash and 90 percent of the net proceeds to star in something called *One Thousand Cups of Crazy German Coffee*. That one made him laugh out loud. The producer had recently acquired the rights to a script that Grant himself had owned for years, before selling it when he decided he was never going to make another movie.

In June 1973, Grant and Gratia von Furstenberg accepted and split a $70,000 settlement from the trucking company the court deemed responsible for the accident that had put them both in the hospital in 1968 just prior to his divorce hearing.

SHORTLY AFTERWARD, in a rare extended interview with *The New York Times*, Grant spoke for the first time in years about his experience with LSD and how he felt it had affected his marriages. "My intention was to make myself happy," Grant told journalist Guy Flatley. "A man would be a fool to take something that didn't make him happy. I took it with a group of men, one of whom was Aldous Huxley. We deceived ourselves by calling it therapy, but we were truly interested in how this chemical could help humanity. I found it a very enlightening experience, but it's like alcohol in one respect; a shot of brandy can save your life, but a bottle of brandy can kill you. And that's what happened when a lot of young people started taking LSD, which is why it became necessary to make it illegal. I wouldn't dream of taking LSD now; I don't need it now."

In 1974 Jennifer began Montessori school, which afforded Grant a little more leisure time but also brought back the feelings of loneliness he had been able to buffer so effectively in the role of doting father. At exactly this time he became involved with a twenty-year-old beauty by the name of Vicki Morgan. Unknown to Grant, Morgan, who apparently had a thing for older, wealthy men, was also involved at the time with department store magnate Alfred Bloomingdale, an elderly millionaire with a penchant for kinky sado-masochistic games. Eerily, a few years later Morgan, like Bouron, was found bludgeoned to death.*

The seventy-year-old Grant then pursued a twenty-six-year-old entertainment reporter, British-born, Hollywood-based Maureen Donaldson. She had first come to America to serve as a nanny for rock star Dee Donaldson, whom she eventually married. They divorced in 1973, after which she briefly worked as a reporter for gossip-monger Rona Barrett's popular and profitable *Hollywood* magazines. In 1974 one of her assignments was to interview Cary Grant.

Donaldson—in her own words "no great beauty"—quickly fell under the spell of her charismatic subject. They began dating, and Grant soon assigned her the task of picking up and delivering Jennifer to Dyan Cannon, so that he could avoid having to come face to face with his ex-wife. While Donaldson may have taken Grant's interest in her for something serious, his motivations were more likely practical and calculated. He was considering suing Cannon for greater custody and believed that if he had a steady girlfriend, especially one who was a former nanny, his chances would be significantly increased.

For the next four years Donaldson was Grant's constant companion, and their names occasionally surfaced in the gossips, where the most persistent rumor was that she was to become Grant's fifth wife. He was always quick to deny it, telling any reporter who directly asked that he was never going to

---

*Her roommate was later charged with her murder.

marry again. When that became clear to Donaldson, the relationship faded, and she disappeared from his life.*

IN 1976 HOWARD HUGHES DIED in his private plane while on a flight to Mexico. Grant was saddened by Hughes's passing and frightened by how, surrounded by his staff and his security guards, he still managed to die, to all intents and purposes, utterly alone. It reinforced Grant's determination not to go the same way.

In 1977, still looking fit if a little fuller around the middle, his thick head of white hair cut short and his skin evenly bronzed, Grant finally won a round in his ongoing court battle with Cannon when the courts loosened the restrictions on his visitation rights with Jennifer. Ironically, that seemed to bring Grant and Cannon closer together than at any time since the night before the Academy Awards. They began taking their daughter out together for Chinese food at Jennifer's favorite restaurant, the child-friendly Madame Wu's in Santa Monica, and those who saw them there remember what looked like happy times for the threesome.

During this period yet another reporter inquired as to whether Grant would ever make another picture, to which he replied, "Jennifer is my best production."

In the spring of 1977, under the pseudonym Cary Robbins, Grant checked into St. John's Hospital in Santa Monica for surgery to repair a hernia, an event whose significance was elevated by the fake name that fooled no one in Hollywood and hence garnered worrisome headlines in the trades about Grant's health until he emerged from the hospital with a big smile on

---

*The year after Grant passed away, Donaldson wrote a so-called "intimate" memoir of her "life" with him, a poor rehash of Grant's life, most of which had been lived before they'd met. In her introduction, Donaldson noted one interesting meeting she had with Dyan Cannon, after the breakup: "'I loved the man,' [Donaldson] told Cannon, 'but couldn't live with him. With one hand he was always pulling me toward him, but with the other he always seemed to be pushing me away. Am I making any sense?' 'Exactly!' Dyan concurred. 'And the funny thing is, everybody else thinks you are the luckiest girl on earth. After all, you've got Cary Grant. The man of every girl's dreams. But they don't understand the baggage that comes along with that—and neither do you, at least at the top of the relationship.'"

his face. He gently chided the crowd of two dozen waiting reporters, telling them they ought to be spending their time looking for a real story. Eleven years after his last movie had been released, Cary Grant's newsworthiness was a tribute to his remarkable popularity.

The year ended on a sad note for Grant, with the news of Charlie Chaplin's passing on Christmas Day. Although they had never become what either would describe as friends — besides their shared status as Hollywood outsiders and loners it's possible Grant's marriage to Cherrill also had something to do with it — Grant never lost the inspiration Chaplin instilled in him.

IN 1978 THE SEVENTY-FOUR-YEAR-OLD Grant began dating a new woman, twenty-eight-year-old Tanzanian-born Barbara Harris. They had met two years earlier on a British-based Fabergé junket. One friend of Grant's described the difference in their ages as a resurfacing of "Grant's Chaplin complex," his attraction to younger women "as periodically dependable as the revival of *Modern Times*."

Grant continued to visit Harris every month in England, where she lived, and after a while invited the attractive brown-haired, hazel-eyed young woman to visit him in Los Angeles. Harris declined all his invitations. To keep seeing her, he increased the frequency of his British Fabergé junkets until late in 1978, when after about a year of dating, she invited him to meet her parents in Devon.

Grant was fifteen years older than her father.

Later that same year Grant, along with Mr. and Mrs. Frank Sinatra and the Gregory Pecks, was invited to Princess Caroline's wedding in Monaco. Everyone in Peck's party, including Grant, arrived at the Pecks' villa at St-Jean-Cap-Ferrat in the South of France alone. After a long conversation between Grant and Peck, during which Grant discussed his reservations about the age difference between himself and Harris, on the first night of Grant's arrival Peck encouraged him to disregard it, call her up, and invite her to join the party. Grant did just that, and to his delight, Harris immediately packed a bag and caught a plane for Nice. Grant drove to the airport by himself to pick her up, and they spent two days alone together before rejoining the others.

After the wedding Grant once again invited Harris to come to Los Angeles with him, and this time she said yes. They flew back to the States, and she stayed at his Beverly Hills home for three weeks, leaving only when her position at Fabergé required her to attend a function in London, after which an apologetic Barrie happily flew her back and forth on his private jet.

The next weekend was a difficult one for Grant. He arranged for the two of them to spend it in Palm Springs with his daughter. Wary of how Jennifer had reacted to his costars whenever she watched his old films, Grant wondered what her reaction would be to a real-life woman he brought into the mix. To his great relief, Jennifer and Harris got along extremely well, as Grant would later describe it, almost like sisters. His mood quickly elevated, and a sparkle no one had seen in his eyes for years was said by friends to have returned.

As did his presence in the gossip columns. Typical of the kind of pieces being written was this one that showed up in the pages of *People* magazine: "In London and L.A. the talk of the town is that Cary Grant's latest *Blonde Venus* is Barbara Harris, 28, whom he met on *Holiday* some months ago and implored to move to the U.S. Figuring that *Ladies Should Listen*, she recently did. Never *Indiscreet*, the two are talking about their romance, but still Harris' mom confirms that it's more than a *Suspicion*. It's no *Charade*." And so on.

In April 1979, Grant made a last-minute decision to appear at that year's Oscar ceremonies after Marlon Brando backed out of presenting Laurence Olivier a special noncompetitive "Honorary Award for the full body of his work, for the unique achievements of his entire career and his lifetime of contribution to the art of film." Directly after Michael Cimino was given his Best Director Oscar for *The Deer Hunter*, Grant appeared at the podium to thunderous applause and a standing ovation. He was clearly moved by the warm reception and needed a few moments to pull himself together. When he finally did begin to speak, his voice was a bit rougher than most remembered. He covered his eyes with thick black-rimmed glasses, Lew Wasserman style, and read softly from the TelePrompTer: "Those of us who have had the joy of knowing [Laurence Olivier] since he came to Hollywood warmly and fondly and yet respectfully call him Larry. He represents the ultimate in acting." At that point a bearded Olivier stepped out from the wings and into yet another standing ovation. Grant handed him the award and slowly disappeared from sight as Olivier made his acceptance speech.

Backstage, the energy was of a different sort. Dyan Cannon had been nominated for her second Best Supporting Actress Oscar, this time for her performance in *Heaven Can Wait*, Warren Beatty's remake of Alexander Hall's magical 1941 comedy *Here Comes Mr. Jordan*, the same film in which Grant had repeatedly turned down the chance to play God. Cannon (who lost to Maggie Smith in *California Suite*) had apparently not been told that her ex-husband was going to stand in for Marlon Brando and was upset about it. She had not approved of his introducing their twelve-year-old daughter to his much younger girlfriend, and she was said to be even more annoyed that Jennifer had liked her. The two former spouses politely nodded to each other but, according to witnesses, did not speak.

AFTER HIS TRIUMPHANT APPEARANCE at the Oscars, rumors swirled that Grant was seriously considering a return to the motion picture screen, and that the vehicle he had chosen was a film version of novelist Irwin Shaw's novel *Nightwork*. The more Grant denied he was going to make the film, the more persistent the rumors became.

In May 1979, Barbara Hutton, Grant's second wife, nearly penniless, died of a heart attack at the age of sixty-two, in her suite at the Beverly Wilshire Hotel while visiting Los Angeles. He could not bring himself to attend her funeral, and his only comment was a statement issued through his office: "Barbara was really a very sweet girl. She could be very funny, and we had some wonderful times together."

Later that same year Grant flew to England to attend the funeral of Lord Louis Mountbatten, who had been assassinated by the Irish Republican Army. It was to be his last trip home.

He was back in Los Angeles for less than two weeks when Mae West died.

Several months later, in May 1980, the bells tolled yet again when Alfred Hitchcock passed away. This was a particularly painful death for Grant. Hitchcock was his favorite director, the one with whom he had shared an unspoken understanding of the art of movie acting. He went into seclusion after Hitchcock's passing and was not seen again in public for weeks.

THAT FALL, CHEAP GOSSIP hit an all-time low when comedian Chevy Chase—who only a few years earlier had been touted by critics as the "next Cary Grant" for his good looks and light comedic touch in movies—committed professional suicide on a late-night show by attacking one of the industry's most beloved figures. It happened the night of September 30, 1980, on Tom Snyder's *Tomorrow* talk show. During the taping of the interview the generally effusive Snyder mentioned the buzz surrounding Chase's burgeoning film career. He could easily see Chase, he said, as the next Cary Grant. A look of obvious disgust crossed the actor's face, as he replied, "I understand he was a homo." Snyder, who was never easy to catch off guard, pulled back, laughed nervously out loud, and then warned Chase that he was on his own. The comic didn't take the hint. Mistaking Snyder's guffaw as a sign of encouragement rather than a warning, he said of Grant, "He was brilliant. What a gal!"

The next day, Grant sued Chase for slander to the unfunny tune of $10 million. Chase's legal defense was based on the First Amendment right to free speech and the protective cloak of satire.

The ugly affair was eventually settled out of court. Although the records were sealed and the amount of the settlement confidential, Grant reportedly received $1 million from Chase, whose film career never recovered from the incident. Grant's only comment after the resolution of the suit was simply to dismiss the whole affair by publicly stating, "True or untrue, I'm old enough not to care."

ON APRIL 15, 1981, three months past his seventy-seventh birthday, Cary Grant married thirty-year-old Barbara Harris on the terrace of his home, overlooking Beverly Hills. The only invited guests were Jennifer, Stanley Fox and his wife, and Grant's part-time Philippine butler and his wife. When the ceremony was over, Grant and Harris drove out to Palm Springs to be the guests of Frank and Barbara Sinatra, who were throwing a combined wedding celebration for the Grants and a twenty-fifth wedding anniversary for Princess Grace and Prince Rainier.

On July 31, Grant hosted the gala reopening of the MGM Grand Hotel, after a fire had all but gutted the Las Vegas gambling site. Word that Grant would personally host the ceremony caused a run on the hotel rooms, and all 2,076 sold out within three hours of the announcement.

On August 8, 1981, it was announced that Cary Grant was to be awarded the prestigious Kennedy Center Honor for Career Achievement in the Performing Arts. The other recipients that year were Count Basie, Helen Hayes, Jerome Robbins, and Rudolf Serkin. The official ceremony was held December 5 at the White House and hosted by President Ronald Reagan, followed by a public reception at the Kennedy Center during which Rex Harrison, paying tribute to Grant, told an audience that included such notables as Douglas Fairbanks Jr., Tennessee Williams, Lillian Gish, Irene Worth, Joshua Logan, and Peter Bogdanovich, "The fact is, there is but one Cary Grant, the original, the supremely gifted man whom we honor tonight for a magnificent career on the screen." Harrison then turned to Grant and publicly asked him to return once more to the screen. The request caused an uproar of approval throughout the auditorium.

Afterward a reporter asked Grant about what Harrison had suggested, and he politely replied that while he was indeed honored, his performing days were over. Another asked him when he was going to write his memoirs (apparently unaware of Hyams's ghostwritten version). "I wouldn't think of it," Grant said. "I'm sure other people will write books, they can go ahead. They'll make me a Nazi spy or a homosexual or some other such thing . . . What the hell."

In 1982, when he was nominated for the American Film Institute Award for Lifetime Achievement, he flatly turned it down unless the institute agreed to forgo the obligatory TV show they made out of it. His stated opinion was that the award was merely an excuse to sell products, and as he already represented Fabergé, it presented a conflict of interest. Instead, he accepted the New York Friars Club honor as its Man of the Year and attended the Sunday evening celebration at the Waldorf-Astoria (which was not broadcast), only after he was assured all the proceeds from the $250-to-$1,000-a-plate dinner would be divided among the Motion Picture and Television Fund, the Children's Diabetes Fund in Denver, and the Jennifer Jones Foundation for

Mental Health. The host of this affair—attended by Katharine Hepburn, Irene Dunne, and Jean Arthur, three of the most reclusive movie stars—was Friar Abbot Frank Sinatra, who referred to Grant that night as "this Cockney baby!" before singing "The Most Fabulous Man in the World" to the tune of "The Most Beautiful Girl in the World." At that point Grant, sitting with his wife, broke down in tears and wept like a baby.

One of the guests on the dais was John Kluge, owner of local television Channel 5 in New York. At two o'clock that morning, as a tribute to Grant and Sinatra, he had the station broadcast the rarely seen *The Pride and the Passion* with no commercial interruption.

In August 1982 news reached Grant that Ingrid Bergman had succumbed to cancer. Friends reported that her passing left him inconsolable for weeks. Worst of all for him was the crushing news, only a month later, of Princess Grace's untimely death in an automobile accident. She had suffered a stroke while driving down the same winding road where they had shot their memorable car scene together for Hitchcock twenty-eight years earlier in *To Catch a Thief*. Grant attended her funeral and wept continually through the magisterial service that was broadcast live around the world.

He intended to spend the last years of his life close to home with only his wife and frequent visitor Jennifer. He loved nothing more than to watch the day's edge slip into the ocean, or receive the occasional visit from a friend, and he studiously avoided anything that reminded him of death. While watching *On Golden Pond* on TV, he turned it off in the middle because, as he later told columnist Cindy Adams, "Henry Fonda's aging character reminded me of me." The next morning he promised Harris that he would live to be one hundred years old.

Tony Curtis, one of the few outsiders Grant allowed to visit regularly, remembered their time together this way: "I stayed close to Cary always and really admired him. There was much to admire. We'd be on his terrace, and I'd tell him the trials and tribulations of being an actor (as if he didn't know), what was going on in my life, this or that party, and he'd just sit there and say,

'Tony, Tony, Tony!' I loved it. I was one of the boys on the street for him. I was one of the voices for him, one of the eyes. Acting was an ongoing subject of conversation between us. 'Tony,' he'd say, 'you must forget that you're making a movie . . . so artful it's artless.' That was Cary Grant's gift to me, and I always loved him for it."

There was one place where Grant occasionally still liked to go, and that was Las Vegas. He would have Barbara pack up the car, and together they would be driven to the MGM Grand, where for the next several days they would take in all the shows on the Strip. Nothing amused him like live club performances, especially by comedians. One he especially liked was Charlie Callas, a particularly manic old-school vaudeville–Borscht Belt comic with bulging eyes and rubber face, whom Grant had become familiar with from Johnny Carson's *Tonight Show*, a program he almost never missed. One night, after seeing Callas's show at the Sands, Grant took Harris backstage to meet him. "I just want to tell you," Grant told Callas, "I think you are the funniest comedian in Las Vegas!"

They struck up a friendship that lasted for the rest of Grant's life, and they exchanged letters on a number of topics, including the art of comedy, the life of a stand-up, and other assorted show-business musings. Whenever Grant went to Vegas, he always looked up the comedian and spent days at his home. Grant especially enjoyed the Jewish dialect Callas was so adept at and asked if he could teach him how to do it. As Callas remembers, "Grant trying to sound Jewish was one of the funniest things I'd ever heard."

THE FRIENDSHIP WITH CALLAS was more than pleasant relaxation. It planted the seed for what Grant eventually decided to do with whatever time he had left. That seed began to germinate one day in 1982, when he got a telephone call from Steve Allen, who had put together a one-man show he took around the country, mostly to college campuses, during which he would reminisce about his career and show a few autobiographical slides. Allen had come down with a severe cold and asked Grant if he could possibly fill in at the DeAnza Community College in Cupertino, about forty miles outside San Francisco. Grant agreed, and the next night, before a full house of 2,500 students, he found himself sitting on a stage answering questions from the audience about his own life and career.

At one point, noting the recent passing of Henry Fonda, Grant returned to the dominant subject that had inevitably taken over his life. He told the audience, "I remember being in New York in the 1920s and watching a parade on Veterans Day of soldiers from the Civil War. Each year there were less and less. I asked Jimmy Stewart the other day if he'd experienced the feeling of everybody leaving us and not knowing what to think about it. He said he hadn't at all.

"But I have."

The evening proved such a success, Grant began working on a ninety-minute one-man show he called A Conversation with Cary Grant. In the fall of 1984, shortly after his eightieth birthday, Jennifer Grant entered Stanford University as a freshman, and Grant decided the time was right to try his new "act" out on the road and, if it worked, tour with it around the country. He wanted it to be like the beginning of his career, when he toured the smaller cities of America as part of a vaudeville troupe, mining the backroads of big-time showbiz. To that end, he grew a full beard that he kept well trimmed and, with Barbara by his side, revisited the atmosphere of his youth, playing places like Texarkana, Joliet, Red Bank, Sarasota, and Schenectady, all regular vaudeville stops on the turn-of-the-twentieth-century circuit. He kept the price of admission to a relatively low twenty-five dollars to encourage younger people to come out and see him.

He always began his presentation with film clips from Bringing Up Baby, The Philadelphia Story, Suspicion, Notorious, and To Catch a Thief, and the night he received his Honorary Oscar. Then the spotlight would come up on him already onstage and seated. He would tell stories to the audience, mostly off the cuff from a few prepared cue-notes, and end the evening taking questions.

In October 1984, after a particularly rigorous touring schedule, a gala for President Reagan at the Century Plaza Hotel in Los Angeles that the Grants attended, and a trip to Monaco for the Princess Grace Red Cross Ball, Grant suffered a slight stroke and was advised by his doctors to give up his touring show. He refused.

IN APRIL 1986, Grant and Harris celebrated their fifth wedding anniversary by renewing their marriage vows. They spent that summer together touring, and because of overwhelming demand, Grant extended his dates through Thanksgiving, after which he promised Harris he would take several months off and do nothing but rest and relax.

As time went on, his presentation became smoother, more charming, and more informative. The most gratifying thing for Grant was that even though he hadn't made a movie in nearly twenty years, the public, especially the college generation that knew him from their film appreciation courses, kept every seat filled. He became more comfortable giving his answers, with occasional flashes of the old charm and wit, and as word of the show spread, he regularly sold out three- and four-thousand-seat venues.

He loved the mix of questions and the notable lack of personal gossip, which students in particular seemed not to be interested in at all. One night someone asked him why more westerns weren't being made. Grant's standard good-natured reply was that he wasn't sure but that he would spread the word around Hollywood to get on the ball. A while later that same evening someone else asked the same question. Grant asked him his name and told him he ought to get together with the other fellow, and would either of them mind if he lay down for a while? The audience roared its approval at his quick wit. To questions about who his favorite leading lady was, Grant, with apologies to all the others, always cited Grace Kelly. As to which role came closest to the "real" Cary Grant, he never varied: "The bum I played in *Father Goose*." Occasionally he sounded as if he were confiding in the closest of friends. Of his taking LSD, he said, "The doctor read a book over in the corner with a little light. He played music associated with my youth. Like Rachmaninoff. It would last three or four hours. I would see nightmares, and the fears, the scenes associated with nightmares. Out of these sessions I learned to forgive my parents for what they didn't know. And my [lifelong] fear of knives. After which I joined humanity as best I could. I no longer have hypocrisies."*

---

*Although he claimed to know the source of his knife phobia, he never revealed it.

One of the most frequently asked questions was whether he would ever return to the movies. "I don't have the energy for it anymore," he told one crowd in San Francisco. "I loved my work, so I had fun making most of my films — especially those I did for Alfred Hitchcock." One evening, when asked about his still superb physical condition, he said that he never exercised: "The best exercise I know of is making love." That was his closing comment, and it brought the audience to its feet.

On November 28, 1986, the final stop of the thirty-six-city fall tour took eighty-two-year-old Grant and thirty-six-year-old Harris to the Blackhawk Hotel in Davenport, Iowa. They spent the morning touring the city under the guidance of local businessman Doug Miller. That afternoon Grant and Harris went to the Adler Theater for a quick technical rehearsal. Afterward an unusually winded and pale Grant told Harris he wasn't feeling well and went to his dressing room to lie down. After an hour he had Harris take him back to the hotel, saying that he still wasn't a hundred percent.

At seven o'clock he asked that the scheduled performance be canceled.

At eight o'clock Miller came to check on Grant and, after seeing how weak he was, called his personal physician, Dr. Duane Manlove. "He was weak, complaining of dizziness and a headache, and had been vomiting," Manlove later recalled. "I examined him and called for a cardiologist."

At eight-fifteen Grant's face began to glaze over, and he started speaking out loud to no one in particular. "He was talking about going back to Los Angeles," Dr. Manlove said. "But I knew that was impossible. He didn't have that much time to live. He was having a major stroke, and it was getting worse."

At eight forty-five cardiologist James Gilson arrived. "I don't need doctors, I just need rest," Grant protested, his voice now barely above a whisper.

Dr. Gilson called an ambulance. At nine o'clock paramedic Bart Lund and two others arrived. According to Lund, "We found Cary Grant lying on a bed — without shoes, wearing slacks, a shirt, and jacket. He was conscious and, despite his age, hardly looked as though he was ill. He told us, 'I'm feeling a little pain in the chest. But I don't think it's anything. I don't want to make a fuss.'"

As he was being taken down the hotel service elevator, they hooked him up to wires and monitors. A glassy-eyed Grant kept calling for Barbara, who was standing right next to him.

At nine-fifteen the ambulance arrived at St. Luke's Hospital emergency room. As Grant was being wheeled into the emergency room, he squeezed his wife's hand. "I love you, Barbara," he said. "Don't worry."

At 11:22 P.M., Cary Grant was pronounced dead.

34

"I don't know how I consider death. So many of my friends have been doing it recently. I hope I do it well . . . I would like to be remembered as a congenial fellow who didn't rock the boat, I suppose."

—CARY GRANT

As word of his passing flashed around the world, tributes from friends began to pour in, paying homage to the little boy from Bristol who grew up in search of love, only to have the whole world fall in love with him. These are among the more notable ones:

Frank Sinatra: "I am saddened by the loss of one of the dearest friends I ever had. I have nothing more to say except that I shall miss him terribly."

Jimmy Stewart: "He was one of the great people in the movie business."

George Burns: "He was one of the greats."

Charlton Heston: "What he did he did better than anyone ever has. He was surely as unique as any film star and as important as anyone since Charlie Chaplin."

Loretta Young: "He was *the* elegant man."

Polly Bergen: "We have just lost the man who showed Hollywood and the world what the word *class* really means. He was the one star that even other stars were in awe of."

Eva Marie Saint: "He was the most handsome, witty, and stylish leading man both on and off the screen. I adored him. It's a sad loss for all of us."

Dean Martin: "He was one of my heroes. He was not only a great actor, he was a refined and polished gentleman. We were very close friends, and I'm going to miss him."

Alexis Smith: "The best movie actor that ever was. There's a term 'romance with a camera,' and I doubt anybody had as great a romance with the camera as he did."

President Ronald Reagan: "We were very saddened by news of the death of our old Hollywood friend. He was one of the brightest stars in Hollywood and his elegance, wit and charm will endure on film and in our hearts. We will always cherish the memory of his warmth, his loyalty and his friendship and we will miss him dearly."

As was his wish, there was no funeral. On Monday, December 2, his body was cremated by the Neptune Society. A small ceremony was held by his wife and daughter to dispose of the ashes.

At his death, Cary Grant was estimated to be worth approximately $60 million. His last will, signed November 26, 1984, left half his estate to his wife, Barbara Harris, the other half to be placed in trust for Jennifer until the age of thirty-five, with the ability to draw up to 50 percent of the principal until then, and the balance delivered thereafter. He left all of his real estate, including the four-acre home in Beverly Hills and its contents, to Harris, $150,000 to be divided among long-term employees, $50,000 to the Motion Picture and Television Relief Fund, and $25,000 to Variety Clubs International. He left $10,000 to Dr. Mortimer Hartman, who had administered many of the LSD treatments Grant took in the late 1950s and early 1960s, and $25,000 to Stanley Fox's son and granddaughter. Grant's extensive custom-made wardrobe, ornaments, and jewelry were all left to Stanley Fox, who was charged with dividing them among Frank Sinatra, Betsy Drake Grant, Irene Selznick, Roderick Mann, Stanley Donen, Kirk Kerkorian, and a few others whose names meant nothing to the public. A trunk filled with personal items associated with Grace Kelly was left to Princess Caroline of Monaco.

SHORTLY AFTER HER FATHER'S DEATH, Jennifer returned to Stanford University, to complete her senior year in political science and history. She then studied law, until she decided to try acting as a career, something Grant had discouraged her from doing while he was alive. She became one of the regulars on the popular TV show *Beverly Hills 90210* and today lives as a single woman in Santa Monica, California.

The highlight of Virginia Cherrill's film career remains Chaplin's *City Lights.* Her last film was Albert Parker's *Troubled Waters,* after which she gave up movies to marry a wealthy British earl. She became the Countess of Jersey and went on to find real meaning in her life by doing selfless, some might say heroic, work during the bombing of London in the darkest years of World War II. Upon the earl's death, Cherrill returned to Hollywood, where she married twice more before choosing to live in wealthy seclusion in Santa Barbara, about ninety miles north of Hollywood. She died there in 1996.

Betsy Drake retired from films and became an "alternative" psychotherapist and the author of several books. She lives in Desert Hot Springs, California.

Dyan Cannon continued with her successful acting career. She married an older businessman in 1980 and retired from films. Three years later, she divorced and returned to her career in movies and television. She lives in Los Angeles.

Randolph Scott went on to a successful career in Hollywood westerns of the '50s. He retired from films in 1962, and was worth several hundred million dollars. That same year he left Los Angeles with his second wife and retired to North Carolina, where he played golf and followed his many investments. He died in 1987, one year after Grant, at the age of eighty-nine. Although he remained friendly with his former roommate, he rarely saw him again after Grant married Barbara Hutton.

TWO YEARS AFTER HIS DEATH, on October 19, 1988, the only formal public memorial ceremony was held for Cary Grant, attended by 940 of his most

famed admirers and friends. They paid tribute to him at a $1,000-a-plate din-
ner at emcee and host Merv Griffin's Beverly Hilton Hotel, with the proceeds
going to the Princess Grace Foundation. Barbara Harris, a foundation
trustee, helped organize the evening. Dyan Cannon was not invited and did
not attend. Among those who did were Frank Sinatra and his wife Barbara,
Monaco's Prince Rainier, his children Princess Stephanie and Prince Albert,
Shirley Temple Black, Griffin's girlfriend Eva Gabor, Jennifer Grant and her
then live-in fiancé television producer Randy Zisk, Gregory Peck, Richard
Baskin, Barbra Streisand, Michael Caine, Jackie Collins, Liza Minnelli, Jack
Haley Jr., Kirk Kerkorian, Angie Dickinson, Dina Merrill, Robert Wagner,
Eva Marie Saint, Maureen Donaldson, and Sammy Davis Jr.

Also in 1988, a pavilion at the Hollywood Park Race Track was dedicated
to Cary Grant. John Forsythe spoke at the ceremony: "Cary Grant was a man
who had such presence and magnetism that every close-up was riveting to
watch — you couldn't take your eyes off him. And did you ever notice that
when he was presenting a trophy down in the winners circle after a big race,
everything stopped at the track. People put down their racing forms and
picked up their binoculars to get a closer look at him. Others ran down to the
winners circle to catch a glimpse of him. Believe me, that rarely happens at
a racetrack. He was also a star in the business community, a star as a member of our board of directors, and perhaps most important of all, he was a star
as a friend."

In the universe of the imagination, as long as there are movies and audiences who seek to find in them the reflection of their highest hopes and their
deepest dreams, Cary Grant's star will indeed shine forever, offering the illu-
sion of the pleasure of his company as it guides us along the most difficult
journey of all: the one into ourselves.

SOURCES

RESEARCH INSTITUTIONS

The following research facilities were used by the author:

The Margaret Herrick Library of the Academy of Motion Picture Arts and Sciences, Beverly Hills, California

The New York Public Library, New York City

The New York Public Library for the Performing Arts, New York City

The British Film Institute

The Bristol Information Center

BIBLIOGRAPHY

Agee, James. *Agee on Film.* Vol. 1. New York: Grosset's Universal Library, 1969.

Ashman, Chuck, and Pamela Trescott. *Cary Grant.* London: W.H. Allen, 1986.

Auiler, Dan. *Vertigo.* New York: St. Martin's Press, 1998.

Barlett, Donald, and James B. Steele. *Empire: The Life, Legend and Madness of Howard Hughes.* Toronto: George J. McLeod, 1979.

Berg, A. Scott. *Goldwyn: A Biography.* New York: Alfred A. Knopf, 1989.

Bergquist, Laura. "The Curious Story Behind the New Cary Grant." *Look,* September 1, 1959.

Bogdanovich, Peter. *Pieces of Time.* New York: Arbor House, 1973.

——. *Who the Devil Made It?* New York: Alfred A. Knopf, 1997.

——. *Peter Bogdanovich's Movie of the Week.* New York: Ballantine, 1999.

Brown, Peter Harry, and Pat H. Broeske. *Howard Hughes: The Untold Story.* New York: Diane Publishing, 1996.

Buehrer, Beverley Bare. *Cary Grant: A Bio-Bibliography.* Westport, Conn.: Greenwood Press, 1990.

Chaplin, Charles. *Charles Chaplin: My Autobiography.* New York: Simon and Schuster, 1964.

Curtis, Tony. *Tony Curtis: The Autobiography*. New York: Morrow, 1998.

Davis, Debra Sharon. "Cary Grant: A Candid Conversation with America's Epitome of Elegance." *Playboy Guide*, Spring-Summer 1981.

Deschner, Donald. *The Films of Cary Grant*. Secaucus, N.J.: Citadel Press, 1973.

Diamondstein, Barbaralee. *The Landmarks of New York*. New York: Harry Abrams, 1993.

Dickens, Homer. *The Films of Katharine Hepburn*. Secaucus, N.J.: Citadel Press, 1971.

Donaldson, Maureen, and William Royce. *An Affair to Remember: My Life with Cary Grant*. New York: Putnam, 1989.

Durgnat, Raymond. *The Strange Case of Alfred Hitchcock, or the Plain Man's Hitchcock*. Cambridge, Mass: MIT Press, 1978.

Eyman, Scott. *Ernst Lubitsch: Laughter in Paradise*. New York: Simon and Schuster, 1993.

Fairbanks, Douglas Jr. *The Salad Days*. New York: Doubleday, 1988.

Gabler, Neal. *An Empire of Their Own*. New York: Crown, 1988.

Gentry, Curt. *J. Edgar Hoover: The Man and the Secrets*. New York: W.W. Norton, 1991.

Godfrey, Lionel. *Cary Grant: The Light Touch*. New York: St. Martin's Press, 1981.

Govoni, Albert. *Cary Grant: An Unauthorized Biography*. Chicago: Henry Regnery, 1971.

Grant, Cary. "Archie Leach." *Ladies' Home Journal*, January/February 1963 (Part 1), March 1963 (Part 2), April 1963 (Part 3). Referred to in text as Grant's "autobiography."

Hadleigh, Boze. *Hollywood Gays*. New York: Barricade Books, 1996.

Hamilton, Ian. *Writers in Hollywood: 1915–1951*. New York: Harper and Row, 1990.

Harris, Warren G. *Cary Grant: A Touch of Elegance*. New York: Doubleday, 1987.

Haskell, Molly. *Holding My Own in No Man's Land*. New York: Oxford University Press, 1997.

Haver, Ronald. *A Star Is Born*. New York: Bonanza Books, 1980.

Higham, Charles. *Kate*. New York: W.W. Norton, 1975.

Higham, Charles, and Roy Moseley. *Cary Grant: The Lonely Heart*. New York: Harcourt Brace Jovanovich, 1989.

Holden, Anthony. *Behind the Oscars*. New York: Simon and Schuster, 1993.

Hotchner, A. E. *Sophia Living and Loving*. New York: William Morrow, 1979.

Jones, Ken D., Arthur F. McClure, and Alfred E. Twomey. *The Films of James Stewart*. New York: Castle Books, 1970.

Kael, Pauline. "The Man from Dream City." *The New Yorker*, July 14, 1975.

Kashner, Sam, and Nancy Schoenberger. *A Talent for Genius: The Life and Times of Oscar Levant*. New York: Villard, 1994.

Kriendler, H. Peter, and H. Paul Jeffers. *"21": Every Day Was New Year's Eve*. Dallas: Taylor Publishing, 1999.

Leff, Leonard J. *Hitchcock and Selznick*. New York: Weidenfeld and Nicolson, 1987.

Leff, Leonard J., and Jerold L. Simoons. *The Dame in the Kimono*. New York: Grove Weidenfeld, 1980.

Levant, Oscar. *Memoirs of an Amnesiac*. New York: G. P. Putnam, 1965.

McBride, Joseph. *Frank Capra: The Catastrophe of Success*. New York: Simon and Schuster, 1992.

McCann, Graham. *Cary Grant: A Class Apart*. New York: Columbia University Press, 1996.

McCarthy, Todd. *Howard Hawks: The Grey Fox of Hollywood*. New York: Grove Press, 1997.

McDougal, Dennis. *The Last Mogul: Lew Wasserman, MCA and the Hidden History of Hollywood*. New York: Random House, 1998.

McGilligan, Patrick. *George Cukor: A Double Life*. London: Faber and Faber, 1991.

Meyers, Jeffrey. *Gary Cooper: American Hero*. New York: Cooper Square Press, 2001.

Milton, Joyce. *Tramp: The Life of Charlie Chaplin*. New York: HarperCollins, 1996.

Moldea, Dan E. *Dark Victory: Ronald Reagan, MCA and the Mob*. New York: Viking, 1986.

Nelson, Nancy. *Evenings with Cary Grant: Recollections in His Own Words, and by Those Who Knew Him Best*. New York: Warner Books, 1993.

Niven, David. *Bring on the Empty Horses*. New York: G. P. Putnam's Sons, 1975.

Parish, James Robert. *The RKO Gals*. New Jersey: Rainbow Books, 1974.

Parish, James Robert, and Ronald L. Bowers. *The MGM Stock Company: The Golden Era*. New York: Arlington House, 1973.

Roberts, Randy, and James Olson. *John Wayne: American*. New York: Free Press, 1995.

Sarris, Andrew. *You Ain't Heard Nothin' Yet*. New York: Oxford University Press, 1998.

Schickel, Richard. *The Men Who Made the Movies*. New York: Atheneum, 1975.

———. *Cary Grant: A Celebration*. New York: Little, Brown, 1983.

———. *D. W. Griffith: An American Life*. New York: Simon and Schuster, 1984.

Server, Lee. *Robert Mitchum: Baby I Don't Care*. New York: St. Martin's Press, 2002.

Shipman, David. *The Great Movie Stars: The Golden Years*. New York: Crown, 1970.

Siegel, Scott, and Barbara Siegel. *The Encyclopedia of Hollywood*. New York: Facts on File, 1990.

Spada, James. *Grace: The Secret Lives of a Princess*. New York: Dolphin Books, 1987.

———. *Peter Lawford: The Man Who Kept the Secrets*. New York: Bantam, 1991.

Spoto, Donald. *The Dark Side of Genius: The Life of Alfred Hitchcock*. New York: Ballantine, 1983.

Summers, Anthony. *Goddess: The Secret Lives of Marilyn Monroe*. New York: Macmillan, 1985.

Thomas, Bob. *King Cohn: The Life and Times of Harry Cohn*. New York: Bantam, 1958.

Tuska, Jon. *The Films of Mae West*. Secaucus, N.J.: Citadel Press, 1973.

Vermilye, Jerry. *Cary Grant*. New York: Galahad Books, 1973.

Wansell, Geoffrey. *Haunted Idol: The Story of the Real Cary Grant*. New York: Morrow, 1984.

Waterbury, Ruth. "The Story of Cary Grant." *Liberty*, March 11, 1939.

Wayne, Jane Ellen. *Cooper's Women*. London: Hale, 1988.

Weller, Sheila. *Dancing at Ciro's*. New York: St. Martin's Press, 2003.

Wiley, Mason, and Damien Bona. *Inside Oscar*. New York: Ballantine Books, 1986.

Wood, Robin. *Hitchcock's Films*. New York: Castle Books, 1969.

NOTES

INTRODUCTION

"the man from dream city." Kael, "The Man from Dream City."

[1]

the Academy of Motion Picture Arts and Sciences. Mayer organized the multiple-studio "house" organization to deal with the fundamental shift in Hollywood toward labor unionism in what had been, for its first twenty years, a freewheeling, management-dominated factory town. The Academy was formally introduced by Mayer at a dinner party held at the Ambassador Hotel on January 17, 1927. Douglas Fairbanks, a charter member of the Academy (and one of the founders of United Artists), came up with the idea of merit awards for achievement as a way to promote movies to the public.

Grant's snubbing by the Academy. Grant was by no means the only major star never to have won a competitive Oscar. Many Hollywood legends — Charlie Chaplin, Buster Keaton, the Marx Brothers, W. C. Fields, Greta Garbo, Fred Astaire, Kirk Douglas, Mickey Rooney, Maurice Chevalier, Bob Hope, Barbara Stanwyck, Robert Mitchum, Errol Flynn, Edward G. Robinson, Danny Kaye, and Jerry Lewis — never won an Oscar for their acting. Alfred Hitchcock never won one for direction. Grant, ever the outsider, made this observation about the Oscars after Fredric March's 1946 win for Best Actor (in William Wyler's *The Best Years of Our Lives* over Grant's longtime friend Laurence Olivier's self-directed *Hamlet*): "There is something embarrassing about all these wealthy people publicly congratulating each other. When it all began, we kidded ourselves and said, 'All right, Freddie March, we know you're making a million dollars. Now come up and get your little medal [for *Dr. Jekyll and Mr. Hyde*] for it.'" Grant's specialty, "light comedy," he was fond of telling friends and interviewers alike, "has little chance for an Oscar."

Aided by a 1948 landmark antitrust lawsuit. The federal lawsuit was *SIMPP v. Paramount Pictures.* The decision in the case was handed down in February 1948 and effectively ended the majors' forty-year domination of the production, distribution, and exhibition of motion pictures.

"poor judgment." The lawsuit was filed on August 8, 1969, in Los Angeles Superior Court against MCA and Universal Studios, asking for damages in excess of $8 million over the sale of four pictures coproduced by Grant and Donen that were financed by Universal prior to their eventually being purchased by MCA. The four films were *The Grass Is Greener, That Touch of Mink, Operation Petticoat,* and *Father Goose.* Sources: *Los Angeles Herald Examiner* and *Variety.* The sale voided the lawsuit.

"personal reasons." Quoted in Sheilah Graham, syndicated gossip column, March 1970.

Cynthia Bouron . . . One columnist claimed to have known it was coming . . . In his March 1970 column in the *Hollywood Citizen-News,* entertainment editor John Austin wrote, "I and my fellow columnists have been aware of this story for weeks, some of us for months . . . Few of us are muckrakers and it is a great shame, a tragedy, in fact, that Cary Grant, at the age of 66 with an honorable career behind him, has been subjected to all this before it has even been established that he is the father of Miss Bouron's child."

Grant secretly flew to the Bahamas . . . Grant zigzagged his way around the world during the Bouron affair, traveling to Bristol, then the Bahamas, stopping in New York at the Warwick Hotel, then back to Beverly Hills, then to Las Vegas and home again. He flew in a private DC-3 that Howard Hughes provided for his unlimited use.

Judge Laurence J. Rittenband. Grant may actually have fled on the advice of his attorney, fearing the hard line that Rittenband was known for, especially when it came to celebrities. Prior to the Bouron case, Rittenband had presided over the Elvis Presley divorce and Marlon Brando's custody battle, and in each instance his decision heavily favored the wife. A few years after the Bouron case, Rittenband would be the presiding judge in the sensational Roman Polanski sex-with-a-minor case, in which, it was rumored, despite an agreed-upon plea bargain he intended to throw the book at the wayward director. Like Grant, Polanski, very likely on the advice of his attorney, fled the country.

The scandal, however, refused to die. Many questions remain unanswered to this day. Bouron was a high-priced call girl and had a long criminal record. The most serious charge against her was a felony arrest for theft in 1967, which was eventually dismissed. She had been married twice and was the mother of two previous children. Her first husband was former stuntman Milos Milocevic, whom she had married in 1964 for a reportedly high five-figure sum, to save him from deportation to his native Yugoslavia, where he faced a fifteen-year prison term for army desertion. Two years later, in February 1966, five months before her pre–agreed-upon divorce from him became final, Milocevic's dead body was found beside that of Barbara Rooney, who was married at the time to actor Mickey Rooney. He apparently committed suicide after killing her. On October 30, 1973, three years after Bouron's failed attempt to bring a paternity suit against Grant, her dead body was found in the trunk of a stolen car in a Hollywood supermarket parking lot. The cause of death was determined by the Los Angeles Coroner's Office to have been bludgeoning with a claw hammer. Finally, the child Bouron accused Grant of fathering, a girl she named Stephanie Andrea Grant Bouron, was described in the police report as being "of strong Negro blood." The murder case was never solved. According to the North Hollywood police, "several friends of the victim stated she would often pick up men at bars or restaurants." When asked for a comment about the discovery of Bouron's body, Grant had none.

a "close friend." John Austin, *Hollywood Citizen-News*, April 2, 1970.

As the night of the Awards approached. Grant gave Dyan Cannon the okay for an exclusive interview with syndicated gossip columnist Sheilah Graham one week after he received his Award. In it, Cannon gave some details of the night she and Grant spent together the night before the ceremonies. According to Cannon, Grant read his acceptance speech to her and asked her approval of its content; and she "read him my loser's speech." Graham ended her column hinting that Grant and Cannon were contemplating getting back together, a bit of deliberate "family man" PR that Grant no doubt encouraged to help repair whatever damage his image might have suffered over Bouron. Grant took early control of his relationship with the Hollywood and national gossip columnists, and it was said that despite his always friendly and cooperative demeanor, he loathed every one of them. He sued Graham in 1940 over a piece she ran suggesting a little bit too strongly that Grant was gay and everybody in Hollywood knew it. He later dropped the lawsuit. His regular "contacts," as he called them, were Hedda Hopper, John Austin, Ben Maddox, Leonard Lyons, Sidney Skolsky, Earl Wilson, Walter Winchell, and Ed Sullivan.

a six-minute montage of clips. The montage of Cary Grant clips was put together by Mike Nichols. The only clip Grant asked Nichols to specifically include was his crying scene from 1941's *Penny Serenade*, a performance for which he was to receive one of his two Oscar nominations. The only film he insisted be excluded was *Singapore Sue*, a short he made while still in New York. It was his first appearance on film, and he always claimed he couldn't stand it.

[2]

"I'm reminded of a piece of advice . . ." Cary Grant, "How to Dress Confidently," *This Week* (supplement to the *Los Angeles Times*), April 1, 1962.

Bristol is the seventh-largest city. Official University of Bristol website — "History, Architecture, Churches, Statues and Landmarks." http://www.bris.ac.uk/.

Archibald Alec Leach. *Alec* is the familiar form of *Alexander* (as *Dick* is to *Richard*) and is the way the name appears in the birth records.

the unexpected death of her firstborn. "It was only recently that I recognized a clue to the cause of my mother's retreat within herself. Some years prior to my birth my parents had another child . . . a baby boy who, alas, died of some sort of convulsions after only a few months of life." Grant, in "Archie Leach."

Archibald Leach was born on January 18, 1904. The birth records of Archibald Alec (Alexander) Grant were not registered until February 29, 1904, five weeks after his arrival—not an unusual amount of time in those days. Nevertheless, this time lapse has resulted in excessive confusion as to his actual birth date, his ethnic background, and his "true" parental heritage—specifically that he was secretly Jewish and/or adopted. The author found no substantial factual evidence supporting either of these claims. Nor has any solid evidence been found for any conspiratorial coverup of "real" origins, parents, heritage, and the like. At least one previous biographer has used reports that Grant was circumcised as "proof" that he was Jewish. If he was circumcised, it is probably because his mother insisted on it after the death of her first son, believing, as many did at the time, that circumcision helped prevent infant infection and disease. No reliable records have thus far been found of any such procedure actually having been performed on the baby Leach for either medical or religious reasons. Furthermore, while it is almost always done within days after birth, circumcision may be performed at any time.

"As a little boy . . ." Quoted in Cleveland Amory, "That Touch of Class," *Parade*, September 22, 1985, pp. 4–9.

Elsie enjoyed keeping little Archie's hair long. "It seemed to me that I was kept in baby clothes much longer than any other child and perhaps, for a while, wasn't sure whether I was a boy or a girl," Grant wrote in "Archie Leach." Grant's meticulous attention to his wardrobe, particularly in his later films such as *That Touch of Mink* and *North by Northwest*, as well as his obsessional pursuit of the finest personal custom tailoring, echo Elias's occupation as a tailor, a sartorial link to his happier childhood memories of his father.

he still often preferred wearing women's nylon panties. Harris, *Cary Grant*, 194, quoting from the unpublished 1959 Joe Hyams interview made during the filming of *Operation Petticoat*.

"My parents tried so hard . . ." Amory, "Touch of Class."

The value of good clothes. Grant's complete quote regarding the value of good shoes: "I learned a lot about clothes and how to buy them from my father. We couldn't afford a great deal when I was a boy growing up in Bristol, England, but we were not unaware of what others who had money were doing. I remember I had bought three or four pairs of shoes. They were not very costly. My father reprimanded me. He said one should always look good and wear well-made things even if one doesn't have a lot of money. He taught me about clothes and that I should buy one good pair of shoes rather than four inexpensive pairs that look cheap and won't last. Shoes are very important. One should always have at least two pairs to switch off now and then. Yes, my father taught me to buy better clothes and less of them." Davis, "Cary Grant."

Left-handedness. According to Leslie Caron, Grant's costar in *Father Goose*, in 1964: "He was basically left-handed, but he had trained himself to be ambidextrous. One time the prop man set a bottle he was to use in the scene by his right hand, and Cary flashed very angrily, 'How do you expect me to pour the bottle with this hand?'" Caron, quoted by Marla Brooks, in *Lefthander*, January/February 1995, 13. In "Archie Leach," Grant expresses gratitude that no one discouraged his natural left-handedness, as was often done in both British and American schools of the early twentieth century, where the preference was seen as an affliction.

"I [made] the mistake of thinking that each of my wives was my mother." Harris, *Cary Grant*, 14; Grant, "Archie Leach."

"came right up the Avon River . . ." Grant, "Archie Leach."

"That's when I *knew*." Grant, "Archie Leach."

That August Archie eagerly signed a three-year contract. "MEMORANDUM OF AGREE-MENT: Made on this day 9th, August, between Robert Pender of 247 Brixton Road, London, on the one part, Elias Leach of 12 Campbell Street, Bristol, on the other part. The said Robert Pender agrees to employ the son of the said Elias Leach, Archie Leach, in his troupe at a weekly salary of 10 shillings a week with board and lodging and every-thing found for the stage, and when not working full board and lodgings. This salary to be increased as the said Archie Leach improves in his profession and he agrees to remain in the employ of Robert Pender till he is eighteen years of age or a six months notice on either side. Robert Pender undertaking to teach him dancing and other accomplishments needful for his work. Archie Leach agrees to work to the best of his abilities. Signed, Bob Pender." Nelson, *Evenings with Cary Grant*, 39.

"cultured English talk." Ernest Kingdon (one of the cousins of young Archie who lived with him and his mother), quoted in Godfrey, *Cary Grant*, 41.

"doggedly strive . . ." Grant, "Archie Leach."

[3]

"I never associated him . . ." Peter Cadbury (a member of the famed chocolate fam-ily and a native Bristolean), interview by Xan Brooks, *Guardian*, August 17, 2001.

the famous B. F. Keith vaudeville circuit. At the time, the most prestigious vaude-ville circuit in America.

Coney Island's famous Steeplechase Park. The gig paid five dollars a day, ten dol-lars on weekends. Grant worked Tuesdays through Fridays, and weekends.

a witness to all this "homosexuality." Higham and Moseley, *Cary Grant*, 37. They claim to have conducted the interview with Burns a few years before his death.

Grant insisted that in 1925 . . . he returned to England. The source of the fanciful story of Archie's return to England in 1925 was Archie Leach himself. While appearing in summer stock in 1930, he was invited to write a profile of himself for the local news-papers and crafted what amounts to a colorful fiction of his early life, including the sup-posed 1925 trip back home. This trip shows up repeatedly in biographies of Grant, based on this profile, embellished with all manner of detail and color, but without any basis in fact. Grant was to continue to use this method of misdirection to throw off all those who sought to write about him, and it usually worked quite effectively. In later works and inter-views, for example, Grant "confessed" that he came from a strong theatrical background and that his father, Elias, was a wealthy clothing manufacturer. One of the strongest "pieces of evidence" Higham and Moseley use to "prove" that Grant was Jewish and that Elsie was not his mother is the 1962 *Who's Who in America* entry on Cary Grant, in which she is identified as Lillian. It is fairly certain that Grant himself was the source of the mix-up in names, as he constantly sought to protect his mother from the prying eyes of writers, researchers, and biographers. Finally, Elsie and Lillian are similar-sounding names, easily mistaken in transcription or translation, an error Grant would not have bothered to correct.

[4]

"I had quite a run of stage successes . . ." Quoted in John Paddy Carstairs, "He's Grand—and He's Grant," *Film Pictorial*, December 17, 1932.

"He was never a very open fellow . . ." Quoted in Wansell, *Haunted Idol*, 65.

"happy acquaintance." Grant, "Archie Leach." According to Grant, it was not Orry-Kelly but another young, hustling actor by the name of Max Hoffman Jr. who introduced him to Reginald Hammerstein. This is, most likely, another instance of Grant's masterful use of misdirection, as all evidence points to Orry-Kelly being the one. It is interesting to note that Grant never refers to or mentions Orry-Kelly by name in any interview or autobiographical writings, including "Archie Leach."

Golden Dawn. The show starred Louise Hunter and Paul Gregory. Archie received generally good notices, including one from *The New York Times*, which called him a "handsome young newcomer." *Golden Dawn* was made into a Warner Bros. movie in 1930 starring Vivienne Segal and Walter Woolf King. It is mostly remembered for being one of the first Hollywood feature films to be shot entirely in color.

Polly with a Past. This show was written by Ina Claire and originally produced on Broadway by David Belasco.

June took an instant dislike to Archie. Quoted in Harris, *Cary Grant*, 41; original source unknown.

Rosalie. By the 1920s Broadway had become a seeding ground for the many national theaters belonging to various producers/theater owners. Before talking pictures, a show that opened on Broadway became the model for a live touring version that would play in every major city in America. For Archie, the opportunity to tour meant national exposure with star billing, a major step up in his theatrical career.

Orry-Kelly, costume designer for *Boom Boom*. It remains a mystery what role, if any, Orry-Kelly played in convincing the Shuberts to sign the still largely unknown Archie Leach away from the Hammersteins.

"Without the ability . . ." Cary Grant, "Archie Leach."

open-air Municipal Opera in St. Louis. Orry-Kelly may have been involved in the Shuberts' decision to send Archie to St. Louis.

[5]

"Some men squeeze a line to death . . ." Michael Curtiz, *Time*, July 27, 1962.

Sternberg and Dietrich. Sternberg directed Dietrich in seven classic movies (eight if the German version of *The Blue Angel* is counted, a film Sternberg reshot in English after the success of *Morocco*). These include *The Blue Angel* (1930, German and English versions), *Morocco* (1930), *Dishonored* (1931), *Shanghai Express* (1932), *Blonde Venus* (1932, with Cary Grant), *Scarlet Empress* (1934), and *Devil Is a Woman* (1935). Both *Scarlet Empress* and *Devil Is a Woman* were box office failures.

"Hate . . . mannerisms . . ." Interview by Suzy Parker, March 31, 1956; in Wayne, *Cooper's Women*, 143.

With the Hays Office gaining power in Hollywood. In the wake of threats by the federal government to appoint a board of censorship similar to the one already in place in England, the Motion Picture Producers and Distributors of America created an authority to self-regulate the film industry. In 1922 the association appointed Postmaster General Will Hays to enforce a predetermined formula of standards. Not everyone greeted Hays's arrival with the official warmth that the studio heads did. Chaplin, always the iconoclast, had signs hung over the men's room of his studio declaring "Welcome ill Hays." It would take ten years for the code to bring about a regulated ethic that became the industry standard. Until then the studios tried on an individual basis to see how far they could stretch the limits of what became known as the Hays Office. Thus in 1929, when profits were beginning to dip, Carl Laemmle tried, without success, to bring Mae West and her controversial show to Hollywood via Universal Studios. Two years later, with the studio on the brink of bankruptcy, Paramount risked everything by taking on the woman and her reputation, along with the property that had enjoyed such success on Broadway. As always it was money, not morals, that ruled Hollywood.

"It wasn't true . . ." Quoted in Cindy Adams, May 1982.

"I copied other styles I knew . . ." Quoted in Davis, "Cary Grant."

"was a homosexual . . ." Dietrich made this statement many times, including in an interview quoted in Higham and Moseley. Rumors of Dietrich's own bisexuality had been floated for years; kissing another woman onscreen while dressed in a man's tuxedo in *Shanghai Express* didn't help, but neither did it threaten her star status. If anything, it gave her an added "takes one to know one" pedigree in evaluating potential lovers. To those who held power in Hollywood, lesbianism was simply titillating and therefore tolerated. No man, they believed, would refuse to buy a ticket to see Marlene Dietrich because she preferred women, but many would refuse to see a Cary Grant flick if they thought he was "queer."

"If women want to wear men's clothes . . ." Quoted in *Los Angeles Times*, January 25, 1933.

[6]

"Was there pressure on you or Cary Grant to wed . . ." Scott, in Hadleigh, *Hollywood Gays*.

Cary and Scott. On at least one occasion their relationship cost them the chance to work together. Paramount had considered teaming the two in a film about the Arctic, *Spawn of the North*, with Carole Lombard in the female lead. But mainly due to the persistent rumors over the duo's sexual preferences, the roles eventually went to Henry Fonda and George Raft. The film was directed by Henry Hathaway and released by Paramount in 1938.

Bachelor Hall. This name, given to the bachelor pad of Grant and Scott, was often attributed to Carole Lombard but actually came from a Paramount PR executive.

"Cary is the gay, impetuous one . . ." Ben Maddox, quoted (without attribution) by Gerald Clarke, in *Architectural Digest*, April 1996, 282.

"carrying this buddy business . . ." Harris, *Cary Grant*, 58.

Grant and Scott's competitive workout routine. The details of the daily workout routine and the bet between them are from an RKO memo written by S. Barret McCormick in 1947, to publicize the chance meeting between Scott and Grant that happened during the filming of *The Bachelor and the Bobby-Soxer*.

[7]

"Her shapely form in a blue . . ." Chaplin, *Charles Chaplin: My Autobiography*. He devotes a mere two paragraphs to Cherrill, one having to do with their meeting on the beach, and one having to do with directing her in *City Lights*. He omits any reference to his romantic pursuit of her.

private diaries. The personal diaries kept by Virginia Cherrill and the extensive audiocassettes she kept for use for a possible memoir were made available to the author by Teresa McWilliams, Cherrill's close friend and next-door neighbor in Santa Barbara for more than forty years.

"Most of the actresses that worked for him . . ." Interview by film historian Gerard Molyneaux, in Milton, *Tramp*, 297.

Chaplin wanting to fire Cherrill and replace her with Georgia Hale. Chaplin had done this sort of thing before. In 1925, during the filming of *The Gold Rush*, he had gotten his leading lady, sixteen-year-old Lita Grey, pregnant and decided to reshoot her scenes with Georgia Hale. Paramount signed Hale on the strength of her performance and cast her in its 1926 production of Herbert Brenon's *The Great Gatsby*. Her career ended with the arrival of talkies, for which, the studio decided, she was vocally unsuited.

The night Cary Grant met her. In most versions of their initial meeting, Grant is described as declaring his "instant love" for Cherrill, one of the many stories about them that is very likely apocryphal. Previous biographers seem to have had a great deal of difficulty discerning the precise source of Grant's quote, or to whom it is supposed to have been told. In Harris, *Cary Grant*, it is unattributed; in Grant, Ashman, and Trescott, *Cary Grant*, it is similarly unattributed, although it is slightly amended to love at "second sight (taking into account the sighting at the fights and the subsequent meeting in the commissary)"; in Higham and Moseley, *Cary Grant*, Grant is "fascinated" by Cherrill, who, in turn, is "warned" by none other than Orry-Kelly, in a quote that is neither sourced nor substantiated (and highly unlikely), to be wary of Grant. "Later on," after their divorce he tells Cherrill—in a quote that sounds more like a line out of a soap opera than a commentary by Orry-Kelly, whose connection, if any, to Cherrill is never established — "We both loved him and lost him, didn't we?" In Godfrey, *Cary Grant*, Grant's initial reaction is that he is "charmed" by her during the commissary meeting; in Wansell, *Haunted Idol*, Grant is quoted (without any attribution whatsoever) as telling unnamed "friends" after the initial meeting at the commissary, "I fell in love with her the moment I saw her." Finally, Govoni, *Cary Grant*, comes to this conclusion: "It was not, in any sense, a love-at-first-sight situation." Again, the conclusion is drawn without any attribution.

Grant's back injury. According to associate director Michael Liesen, Grant had been "inattentive" and was injured when an explosion was triggered prematurely. The rest of the cast was unhurt because they had followed instructions and were standing on their spots, whereas Grant had absentmindedly drifted off his. See Godfrey, *Cary Grant*, 62.

Virginia Cherrill had the best sense of humor. McWilliams, recalling a conversation she had with Cary Grant in 1982 at the Hollywood Park racetrack. Unless otherwise noted, all McWilliams quotes are from author interviews.

Grant's bed. Waterbury, "Story of Cary Grant."

"The only thing I got . . ." Levant, *Memoirs*, 91.

"I can't say that I'm in love with Miss West . . ." *Los Angeles Times*, October 16, 1933. Grant kept his word and never worked with Mae West on another film. In the eleven films she made, he was the only leading man to appear with her onscreen more than once.

[8]

"The first day that Cary, the perfectionist . . ." Niven, *Bring on the Empty Horses.*

Grant's trip to England. Sources on Grant's trip to England include papers, articles, and other related documents archived in the Academy of Motion Picture Arts and Sciences; the materials on file at the British Film Institute research division; research documents in Bristol; court records in England, Los Angeles, and the United States; author interviews with Teresa McWilliams; and the private, unpublished diaries and papers of Virginia Cherrill.

Fishponds. The institution was one of the worst medical facilities in all of Great Britain. The rooms were filthy, the patients unattended, the food lousy. Elias chose it because it was a state-run facility that cost him exactly one pound a year.

Grant was devastated. Some have suggested that Grant knew of his mother's incarceration since childhood, that he had been told of it by his father, and that he accepted his father's new life in Southampton as part of their accord. There is no evidence of this, nor does it seem the least bit plausible. Grant would certainly have been in contact with his mother during the nineteen-year period of their separation. The best proof that Grant did not know his mother was alive — besides the psychological behavior her abandonment caused him — is the simple, incontrovertible fact that prior to learning she was alive, he never visited her, wrote to her, or sent her money.

the day of his wedding. It's possible that one of the reasons Grant married Cherrill in London was to avoid the California equal-division-of-property statutes. But as Grant was shortly to discover, full-time residency and place of income were the overriding legal considerations.

[9]

"Movie stars operate in an ether . . ." Peter Rainer, *Los Angeles Herald-Examiner*, December 1, 1986.

Cherrill's claims of Grant's violence. The story has been published in various forms elsewhere, most notably in Higham and Moseley, *Cary Grant*, but without a shred of supporting evidence. No police report was ever filed. No medical report exists. Grant's fit of violence may have taken place, but if Grant was leaning ever so slightly toward divorce, Cherrill probably was, too, and incidents of violence nearly always serve as an avenue of sympathy for the victim at civil trial.

"I had been at a party with friends . . ." This quote appeared in several newspapers and in Wansell, *Haunted Idol*, 102.

"You know what whiskey . . ." Quoted in Godfrey, *Cary Grant*, 66.

The Grant/Cherrill divorce proceedings. Public records on file at the Los Angeles County Superior Court.

[10]

"My first great chance came in 1936 . . ." Quoted in Grant, "What It Means to Be a Star," *Films and Filming*, July 1961.

"Cary was the perfect central-casting fag . . ." The source of the quote insists upon being and will remain anonymous.

"too effete." The quote appears in various forms in numerous publications, including Harris, *Cary Grant*, 71. The source here is the offspring of a well-known Hollywood figure of the time, who wishes to remain anonymous.

Grant accepted radio work. Grant may have had other motives for suddenly changing his mind about appearing for free on the airwaves. He had heard that Virginia Cherrill was in New York alone, and he couldn't resist having a paid excuse to make the trip east, in the hope of somehow running into her and reconciling, neither of which happened.

"I could never get weak-kneed . . ." McGilligan, *George Cukor*, 86.

"the queen of the roost." Ibid., 125.

Frank Horn. Ibid., 127.

"Until then he was a successful young leading man . . ." Schickel, *Men Who Made the Movies*, 182.

Cukor . . . claimed . . . that he had discovered Grant. For the rest of his life Cukor insisted that *Sylvia Scarlett* was the film that "discovered" Cary Grant and that therefore he, Cukor, was responsible for Grant's long and illustrious Hollywood career. Sarris, in *You Ain't Heard Nothin' Yet*, reflects on all those who claimed Grant as their discovery:

"Mae West has tried to claim credit for 'discovering' Grant for *She Done Him Wrong* but he had already made seven movies before the West come-on certified his stud status. The late George Cukor insisted that *Sylvia Scarlett* put Grant over with the moguls. Since the movie itself was such a commercial and critical dud at the time, and almost destroyed Katharine Hepburn's career, Cukor's assertion seems downright bizarre. Nor did Grant's involvement with Marlene Dietrich and Josef von Sternberg in *Blonde Venus* do much for his own image. Although he was listed in casts with such yesteryear icons as Carole Lombard, Sylvia Sidney, Tallulah Bankhead, Jean Harlow, Frances Farmer, and even Grace Moore, he was most effective in a light-fun way with Nancy Carroll in *Hot Saturday* and *The Woman Accused*, and with Joan Bennett in *Big Brown Eyes* and *Wedding Present*."

"*Sylvia Scarlett* was my breakthrough . . ." Quoted in Nelson, *Evenings with Cary Grant*, 83.

[11]

"I am most keenly reminded . . ." Bogdanovich, *Who the Devil Made It?*, 382.

"If I had stayed at Paramount . . ." Nelson, *Evenings with Cary Grant*, 84.

Grant's decision to leave Paramount. He would not make another movie for Paramount until 1954, when he came out of retirement to star in Alfred Hitchcock's *To Catch a Thief*.

[12]

"As the tall, dark, and handsome male star . . ." Steven Cohan, "Cary Grant in the Fifties: Indiscretions of the Bachelor's Masquerade," *Screen* 33, no. 4 (Winter 1992).

Signing with Frank Vincent. According to Higham and Moseley, *Cary Grant*, Grant was not actually represented by Vincent and Edington but was their partner, having secretly invested much of his savings in the business. Higham and Moseley claim as their source Kendall Carly Browne, Vincent's longtime personal secretary, who "confirmed" that Grant was, in fact, his own agent and split his standard 10 percent commission three ways.

Harry Cohn. Cohn (often referred to as "Horrible" Harry Cohn), his brother Jack, and Joe Brandt had at one time all worked for Carl Laemmle, the founder of Universal Pictures. Cohn began Columbia Pictures in 1924 from C.B.C. Films Sales Company, which he had founded in 1920. C.B.C. stood for Cohn, Brandt, and Cohn. Harry Cohn changed the name after a major financial reorganization, and because everyone in Hollywood referred to it as "Corned Beef and Cabbage."

a vulgarian, womanizer, and tantrum-throwing tyrant. Sarris, *You Ain't Heard Nothin' Yet*, 29.

"Howard was the most restful man . . ." Quoted in Brown and Broeske, *Howard*

Hughes, 125. A necessary word about the nature of the Grant-Hughes relationship, erroneously described in Higham and Moseley. Brown and Broeske express it best: "Following Grant's death in November 1986, writers began depicting their association as a lascivious homosexual affair. Several of them claimed that Hughes and Scott were lovers. Cary and Howard supposedly fell into each other's arms when the romance between Scott and Grant cooled. *But there are no direct sources to prove a Hughes-Grant affair . . . three exhaustive studies of Howard's life found no hints of bisexuality* [emphasis added] . . . 'Howard had so many enemies, including the FBI, that even the most discreet homosexual encounter would have been uncovered,' said Robert Maheu, the former FBI special agent who became Hughes's second-in-command in the 1950s. And Noah Dietrich told his biographers that he had heard the rumors but knew them to be false." Brown and Broeske claim to have read Hughes's entire 2,059-page FBI file, which was personally supervised by J. Edgar Hoover. They insist there is no trace of any homosexual activity on Hughes's part, nor in the 100,000-page legal, sexual, and psychological abstract ordered by the Hughes estate. Curiously, one of Higham and Moseley's "sources" for "proof" of Hughes's homosexuality and his supposedly ongoing affair with Cary Grant was Noah Dietrich, one of Hughes's personal aides, who died before they named him as one of their sources. To date, the author has found no evidence of Hughes's homosexuality, and no one who claims to know of any affair between Hughes and Grant. Brown and Broeske also strongly question Grant's "homosexual" affair with Scott, but their research here is marginal at best.

the famed Trocadero nightspot. The famed restaurant and club was located at 8610 Sunset Boulevard. Along with Ciro's (8433 Sunset) and Mocambo (8588 Sunset), it was the favorite spot for the show-business crowd during the height of the studio era. The Trocadero was one of Grant's favorite places to relax, as was the Brown Derby restaurant, located near Hollywood and Vine.

"For years I had begged Paramount . . ." Quoted in Carroll, *Motion Picture*, February 1941.

Phyllis Brooks on first seeing Cary Grant. "The first time I saw Cary was at Marion Davies' . . . he was there with Ginger Rogers. He was so tanned he was almost black, while Ginger was lobster red from the sun. It was funny." Brooks is quoted in Nelson, *Evenings with Cary Grant*, 89.

"the love of her life." Ibid., 89.

"the Brooks." Waterbury, "Story of Cary Grant," 55.

[13]

"The great majority of screwball comedies . . ." Sarris, *You Ain't Heard Nothin' Yet*, 96–97.

Irene Dunne. Dunne's other film roles prior to *The Awful Truth* include John Stahl's *Back Street* (1932), John Cromwell's *Ann Vickers* (1933), William Seiter's *Roberta* (1935), and James Whale's *Show Boat* (1936). *The Awful Truth* was her twenty-third movie. She would costar opposite Grant twice more, before playing what would become her signature role, Mama in George Stevens's *I Remember Mama* (1948). She was nominated a total of five times for an Academy Award for Best Actress, including for *The Awful Truth*, but never won.

"Frustration arises inevitably . . ." Sarris, *You Ain't Heard Nothin' Yet*, 95. The best short essay on screwball comedy (with essential references) may be found here on pages 89–100.

Frank Capra, who was threatening to walk out on . . . Columbia. Although his relationship with Cohn was a difficult one, Capra continued to make films for Columbia until 1939. In 1934 *It Happened One Night* was the first picture to win all four of the major Academy Awards—Best Picture, Best Director (Capra), Best Actor (Clark Gable), and Best Actress (Claudette Colbert). Capra won again as Best Director in 1936 for *Mr. Deeds Goes to Town*. That picture was nominated as well but lost to Robert Z. Leonard's *The Great Ziegfeld*. Capra won Oscars for *You Can't Take It With You* (1938, Best Director, Best Picture) and nominations for Best Director and Best Picture in 1939 for *Mr. Smith Goes to Washington*. In 1946, as an independent (Liberty Films), he was nominated as Best Director and Best Picture for *It's a Wonderful Life*.

"a comedy of remarriage." Film critic and historian Richard Schickel quotes Cavell on screwball in Schickel, *Cary Grant*, 72–73.

Sons of the Desert. This 1933 Hal Roach comedy was directed by William Seiter and distributed by MGM. In the film, Laurel and Hardy lie about a convention they want to go to, telling their wives that Ollie must go for a curative rest to the mountains. The lie snowballs and nearly causes the two "boys" to lose their wives, before a confession by Laurel more or less redeems them.

Grant and McCarey. Peter Bogdanovich interviewed McCarey in 1969, shortly before his death, and asked the director what it was like to work with Grant on *The Awful Truth*. McCarey responded with a one-word answer: "Impossible." When Bogdanovich asked him in what way, McCarey cited Grant's insecurity. The complete interview may be found in Bogdanovich, *Who the Devil Made It?*

The Awful Truth and the Hays Office. The film tested the limits of the Hays Office in more ways than one. Not only did it hint at unpunished adulterous behavior on the part of its lead, it also dealt comically with divorce, a subject that the censors always found questionable in comedy. The Hays Office much preferred separation by death and a noble widow or widower to even the suggestion of a happy survivor of a bad marriage. Giddy single exes, like double beds, did not often get by the official watchdogs. The film also contained what was, for its day, a very racy bedroom scene between Grant and Dunne, in which the dialogue was colorful and both stars were dressed only in their nightclothes. Dunne, to the consternation of the Hays Office, looked quite fetching in her nightie.

"remarkable for the extent . . ." Andrew Britton, "Cary Grant: Comedy and Male Desire," *Cine-Action!* 7 (1986).

"resplendent but characterless . . ." Kael, "Man from Dream City."

[14]

"Cary Grant represents a man we know." Alfred Hitchcock, from an interview by Peter Bogdanovich, *Esquire*, August 1962.

Radio adaptation of *The Awful Truth*. The radio version proved so popular that Lux repeated it several times. Then, in a highly unusual move that demonstrated nothing so much as the enduring popularity of the film, the Gulf Screen Guild Playhouse purchased the radio rights and did an entirely new version, retaining only Ralph Bellamy from the original cast, with Robert Young and Carole Lombard cast as the Warriners.

while Scott was making Rouben Mamoulian's. The connective strands fascinate. After *The Last of the Mohicans*, Scott made one more film at Paramount, Rouben Mamoulian's *High, Wide, and Handsome*, which costarred Irene Dunne, just before she was let go in the general bloodletting that took place at the struggling studio. Dunne moved to Columbia, where she was immediately cast opposite Grant in *The Awful Truth*. Scott then moved to Fox, where he appeared in *Rebecca of Sunnybrook Farm*.

***Bringing Up Baby*.** Some of the background on production and finances is from McCarthy, *Howard Hawks*. Other sources as cited.

the two had to "lock-step" their way to the manager's office. The Hays Office finally approved the scene because of its heavy comic content, after being convinced by Hawks that absolutely no erotic intent was attached to or suggested by the scene.

[15]

"Only one actor was agile enough . . ." "Appreciations," *New York Times*, July 1, 2003, editorial page.

"Sure, the government gets eighty-one cents . . ." Quoted in Waterbury, "Story of Cary Grant." The interview was conducted in the spring of 1938, before Grant's sudden departure in October for London.

***The Awful Truth* was nominated for Best Picture . . .** The other Best Picture nominees for 1937 were Victor Fleming's *Captains Courageous*, William Wyler's *Dead End*, Sidney Franklin's *The Good Earth*, Henry King's *In Old Chicago*, Frank Capra's *Lost Horizon*, Henry Koster's *One Hundred Men and a Girl*, Gregory La Cava's *Stage Door*, William Wellman's *A Star Is Born*, and the winner, William Dieterle's *The Life of Emile Zola*. The other Best Actress nominees were Greta Garbo (George Cukor's *Camille*), Janet Gaynor (*A Star Is Born*), Barbara Stanwyck (King Vidor's *Stella Dallas*), and the winner, Luise Rainer (*The Good Earth*). The other Best Supporting Actor nominees were Thomas Mitchell (John Ford and Stuart Heisler's *The Hurricane*), H. B. Warner (*Lost Horizon*), Roland Young (*Topper*, another Cary Grant movie), and the winner, Joseph Schildkraut (*The Life of Emile Zola*). The other Best Director nominees were William Dieterle (*The Life of Emile Zola*), Sidney Franklin (*The Good Earth*), Gregory La Cava (*Stage Door*), and William Wellman (*A Star Is Born*).

Grant at the 1938 Academy Awards. As their player contracts expired, more and more actors attempted to go "the Cary Grant route," something the studio heads feared might one day bring down the structure of the entire system. Within a month of that year's ceremonies, the U.S. government formally instituted an antitrust suit against the studios, claiming that their absolute control over the three branches of their business—the production, distribution, and exhibition of movies—constituted an illegal monopoly that prevented independent filmmakers and theater owners from fairly competing for talent, distribution, and houses to screen their product. In 1948 the case finally came before the Supreme Court, and the studios signed a consent decree that ended their iron grip on Hollywood filmmaking forever. (See notes for "One.")

a party at "21" to meet Alfred Hitchcock. Hitchcock first arrived in America on August 22, 1938, aboard the *Queen Mary*. He was accompanied by his wife, Alma, and their daughter, Patricia.

"One of the marks of a great director . . ." Haskell, *Holding My Own,* 25.

Cary Grant's 1939 visit to London and Bristol. Some of the information for this sequence of events comes from McCann, *Cary Grant.* Additional material comes from an article by Philip French, in *London Observer,* August 25, 1996. The author contacted the FBI on several occasions, under the auspices of the Freedom of Information Act, to obtain Cary Grant's FBI file. The official response was a carefully worded statement that said no such file existed. In a letter dated January 17, 2003, in response to "Request #0971956-000, regarding Cary Grant," the FBI stated, "Based on the information furnished, a search of the automated indices to our central records system files at FBI headquarters located no records responsive to your FOIPA request to indicate you and/or the subject(s) of your request have ever been of investigatory interest to the FBI."

"picture of another sucker." Quoted in an article by Norma Abrams and Gerald Duncan, *New York Daily News,* December 12, 1938.

[16]

"If you haven't seen Cary Grant . . ." Bogdanovich, *Movie of the Week,* 97.

As Peter Bogdanovich rightly points out. Ibid.

"They both wanted the beach house . . ." Interview by the author. The source of this quote wishes to remain anonymous.

[17]

"Cukor's strategy was to keep Cary Grant . . ." McGilligan, *George Cukor,* 162.

"Plenty of room up front." This was one of Grant's favorite parables. He told it for years. It first found its way into print in an interview conducted by Duncan Underhill for the *New York World-Telegram,* January 24, 1942.

"Cash and Cary." The idea that Grant, who had previously married one of the most beautiful women in Hollywood, would be interested in the rather homely Barbara Hutton led everyone, including the gossip columnists, to suspect that his motives were other than true love. The phrase "Cash and Cary" became something of a joke in Hollywood, whenever the Grant-Hutton relationship was spoken of, which was quite often. Its appearances in the gossip columns amused neither Hutton nor Grant.

Goldwyn was . . . "mad for the material." Berg, *Goldwyn*, 316.

"I am heartbroken . . ." Ibid.

"When I go to the movies . . ." Grant, interviewed by Carroll, *Motion Picture*, February 1941.

"Irene and I sit here and worry . . ." Ibid.

Grant's relatives killed. The bombing raid on Bristol was reported in the *Los Angeles Examiner* and the *New York Daily News*, January 28, 1941.

[18]

"The consensus was that audiences . . ." Hitchcock, quoted in "Murder—With English on It," *New York Times Magazine*, March 3, 1957.

"a minor figure in a fast film industry . . ." Quoted in Spoto, *Dark Side of Genius*, 222.

[19]

"Cary Grant is a great comedian . . ." Quoted in Schickel, *Men Who Made the Movies*.

"a dear, dear man." Quoted in McBride, *Frank Capra*, 445.

Grant's special affection for Jean Adair. Details of this story are from the *New York Daily Mirror*, September 11, 1944.

Grant wearing only the tops of his pajamas. From a syndicated Tintypes column by Sidney Skolsky, "Hollywood Is My Beat," January 3, 1946.

"among the industry's . . . most pro-Communist offerings." Internal FBI memorandum, May 11, 1944.

"known Communist connections . . ." Internal FBI memorandum, November 20, 1944.

"no chance of reconciliation." Quoted in Florabel Muir, *New York Daily News*, August 16, 1944.

[20]

"I can't portray Bing Crosby . . ." Quoted in Kent Schuelke, "Cary Grant," *Interview*, January 1987. This was one of Grant's final sit-downs, conducted four months before his death.

"Why, Cary Grant, of course!" Cole Porter's often-quoted comment likely came after Grant had already been offered the part. In fact, Porter's first choice was his very close friend Fred Astaire, who wanted no part of it.

"I know of not one single soul . . ." Govoni, *Cary Grant*, 131. It is safe to say there was no love lost between Wilder and Grant. Years later, when interviewed by Al Cohn at

Newsday (December 19, 1964), Grant was reminded of Wilder's comment and tersely replied, "Well, maybe *he* hasn't been to my house. Maybe he doesn't know the same people I know." While Grant never appeared in a Billy Wilder film, in 1958 Wilder directed *Some Like It Hot*, in which Tony Curtis did a devastatingly accurate impersonation of Grant, as a character who had trouble making love to women.

Hughes had the bathrooms custom-built. Brown and Broeske, *Howard Hughes*, 302.

Cook's budget and cold turkey sandwiches. Lloyd Shearer, "Intelligence Report," *Parade*, March 12, 1989.

"there wasn't a paper . . ." Quoted in Barlett and Steele, *Empire*, 164.

peanut butter and jelly sandwiches at "21." Walter Weiss [maître d'] obituary, *The New York Times*, October 15, 2002.

"It was all very flattering . . ." Quoted in Brown and Broeske, *Howard Hughes*, 251.

[21]

"*Notorious* resumes the general visual key . . ." Durgnat, *Strange Case of Alfred Hitchcock*, 195.

"carefully trained and coached . . ." Margaret McDonnell (a contract story editor), a memo to David O. Selznick, August 7, 1944. In the memo McDonnell conveyed Hitchcock's idea for a new movie she had discussed with him at "a long lunch last Friday." This germ of an idea may be seen again in several later Hitchcock films, by both genders, and across generations, most vividly in *Strangers on a Train, To Catch a Thief, Vertigo, North by Northwest,* and *Psycho*.

"a kissing sequence that made . . ." Sarris, *You Ain't Seen Nothin' Yet*, 257.

[22]

"I'd been flying for a lot longer . . ." Quoted in McCarthy, *Howard Hawks*, 156–57.

"All we did was to change plans . . ." Hedda Hopper, *Chicago Tribune*, June 26, 1947.

Grant joins MCA. This arrangement was to last only three years. While it started off well, Stein's vision of the agency as a packager of its own talent ultimately proved unacceptable to Grant.

"a rather conceited, impudent . . ." Telegram, Grant to Samuel Goldwyn, January 2, 1947.

[23]

"I've been called the longest lasting young man . . ." Cary Grant, "What It Means to Be a Star," *Films and Filming*, July 1961.

"Cary came out weighing . . ." Quoted in McCarthy, *Howard Hawks*, 461. See also ibid., chap. 29.

"One problem with the show . . ." William Frye, interview by the author.

[24]

"Selectivity always suggests art . . ." Schickel, *Cary Grant.*

the directing debut of Richard Brooks. *Crisis* was the inauspicious start to a very successful Hollywood career. Among the films Brooks would go on to direct are *The Last Time I Saw Paris* (1954), *Blackboard Jungle* (1955), *Something of Value* (1957), *Elmer Gantry* (1960), and *In Cold Blood* (1967).

A *Star Is Born.* Some of the background information given here comes from Haver, *Star Is Born,* 191–205, and McGilligan, *George Cukor,* 218–24. The meeting between Cukor and Grant is almost always mistakenly reported as happening much later, *after* the film's 1954 release. The meeting actually took place in December 1952, when Cukor (who had been offered the original 1937 version but turned it down) began interviewing actresses to play the role of Esther. The first actress he saw, in December 1952, was Judy Garland. That same month he began his ultimately unsuccessful campaign to enlist the acting services of Cary Grant.

"This is the part you were born to play!" and Grant's response. McGilligan, *George Cukor,* 219.

"one of those periodically increasing episodes . . ." Interview by the author. The source wishes to and will remain anonymous.

"Heavy romance on the screen . . ." Quoted in Lon Jones, *Star Weekly,* January 1952.

Cropped Grant-Monroe-DiMaggio photo. Summers, *Goddess,* 66–67.

"Cary was being very mysterious." William Frye, interview by the author.

"It was the period of blue jeans . . ." Quoted in Robert C. Roman, "Cary Grant," *Films in Review,* December 1961.

"[Chaplin] has given great pleasure to millions . . ." Grant, press conference to announce his retirement from film, *New York Daily News,* February 6, 1953.

[25]

"The results of living in reality . . ." Quoted in Earl Wilson's syndicated column, "It Happened Last Night," circa 1971.

Details of Grant's Palm Springs home and life. Betsy Drake, as told to Liza Wilson, "My Life with Cary Grant," *American Weekly,* August 4, 1957.

Grace Kelly. During her off days, when her presence wasn't required for shooting, Kelly liked to go over to the tiny principality of Monaco, to gamble in the state casino and visit the state gardens. While on one such visit, she was introduced to Prince Rainier Grimaldi, who insisted on giving her a personal tour of the Grimaldi castle, overlooking the waters of the Mediterranean.

[26]

"I had a theme in most of my movies . . ." *New York Times,* July 21, 1955.

"The movies are like the steel business . . ." Interview in *Pix,* December 10, 1955.

"the easiest decision I ever had to make." Quoted in Hotchner, *Sophia*, 105.

Drake's telegram to Grant. Betsy Drake, as told to Liza Wilson, "My Life with Cary Grant," *American Weekly*, August 4, 1957.

"We fell in love . . ." Hotchner, *Sophia*, 110–12.

[27]

"Nobody doesn't like Cary Grant . . ." Warren Hoge, "The Other Cary Grant," *The New York Times Magazine*, July 31, 1977.

"I'd taken advice . . ." Interview by Peter Shield, *Sunday Graphic*, October 19, 1958. Portions of this interview appear in Godfrey, *Cary Grant*, 152–53.

"It was all just some sort of extended daydream . . ." William Frye, interview by the author.

[28]

"In *North by Northwest* during the scene . . ." Hitchcock, speech to the Screen Producers Guild, March 7, 1965, upon the occasion of his receiving the Guild's twelfth Milestone Award.

"to accept the responsibility for my own actions . . ." Grant, "Archie Leach." Additional information and quotes from Grant's diaries are from John Whalen, "The Trip," *Los Angeles Weekly*, July 9, 1998.

[29]

"I've heard the fag rumor . . ." Quoted in Jeffrey Robinson, "Cary Grant: 'I've Lived My Life,'" *Redbook*, March 1987, p. 28.

Joint statement of separation. The statement was issued jointly by Grant and Drake and appeared in the *Los Angeles Times*, October 17, 1958.

"I was doing so swell those days . . ." Curtis, *Tony Curtis*.

"I never worked it deliberately . . ." Ibid.

Grant's "autobiography." Grant, "Archie Leach."

Instead, the magazine went ahead and ran its lengthy contracted LSD story. Bergquist, "Curious Story."

[30]

"I was a self-centered boor . . ." Lecture to an audience of students at UCLA, July 14, 1962.

"tycoon, bargaining with a mind . . ." Bergquist, "Curious Story."

Details of Grant's Universal contract. *Newsday*, December 19, 1964.

"The final outrage . . ." McDougal, *Last Mogul*, 259–60.

Grant films grossed more than $10 million at Radio City. *Variety*, January 6, 1960.

"there is no doubt that I am aging . . ." Quoted in *The New York Times*, February 2, 1961.

Mitchum and Grant's relationship during *The Grass Is Greener*. Some information and the Mitchum quote come from Server.

"Cary played a titled Englishman . . ." Quoted in *The New Yorker*, January 13, 2000.

Grant and Drake visiting Monaco. Some of the information and the quote is from Spada, *Grace*, 226–27. Other sources wish to and will remain anonymous.

[31]

"How old Cary Grant? . . ." In 1962, *Time*, doing a story on Grant, was said to have wired the question to Grant, who sent back his "Old Cary Grant" reply. The story is apocryphal; no telegram was ever sent to Grant; nor did he ever reply in kind.

"I had just returned from Rome . . ." Interview by Henry Gris, *Coronet*, March 1971.

"Cary called me . . ." Ibid.

"I bombed right in front of Wald." Quoted in Dean Gautschy, *Los Angeles Herald-Examiner*, September 28, 1963.

"No matter how good I am . . ." Quoted in Al Cohn, *Newsday*, December 19, 1964.

"consistently better than ordinary . . ." Andrew Sarris, *Village Voice*, January 1, 1964.

"I don't know . . ." Grant, quoted by Charles Champlin, *Los Angeles Times*, December 1, 1996 (obit.).

"I'm only telling you . . ." Interview by Roderick Mann, *Sunday Graphic*, July 31, 1965.

[32]

"I don't like to see men of my age . . ." Interview by Sheilah Graham, *Hollywood Citizen-News*, February 8, 1966.

"One does join in the stream of life . . ." Quoted in *New York Daily News*, February 28, 1966.

"I was sitting up front in the car . . ." Interview by *Ticketron*, 1972.

Grant and Cannon disagree before the press. Reported in *Variety*, August 10, 1966.

Grant declared that the institution of marriage was dying. *Los Angeles Times*, August 7, 1966.

"He struck me as an angry . . ." Interview by the author. Information regarding Grant's relationship with Taplinger, Flynn, Blackman, and Barrie is from various sources, as noted, including this interview. All Flynn quotes in this chapter are from my interview with her.

Cannon's testimony. This and all other testimony quoted is from court records, Los Angeles Superior Court.

Friendship with George Barrie. Barrie first called Grant after reading an interview in which Grant objected to women using hairspray. After Grant's statement, the company's stock had fallen one full point. Once they got to know each other they became frequent social companions. Grant always said he admired Barrie for having built his cosmetics empire from scratch.

[33]

"Every one of my wives left me . . ." Interview in *The New York Times*, 1971.

"My first wife . . ." Quoted in Donaldson, 202–203.

"she never smoked . . ." Quoted in *Variety*, January 24, 1973.

"I was there the night Mr. Grant called . . ." Joey Reynolds, interview by the author.

"Jennifer once walked up to the screen . . ." Interview by Al Cohn, *Newsday*, September 14, 1975.

"My intention was to make myself happy . . ." Guy Flatley, "About Cary Grant: From Mae to September," *New York Times*, July 22, 1973.

"Jennifer is my best production." Quoted in Warren Hoge, "The Other Cary Grant," *The New York Times Magazine*, July 31, 1977.

"as periodically dependable . . ." The quipper wishes anonymity.

"I wouldn't think of it . . ." Interview by Tom Shales for the *Washington Post*, reprinted in the *Los Angeles Times*, December 25, 1981.

"I stayed close to Cary always . . ." Curtis, *Tony Curtis*.

Grant and Charlie Callas. Charlie Callas, interview by the author.

Grant trying to sound Jewish . . . Ibid.

"I remember . . ." Lecture at Flint Center, DeAnza Community College, Cupertino, California, November 3, 1982.

"I don't have the energy for it . . ." Lecture at the Masonic Auditorium at San Francisco, as reported by Jennings Parrott in the *Los Angeles Times*, January 31, 1985. A detailed recapitulation of Grant's presentations may be found in Nelson, *Evenings with Cary Grant*.

Comments of doctors during Grant's stroke. There are several sources for the comments of Drs. Manlove and Gilson, and paramedic Lund, including the *Los Angeles Times*, *People*, and Warren G. Harris, *Good Housekeeping*, September 1987.

[34]

"I don't know how I consider death . . ." *People*, December 15, 1986.

"I would like to be remembered as a congenial fellow . . ." Quoted by Kent Schuelke, *Interview*, "Cary Grant," January 1987.

FILMOGRAPHY

FEATURE FILMS

THIS IS THE NIGHT (1932, year of release). Paramount Publix. Directed by Frank Tuttle. Produced by Benjamin Glazer. Screenplay by Avery Hopwood and Benjamin Glazer, from *Pouche*, by René Peter and Henri Falk, also George Marion Jr. and René Peter. Principal cast: Lily Damita, Charles Ruggles, Roland Young, Thelma Todd, Cary Grant, Irving Bacon. B&W.

SINNERS IN THE SUN (1932). Paramount Publix. Directed by Alexander Hall. Produced by Paramount Publix. Screenplay by Vincent Lawrence, Waldemar Young, and Samuel Hoffenstein, from a story by Mildred Cram. Principal cast: Carole Lombard, Chester Morris, Adrienne Ames, Alison Skipworth, Walter Byron, Reginald Barlow, Zita Moulton, Cary Grant. B&W.

MERRILY WE GO TO HELL (1932). Paramount Publix. Directed by Dorothy Arzner. Produced by Paramount Publix. Screenplay by Edwin Justus Mayer, from *I, Jerry, Take Thee, Joan*, by Cleo Lucas. Principal cast: Sylvia Sidney, Fredric March, Adrianne Allen, Skeets Gallagher, Florence Britton, Esther Howard, George Irving, Kent Taylor, Charles Coleman, Leonard Carey, Cary Grant. B&W.

DEVIL AND THE DEEP (1932). Paramount Publix. Directed by Marion Gering. Produced by Paramount Publix. Screenplay by Benn Levy and Harry Hervey. Principal cast: Tallulah Bankhead, Gary Cooper, Charles Laughton, Cary Grant, Gordon Westcott, Paul Porcasi, Juliette Compton, Arthur Hoyt, Dorothy Christy. B&W.

BLONDE VENUS (1932). Paramount Publix. Directed by Josef von Sternberg. Produced by Paramount Publix (Josef von Sternberg, uncredited). Screenplay by Jules Furthman and S. K. Lauren, from a story by Josef von Sternberg. Principal cast: Marlene Dietrich, Herbert Marshall, Cary Grant, Dickie Moore, Gene Morgan, Rita La Roy, Sidney Toler, Cecil Cunningham. B&W.

HOT SATURDAY (1932). Paramount Publix. Directed by William A. Seiter. Produced by Paramount Publix. Screenplay by Seton I. Miller, Josephine Lovett, and Joseph

Moncure March, from the novel by Harvey Fergusson. Principal cast: Nancy Carroll, Cary Grant, Randolph Scott, Edward Woods, Lilian Bond, William Collier Sr., Jane Darwell, Rita La Roy, Grady Sutton. B&W.

MADAME BUTTERFLY (1932). Paramount Publix. Directed by Marion Gering. Produced by Paramount Publix. Screenplay by Josephine Lovett and Joseph Moncure March, from a story by John Luther Long and the play by David Belasco. Principal cast: Sylvia Sidney, Cary Grant, Charles Ruggles, Sándor Kállay, Irving Pichel, Helen Jerome Eddy, Edmund Breese, Sheila Terry. B&W.

SHE DONE HIM WRONG (1933). Paramount Publix. Directed by Lowell Sherman. Produced by Paramount Publix. Screenplay by Harvey Thew and John Bright, adapted from the play *She Done Him Wrong*, by Mae West. Principal cast: Mae West, Cary Grant, Gilbert Roland, Noah Beery, Rafaela Ottiano, David Landau, Rochelle Hudson, Owen Moore, Fuzzy Knight, Louise Beavers, Dewey Robinson, Grace La Rue. B&W.

WOMAN ACCUSED (1933). Paramount Publix. Directed by Paul Sloane. Produced by Paramount Publix. Screenplay by Bayard Veiller, based on a story by Polan Banks, from a *Liberty* magazine serial: individual episodes by Rupert Hughes, Vicki Baum, Zane Grey, Viña Delmar, Irvin S. Cobb, Gertrude Atherton, J. P. McEvoy, Ursula Parrott, Polan Banks, and Sophie Kerr. Principal cast: Nancy Carroll, Cary Grant, John Halliday, Irving Pichel, Louis Calhern, Norma Mitchell, Jack La Rue, Frank Sheridan, John Lodge, Lona Andre. B&W.

THE EAGLE AND THE HAWK (1933). Paramount Publix. Directed by Stuart Walker. Produced by Paramount Publix. Screenplay by Bogart Rogers and Seton I. Miller, from a story by John Monk Saunders. Principal cast: Fredric March, Cary Grant, Jack Oakie, Carole Lombard, Sir Guy Standing, Forrester Harvey, Virginia Hammond. B&W.

GAMBLING SHIP (1933). Paramount Publix. Directed by Louis J. Gasnier and Max Marcin. Produced by Paramount Publix. Screenplay by Max Marcin, Seton I. Miller, and Claude Binyon, from stories by Peter Ruric. Principal cast: Cary Grant, Benita Hume, Roscoe Karns, Glenda Farrell, Jack La Rue, Arthur Vinton, Edward Gargan. B&W.

I'M NO ANGEL (1933). Paramount Publix. Directed by Wesley Ruggles. Screenplay by Mae West and Lowell Brentano. Produced by Paramount Publix. Principal cast: Mae West, Cary Grant, Edward Arnold, Ralf Harolde, Russell Hopton, Gertrude Michael, Kent Taylor, Dorothy Peterson, Gregory Ratoff, Gertrude Howard, Nat Pendleton. B&W.

ALICE IN WONDERLAND (1933). Directed by Norman Z. McLeod. Produced by Paramount Publix. Screenplay by Joseph L. Mankiewicz and William Cameron Menzies, from the writings of Lewis Carroll. Principal cast: Charlotte Henry, Richard Arlen, Roscoe Ates, Gary Cooper, Leon Errol, Louise Fazenda, W. C. Fields, Skeets Gallagher, Cary Grant, Sterling Holloway, Edward Everett Horton, Roscoe Karns,

Baby LeRoy, Mae Marsh, Polly Moran, Jack Oakie, Edna May Oliver, May Robson, Charles Ruggles, Alison Skipworth, Ned Sparks. B&W.

THIRTY DAY PRINCESS (1934). Paramount Publix. Directed by Marion Gering. Produced by B. P. Schulberg, Schulberg Productions. Screenplay by Preston Sturges, Frank Partos, Sam Hellman, and Edwin Justus Mayer, from a story by Clarence Budington Kelland. Principal cast: Sylvia Sidney, Cary Grant, Edward Arnold, Henry Stephenson, Vince Barnett, Edgar Norton, Lucien Littlefield. B&W.

BORN TO BE BAD (1934). United Artists. Directed by Lowell Sherman. Produced by 20th Century. Screenplay by Ralph Graves and Harrison Jacobs. Principal cast: Loretta Young, Cary Grant, Jackie Kelk, Henry Travers, Russell Hopton, Andrew Tombes, Marion Burns, Paul Harvey. B&W.

KISS AND MAKE UP (1934). Paramount Publix. Directed by Harlan Thompson. Produced by B. P. Schulberg. Screenplay by Harlan Thompson, George Marion Jr., and Jane Hinton, from a story by István Békeffy. Principal cast: Cary Grant, Helen Mack, Genevieve Tobin, Edward Everett Horton, Lucien Littlefield, Mona Maris, Toby Wing. B&W.

LADIES SHOULD LISTEN (1934). Paramount Publix. Directed by Frank Tuttle. Produced by Douglas MacLean. Screenplay by Claude Binyon and Frank Butler, from a play by Alfred Savoir and Guy Bolton. Principal cast: Cary Grant, Frances Drake, Edward Everett Horton, Rosita Moreno, George Barbier, Nydia Westman, Charles Ray, Clara Lou Sheridan. B&W.

ENTER MADAME (1935). Paramount Publix. Directed by Elliott Nugent. Produced by Benjamin Glazer. Screenplay by Charles Brackett and Gladys Lehman, from a play by Gilda Varesi Archibald and Dorothea Donn-Byrne. Principal cast: Elissa Landi, Cary Grant, Lynne Overman, Sharon Lynn, Michelette Burani, Paul Porcasi, Adrian Rosley, Cecilia Parker, Frank Albertson, Diana Lewis. B&W.

WINGS IN THE DARK (1935). Paramount Pictures. Directed by James Flood. Produced by Arthur Hornblow Jr. Screenplay by Jack Kirkland, Frank Partos, Dale Van Every, and E. H. Robinson, from a story by Nell Shipman and Philip Hurn. Principal cast: Myrna Loy, Cary Grant, Roscoe Karns, Hobart Cavanaugh, Dean Jagger, Samuel S. Hinds, Bert Hanlon, Graham McNamee. B&W.

THE LAST OUTPOST (1935). Paramount Pictures. Directed by Charles Barton and Louis Gasnier. Produced by E. Lloyd Sheldon. Screenplay by Philip MacDonald, Frank Partos, and Charles Brackett, from a story by F. Britten Austin. Principal cast: Cary Grant, Claude Rains, Gertrude Michael, Kathleen Burke, Colin Tapley, Akim Tamiroff, Billy Bevan, Margaret Swope. B&W.

SYLVIA SCARLETT (1936). RKO Radio. Directed by George Cukor. Produced by Pandro S. Berman. Screenplay by Gladys Unger, John Collier, and Mortimer Offner, from the novel by Compton MacKenzie. Principal cast: Katharine Hepburn, Cary Grant, Brian Aherne, Edmund Gwenn, Natalie Paley, Dennie Moore, Lennox Pawle. B&W.

BIG BROWN EYES (1936). Paramount Pictures. Directed by Raoul Walsh. Produced by

Walter Wanger. Screenplay by Raoul Walsh and Bert Hanlon, from a story by James Edward Grant. Principal cast: Cary Grant, Joan Bennett, Walter Pidgeon, Lloyd Nolan, Alan Baxter, Marjorie Gateson, Isabel Jewell, Douglas Fowley. B&W.

SUZY (1936). MGM. Directed by George Fitzmaurice. Produced by Maurice Revnes. Screenplay by Dorothy Parker, Alan Campbell, Horace Jackson, and Lenore Coffee, from a novel by Herbert Gorman. Principal cast: Jean Harlow, Franchot Tone, Cary Grant, Lewis Stone, Benita Hume, Reginald Mason, Inez Courtney, Una O'Connor. B&W.

WEDDING PRESENT (1936). Paramount Pictures. Directed by Richard Wallace. Produced by B. P. Schulberg. Screenplay by Joseph Anthony, from a story by Paul Gallico. Principal cast: Joan Bennett, Cary Grant, George Bancroft, Conrad Nagel, Gene Lockhart, William Demarest, Inez Courtney, Edward Brophy, Lois Wilson. B&W.

WHEN YOU'RE IN LOVE (1937). Columbia. Directed by Robert Riskin. Produced by Everett Riskin. Screenplay by Robert Riskin, from a story by Ethel Hill and Cedric Worth. Principal cast: Grace Moore, Cary Grant, Aline MacMahon, Henry Stephenson, Thomas Mitchell, Catherine Doucet, Luis Alberni, Emma Dunn, Frank Puglia. B&W.

THE AMAZING QUEST OF ERNEST BLISS (AKA ROMANCE AND RICHES) (1937). Grand National. Directed and produced by Alfred Zeisler. Screenplay by John L. Balderston, from a short story, "The Amazing Quest of Ernest Bliss," by E. Phillips Oppenheim. Principal cast: Cary Grant, Mary Brian, Peter Gawthorne, Henry Kendall, Iris Ashley, Leon M. Lion, John Turnbull. B&W.

TOPPER (1937). MGM. Directed by Norman Z. McLeod. Produced by Hal Roach. Screenplay by Jack Jevne, Eric Hatch, and Eddie Moran, from *The Jovial Ghosts* by Thorne Smith. Principal cast: Constance Bennett, Cary Grant, Roland Young, Billie Burke, Alan Mowbray, Eugene Pallette, Arthur Lake, Hedda Hopper, Virginia Sale, Hoagy Carmichael. B&W.

THE TOAST OF NEW YORK (1937). RKO Radio. Directed by Rowland V. Lee. Produced by Edward Small. Screenplay by Dudley Nichols, John Twist, and Joel Sayre, from *The Book of Daniel Drew* by Bouck White and *Robber Barons* by Matthew Josephson. Principal cast: Edward Arnold, Cary Grant, Frances Farmer, Jack Oakie, Donald Meek, Thelma Leeds, Clarence Kolb, Billy Gilbert, George Irving, Oscar Apfel, Dewey Robinson, Gavin Gordon, Joyce Compton. B&W.

THE AWFUL TRUTH (1937). Columbia. Directed and produced by Leo McCarey. Screenplay by Viña Delmar, from a story by Arthur Richman. Principal cast: Irene Dunne, Cary Grant, Ralph Bellamy, Alexander D'Arcy, Cecil Cunningham, Esther Dale, Joyce Compton, Mary Forbes, Zita Moulton, Bess Flowers. B&W.

BRINGING UP BABY (1938). RKO Radio. Directed by Howard Hawks. Produced by Howard Hawks and Cliff Reid. Screenplay by Dudley Nichols and Hagar Wilde. Principal cast: Katharine Hepburn, Cary Grant, Charles Ruggles, Walter Catlett,

Barry Fitzgerald, May Robson, Fritz Feld, Leona Roberts, George Irving, Tala Birell. B&W.

HOLIDAY (1938). Columbia. Directed by George Cukor. Produced by Everett Riskin. Screenplay by Donald Ogden Stewart and Sidney Buchman. Principal cast: Katharine Hepburn, Cary Grant, Doris Nolan, Lew Ayres, Edward Everett Horton, Henry Kolker, Binnie Barnes, Jean Dixon, Henry Daniell. B&W.

GUNGA DIN (1939). RKO Radio. Directed and produced by George Stevens. Screenplay by Ben Hecht, Charles MacArthur, Joel Sayre, and Fred Guiol, inspired by the poem by Rudyard Kipling. Principal cast: Cary Grant, Victor McLaglen, Douglas Fairbanks Jr., Sam Jaffe, Eduardo Ciannelli, Joan Fontaine, Montagu Love, Robert Coote, Abner Biberman, Lumsden Hare, Ann Evers. B&W.

ONLY ANGELS HAVE WINGS (1939). Columbia. Directed and produced by Howard Hawks. Screenplay by Jules Furthman, from a story by Howard Hawks. Principal cast: Cary Grant, Jean Arthur, Richard Barthelmess, Rita Hayworth, Thomas Mitchell, Sig Ruman, Victor Kilian, John Carroll, Allyn Joslyn, Donald Barry, Noah Beery Jr., Milisa Sierra. B&W.

IN NAME ONLY (1939). RKO Radio. Directed by John Cromwell. Produced by George Haight. Screenplay by Richard Sherman from the novel *Memory of Love* by Bessie Breuer. Principal cast: Carole Lombard, Cary Grant, Kay Francis, Charles Coburn, Helen Vinson, Katharine Alexander, Jonathan Hale, Nella Walker, Peggy Ann Garner. B&W.

HIS GIRL FRIDAY (1940). Columbia. Directed and produced by Howard Hawks. Screenplay by Charles Lederer, from *The Front Page* by Ben Hecht and Charles MacArthur. Principal cast: Cary Grant, Rosalind Russell, Ralph Bellamy, Gene Lockhart, Porter Hall, Ernest Truex, Cliff Edwards, Clarence Kolb, Roscoe Karns, Frank Jenks, Regis Toomey, Abner Biberman, Frank Orth, John Qualen, Helen Mack, Alma Kruger, Billy Gilbert, Pat West. B&W.

MY FAVORITE WIFE (1940). RKO Radio. Directed by Garson Kanin. Produced by Leo McCarey. Screenplay by Sam and Bella Spewack, from *Enoch Arden* by Alfred Tennyson. Principal cast: Irene Dunne, Cary Grant, Randolph Scott, Gail Patrick, Ann Shoemaker, Scotty Beckett, Mary Lou Harrington, Donald MacBride, Pedro de Cordoba. B&W.

THE HOWARDS OF VIRGINIA (1940). Columbia. Directed and produced by Frank Lloyd. Screenplay by Sidney Buchman, from *The Tree of Liberty* by Elizabeth Page. Principal cast: Cary Grant, Martha Scott, Sir Cedric Hardwicke, Alan Marshal, Richard Carlson, Paul Kelly, Irving Bacon, Elizabeth Risdon, Anne Revere, Richard Gaines, George Houston. B&W.

THE PHILADELPHIA STORY (1940). MGM. Directed by George Cukor. Produced by Joseph L. Mankiewicz. Screenplay by Donald Ogden Stewart, based on the play by Philip Barry. Principal cast: Cary Grant, Katharine Hepburn, James Stewart, Ruth Hussey, John Howard, Roland Young. B&W.

PENNY SERENADE (1941). Columbia. Directed by George Stevens. Produced by Fred Guiol and George Stevens. Screenplay by Morrie Ryskind, based on a story by Martha Cheavens. Principal cast: Cary Grant, Irene Dunne, Beulah Bondi, Edgar Buchanan, Ann Doran. B&W.

SUSPICION (1941). Columbia. Directed by Alfred Hitchcock. Produced by Alfred Hitchcock (uncredited). Screenplay by Samson Raphaelson, Joan Harrison, Alma Reville (and Hitchcock, uncredited), based on Francis Iles's novel *Before the Fact*. Principal cast: Cary Grant, Joan Fontaine, Sir Cedric Hardwicke, Nigel Bruce, Dame May Whitty. B&W.

THE TALK OF THE TOWN (1942). Columbia. Directed by George Stevens. Produced by George Stevens and Fred Guiol. Screenplay by Irwin Shaw and Sidney Buchman, based on a story by Sidney Harmon. Principal cast: Cary Grant, Jean Arthur, Ronald Colman, Edgar Buchanan, Glenda Farrell. B&W.

ONCE UPON A HONEYMOON (1942). RKO Radio. Directed and produced by Leo McCarey. Screenplay by Sheridan Gibney, based on a story by Leo McCarey. Principal cast: Cary Grant, Ginger Rogers, Walter Slezak, Albert Dekker, Albert Bassermann. B&W.

MR. LUCKY (1943). RKO Radio. Directed by H. C. Potter. Produced by David Hempstead. Screenplay by Milton Holmes and Adrian Scott, based on a story by Milton Holmes. Principal cast: Cary Grant, Laraine Day, Charles Bickford, Gladys Cooper, Alan Carney. B&W.

DESTINATION TOKYO (1943). Warner Bros. Directed by Delmer Daves. Produced by Jerry Wald. Screenplay by Delmer Daves and Albert Maltz, based on a story by Steve Fisher. Principal cast: Cary Grant, John Garfield, Alan Hale, John Ridgely, Dane Clark. B&W.

ONCE UPON A TIME (1944). Columbia. Directed by Alexander Hall. Produced by Louis F. Edelman. Screenplay by Lewis Meltzer and Oscar Saul. Principal cast: Cary Grant, Janet Blair, James Gleason, Ted Donaldson, William Demarest. B&W.

NONE BUT THE LONELY HEART (1944). RKO Radio. Directed by Clifford Odets. Produced by David Hempstead. Screenplay by Clifford Odets, based on a novel by Richard Llewellyn. Principal cast: Cary Grant, Ethel Barrymore, Jane Wyatt, June Duprez, Barry Fitzgerald. B&W.

ARSENIC AND OLD LACE (1944). Warner Bros. Directed and produced by Frank Capra. Screenplay by Julius J. Epstein and Philip G. Epstein, with contributions from Howard Lindsay and Russell Crouse, based on the play by Joseph Kesselring. Principal cast: Cary Grant, Josephine Hull, Jean Adair, Raymond Massey, Priscilla Lane, Jack Carson, Peter Lorre, Edward Everett Horton. B&W.

NIGHT AND DAY (1946). Warner Bros. Directed by Michael Curtiz. Produced by Arthur Schwartz. Screenplay by Charles Hoffman, Leo Townsend, and William Bowers. Principal cast: Cary Grant, Alexis Smith, Monty Woolley, Ginny Simms, Jane Wyman, Mary Martin. Technicolor.

NOTORIOUS (1946). RKO Radio. Directed and produced by Alfred Hitchcock.

Screenplay by Ben Hecht. Principal cast: Cary Grant, Ingrid Bergman, Claude Rains, Louis Calhern, Madame Leopoldine Konstantin. B&W.

THE BACHELOR AND THE BOBBY-SOXER (1947). Directed by Irving Reis. Produced by Dore Schary. Screenplay and original story by Sidney Sheldon. Principal cast: Cary Grant, Myrna Loy, Shirley Temple, Rudy Vallee, Ray Collins. B&W.

THE BISHOP'S WIFE (1947). RKO Radio. Directed by Henry Koster. Produced by Samuel Goldwyn. Screenplay by Robert E. Sherwood and Leonardo Bercovici, based on a novel by Robert Nathan. Principal cast: Cary Grant, Loretta Young, David Niven, Monty Woolley, James Gleason.

MR. BLANDINGS BUILDS HIS DREAM HOUSE (1948). Directed by H. C. Potter. Produced by Dore Schary. Screenplay by Norman Panama and Melvin Frank, based on a novel by Eric Hodgins. Principal cast: Cary Grant, Myrna Loy, Melvyn Douglas, Reginald Denny, Connie Marshall. B&W.

EVERY GIRL SHOULD BE MARRIED (1948). RKO Radio. Directed by Don Hartman. Produced by Don Hartman and Dore Schary. Screenplay by Stephen Morehouse Avery and Don Hartman, based on a short story by Eleanor Harris. Principal cast: Cary Grant, Betsy Drake, Franchot Tone, Diana Lynn, Eddie Albert. B&W.

I WAS A MALE WAR BRIDE (AKA YOU CAN'T SLEEP HERE) (1949). 20th Century–Fox. Directed by Howard Hawks. Produced by Sol C. Siegel. Screenplay by Charles Lederer, Leonard Spigelgass, and Hagar Wilde, based on a short story by Henri Rochard. Principal cast: Cary Grant, Ann Sheridan, Marion Marshall, Randy Stuart, William Neff. B&W.

CRISIS (AKA BASRA) (1950). MGM. Directed by Richard Brooks. Produced by Arthur Freed. Screenplay by Richard Brooks, based on a story by George Tabori. Principal cast: Cary Grant, José Ferrer, Paula Raymond, Ramon Novarro, Gilbert Roland. B&W.

PEOPLE WILL TALK (AKA THE DR. PRAETORIOUS STORY) (1951). 20th Century–Fox. Directed by Joseph L. Mankiewicz. Produced by Darryl F. Zanuck. Screenplay by Joseph L. Mankiewicz, based on the play *Dr. Praetorius* by Curt Goetz. Principal cast: Cary Grant, Jeanne Crain, Finlay Currie, Walter Slezak, Hume Cronyn. B&W.

ROOM FOR ONE MORE (AKA THE EASY WAY) (1952). Warner Bros. Directed by Norman Taurog. Produced by Henry Blanke. Screenplay by Jack Rose and Mel Shavelson. Based on a book by Anna Perrot Rose. Principal cast: Cary Grant, Betsy Drake, Iris Mann, George Winslow, Lurene Tuttle. B&W.

MONKEY BUSINESS (1952). 20th Century–Fox. Directed by Howard Hawks. Produced by Sol C. Siegel. Screenplay by Ben Hecht, I. A. L. Diamond, and Charles Lederer. Principal cast: Cary Grant, Ginger Rogers, Charles Coburn, Hugh Marlowe, Marilyn Monroe. B&W.

DREAM WIFE (1953). MGM. Directed by Sidney Sheldon. Produced by Dore Schary. Screenplay by Sidney Sheldon, Herbert Baker, and Alfred L. Levitt. Principal cast: Cary Grant, Deborah Kerr, Walter Pidgeon, Betta St. John, Buddy Baer. B&W.

To Catch a Thief (1955). Paramount. Directed and produced by Alfred Hitchcock. Screenplay by John Michael Hayes (and Alfred Hitchcock, uncredited), based on a novel by David Dodge. Principal cast: Cary Grant, Grace Kelly, Jessie Royce Landis, John Williams, Brigitte Auber. Technicolor.

The Pride and the Passion (1957). United Artists/Stanley Kramer Pictures. Directed and produced by Stanley Kramer. Screenplay by Edward and Edna Anhalt, based on the novel *The Gun* by C. S. Forester. Principal cast: Cary Grant, Frank Sinatra, Sophia Loren, Theodore Bikel, John Wengraf. Technicolor.

An Affair to Remember (1957). 20th Century–Fox. Directed by Leo McCarey. Produced by Jerry Wald. Screenplay by Delmer Daves and Leo McCarey. Principal cast: Cary Grant, Deborah Kerr, Richard Denning, Cathleen Nesbitt, Neva Patterson. Color by Deluxe.

Kiss Them for Me (1957). 20th Century–Fox. Directed by Stanley Donen. Produced by Jerry Wald. Screenplay by Julius J. Epstein, based on the novel *Shore Leave* by Frederic Wakeman and the play by Luther Davis. Principal cast: Cary Grant, Jayne Mansfield, Suzy Parker, Leif Erickson, Ray Walston. Color by Deluxe.

Indiscreet (1958). Warner Bros./Grandon Productions. Directed and produced by Stanley Donen. Screenplay by Norman Krasna, based on his play *Kind Sir*. Principal cast: Cary Grant, Ingrid Bergman, Cecil Parker, Phyllis Calvert, Megs Jenkins. Technicolor.

Houseboat (1958). Paramount/Scribe. Directed by Melville Shavelson. Produced by Jack Rose. Screenplay by Melville Shavelson and Jack Rose. Principal cast: Cary Grant, Sophia Loren, Martha Hyer, Harry Guardino, Paul Petersen. Technicolor.

North by Northwest (1959). MGM. Directed and produced by Alfred Hitchcock. Screenplay by Ernest Lehman. Principal cast: Cary Grant, Eva Marie Saint, James Mason, Jessie Royce Landis, Leo G. Carroll. Technicolor.

Operation Petticoat (1959). Universal/Granart. Directed by Blake Edwards. Produced by Robert Arthur. Screenplay by Stanley Shapiro and Maurice Richlin. Principal cast: Cary Grant, Tony Curtis, Joan O'Brien, Dina Merrill, Gene Evans. Eastmancolor.

The Grass Is Greener (1960). Universal/Grandon. Directed and produced by Stanley Donen. Screenplay by Hugh and Margaret Williams, based on their play. Principal cast: Cary Grant, Deborah Kerr, Robert Mitchum, Jean Simmons, Moray Watson. Technicolor.

That Touch of Mink (1962). Universal/Granlex/Arwin/Nob Hill. Directed by Delbert Mann. Produced by Stanley Shapiro, Martin Melcher, and Robert Arthur. Screenplay by Stanley Shapiro and Nate Monaster. Principal cast: Cary Grant, Doris Day, Gig Young, Audrey Meadows, Dick Sargent, John Astin, Alan Hewitt. Eastmancolor.

Charade (1964). Universal/Stanley Donen. Directed and produced by Stanley Donen. Screenplay by Peter Stone, based on a story by Peter Stone and Marc Behm. Principal cast: Cary Grant, Audrey Hepburn, Walter Matthau, James Coburn, George Kennedy. Technicolor.

Father Goose (1964). Universal/Granox. Directed by Ralph Nelson. Produced by

Robert Arthur. Screenplay by Peter Stone and Frank Tarloff, based on a story by S. H. Barnett. Principal cast: Cary Grant, Leslie Caron, Trevor Howard, Jack Good, Verina Greenlaw. Technicolor.

WALK, DON'T RUN (1966). Granley. Directed by Charles Walters. Produced by Sol C. Siegel. Screenplay by Sol Saks, based on a story by Robert Russell and Frank Ross. Principal cast: Cary Grant, Samantha Eggar, Jim Hutton, John Standing, Miiko Taka. Technicolor.

SHORT FILMS AND CAMEO APPEARANCES

SINGAPORE SUE (1932). Paramount. Written and directed by Casey Robinson. Cary Grant in a minor part. Starring Anna Chang. B&W.

PIRATE PARTY ON CATALINA ISLE (1936). MGM. Produced by Louis Lewyn. Continuity and dialogue by Alexander Van Horn. Musical direction by Abe Meyer. With Chester Morris (Master of Ceremonies), Marion Davies, Cary Grant, Randolph Scott, Virginia Bruce, Lee Tracy, Errol Flynn, Lili Damita, Sid Silvers, Eddie Peabody, Leon Errol, Robert Armstrong, Charles "Buddy" Rogers and his Band. Technicolor.

TOPPER TAKES A TRIP (1939). United Artists. Directed by Norman Z. McLeod. Produced by Milton Bren. Grant was originally slated to star in this sequel but did not. A short clip from the original *Topper* with Grant was used to introduce the film; it is Grant's only appearance in the sequel. B&W.

ROAD TO VICTORY (1944). Warner Bros. Ten-minute propaganda film starring Bing Crosby, Cary Grant, Frank Sinatra, Charles Ruggles, Dennis Morgan, Irene Manning, Jack Carson, Jimmy Lydon, and Olive Blakeney. B&W.

WITHOUT RESERVATIONS (1946). RKO. Grant makes an uncredited cameo appearance in this Claudette Colbert–John Wayne film directed by Mervyn LeRoy. B&W.

THE BIG PARADE OF COMEDY (1963). MGM. Two sequences from previous Cary Grant films, *Suzy* and *The Philadelphia Story*. Grant sequences in B&W.

TRIBUTE TO AND SOLICITATION FOR THE WILL ROGERS MEMORIAL HOSPITAL (1965). B&W.

ELVIS: THAT'S THE WAY IT IS (1970). Brief uncredited appearance as himself. Technicolor.

THAT'S ENTERTAINMENT (1974). UA/MGM. Sequences from *Suzy* and *Pirate Party on Catalina Isle*. Grant sequences in B&W and Technicolor.

THAT'S ENTERTAINMENT, PART II (1976). UA/MGM. Sequence from *The Philadelphia Story*. Grant sequence in B&W.

TELEVISION APPEARANCES

ACADEMY AWARDS PRESENTATIONS. Cary Grant's live appearances at Academy Awards ceremonies were televised five times: in 1957, when he accepted the Academy Award for Ingrid Bergman at the twenty-ninth annual Awards; in 1958, as the presenter of the Best Actor Oscar to David Niven *(Separate Tables)*, at the thirtieth annual Awards; in 1970 at the forty-second annual Awards, when he accepted his Honorary Oscar; in 1985 at the fifty-seventh annual Awards as the presenter of an Honorary Oscar to James Stewart; and in 1979 at the fifty-first annual Awards, to present an Honorary Oscar to Laurence Olivier.

DAVE AND CHARLIE (1970). Sitcom. Unbilled guest appearance. The show starred Cliff Arquette (as Charlie Weaver) and David Wilcock, two former radio stars. Grant loved the show and insisted on appearing on an episode as a background hobo.

BROTHER, CAN YOU SPARE A DIME? (1975). Archive footage.

HOORAY FOR HOLLYWOOD (1975). Archive footage.

IT'S SHOWTIME (1976). Archive footage.

THAT'S ACTION (1977).

HAS ANYBODY HERE SEEN CANADA? A HISTORY OF CANADIAN MOVIES 1939–1953 (1979). Archive footage at Oscar dinner, 1942, with Rosalind Russell.

KEN MURRAY SHOOTING STARS (1979). Archive footage.

AMERICAN FILM INSTITUTE SALUTE TO ALFRED HITCHCOCK (1979).

SINATRA: THE FIRST 40 YEARS (1980).

KENNEDY CENTER HONORS: A CELEBRATION OF THE PERFORMING ARTS (1981). Honoree.

GEORGE STEVENS: A FILMMAKER'S JOURNEY (1985).

AMERICAN FILM INSTITUTE SALUTE TO GENE KELLY (1985).

CINEMAX: CARY GRANT: A CELEBRATION OF A LEADING MAN (1988).

FAME IN THE TWENTIETH CENTURY (1993). Uncredited archive footage.

SEVENTIETH ANNUAL ACADEMY AWARDS (1998). Archive footage.

HITCHCOCK, SELZNICK, AND THE END OF HOLLYWOOD (AKA AMERICAN MASTERS: HITCHCOCK, SELZNICK, AND THE END OF HOLLYWOOD) (1999). PBS. Archive footage.

HOLLYWOOD SCREEN TESTS: TAKE 2 (1999). Uncredited archive footage.

A&E BIOGRAPHY: SOPHIA LOREN—ACTRESS ITALIAN STYLE (1999). Archive footage.

MARILYN MONROE: THE FINAL DAYS (2001). Uncredited archive footage.

SHIRTLESS: HOLLYWOOD'S SEXIEST MEN (2002). Uncredited archive footage.

RADIO APPEARANCES

THE CIRCLE (1939). An NBC network talk show.

THE HOLLYWOOD GUILD (1939). On the CBS radio network.

THE LUX RADIO THEATER

    Adam and Eve (May 5, 1935) First broadcast.

    Madame Butterfly (March 8, 1937)

    Theodora Goes Wild (June 13, 1938)

    Only Angels Have Wings (May 28, 1939)

    The Awful Truth (September 11, 1939)

    In Name Only (December 11, 1939)

    I Love You Again (June 30, 1941)

    Here Comes Mr. Jordan (January 26, 1942)

    The Philadelphia Story (July 20, 1942). Special victory show for the U.S. government.

    Talk of the Town (May 17, 1943)

    Mr. Lucky (October 18, 1943)

    Bedtime Story (February 26, 1945)

    Bachelor and the Bobby Soxer [*sic*] (June 13, 1949)

    Every Girl Should Be Married (June 27, 1949)

    Mr. Blanding [*sic*] *Builds His Dream House* (October 10, 1950)

    I Confess (September 21, 1953)

    People Will Talk (January 25, 1954)

    Welcome, Stranger (April 5, 1954)

GRANT AND THE ACADEMY AWARDS

Even before resigning from the Academy, Grant had privately expressed his disdain for the industry's self-serving practice of giving out awards to itself. In 1946 Harold Russell won a special Oscar for his performance in William Wyler's *The Best Years of Our Lives* in addition to a regular Oscar for Best Supporting Actor for the same performance; Grant's performances in two films that year, Michael Curtiz's *Night and Day* and Hitchcock's *Notorious,* were ignored by the Academy. Grant thereupon remarked to a friend, "Where can I get a stick of dynamite?"

Grant did not officially rejoin the Academy until September 1970, five months after receiving his Lifetime Achievement Oscar, and only after receiving a long and conciliatory letter from Academy Award–winning screenwriter Daniel Taradash, the newly elected Academy president who succeeded Gregory Peck. Taradash implored Grant to return to the fold. Only then did Grant reluctantly agree to end his thirty-five-year self-imposed exile. In response to Taradash, Grant wrote, "At the time because of what may have since become outmoded principles, I deplored commercializing a ceremony, which, in my estimation, should have remained unpublicized and privately shared among the artists and craftsmen of our industry. I'm not at all sure that my beliefs have changed; just the times."

FILM NOTES

Highest estimated earnings by movie stars during the four decades Cary Grant made films:

1930s: Mae West. $480,833 per annum
1940s: Betty Grable. $800,000 per annum
1950s: James Stewart. $1 million plus per film
1960s: Cary Grant. $3 million per film

Highest-grossing films starring Cary Grant, based on the first initial theatrical domestic release. The list was compiled in 1972 by *Weekly Variety,* based on theatrical receipts in the United States and Canada. It should be noted that it has not been corrected for inflation, and that during Grant's thirty-five-year career, the average price of admission fluctuated between five and seventy-five cents. Nevertheless, Grant's later films managed to outgross his earlier ones consistently. None of the forty-seven films he made before *Notorious* (1946) make the list.*

Operation Petticoat (1960) $9,500,000
That Touch of Mink (1962) $8,500,000
North by Northwest (1959) $6,310,000
Charade (1963) $6,150,000
Father Goose (1965) $6,000,000
Notorious (1946) $4,800,000
The Bachelor and the Bobby-Soxer (1947) $4,500,000
To Catch a Thief (1955) $4,500,000
The Pride and the Passion (1957) $4,500,000
I Was a Male War Bride (1949) $4,100,000
Night and Day (1946) $4,000,000
Walk, Don't Run (1966) $4,000,000

*Sources: *Guinness Book of the Movies, Guinness Book of Records,* Herrick Library, Rebel Road Library, Archive of Film and Music, *The Films of Cary Grant* by Donald Deschner.

FINAL THOUGHTS AND

ACKNOWLEDGMENTS

I WAS JUST A BOY when I first became aware of Cary Grant. The film was *North by Northwest*. I saw it in its initial run one Friday night at the Loew's Paradise on the Grand Concourse in the Bronx. Because I was underage, I asked an adult if he would buy me my ticket. He agreed, I gave him the three quarters I had saved, got in, bought some popcorn (fifteen cents with real butter) and a Coke (ten cents), found a seat toward the front of the enormous theater with the artificial stars in its beautiful faux "sky," and settled in to be transported. By then, although my access was by today's standards severely limited — no cable, no video, no DVDs, no Turner Classic Movies, and relatively few and far between revival houses, I was well hooked on the movies, on Alfred Hitchcock, and, after this film, on Cary Grant.

North by Northwest was, along with a handful of others (*High Noon, On the Waterfront, From Here to Eternity, Shane, Sons of the Desert*), one of the seminal films of my formative years that were so powerful and affecting they managed to change the emotional and creative direction of my life. With *North by Northwest*, it was not because of anything in its convoluted plot or sophisticated multitracked themes. I was too young to "get" all the multiple-theme doppelgängers, the "hidden" dark artistry of Alfred Hitchcock, the peculiar resistance to the love-lipsticked Eva Marie Saint — but was immediately and completely spellbound by the unbelievable, if for me still inexplicable, charismatic allure of its three stars, the evil James Mason, the provocative Ms. Saint, and the handsome Mr. Grant. For the first time, despite the very real presence of my father in our small and cramped apartment, I understood my mother's open, hopeless, and unconditional love for Cary Grant.

After graduating from the High School of Performing Arts and receiving my B.A. at the City University of New York, I lost two years recovering from a serious accident before I applied for and won in 1970 a fellowship at Columbia University's Graduate School of the Arts. Thus I began my new five-year educational marathon — two years spent earning my M.F.A. in writing, three more to study film history and criticism in the School of the

Arts' Ph.D. program under the aegis of someone who was to completely change my thinking about movies. His name was Andrew Sarris, at the time the film critic for *The Village Voice* newspaper and a professor at Columbia University, where he had joined the faculty of the School of the Arts after having shaken up the cinematic universe with his monumental *The American Cinema*, a book that propounded the "Auteur Theory" and that became for me, and an entire generation of students and filmmakers, cinema's holy grail. Although auteurism is, today, as standard an approach to film as low carbohydrates is to dieting, at the time Sarris's work had the power to outrage the mainstream while at the same time awakening it to the realization of the true artistry of the American cinema.

As much as I loved the surface of the silver screen, Sarris taught me about another layer of movies, those that lurk beneath the shimmering surface and connect directly to the soul. Uncovering these provocatively textured layers of emotion released their greater power and meaning, and the heat of the director's vision fanned the flames of my own creative fires. Sarris also taught me how film's dreams of reality help reveal the reality in my own dreams.

For many years after my time at Columbia I tried to see at least one movie every day of my life. Eventually I reemerged from this subtextural delirium and returned once more to the primal source of my attraction to it, the compelling, wondrous, and irresistible force of the messengers of their meaning. Having been immersed for so long in the examination of the emotional bones that lay beneath the perfect skin of its larger-than-life stars, I once more got the picture, as it were, after seeing a screening of *North by Northwest* in the mid-'80s at a Hitchcock festival in one of New York's revival theaters. It was then I realized all over again that no one ever looked better, had a greater face or deeper soul, than the cinematic miracle that was Cary Grant. And that the real magic of movies and actors was how they showed you both.

THE RESEARCH FOR THIS BIOGRAPHY was conducted over a five-year period of interviews, library and private collection research, and, of course, repeated viewings of Cary Grant movies (of which, by my count, I have now seen sixty-three of the seventy-two).* As a biographer I probably put less stock than others in firsthand "eyewitness" recollections of those who knew, or claim to have known, Cary Grant. For one thing, nearly twenty years have passed since his death in 1986 at the age of eighty-two. By the time I began this book, relatively few people from his early and middle years were still alive and able to tell their tales. Some of the others who did, as I have sometimes painfully discovered in my career, shared an unfortunate (but prevalent) tendency to either rewrite his-

---

*It is easier, of course, to list those I have not seen than those I have. These include *This Is the Night, Sinners in the Sun, Merrily We Go to Hell, Devil and the Deep, Hot Saturday, Gambling Ship, Kiss and Make Up, Ladies Should Listen,* and *Wedding Present*. Most if not all of these were either lost or discarded in the confusing years of Paramount's poverty-stricken era, when Grant was a contract player. I have seen, in one form or another, every Cary Grant film since *When You're in Love*.

tory for the sake of the departed, or elevate their own position in his saga. Any decent biographer shares the same fraternal joke: that he or she has met at least a dozen of his or her subject's "best friends," "closest companions," or "most trusted confidants." When I wrote *Death of a Rebel*, my first biography, of Phil Ochs, although he died in a web of severe loneliness, I somehow came across dozens of "best" and "closest" friends.

Far more important, I believe, is an accurate documentation of events, and equally important, the ability to understand and determine the meaning of those events. When Grant died, there was an unfortunate but inevitable rush of hopelessly inaccurate accountings of his death, with the "big secret" of his life revealed "at last," the "hidden" fact of his homosexuality. A generation later, this subject no longer produces the shock and often accompanying outrage it did in the months after his passing. What it does do now is offer a clearer window into the way Hollywood reacted to the gay issue in Grant's lifetime, and in a larger sense the way it was generally regarded by the twentieth century's so-called mainstream culturalists.

As for his work for the FBI, another poorly researched "sensation" that first surfaced in the immediate wake of Grant's passing, the painful lesson we have come to learn is that virtually no one in the entertainment industry of the thirties, forties, fifties, and sixties was able to escape the long and grisly arm of the monstrous (and monstrously powerful) J. Edgar Hoover. As I have done in the past, I used the Freedom of Information Act for a source of invaluable information. The FOIA is a direct, if hard-fought-for, application of the Constitution that in a free world guarantees the public's essential right to know, a by-product of our First Amendment. I have used the FOIA for four books — *Death of a Rebel*, *Rockonomics*, *Walt Disney: Hollywood's Dark Prince*, and this biography of Cary Grant. I must report that despite numerous court decisions in favor of the public's right to access, the FBI continues to make it extremely difficult, if not impossible, for journalists to receive meaningful and important documents, and that they retain a seemingly unchallenged right to alter and withhold whatever information they feel is not in the best interest of the public.

In the case of Cary Grant, they have continued to insist that despite all evidence to the contrary, there never was any file kept on Cary Grant (more likely, if it does not exist it was destroyed along with thousands of others by J. Edgar Hoover, at his direction, shortly before and after his death). Fortunately, I was able to piece together much of what I needed from files made available to me by people outside of the government who had, from time to time, gained access to the FBI's dossiers on others, and they are noted in the Sources section of the book.

One final, troubling note about the Grant/Hoover relationship. Throughout most of the ten-year anti-Communist inquisition the government inflicted upon Hollywood, from approximately the mid-forties to the mid-fifties, while McCarthy took center stage as the country's self-styled savior, Hoover's influence, if not presence, always lurked just behind the scenes. And yet, throughout his career, after his Depression gangster years, he never pursued any organized crime figures, and no one was ever asked in all of the hearings that took place under the auspices of HUAC if they "were now or ever have been a Nazi."

Finally, it appears that strings were pulled during the HUAC years to protect Grant, who had become an invaluable property (if not a loyal one) to some of Hollywood's most important filmmakers. On a darker note, Hoover, who was gay, may simply have fallen in love with Cary Grant and wanted to protect him. Stranger things, as we now know, have occurred in the history of twentieth-century American law enforcement.

THERE ARE SEVERAL PEOPLE I wish to thank for their help, assistance, guidance, and encouragement during the writing of this book. Because so many requested anonymity, out of respect for them and for Cary Grant, I have honored those requests. Of those I can mention, I will. They include Peter Bogdanovich, Charlie Callas, Cindy Hubach, Teresa McWilliams, Ward Morehouse, William Frye, Joey Reynolds, Chi-Li Wong, Virginia Cherrill (her private diaries and audiotapes generously supplied by Ms. McWilliams), Luisa Flynn, and Satsko. To the rest, you know who you are, and I thank you all.

I wish to thank the Authors Guild and my fellow Friars, especially Mickey Freeman.

I also wish to thank my publisher Shaye Arehart, my editors Julia Pastore and Teryn Johnson, production editor Mark McCauslin, designer Lauren Dong, production supervisor Leta Evanthes, copyeditor Janet Biehl, proofreader Robin Slutzky, my photographer Brenda Killenbeck, and my agent Mel Berger.

And especially to all my friends who have stayed loyal to me throughout the years, I thank you as well.

INDEX

Italicized page numbers indicate photographs

ABOUT THE AUTHOR

MARC ELIOT has been writing about pop culture for over twenty-five years and is the author of more than a dozen books, including *To the Limit: The Untold Story of the Eagles, Down 42nd Street: Sex, Money, Culture, and Politics at the Crossroads of the World*, the *New York Times* bestselling Erin Brockovich autobiography, *Take It from Me*, and the critically acclaimed, award-winning biography *Walt Disney: Hollywood's Dark Prince*. His work has appeared in *Penthouse, LA Weekly, California Magazine*, and the *Metropolitan Review*, as well as in numerous other publications both here and abroad. He divides his time among Los Angeles, New York City, and upstate New York. Visit his website at www.marceliot.net.